What Are Sound Waves?

Robin Johnson

Crabtree Publishing Company
www.crabtreebooks.com

Author
Robin Johnson

Publishing plan research and development
Reagan Miller

Editorial director
Kathy Middleton

Editor
Kathy Middleton

Proofreader
Shannon Welbourn

Design
Samara Parent

Photo research
Samara Parent

**Production coordinator
and prepress technician**
Samara Parent

Print coordinator
Margaret Amy Salter

Photographs
Andrew Lambert Photography / Science Source/
    Photo Researchers: page 14 (left)
Thinkstock: pages 3, 8, 15 (bottom), 16, 22 (both)
All other images by Shutterstock

Library and Archives Canada Cataloguing in Publication

Johnson, Robin (Robin R.), author
        What are sound waves? / Robin Johnson.

(Light and sound waves close-up)
Includes index.
Issued in print and electronic formats.
ISBN 978-0-7787-0522-2 (bound).--ISBN 978-0-7787-0526-0 (pbk.).--
ISBN 978-1-4271-9011-6 (html).--ISBN 978-1-4271-9015-4 (pdf)

        1. Sound-waves--Juvenile literature. I. Title.

QC243.2.J64 2014   j534   C2014-900811-2
                                         C2014-900812-0

Library of Congress Cataloging-in-Publication Data

Johnson, Robin (Robin R.), author.
    What are sound waves? / Robin Johnson.
        pages cm -- (Light and sound waves close-up)
    Includes index.
    ISBN 978-0-7787-0522-2 (reinforced library binding) --
    ISBN 978-0-7787-0526-0 (pbk.) -- ISBN 978-1-4271-9015-4 (electronic pdf) --
    ISBN 978-1-4271-9011-6 (electronic html)
    1. Sound-waves--Juvenile literature. I. Title.

QC243.2.J64 2014
534--dc23
                                         2014004280

Crabtree Publishing Company

www.crabtreebooks.com   1-800-387-7650

Printed in Canada/072015/EF20150617

**Published in Canada
Crabtree Publishing**
616 Welland Ave.
St. Catharines, Ontario
L2M 5V6

**Published in the United States
Crabtree Publishing**
PMB 59051
350 Fifth Avenue, 59th Floor
New York, New York 10118

**Published in the United Kingdom
Crabtree Publishing**
Maritime House
Basin Road North, Hove
BN41 1WR

**Published in Australia
Crabtree Publishing**
3 Charles Street
Coburg North
VIC 3058

Contents

What is sound?

Sound is all the noises you hear around you. There are many kinds of sounds. When a clown honks his big red nose, it makes a silly sound. When a lion roars, it makes a scary sound. If you are reading this book out loud, you are making sounds about sound!

4

Now hear this!

The world is full of sounds! Close your eyes and listen to the sounds around you. Are people talking? Is a dog barking? Is a plane buzzing by? What do each of these different sounds make you think about?

Music is sound that makes you want to dance!

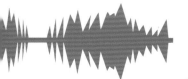 

Sounds good!

Sounds are an important part of life. They help you understand the world around you. When you hear the siren of an ambulance, you know that help is on the way to someone in trouble. When you hear the music of an ice cream truck, you know that tasty treats are nearby!

Safe and sound

Sounds also warn people and animals that they are in danger. When you hear the ringing of a fire alarm, the sound tells you to leave the building because there might be a fire. When a beaver slaps its big, flat tail on the water, the sound warns other beavers that a **predator** is nearby.

What do you think?

Name some sounds you hear each day. What do they tell you about your world?

beaver

wolf

We communicate

People and animals use sounds to **communicate**. To communicate is to share ideas and information. Most people communicate by talking. You whisper secrets softly in your sister's ear. In the game of hide and seek, you shout to your friends that you are coming to find them, ready or not!

When you play Marco Polo, the person who is "it" closes their eyes and yells "Marco." When everyone else answers "Polo," "Marco" must follow the sounds of the other players' voices to tag them.

Other sounds

People and animals also use other sounds to communicate. You giggle when you are happy. Babies cry when they are hungry. Dogs growl when they are angry or scared. What other sounds show how people or animals are feeling?

Dolphins "talk" to each other using clicks, whistles, grunts, barks, and squeaks.

9

Sound is energy

Sound is a form of **energy**. Energy is the power needed to do work. You need energy to move, play, and talk. You need a lot of energy to run, jump, and climb. You even need energy to learn about sound!

Out of energy

Sound is energy you can hear. Every sound runs out of energy over time and eventually stops. If sounds did not run out of energy, they would keep bouncing from place to place forever. We would hear the same sounds over and over again.

What do you think?

Light and heat are other types of energy. They light up and warm your home. What else do you need energy for?

The world would be a very noisy and confusing place if sounds never stopped!

11

Objects vibrate

Sound energy is made only when objects **vibrate**. To vibrate is to shake or move quickly back and forth. You can see guitar strings vibrate when you strum or pluck them with your fingers. The moving strings make music sounds.

string vibrating

What is the matter?

Everything is made of **matter**. Matter is anything that takes up space and can be seen or touched. All matter vibrates. When you knock on a door, the door vibrates. When you bounce a ball, the ball vibrates. The movements are often too small to see or feel, however.

What do you think?

*You can feel the **vibration** when you ride your scooter across a wooden floor. What other activities make you feel vibration?*

Making waves

Sound travels in waves. **Sound waves** are created when an object vibrates. We can hear when the sound wave travels from the object to our ear. Sound waves can travel through air, water, and even solid objects such as walls!

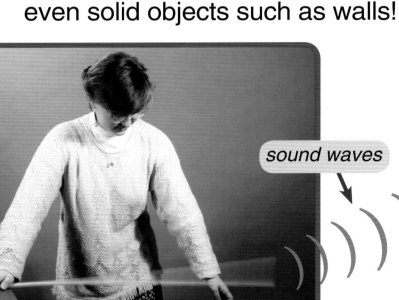

sound waves

The vibration of the ruler creates sound waves that travel to your ear.

Loud or soft

Volume is how loud or quiet a sound is. A strong vibration has more energy and makes a loud sound. A vibration with less energy makes a soft sound. The volume also depends on how close the listener is to the sound. For example, you can hear the actors in a play better if you sit close to the stage instead of far away.

How do we hear?

Ears catch sound waves as they pass. The waves enter the outer part of the ear. They travel down a tube called the **ear canal**. Then they hit the **eardrum**. The eardrum is a thin flap of skin that vibrates when it is hit by sound waves.

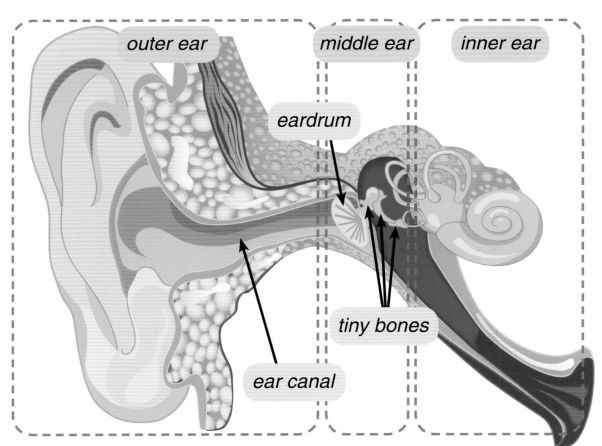

outer ear

middle ear

inner ear

eardrum

tiny bones

ear canal

Inside your ear

When the eardrum vibrates, it causes tiny bones in the middle part of the ear to vibrate too. This helps make the sound easier to hear as it gets passed along. The sound signals get carried to your brain. Then your brain tells you what sounds you are hearing.

You have two ears so you can catch sounds all around you. It helps you tell which direction sounds are coming from.

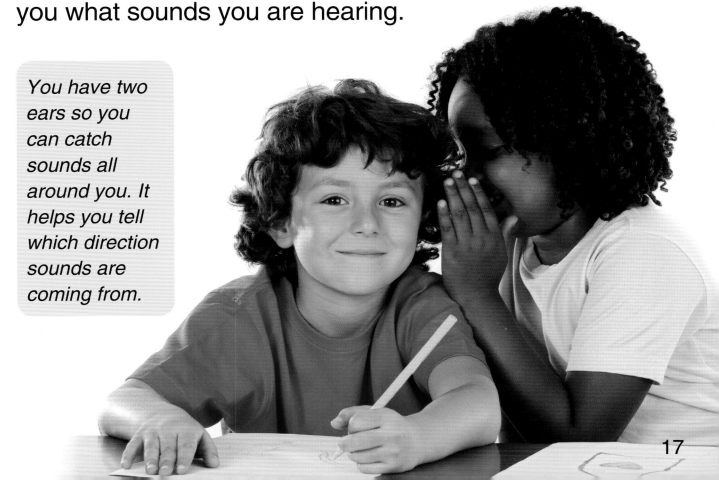

On shaky ground

You have learned that matter vibrates and makes sound. Did you know that sound also makes matter vibrate? Loud noises have a lot of energy. Strong vibrations from loud sounds can rattle windows and move objects. They can even shake the ground!

Sound vibrations can sometimes make snow slide down a mountain in a dangerous avalanche.

See and feel the beat

To see sound waves in action, tape a piece of paper to the front of a speaker. Turn the music up. Sound waves will make the paper jump! You can also hum a tune to feel sound. Put your fingers on your throat while you hum. Do you feel the vibrations?

Make a paper-cup phone

Telephones let you communicate with people who are far away. Follow these steps to make your own phone with paper cups. Then call your friends and tell them what you learned about sound waves!

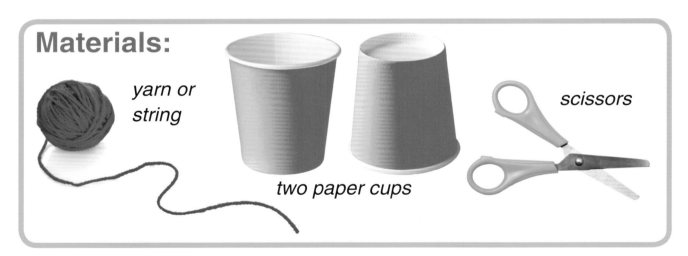

Materials:

yarn or string

two paper cups

scissors

What to do:

1. Cut a long piece of string.

2. Make a small hole in the bottom of each paper cup.

3. Poke one end of the string through each hole. Tie a knot on each end of the string inside the cups so the string cannot slip out.

4. Hold one cup and ask a friend to take the other cup. Pull the cups apart gently so the string is stretched tightly.

5. Speak into one cup while your friend puts the other cup to their ear. Then listen while your friend speaks into their cup. You will not believe your ears!

Sound waves from your voice make the bottom of your cup vibrate. The vibrations travel along the string to your friend's cup. Your friend's ear picks up the vibrations, and their brain tells them what you said!

21

Call again

Try using other materials to make your phone. Use plastic cups or metal cans. Use kite string or fishing line. How does the sound change? Write down what you hear in a notebook. You will learn that sound travels differently through different objects.

String! String! Your phone is ringing!

What do you think?

Will your phone work if the string touches a wall or other object? Why? What will happen to the sound waves?

Learning More

Books

Amazing Sound by Sally Hewitt. Crabtree Publishing Company, 2008.

Sound by Sally M. Walker. Lerner Publications, 2005.

Sound Waves by Ian F. Mahaney. Rosen Classroom, 2007.

What Is Hearing? by Molly Aloian.
Crabtree Publishing Company, 2013.

What Is Sound? by Charlotte Guillain. Heinemann, 2009.

Websites

Science Kids: The Science of Sound for Kids
www.sciencekids.co.nz/sound.html

Science Kids at Home
www.sciencekidsathome.com/science_topics/what_is_sound.html

Kids Health: Your Ears
http://kidshealth.org/kid/htbw/ears.html#

Words to know

communicate (kuh-MYOO-ni-keyt) *verb* To share ideas and information

ear canal (eer kuh-NAL) *noun* The tube that carries sound to the ear

eardrum (EER-druhm) *noun* Part of the ear that vibrates and moves tiny bones inside the ear

energy (EN-er-jee) *noun* The power to do work

matter (MAT-er) *noun* Something that takes up space

predator (PRED-uh-ter) *noun* An animal that hunts other animals

sound wave (sound weyv) *noun* Something that carries sound from place to place

vibrate (VAHY-breyt) *verb* To move quickly back and forth

vibration (vahy-BREY-shuh n) *noun* A fast movement back and forth

volume (VOL-yoom) *noun* How loud or quiet a sound is

A *noun* is a person, place, or thing.
A *verb* is an action word that tells you what someone or something does.

Index

Ecological Studies

Analysis and Synthesis

Edited by

W. D. Billings, Durham (USA) F. Golley, Athens (USA)
O. L. Lange, Würzburg (FRG) J. S. Olson, Oak Ridge (USA)

Volume 25

Microbial Ecology of a Brackish Water Environment

Edited by
G. Rheinheimer

Contributors
M. Bölter · K. Gocke · H.-G. Hoppe · J. Lenz
L.-A. Meyer-Reil · B. Probst · G. Rheinheimer
J. Schneider · H. Szwerinski · R. Zimmermann

With 77 Figures

Springer-Verlag Berlin Heidelberg New York 1977

Editor and contributors:
Institut für Meereskunde
an der Universität Kiel
Abt. Marine Mikrobiologie,
Marine Planktologie
Düsternbrooker Weg 20
D-2300 Kiel 1/FRG

ISBN 3-540-08492-4 Springer-Verlag Berlin Heidelberg New York
ISBN 0-387-08492-4 Springer-Verlag New York Heidelberg Berlin

Library of Congress Cataloging in Publication Data, Main entry under title: Microbial ecology of a brackish water environment. (Ecological studies; v. 25). Includes bibliographies and index. 1. Marine microbiology. 2. Microbial ecology. 3. Brackish water biology. I. Rheinheimer, Gerhard, 1927–. II. Series. QR106.M5. 1978. 576'.19'2. 77-16400.

Typesetting, printing, and binding: Brühlsche Universitätsdruckerei, Lahn-Gießen.
2131/3130—543210

Preface

A knowledge, which is as accurate as possible of microbial ecology is indispensible for ecosystem research and environmental protection. This is particularly true for coastal waters, whereby brackish water areas occupy a special position.

After several years of preliminary studies on the composition and distribution of the microflora – algae, fungi, and bacteria – a comprehensive investigation on the primary production, bacterial development and microbial uptake and decomposition of substances in the Kiel Bight was carried out, during which ten scientists from the Institut für Meereskunde of Kiel University participated. Here for the first time numerous hydrographical, chemical and microbiological parameters could be measured on the same water samples. The aim of this joint project was to gain an insight into the manifold functions of the microorganisms in the uptake and degradation of organic substances and in the connections between pollution, production, and remineralization.

The results of the investigations led not only to new knowledge of the role of the microorganisms in the brackish water ecosystem, but also to a revision of earlier conceptions, especially on the influence of wastes on the microflora and its role in the self-purification of coastal waters.

Such a time-limited investigation, however, cannot clarify all the questions on the complex relationships between the microorganisms and their biotope. Therefore, the present volume should also be understood as a stimulus for new and further-reaching research on the microbial ecology of coastal waters. Thereby the most important methods are described, as well as the practical experience obtained.

The investigations were performed mostly in the western Baltic Sea and adjacent areas in the temperate climatic zone of Europe. Thus mainly the relevant publications from this region were taken into consideration. In Volume 24 of *Ecological Studies* a coastal marine ecosystem model of the American east coast (Narragansett Bay) is developed by Kremer and Nixon where further American publications are given.

Acknowledgements. The investigations were partly sponsored by the Ministry for Research and Technology of the Federal Republic of Germany.

The results of the theses from M. Bölter and R. Zimmermann which were written at Kiel University under supervision of the editor are included for this study (Chaps. 10, 12, and 13).

Editor and authors should like to thank all those members of the staff of the Institut für Meereskunde of Kiel University who participated in the investigations aboard the ships and in the laboratories, or helped in preparing the results for the manuscript. Our particular thanks are due to Karl Bach, Werner Dzomla, Alfred Eisele, Inge Flittiger, Peter Fritsche, Margit Karl, Ruth Kreibich, Ingeborg Koch, Regine Koppe, Ruth Kuhlmann, Margret Kusche, Edith Mempel, Erika Nietz, Barbara Schönknecht, Gerd Thiel and the crews of the research vessels "Alkor" and "Hermann Wattenberg".

The editor is much indebted to the publisher for understanding and co-operation.

Kiel, September 1977   G. RHEINHEIMER

Contents

6. Determination of Organic Substances and Respiration Potential

7. Primary Production

8. Plankton Populations

9. Fungi

10. Estimation of Bacterial Number and Biomass by Epifluorescence Microscopy and Scanning Electron Microscopy

1. Introduction

G. RHEINHEIMER

With the work *Biology of Brackish Water* by Remane and Schlieper (1971) a comprehensive representation of the ecology and physiology of brackish water organisms is given. According to the knowledge at that time, the work is mainly concerned with animal organisms and secondly with the algae. Genuine microorganisms such as bacteria and fungi, however, receive only a few lines, and the phytoplankton is also given relatively brief consideration. A study of the remaining brackish water literature shows that knowledge of the microbial ecology of brackish water is still rather limited. Generally up to the present mostly investigations on special problems have been carried out. Many of these refer to smaller estuaries with rather high salinity. A number of interesting papers have been compiled e.g., from the symposium *Estuarine Microbiology* (Stevenson and Colwell, 1973).

Since brackish water is found to a considerable extent along the sea coast areas, in intra-continental waters such as the Hudson Bay, the Baltic Sea and the Black Sea as well as in numerous bays and fjords, and in the river estuaries, it is thus exposed in a special way to waste water and refuse loads. Therefore the self-purification in these waters takes on special relevance in maintaining the cleanliness of the sea. For this reason a more accurate knowledge of the microbial ecology of coastal waters—particularly for areas containing brackish water—is urgently necessary.

Thus, after several years of preliminary studies in the Baltic Sea and Elbe estuary, a detailed investigation on the primary production, bacterial development and microbial uptake of substances as well as on the composition and activity of the bacteria, fungi and phytoplankton populations was carried out from January 1974 to March 1975 in the Kiel Bight. Altogether ten scientists from the Institut für Meereskunde of the Kiel University participated in this project.

Endeavors were made to utilize all methods and apparatus which were available and to employ a judicious combination of both modern and classical methods. Thereby on the one hand as much new data as possible should be gained—while at the same time the possibility of comparison to earlier works would also be given. By the simultaneous use of diverse microbiological methods, a better knowledge of the meaning of the data obtained and thus also the value of the newer and older methods is made possible. In particular the more recent methods, some of which were newly developed or modified for these investigations, are described in the corresponding chapters and are supplied with the necessary literature references.

Earlier investigations in the western Baltic Sea as well as in the Elbe and Weser estuaries have shown that the microflora here consists mostly of halophilic marine organisms and—to a less extent—brackish water forms, while salt-tolerant freshwater forms play only a relatively subordinate role despite the strong influence from the land. The number of genuine brackish water species is as small among the algae as well as among the animals (see Remane and Schlieper, 1971)—although they may occur in high numbers of individuals.

Autecological studies on numerous saprophytic bacteria showed, however, that there are a relatively large number of specific brackish water forms here which have salinity optima mostly between 10 and 20‰. These are halophilic organisms which either grow only badly or not at all in freshwater media and are frequently suppressed by salinities above 30‰. Thus in the long run, they are unable to develop in real sea water, whose average salinity is 35‰ (Ahrens and Rheinheimer, 1967; Ahrens, 1969; Meyer-Reil, 1973; Rheinheimer, 1966, 1971, 1975). The proportion of brackish water bacteria in the Baltic Sea increases with the decreasing salinity towards the east, while the genuine marine bacteria with salinity optima between 25 and 40‰ decrease (see Magaard and Rheinheimer, 1974). Genuine marine bacteria are often clearly suppressed at salinities less than 15‰; thus in the middle and northern Baltic Sea as well as in many other brackish water areas, they do not meet optimal growth conditions and accordingly are displaced largely by the brackish water forms.

An example for the distribution of brackish water bacteria is given by the members of a group of bacteria which form characteristic brown pigmented colonies of about 1 mm with a pale translucent margin on yeast extract–peptone agar, and accordingly are easy to recognize and count on agar plates. These bacteria form star-shaped aggregates and are therefore placed in the genus *Agrobacterium*. They are found especially in the Kiel Bight and the bordering areas of the western Baltic Sea, where the salinity of the water ranges between 10 and 25‰. These bacteria occur less frequently in the northwestern Baltic Sea where the salinity is lower, or in the Kattegat with its higher salinity. They could not be determined in the open North Sea and in the North Atlantic. Corresponding forms, however, have been found in the brackish water of the Elbe and Weser estuaries (Ahrens, 1969, 1970; Rheinheimer, 1975).

In spite of the strong land influence the importance of terrestrial bacteria in the western Baltic Sea is minimal. Although they enter the coastal waters in large numbers with waste water, rivers and land erosion, investigations at the municipal waste water outlet from the Kiel city at Bülk (see Fig. 2.1) show that the bacteria carried into the brackish Baltic Sea water die off very rapidly and are replaced instead by halophilic marine and brackish water bacteria (cf. Rheinheimer, 1975). Only in the direct vicinity of the outlet do the waste water-conveyed bacteria play a role in the breakdown of organic wastes. Already at a distance of 1–2 km away, however, their proportion of the total saprophyte flora amounts only to a few percent. This strong decrease is only partly due to the effect of dilution. This could be calculated from measurements made by oceanographers on the mixing processes (see Sadjedi, 1971).

A large proportion of the allochthonous bacteria dies off after a short time. This is probably due above all to the bactericidic properties of brackish and sea water for non-marine bacteria. Thereby in addition to the salinity, heavy metal complexes play an important role (Macleod, 1965). Also the comparatively low nutrient concentrations may be of importance in the rapid disappearance of the bacteria entering coastal waters via waste water. Bacteriophages apparently play only a subordinate role, as could be demonstrated in the Kiel Bight. The number of coliphages here, for example, decreased more rapidly than the coli bacteria themselves.

A few osmophilic bacteria seem to have a longer duration of survival (see Rheinheimer, 1975); these bacteria develop optimally at osmotic values which correspond to those of brackish or sea water—yet they require neither sodium nor chloride ions for their development. Such osmophilic bacteria have been found in the Baltic Sea as well as in the Kattegat (see Meyer-Reil, 1973). Yet in the long run these are also suppressed by halophilic brackish water or marine bacteria. Thereby the comparatively low nutrient concentrations in the coastal waters may again be of importance, as they are for the most part insufficient for those osmophilic bacteria adapted to the high nutrient content of waste water.

Among the fungi, brackish water forms also occur, which develop optimally at salinities between 10 and 25‰. However, the salinity ranges possible for the growth of fungi are as a rule greater than those of bacteria. For this reason a relatively large number of salt-tolerant freshwater fungi also occur in the Baltic Sea in addition to the halophilic marine and brackish water forms.

It seems that there are no genuine brackish water species existing among the phyto and zooplankton. However, a number of euryhaline species is growing well in mesohaline waters—especially among the diatoms. However the number of species is decreasing with the salinity and some of them show a reduction in size (cf. Remane and Schlieper, 1971). Halotolerant freshwater species only play a role in β-mesohaline and oligohaline waters with less than 10‰ salinity.

Compared with most of the earlier investigations on problems of microbial ecology of brackish water, in this study particular stress was laid upon the activity of heterotrophic microorganisms and their dependence on the different biotic and abiotic parameters. Therefore much time was spent to find suitable methods for the determination of the activity of bacterial populations before starting the proper investigations. Of special interest is the amount of active cells on the total bacteria counts, as well as the numbers of those microorganisms which are able to take up certain organic compounds. In order to understand the brackish water ecosystem and its energy flows, detailed knowledge on the uptake and decomposition of matter by heterotrophic microorganisms is urgently necessary. Therefore the methodical work was concentrated on micro-autoradiography and the determination of maximal uptake velocity, turnover times, growth rates and generation times.

To demonstrate the multiple relations between the composition and decomposition of organic matter by microorganisms the results of this study are compiled to a model of the brackish water ecosystem (see Fig. 19.1).

References

Ahrens, R.: Ökologische Untersuchungen an sternbildenden *Agrobacterium*-Arten aus der Ostsee. Kieler Meeresforsch. **25**, 190–204 (1969)

Ahrens, R.: Weitere sternbildende Bakterien aus Brackwasser. Kieler Meeresforsch. **26**, 74–78 (1970)

Ahrens, R., Rheinheimer, G.: Über einige sternbildende Bakterien aus der Ostsee. Kieler Meeresforsch. **23**, 127–136 (1967)

Magaard, L., Rheinheimer, G.: Meereskunde der Ostsee. Berlin-Heidelberg-New York: Springer, 1974

Macleod, R. A.: The question of the existence of specific marine bacteria. Bact. Rev. **29**, 9–23 (1965)

Meyer-Reil, L. A.: Untersuchungen über die Salzansprüche von Ostseebakterien. Botanica Marina **26**, 65–76 (1973)

Remane, A., Schlieper, C.: Biology of brackish water. Die Binnengewässer V. **25**. New York: Wiley, 1971

Rheinheimer, G.: Einige Beobachtungen über den Einfluß von Ostseewasser auf limnische Bakterienpopulationen. Veröff. Inst. Meeresforsch. Bremerh. Sbd. **2**, 237–244 (1966)

Rheinheimer, G.: Über das Vorkommen von Brackwasserbakterien in der Ostsee. Vie et Milieu. Suppl. **22**, 281–291 (1971)

Rheinheimer, G.: Mikrobiologie der Gewässer. 2nd ed. Stuttgart: Fischer, 1975

Sadjedi, F.: Qualitative und quantitative Untersuchungen zum Vorkommen der coliformen Bakterien im Bereich der westlichen Ostsee. Thesis Univ. Kiel 1971

Stevenson, L. H., Colwell, R.: Estuarine Microbiology. Univ. South Carolina Press, 1973

2. The Kiel Bight as Research Area

G. Rheinheimer

As research area the Kiel Bight (Fig. 2.1) was chosen, which can serve as an example of a coastal body of water carrying brackish water with very little differences between high and low tides, but still with a relatively strong exchange of water. It represents the western part of the Baltic Sea and is included in the Belt Sea area (Fig. 2.2). The Kiel Bight shows correspondingly strong irregular salinity changes, which vary approximately between 10 and 25‰. A detailed description of the hydrographic conditions is given in Chapter 3.3. There are only few small rivers flowing into the Kiel Bight area (e.g., the Schwentine river into the Kiel Fjord). Of more importance for this study is the municipal waste water outlet of Kiel at Bülk (see Fig. 2.1). At that time the waste water of about 300,000 inhabitants was only treated mechanically.

For the investigations five stations were chosen along a transect from the inner Kiel Fjord to the middle of the Kiel Bight, which represent well the different conditions in this area of the sea (Table 2.1).

Station 1 is located in the central part of the inner Kiel Fjord opposite the Reventlou Brücke within the Kiel city limits. It is a sea area relatively strongly burdend with wastes, exhibiting a more or less heavy pollution depending on the wind conditions and currents. Accordingly, relatively strong short-term variations in nutrient concentrations and amount of bacteria can also be found (see Gocke, 1975). This part of the Kiel Fjord, however, is already considerably less contaminated than its innermost section, the so-called Hörn (see Rheinheimer, 1975). The sediment consists of mud. During the period of investigation dredging operations were being carried out in the inner Kiel Fjord. The originally feared influence on Station 1, however, was confined to a minimal increase in the turbidity (see Chap. 5), so that the rest of the results were not thereby affected.

Station 2 is located in the outer Kiel Fjord opposite Laboe, a small town with lively tourist traffic during the summer and also some fishing. Steady ship traffic dominates on the fjord here, especially to and from the Kiel Canal. The quality of the water is already better than in the inner Kiel Fjord. Nevertheless various polluting factors such as shipping and smaller inflows from land do have an effect, as well as influences from the municipal waste water outlet at Bülk (see Fig. 2.1) during northwesterly winds. The sediment consists of mud.

Station 3 is located in the southern Kiel Bight approximately at the position of the former Kiel lightship near the present lighthouse. The waste load of Baltic Sea water is usually minimal here in spite of the nearby land. With an outward-flowing current, influences from the more heavily contaminated Kiel Fjord can be seen, and with southwesterly winds also those from the waste water outlet at Bülk.

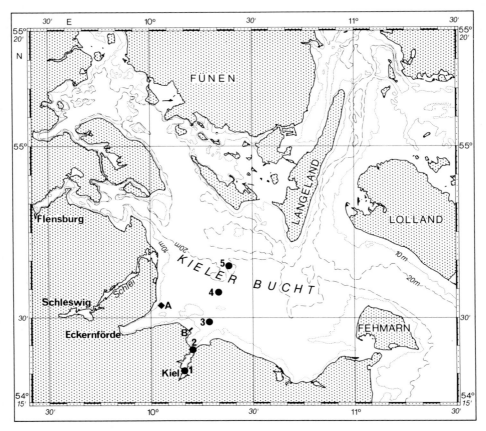

Fig. 2.1. Map of the Kiel Bight (Kieler Bucht) with Stations 1–5 and A.
B Waste water outlet at Bülk

Table 2.1. The five stations investigated

Station	Sea area	Location	Position	Depth
1	Inner Kiel Fjord	Reventlou Brücke	54°20.1′N 10°09.6′E	12 m
2	Outer Kiel Fjord	Laboe	54°24.2′N 10°12.5′E	14 m
3	Kiel Bight	Lightship Kiel	54°29.2′N 10°17.3′E	20 m
4	Kiel Bight	Kieler Bucht Mitte I	54°34.7′N 10°20′ E	14 m
5	Kiel Bight	Kieler Bucht Mitte II	54°39′ N 10°23′ E	22 m

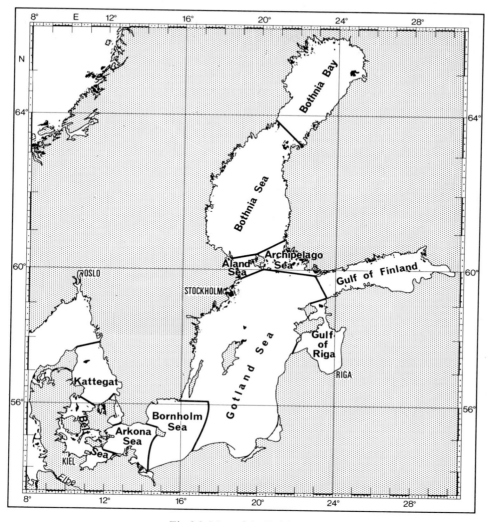

Fig. 2.2. Map of the Baltic Sea

The latter could be demonstrated here above all at a depth of ± 10 m—for example in an increased ammonia concentration. The sediment consists of mud.

Station 4 is located in the central Kiel Bight in a relatively shallow area above sandy sediment. The water here is relatively clean. Polluting influences are only effective to a small extent and are mostly due to shipping.

The sediment of this location has been investigated in detail (see Weise and Rheinheimer, 1977). The grain size analysis from a sample taken on Nov. 21, 1974 gave an average value of 0.410 µm. Roudness index: angular 4%, subangular 32%, subrounded 45%, rounded 16%, well-rounded 3%. Water content 21%, ignition loss 0.35%, organic matter 6.82 mg cm^{-3} wet sediment. With the aid of a scanning electron microscope the relationships between the microtopography and the colonization density of the individual sand grains, as well as the attachment mechanisms of the bacteria was investigated. Sand grains with a medium degree of roundness showed the greatest colonization density. The bacteria were for the most part attached directly to the grain surface and were frequently fastened with slime threads or special fine structures. They were also found to a smaller extent on detritus areas and as "Aufwuchs" on diatoms.

Station 5 also lies in the central Kiel Bight, although somewhat farther northward. It is located above the trench which runs from the Little Belt across the Fehmarn Belt into the Mecklenburg Bight and Lübeck Bight. The station is above fine muddy sediment, the water is relatively clean, and polluting factors are not of any great significance. Contaminations however, can be found more frequently here than at Station 4. This is probably a result of the current conditions within the trench system.

For the interpretation of the investigation results, those from other studies made in recent years on the Belt Sea, the Arkona, Bornholm and Gotland Seas, the Kattegat, and the Limfjord as well as the Elbe and Weser estuaries were taken into consideration (see Fig. 2.2). These are brackish water areas with differing hydrographic conditions and very different salinities which range, seen as a whole, between 0.5 and 30‰.

The investigations in the Kiel Bight were carried out during the time from January 1974 to March 1975. At least once a month profile cruises were made with the research vessels "Alkor" or "Hermann Wattenberg" from the Institut für Meereskunde of the Kiel University in order to obtain the necessary samples which, as far as possible were investigated immediately on board. During the months of February, June and August 1974, additional research cruises could be carried out. A more frequent series of samplings was not possible due to the great amount of work involved, particularly in determining the microbiological parameters, although this would have been desirable because of the great variability of the hydrographic conditions in the Kiel Bight (see Chap. 3.3). Likewise due to the work involved, the sediment analyses were carried out only at Stations 1, 4, and 5, which include, however, the characteristic sediment forms found in the study area. Several parameters involving particularly intensive work, such as primary production, heterotrophic activity, growth rates, the autoradiographic analysis and others could only be determined on part of the samples. Samples from Stations 1 and 5 were used whenever possible since they are considered characteristic for the relatively heavily polluted inner Kiel Fjord and for the relatively clean central Kiel Bight area. Details can be found in Table 2.2 in which all parameters are listed as well as the samples and stations which were investigated and the chapters which deal with them.

For the determination of the saprophytes, coliform, and yeast counts, water samples were taken in sterile glass bottles by means of a modified ZoBell sampling apparatus, and were immediately prepared for analysis. The water samples for determination of the remaining microbiological parameters were taken with a larger bacteriological sampling apparatus with 5-l capacity (see Fig. 2.3) which was constructed for this study by Gocke and Bach. Immediately after the sampling, vessels were filled under sterile conditions with the necessary amounts of water

Table 2.2. The hydrographical, chemical and biological parameters investigated

	Stations	Substrate	Chapter
Water temperature	1–5	w	3
Salinity	1–5	w	3
Oxygen	1–5	w	4
Ammonia	1–5	w	4
Nitrite	1–5	w	4
Nitrate	1–5	w	4
Orthophosphate	1–5	w	4
Seston	1, 2, 4, 5	w	5
Chlorophyll a	1, 2, 4, 5	w	5
Carbon (particulate)	1, 2, 4, 5	w	5
Nitrogen (particulate)	1, 2, 4, 5	w	5
Protein (particulate)	1, 2, 4, 5	w	5
Carbohydrates (particulate)	1, 2, 4, 5	w	5
Lipids (particulate)	1, 2, 4, 5	w	5
ATP	1, 2, 4, 5	w	5
Dehydrogenase activity (DHA)	1, 2, 4, 5	w	6
BOD (14)	1, 5	w	6
COD	1–5	w	6
Primary production	1, 3	w	7
Phytoplancton cell number	1, 2, 4, 5	w	8
Number of yeasts	1, 5	w	9
Number of red yeasts	1, 5	w	9
Detritus area	1, 5	w	10
Bacterial biomass	1, 5	w	10
Total number of bacteria (direct counts)	1–5	w	10
Total number of saprophytes	1–5	w, s	11
Colony counts on medium ZS	1–5	w, s	11
Colony counts on medium ZB	1–5	w, s	11
Colony counts on medium ZL	1–5	w, s	11
Colony counts on medium N	1–5	w, s	11
Coliforms on Gassner-Agar	1–5	w, s	11
Coliforms on nutrient pads (type Endo)	1–5	w	11
Number of cellulose decomposers	1–5	w	12
Number of chitinoclasts	1–5	w	12
Number of bacteria spores	1–5	w	12
Number of active bacteria (microautoradiography)	1, 2, 5	w	14
Max. uptake velocity (glucose, aspartic acid, acetate)	1, 5	w	15
Approximate substrate concentration ($K_t + S_n$) (glucose, aspartic acid, acetate)	1, 5	w	15
Turnover-time (glucose, aspartic acid, acetate)	1, 5	w	15
Turnover-time (pool of dissolved amino acids)	1, 5	w	15
Number of cells capable of growth	1, 5	w	16
Bacterial growth rates	1, 5	w	16
Generation times of bacteria	1, 5	w	16
Bacterial biomass production	1, 5	w	16
Nitrification potential	1, 5	w, s	17
Number of desulfurizing bacteria	1, 5, 1 a	w, s	18

w: water; s: sediment

Fig. 2.3. Bacteriological sampling apparatus for 5-l samples

needed for the various investigations. The further analysis is described in the chapters in question. The sampling of the water for the chemical and planktological determinations was performed by means of hydrographic samplers from the Hydrobios Company, Kiel.

Although the use of different samplers could not be avoided, nevertheless the water for the investigation of all parameters originated from the same water body at the individual stations and depths. This was assured by means of comparative preliminary investigations.

Sampling of sediment was performed with a Van Veen grab. Thereby particular care was taken that only material with an undisturbed sediment surface was used in the analysis.

A certain problem is presented by the data on the water depths, since these may undergo fluctuations of up to 2 m depending on the wind conditions (see Chap. 3). Therefore the greatest sampling depth at a given time corresponds more or less to the height above the sea floor. The depths presented in Table 2.1 are average values.

During this study the weather was characterized by very mild winters and a relatively cool summer. Because of this, air and water temperatures showed less differences than in other years. According to the monthly weather reports for Schleswig-Holstein of the Deutsche Wetterdienst from January to April 1974 and from November 1974 to March 1975 the weather was too warm compared with the averages of many years. On the other hand, temperatures were too low from May to October 1974. Rainfall was very low from February to May and in August 1974 and again in February and March 1975. In the other months there was too much rain.

The weather conditions during this study differed significantly from the averages of long standing, as also the previous and following years which were unusual, however, in another way. In this connection the extremely warm and dry summers 1975 and 1976 may be referred to.

References

Gocke, K.: Studies on short-term variations of heterotrophic activity in the Kiel Fjord. Mar. Biol. **33**, 49–55 (1975)

Rheinheimer, G.: Mikrobiologie der Gewässer. Stuttgart: Fischer, 1975

Weise, W., Rheinheimer, G.: Scanning electron microscopy and epifluorescence investigation of bacterial colonization of marine sand-sediments. Microb. Ecol. in press (1977)

3. Hydrographic Conditions

J. LENZ

3.1 The Baltic Sea as an Estuary

With an area of 422,000 km², the Baltic Sea ranks between Hudson Bay (1,232,000 km²) and the Black Sea (420,000 km²) as the second largest brackish sea in the world (cf. Seibold, 1970). From north to south it extends over 12 degrees of latitude from 66°N to 54°N and on the east–west axis from 30°E to 10°E. The average depth is 55 m and the total water volume approximately 23,000 km³. The Baltic Sea consists of a series of basins of varying depth, the deepest point lying in the Gotland Basin. The Kattegat and the Belt Sea, which comprise the transitional area between the Baltic and the North Sea, are comparatively shallow. A key role in water exchange here is played by sills 11-m, 26-m, and 8-m deep situated in the three straits Little Belt, Great Belt and Öre-Sund, respectively. Another sill, the so-called Darsse sill (18 m) lies between the Mecklenburg Bight and the Arkona Basin.

The Baltic Sea lies in a humid climatic zone with a considerable surplus of rainfall. This surplus is eventually transported into the sea by the numerous rivers of northeast Europe. The drainage area of the Baltic is roughly four times that of its own expanse (cf. Brogmus, 1952). The seven largest rivers emptying into the Baltic, the Angermann-Elf in North Sweden and the Kemi-Elf in North Finland as well as the Neva, the Dvina, the Memel, the Vistula and the Oder, contribute about 44% of the total fresh water input (Brogmus, 1952). These river waters are traceable for some distance into the North Sea and North Atlantic.

This freshwater influx imparts to the Baltic the character of an estuary, the salient feature of an estuary being the flowthrough of river water into the open sea. The ensuing mixing produces the brackish water characteristic of an estuary in its function as a transitional region between two different habitats, limnic and marine. Cameron and Pritchard (1963) have defined an estuary as a partially enclosed water body with an open connection to the sea, where sea water is diluted in a measurable degree by the influx of fresh water from the shore. This definition may be fittingly applied to the Baltic as well as to the other brackish seas.

The paramount factor in the hydrography of an estuary is the dynamic equilibrium between fresh water outflow at the surface and sea water inflow in the depths. This countermotion of water masses is due to the lighter fresh or brackish water spreading over the surface, whereby a pressure gradient is created against the heavier sea water. Strata of equal density tilted by the outflow—as recogniza-

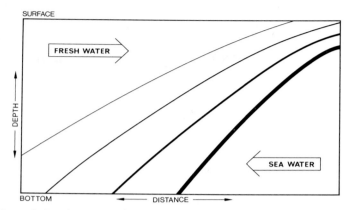

Fig. 3.1. Schematic longitudinal section through an estuary showing the oblique isopycnics
(after Dietrich et al., 1975)

ble from the isopycnal curves—strive to reoccupy their original horizontal posi-
tions (Fig. 3.1). In response to this, a countercurrent is set up in the depths,
whereupon the heavier water underflows the lighter. Thus we see that gravita-
tional forces act against the density incline, producing a state of interdependence
between inflow and outflow. In effect this means that wherever possible, salt water
enters at the depths to counterbalance the diluting effect of river runoff at the
surface.

This basic pattern is subject to alteration according to the specificities of each
estuary, chief amongst which are bottom topography, the quantity and rate of
fresh water input and the mixing of water masses through the action of wind and
tides with the resultant density gradients. Stommel (1953) and Dietrich et al.
(1975) formulate four main types of estuaries. The Baltic occupies an intermediate
position between type C, the fjord-type with a high sill at its entrance and nearly
constant salinity in its deeper parts, and type D, likewise two-layered, but with a
wedge-shaped salinity distribution in the depths, i.e., salinity decreases towards
the interior of the estuary. A gradual salinity decrease of this kind, typical of
rivermouths with little tidal mixing, is also to be observed in the deep waters of
the Baltic towards the Gulfs of Finland and Bothnia.

The estuarine regions of the southern North Sea, for example the mouths of
the rivers Elbe and Weser, fall into the category of types A and B. The outer
sectors of these rivermouths, which are characterized by shallow depths and, as a
consequence of intensive tidal mixing, by an unstratified water column, as well as
a gradual salinity increase with distance from the shore, may be classified as
type A. Towards the estuary interiors, type A gives way to type B. Here the water
column is generally two-layered; on average, outflow prevails at the surface and
inflow in the lower depths. However, even here in the interior, tidal mixing plays
an important part. The extent of stratification varies with ebb and flow (see
Dietrich et al., 1975).

In this context, attention may be called to another essential difference between
the Baltic and the large river estuaries of the North Sea. This pertains to the heavy

sediment load borne by these rivers and the large amount of inorganic nutrient salts thereby delivered to the southern North Sea. These estuarine regions therefore possess a far higher productivity than the Baltic. Chapter 11 in Remane and Schlieper (1971) contains a competent description of the relationship between hydrography and productivity in both regions. A synoptic discussion of physical, chemical, and biological changes on a transect through a typical North Sea river estuary may be found in Kühl and Mann (1961).

3.2 General Hydrographical Features of the Baltic

It will be conducive to an understanding of the hydrographic influences affecting our study area, the Kiel Bight and the Kiel Fjord, if we first outline the most prominent hydrographical features of the Baltic Sea at large. A detailed presentation of the subject will be found in several contributions to the volume *Meereskunde der Ostsee*, edited by Magaard and Rheinheimer (1974), a work to which we shall repeatedly have recourse in the following.

As already mentioned, water exchange in the Baltic is severely hampered by the relatively narrow and, even worse, shallow straits in the Belt Sea. These straits above all inhibit the inflow of high-salinity deep waters. As a result, there is a marked freshening of the Baltic waters towards the north.

Brogmus (1952) has set up a water budget for the Baltic excluding the Kattegat region, thereby reducing area and volume to $386,000 \, km^2$ and $22,190 \, km^3$, respectively. On the gain side we have firstly the fresh water input through precipitation and river discharge and secondly, the salt water inflow; on the loss side we register evaporation and outflow of brackish water.

Table 3.1 presents an estimation of these factors. Since no measurements of precipitation and evaporation in the open sea are available, they had to be indirectly inferred from data collected from the coastal stations. Obviously, the ratio precipitation: evaporation over the open sea will be substantially different from that for the coastal regions. Precipitation is less over the open sea since various terrestrial factors responsible for causing rainfall in nearshore areas are absent. Evaporation in contrast is generally higher. Making allowance for these disparities, Brogmus in his study, apparently by coincidence, arrives at a balance between the two.

Table 3.1. Water budget $(km^3 \, y^{-1})$ for the Baltic (after Brogmus, 1952)

Gain			Loss	
Inflow	737	(53%)	Outflow	1,216 (87%)
Precipitation	183	(13%)	Evaporation	183 (13%)
River discharge	479	(34%)		
Total	1,399	(100%)	Total	1,399 (100%)

Table 3.2. The water exchange at various cross-sections in the Baltic (after Brogmus, 1952)

Position of cross-section	Between Kattegat and Belt Sea	Between Belt Sea and Baltic proper	Entrance Gulf of Finland	Entrance Gulf of Bothnia
Salinity ($^o/_{oo}$) of outflowing water	20.0	8.7	5.8	5.3
Salinity ($^o/_{oo}$) of inflowing water	33.0	17.4	8.0	6.1
River water influx (km^3/year)	479	472	131	199
Outflow (km^3/year)	1,216	944	476	1,517
Inflow (km^3/year)	737	472	345	1,318
Calculated import of oceanic water (35$^o/_{oo}$) (km^3/year)	639	156	26	35
% of total import	100	24.4	4.0	5.4

The table shows us that more than half (60%) of the outflowing water volume is replaced by inflow. The river discharge, comprising 40% of total outflow volume, has, by the time it reaches the outlet of the Baltic near Skagen, acquired a salinity of 20‰ through mixing. The excess of water in the Baltic expresses itself in a significant gradient in sea level. Between Skagen and the interiors of the Gulfs of Finland and Bothnia, there is a rise in sea level of 30 to 35 cm.

Postulating a state of equilibrium and with an estimate of the fresh water input, the volumes of inflow and outflow can be calculated from the mean salinities of the two water masses. The loss in salinity through the outflowing surface waters is replaced by the inflowing deep waters. In this way, Brogmus (1952) assessed the scales on which water exchange takes place over four cross-sections in the Baltic (see Table 3.2).

The characteristic salinity distribution for the Baltic is well recognizable from the table, namely, the increasing salinity in the surface waters towards the outlet and the gradual freshening of the deep waters from the Kattegat towards the northeast. In addition, the table shows us that the Gulf of Bothnia receives the largest influx of river water, followed by the central Baltic and the Gulf of Finland. Only a very small portion of total river runoff empties into the Belt Sea. The extent of water exchange varies considerably from one region to the other, depending on fresh water influx and the degree of mixing. At the mouth of the Gulf of Bothnia, where the difference in salinity between surface and depths is at its minimum, exchange is more intensive than elsewhere. The calculated constituent of ocean water (35‰) in the volume of inflow indicates the amount of salt that must be brought in, in order to compensate the loss through outflow. This so-called salt flux decreases rapidly with the gradual freshening of the waters towards the northeast. At Gedser, the total salt flux is only a quarter of what it was, and less than a tenth reaches the Gulfs of Bothnia and Finland.

So far we have been concerned only with the generalities of water exchange between the Baltic and the North Sea. In reality, though, we are confronted with a multiplicity of interlocking processes both periodic and aperiodic in nature. An example of periodic processes are the seasonal fluctuations; chief among the aperiodic phenomena are the short-term changes such as occur most typically in the Belt Sea region. This is because currents in this shallow transitional area, which acts as a connecting pipe between two large water reservoirs, respond to the most subtile differences in level between the two seas (cf. Dietrich, 1951).

The short-term current pattern in the Western Baltic is decisively influenced by the large-scale distribution of atmospheric pressure and the location of high-pressure and low-pressure areas over the North Sea and the Baltic, together with the winds thereby generated. A difference in atmospheric pressure of 1 mb corresponds to a rise or fall in water level of roughly 10 mm. An additional factor is the piling-up effect of the wind. Strong and persistent winds, especially when blowing from east or west, drive the water masses across the Baltic and pile them up at the opposite end. When high pressure prevails over Central Europe and low pressure over Scandinavia, westerly winds drive the water into the Eastern Baltic and induce the surface current normally flowing outwards to reverse its course. When pressure conditions are reversed, the water masses are piled up in the western Baltic, giving rise to an augmented outflow (Thiel, 1953).

These changes in water level due to meteorological conditions are normally restricted to ± 1 m in the southern Belt Sea. In extreme cases, though, the amplitude may be much wider (Thiel, 1953). Water pile-up may frequently lead to seiches being observed. These manifest themselves in a series of regular, pulse-like oscillations in water level. Depending on the seiche type, the oscillation period varies between 13 and 39.4 h (cf. Magaard, 1974). Tides play only a minor role in the western Baltic, their range averaging merely 10–15 cm. In the Baltic proper the tidal range is reduced to a few cm only.

A very important aspect of the hydrography of the Baltic concerns the renewal of the deep waters in the basins. The inflowing saltier water, though underflowing the surface water, is generally not dense enough to displace the bottom water in the deeper basins. It therefore either spreads over the bottom waters or displaces only its upper strata. The bottom waters are thus renewed only when an unusually powerful inflow with a greater than normal salt-load crosses the Darsse Sill into the Baltic proper. This renewal is aperiodic in its occurrence. It occurs spasmodically, sometimes on a very vast scale (Wyrtki, 1954).

When a greater than usual salt flux is thus introduced into the Baltic, it fertilizes the surface waters, which are otherwise rather deficient in inorganic nutrient salts. Through the exchange process part of the nutrient-enriched deep waters otherwise not involved in the winter vertical circulation are drawn upwards into the euphotic zone. Major influxes of salt, as observed during the early thirties and sixties, had far-reaching biological consequences. They not only led to a sharp rise in productivity, but also brought about a temporary change in faunal composition with repercussions on the fishery yields (see Segerstråle, 1969).

Sometimes, though, it may take years for the bottom layers to be completely renewed. Oxygen consumption following on remineralization processes may, under conditions of sustained stagnation, cause a total depletion of oxygen, resulting in the development of hydrogen sulfide. In the deepest basins of the central Baltic below a depth of 125 m, anoxic conditions such as are characteristic of the Black Sea may temporarily prevail. There is some reason to believe that anoxic periods have gained in frequency over the last decades, though it cannot yet be decided whether enhanced nutrient enrichment through the activities of man is responsible, or a decreased renewal rate due to hydrographic factors (Grasshoff, 1974).

3.3 The Kiel Bight

The Kiel Bight forms the southwestern part of the Belt Sea with two outlets to the north, the Little Belt and the Great Belt, and one to the east, the Fehmarn Belt. These straits also determine sea floor topography inasmuch as they are connected by a channel system roughly 30 m deep, with a trough running into the Eckernförde Bight, while the remaining parts of the Kiel Bight generally lie above the 20 m depth level (Fig. 2.1). The mean depth is about 20 m and the total area approximately 3000 km^2. This implies a water volume of 60 km^3. A detailed description of the hydrographic regime for this area has been given by Krug (1963).

The Coriolis force causes the outflowing Baltic water to be deflected to the right towards the Swedish coast. Its main exits are therefore the Öre Sund and the Great Belt. The inflowing water is likewise deflected to the right, thus traveling up more on the Danish side. Another factor controlling the inflow of saltier, heavier water is the presence of the sills at the outlets of the Baltic. Thus the Öre Sund with its high sill lying only 7–8 m deep normally prevents inflow altogether.

Consequently, a large part of the outflow and nearly the entire inflow pass through the Kiel Bight. This fact in itself suggests that the Bight undergoes strong hydrographic changes. When we compare the water volume of the Kiel Bight with the volumes for yearly inflow and outflow quoted in the preceding section, we see that the Kiel Bight is flushed in both directions several times a year. It is important to consider this circumstance in connection with the distribution of nutrients, micro-organisms and plankton, for we must remember that we are not dealing with one and the same static water body, but with different, albeit similar water masses fed from two sources, the Central Baltic and the Kattegat. The northeastern part of the Kiel Bight, which connects the Great Belt with the Fehmarn Belt, is more involved in these exchange processes than the southwestern part, where our studies were conducted.

Inflow and outflow are associated with major changes in salinity. Salinity extremes in the Kiel Bight range from 10‰ to 30‰; these extremes, though, occur at different depth levels. By rule of thumb we can take salinity in the upper layer as varying between 10‰ and 20‰ and in the bottom water below 25 m between 20‰ and 30‰.

The annual temperature range is similarly wide, extending over approximately 20° C in the surface layer. However, the extreme values – 1.2° and 20° C are not regularly attained. Only as a rare exception does ice form on the open water, most recently in the winter of 1962/63. The annual temperature curve for the deep water is far less pronounced, the amplitude being of the order of 10°. A very characteristic feature of the Kiel Bight and the entire transitional region between Baltic and North Sea is the thermohaline stratification throughout the greater part of the year. The water column very often shows a distinctly laminary structure. On such occasions we may observe not only one but several discontinuity layers, often recognizable on the echo-sounder (Lenz, 1965).

Seasonality in water stratification is well demonstrated by the routine studies on plankton and hydrography carried out over a 19-year period by the late Professor Krey at the permanent station Boknis Eck at the entrance to Eckern-

Table 3.3. Mean seasonal cycle of salinity ($^0/_{00}$) in the surface and bottom layer of the 28-m deep permanent station Boknis Eck (Kiel Bight) from unpublished data by Krey (†)

Months	Jan.	Feb.	March	April	May	June	July	Aug.	Sept.	Oct.	Nov.	Dec.
A. Surface layer (0.5 m)												
$\bar{x}$	18.8	18.0	16.5	16.3	14.8	14.2	15.1	15.1	16.4	17.3	18.8	19.1
s	1.4	1.5	1.6	2.8	1.1	1.5	1.9	2.1	1.9	2.0	1.8	1.6
B. Bottom layer (26 m)												
$\bar{x}$	21.3	20.2	19.1	19.6	20.6	21.0	23.2	23.7	23.3	22.8	21.7	21.0
s	2.1	1.9	2.0	3.0	2.7	2.3	2.4	1.8	1.7	1.3	2.4	2.4
C. Vertical gradient												
$\Delta\bar{x}$	2.5	2.2	2.6	3.3	5.8	6.8	8.1	8.6	6.9	5.5	2.9	1.9

Monthly means ($\bar{x}$) for the period 1957–1975 with standard deviation (s) and mean vertical gradient ($\Delta\bar{x}$)

förde Bight (Fig. 2.1—St. A). Monthly sampling included the measurement of salinity at six depth levels. Table 3.3 presents the mean annual cycle as derived from these data. In order to characterize the extent of vertical stratification, surface and bottom layer values have been arranged opposite each other.

Both depths show regular seasonal salinity cycles, which, however, do not run parallel. After a convergence in winter, due mainly to the intensive vertical mixing at this season, there follows a divergence in summer, arising from the dynamic equilibrium between outflow and inflow already spoken of. The freshening of the surface waters through increased runoff from the land in spring and early summer is offset by a rise in salinity in the depths. The month of August marks the maximum extent of vertical stratification.

The time lag between salinity minimum at the surface and maximum in the deep is explicable by the warming of the surface layer in summer. The resultant fall in density compensates for the slight salinity increase from June to August in the surface layer in consequence of higher evaporation.

The standard deviation quoted can with some reservation—for we do not know how far one value is representative of the whole month—be taken as an index for the yearly salinity fluctuations in a given month. At any rate, we generally note greater variations in salinity for the lower layer than for the upper. The freshening of the surface layer in May/June and the sharp rise in salinity in the depths are the features that recur most regularly.

The stability of water stratification in the depths in late summer is reflected in the fact that differences in salinity from month to month are only slight. At this season a severe deficiency of oxygen often develops in the deeper parts of the Kiel Bight (cf. Krey and Zeitzschel, 1971). Not infrequently, total oxygen depletion occurs, followed by formation of hydrogen sulfide (see Chap. 18).

Another point is that the data from Boknis Eck presented here show salinity in some years as diverging substantially from the mean values. Attention was drawn to this by Krey (1961). Between 1958 and 1960, the annual average at Boknis Eck rose by 3.3‰, accompanied by a significant increase in phosphate content as well as in the plankton biomass. Generally, a salinity rise in the euphotic zone augments productivity, since water from the Kattegat is considerably richer in inorganic nutrients than the surface waters of the Central Baltic.

Regarding the water budget of the Baltic, an analysis of long-term observation series would in all probability reveal the same sequence of cause and effect as brought to light by Schott (1966) for the long-term changes in surface salinity in the southern North Sea. The decisive factor is runoff from the land, which in turn depends on precipitation over the drainage area. Since in our latitudes precipitation is brought on chiefly by the westerlies, the chain of cause and effect may be carried further via the action of the westerlies to large-scale changes in atmospheric circulation.

Whereas for the Baltic proper an increase in runoff from the land brings in its wake a progressive freshening, its implications for the Kiel Bight—as part of the Belt Sea—is a stronger compensatory inflow in the depths and a simultaneous rise in salinity. Winter vertical mixing may distribute this higher salt content over the entire water column.

3.4 The Kiel Fjord

The Kiel Fjord is a narrow extension of the southwestern part of the Kiel Bight, running about 17 km from north to south and terminating at its southern end in the town of Kiel (see Fig. 2.1). From its mouth, roughly 8 km wide, the Kiel Fjord tapers in a funnel shape up to its narrowest part at Friedrichsort, the width here being only little more than 1 km. This constriction at Friedrichsort divides the fjord into two more or less equal sections, at the same time forming the demarcation between the outer and the inner fjord. The latter broadens out again inwards to a width of about 2.5 km, ending in a narrow tongue projecting into the center of the town of Kiel.

As regards bottom topography, the Kiel Fjord is open towards the Kiel Bight, there being no sill to act as a barrier. Its average depth is 15 m. As a prolongation of the fjord, there extends into the Kiel Bight a 17–20 m deep basin. This basin is enclosed by low banks between 10 and 13 m deep. Only in the northeast is there a 15-m deep, relatively narrow outlet leading into the deeper parts of the Kiel Bight. The indirect consequence of this for the Kiel Fjord is that water exchange between the fjord and the deeper parts of the Bight is not as unimpeded as at the surface.

Freshwater input into the Kiel Fjord comes only from one minor source, the river Schwentine. The rainwater drainage of the Kiel municipality contributes a negligible quantity. Similarly, overflow water from the Kiel Canal is irrelevant, since the water in question is brackish, albeit with a lower salt content.

The topography and hydrography of the Kiel Fjord has been treated by Kändler (1959), our description here being based on his study. For six successive years from 1952 to 1957, three stations were occupied at about monthly intervals to measure the vertical distribution of temperature and salinity. We shall here single out the mean annual curves for the 1 m and 14 m depth levels at Station 1 in the inner Fjord according to his study.

February is the coldest month, surface and deep waters having very nearly the same temperature (3° C). In July the surface temperature is highest (18° C), whereas it takes the 14-m depth layer up to September to warm up to its maximum of 13° C. The annual salinity distribution shows a parallel trend for both depths, the mean difference being 2–3‰. With a maximum in winter and minimum in May, it follows the same basic pattern as salinity in the surface water of the Kiel Bight (cf. Table 3.3).

The parallelism in seasonal salinity fluctuations between surface and 14-m depth level proves that the deep waters of Kiel Bight do not normally penetrate into the inner Kiel Fjord in summer. In contrast, they can be clearly traced in the basin at the mouth of the outer Fjord (St. 3) at a depth of 17 m. The boundary layer between inflow and outflow evidently lies somewhere in the depth range between 14 and 17 m.

What is true for the Kiel Bight also applies to the Kiel Fjord: we are confronted with continually shifting water masses, a fact that greatly hampers the study of biological processes in one and the same water body over a longer period of time. How marked these short-term fluctuations are, is plainly demonstrated by the daily records of surface temperature and salinity taken from the Reventlou Brücke in the inner fjord during the same study period (Ohl, 1959).

These records show us that a change in salinity is frequently associated with a simultaneous change in temperature. From this it follows that these fluctuations are not caused by meteorological processes (warming up or cooling down, precipitation or evaporation), but by one water mass having been replaced by another.

From Ohl's diagrams (1959), from which the greatest extrema were eliminated through pentad averaging, we further note that the residence time of a fairly constant water body in the inner Fjord is about one to two weeks. The extrema, though, range from one day to maximally six weeks. The maximal value, however, represents an exceptional situation in winter 1957. From mid-January to the end of February, the fluctuations in surface salinity were so slight as to justify the assumption of the water body having remained static during this period.

3.5 Study Period 1974/75

In the following we shall present the temperature and salinity distribution as recorded during the joint study period from January 1974 to March 1975. Sampling was carried out at about monthly intervals across a transect starting from the inner Kiel Fjord (St. 1) up to the central Kiel Bight (St. 5, see Fig. 2.1). The observation depths are the same as those for the other parameters. The temperature values are rounded-off Nansen cast measurements; salinity values are salinometer readings (Tables 3.4 and 3.5).

Figure 3.2 depicts seasonal change by means of an isopleth diagram. For space reasons we have omitted the values for Station 3 (Kiel lighthouse), as coverage here was generally less thorough than at the remaining four stations.

Temperature distribution shows a regular seasonal cycle. Despite the rather wide-spaced isopleths and the shallow depths at the first three stations, the time lag between surface and depths in warming up and cooling down can be discerned from the diagram. Differences between the stations are slight. The lower layers at the two stations in the central Kiel Bight (Sts. 4 and 5) have lower temperatures in

Table 3.4. Temperature °C

Date	Station 1		Station 2		Station 3			Station 4		Station 5		
	2 m	10 m	2 m	10 m	2 m	10 m	18 m	2 m	10 m	2 m	10 m	18 m
Jan. 24, 1974	3.70	3.60	3.60	3.40	2.90	2.90	2.90	3.00	2.80	3.00	2.90	2.60
Feb. 14	4.35	3.75	—	—	—	—	—	3.30	3.10	3.10	3.10	3.30
Feb. 28	3.70	3.80	3.10	3.10	2.90	2.90	3.00	3.10	3.00	2.90	3.00	3.20
March 21	4.40	4.10	3.80	3.70	3.50	4.30	3.60	3.90	3.20	3.70	4.40	3.10
April 18	8.60	7.30	8.60	7.80	7.00	6.80	4.40	7.60	6.70	7.30	6.80	5.40
May 16	10.90	9.60	10.40	10.00	9.70	9.00	8.80	9.95	9.30	10.10	8.70	6.40
June 11	12.80	11.60	12.80	12.10	12.30	12.30	10.80	12.40	12.30	12.30	12.30	11.60
June 25	17.70	17.00	—	—	—	—	—	17.35	11.20	17.20	15.70	10.50
July 11	16.70	15.40	16.10	16.10	15.50	15.40	12.60	—	—	15.50	15.50	15.10
Aug. 7	—	—	—	—	—	—	—	—	—	—	—	—
Aug. 29	17.70	15.80	17.70	16.50	15.00	16.80	16.00	18.30	17.50	17.45	17.50	15.10
Sept. 12	15.50	15.70	15.90	15.90	15.90	15.70	15.50	16.00	16.00	15.90	15.70	15.60
Oct. 24	10.50	10.50	10.10	10.10	10.60	10.25	10.25	10.40	10.60	10.35	10.35	11.20
Nov. 21	7.50	7.90	7.60	7.80	7.00	7.50	7.80	7.50	8.00	7.50	7.45	8.20
Dec. 10	6.50	6.60	6.70	8.20	6.50	6.50	6.50	6.50	7.00	6.50	6.50	7.00
Jan. 23, 1975	5.30	5.20	5.30	5.10	—	5.00	5.00	—	—	—	5.10	5.00
Feb. 12	3.60	5.10	3.95	4.70	4.10	4.70	4.70	4.15	4.65	4.10	3.70	4.80
March 10	5.50	4.10	4.20	4.10	3.80	3.70	4.30	4.20	3.50	3.90	3.30	—

Table 3.5. Salinity °/₀₀

Date	Station 1		Station 2		Station 3			Station 4		Station 5		
	2 m	10 m	2 m	10 m	2 m	10 m	18 m	2 m	10 m	2 m	10 m	18 m
Jan. 24, 1974	15.26	17.76	14.63	15.13	15.13	15.26	18.41	16.08	16.26	15.51	16.77	19.54
Feb. 14	16.45	17.58	—	—	—	—	—	17.20	17.58	16.58	17.08	19.84
Feb. 28	16.77	17.02	17.17	17.15	16.88	17.27	17.27	15.13	15.13	16.32	16.39	18.66
March 21	15.60	16.37	16.87	17.13	15.54	15.98	16.81	14.34	15.86	15.60	16.24	16.49
April 18	13.66	15.06	14.80	15.31	14.80	15.06	16.08	14.29	14.68	14.31	14.68	16.21
May 16	14.10	15.06	14.99	15.38	14.86	15.76	15.76	14.22	14.99	14.61	14.93	17.81
June 11	15.25	16.66	15.12	16.53	15.63	15.89	21.14	16.27	16.27	16.02	16.15	22.42
June 25	15.95	15.95	—	—	—	—	—	14.54	21.23	14.92	15.89	22.45
July 11	16.40	16.79	16.02	16.08	17.30	17.43	21.01	17.68	17.94	18.25	18.32	20.82
Aug. 7	19.62	20.54	—	—	—	—	—	—	—	—	—	—
Aug. 29	15.30	20.67	14.65	20.40	10.46	19.88	20.93	10.73	17.66	10.73	14.34	22.24
Sept. 12	18.50	19.86	16.69	19.93	15.79	20.32	20.83	14.10	17.08	14.75	18.70	20.96
Oct. 24	17.32	18.25	18.12	18.12	18.12	18.12	18.38	16.25	16.92	16.92	17.45	18.51
Nov. 21	17.17	17.53	17.27	17.79	17.40	17.73	18.15	17.44	18.70	17.66	17.79	18.18
Dec. 10	17.86	18.12	17.08	17.47	17.34	17.47	17.73	17.21	17.47	17.08	17.08	18.12
Jan. 23, 1975	20.40	20.40	19.82	20.14	20.60	20.67	20.67	20.80	20.90	20.32	20.64	20.77
Feb. 12	15.00	19.23	14.49	18.85	10.90	16.92	20.06	9.87	18.40	10.13	10.64	20.45
March 10	13.13	16.63	13.60	17.03	12.54	14.78	20.99	11.15	12.74	11.55	13.33	20.86

June/July than the two stations in the Kiel Fjord. The salinity diagram (Fig. 3.2) shows us that this is due to the influx of saltier deep water. Analogously, the temperature maximum at the end of August is coupled with a salinity minimum, pointing to an intrusion of low-salinity Baltic water into the Kiel Bight.

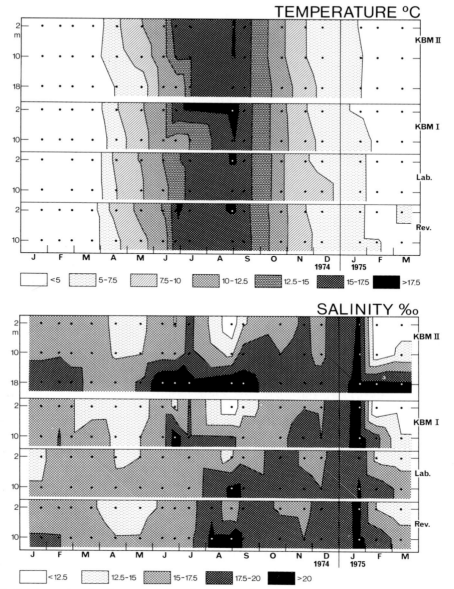

Fig. 3.2. Annual cycle of temperature and salinity at Station I (*Rev.*) and Station 2 (*Lab.*) in the Kiel Fjord and at Station 4 (*KBM I*) and Station 5 (*KBM II*) in the Kiel Bight (cf. Fig. 2.1)

The winters of 1974 and 1975 were unusually mild (see Chap. 2). For 1974 the lowest water temperature was 2.6° C and in 1975 temperatures did not fall below 3.3° C. At the end of January 1975, the temperature was still as high as 5° C (cf. Table 3.4). On the other hand, the summer of 1974 was comparatively cool. The daily temperature records from the lightship "Fehmarnbelt" show that the maximum value in the surface layer was a mere 17.7° C.

A comparison of the stations reveals that the inner Kiel Fjord (St. 1), probably owing to its more sheltered position, tends to have warmer surface temperatures than the stations lying farther out. The temperature difference for the surface waters between Stations 1 and 5 averages 0.5° C, the maximum measured being 1.6° C in March 1975. In autumn and winter, however, the situation may be reversed, since cooling is more rapid near the shore than out in the open sea.

The salinity cycle, which mirrors the variability of the water masses in our area, naturally shows considerably greater irregularity than temperature, since the temperature cycle in the Kiel Bight differs only insignificantly from that of the adjacent areas. The three main features of salinity distribution in the Kiel Bight are fairly well recognizable from Figure 3.2. The first is the almost homogenously mixed water column in winter, the second the salinity minimum in early summer through runoff from the land, which as a probable result of the mild winter can in our case be observed as early as April/May, being traceable down to 18 m depth. Thirdly, we have the summer maximum in vertical stratification. Here we clearly notice build-up in stratification with depth. In the Kiel Fjord, incoming saltier water rises as far up as the 10-m depth level in late summer.

An opposed to these regular features, the two intrusions of low-salinity out-flow water in August 1974 and February/March 1975 are to be regarded as exceptional. On both occasions, surface salinity at the three outer stations (Sts. 3–5, cf. Table 3.5) sank to less than 11‰. On both occasions at Station 5, the rule was confirmed of a strong outflow at the surface being offset by inflow in the depths. The salinity gradient between surface (2 m) and 18-m depth was as much as 10‰ and over.

The events in the spring of 1975 were so unusual that we shall consult the meteorological data recorded from Kiel lighthouse (force and direction of winds) as a help to interpretation. We are indebted to the Department of Meteorology of the Institute for having put these at our disposal.

In January westerly and southerly winds of medium force prevailed, occasion-ally rising up to wind force 8. They led to water level in the Western Baltic being depressed, therewith favoring the inflow of saltier water (cf. Wyrtki, 1952). Thus at the end of January, we obtained distinctly raised salinity values from all stations.

At the beginning of February, weather conditions reversed. From the 2nd to the 12th of February the wind blew almost uninterruptedly from east or north. The exceedingly strong outflow observed on the 12th of February is probably attributable to the joint effect of two factors. The stable weather conditions favor-ing the outflow probably play the lesser role here. The decisive influence appears to have been exerted by the greater than usual volume of fresh water runoff from the land following on the very mild winter. Surplus water from precipitation was not, as in other years, converted into snow and ice. Since there were neither strong nor sustained west winds in the second half of February and early March, outflow persisted up to the following months.

As already mentioned, the extensive outflow at the surface goes hand in hand with a pronounced salinity stratification. The regular winter vertical mixing has been prematurely brought to an end. This circumstance has far-reaching conse-quences as far as the onset and intensity of the spring bloom of phytoplankton is concerned. On account of the comparatively little light available in February and early March, the bloom cannot begin on a full scale unless water stratification is well established. In homohaline waters, therefore, the inception of the plankton bloom depends on the warming of the surface layer and the formation of a thermocline. In deep water bodies in our latitudes, the spring warming up does not generally begin to show effect until the end of March or beginning of April.

The different hydrographic conditions prevailing in the springs of 1974 and 1975, depicted in Figure 3.2, accordingly influence the development of the spring bloom (cf. Chap. 5, Fig. 5.1). In contrast to 1974, the data for 1975 show us—already in early March and at all stations—the commencement of a classical spring bloom.

In conclusion we may compare the salinity distribution at the two inner stations (Sts. 1 and 2) with that observed at the two outer stations (Sts. 4 and 5). As to be expected from the descriptions already given of the two regions, no fundamental differences exist between the Kiel Fjord and the Kiel Bight. Only the rate of water exchange appears sometimes to vary. It remains to be mentioned that, on the whole, the winter of 1974/75 was marked by a higher salinity than the previous winter. Evidently, this is another instance of the variations in salinity from year to year in the Kiel Bight, the significance of these annual fluctuations having been already discussed (Sect. 3.3).

References

Brogmus, W.: Eine Revision des Wasserhaushaltes der Ostsee. Kieler Meeresforsch. **9**, 15–42 (1952)

Cameron, W. M., Pritchard, D. W.: Estuaries, 306–324. In: Hill, M. N. (ed.), The Sea. Vol. II. New York-London: Interscience Publ., 1963

Dietrich, G.: Oberflächenströmungen im Kattegat, im Sund und in der Beltsee. Dt. Hydrograph. Z. **4**, 129–150 (1951)

Dietrich, G., Kalle, K., Krauss, W., Siedler, G.: Allgemeine Meereskunde. 3rd ed. Berlin-Stuttgart: Bornträger, 1974

Grasshoff, K.: Chemische Verhältnisse und ihre Veränderlichkeit, 85–101. In: Magaard, L., Rheinheimer, G. (eds.), Meereskunde der Ostsee. Berlin-Heidelberg-New York: Springer, 1974

Kändler, R.: Hydrographische Beobachtungen in der Kieler Förde 1952–1957. Kieler Meeresforsch. **15**, 145–156 (1959)

Krey, J.: Beobachtungen über den Gehalt an Mikrobiomasse und Detritus in der Kieler Bucht 1958–1960. Kieler Meeresforsch. **17**, 163–175 (1961)

Krey, J., Zeitzschel, B.: Long-term observations of oxygen and chlorophyll a in Kiel Bight. 12 pp. ICES, CM 1971, L:11 (Plankton Committee) (1971)

Krug, J.: Erneuerung des Wassers in der Kieler Bucht im Verlaufe eines Jahres am Beispiel 1960/61. Kieler Meeresforsch. **19**, 158–174 (1963)

Kühl, H., Mann, H.: Vergleichende hydrochemische Untersuchungen an den Mündungen deutscher Flüsse. Verh. Intern. Verein Limnol. **14**, 451–458 (1961)

Lenz, J.: Zur Ursache der an die Sprungschicht gebundenen Echostreuschichten in der Westlichen Ostsee. Ber. Dt. Wiss. Kommn. Meeresforsch. **18**, 111–161 (1965)

Magaard, L.: Wasserstandsschwankungen und Seegang, 67–75. In: Magaard, L., Rheinheimer, G. (eds.), Meereskunde der Ostsee. Berlin-Heidelberg-New York: Springer, 1974

Magaard, L., Rheinheimer, G. (eds.): Meereskunde der Ostsee. Berlin-Heidelberg-New York: Springer, 1974

Ohl, H.: Temperatur- und Salzgehaltsmessungen an der Oberfläche des Kieler Hafens in den Jahren 1952 bis 1957. Kieler Meeresforsch. **15**, 157—160 (1959)

Remane, A., Schlieper, C.: Biology of Brackish Water. 2nd ed. (Die Binnengewässer Vol. 25). Stuttgart: Schweizerbart'sche Verlagsbuchhandlung, 1971

Schott, F.: Der Oberflächensalzgehalt in der Nordsee. Dt. Hydrogr. Z., Erg. H. (A) **9**, 1–58 (1966)

Segerstråle, S. G.: Biological Fluctuations in the Baltic Sea. Progr. Oceangr. **5**, 169–184 (1969)

Seibold, E.: Nebenmeere im humiden und ariden Klimabereich. Geol. Rdsch. **60**, 73–105 (1970)

Stommel, H.: Computation of pollution in a vertically mixed estuary. Sewage Industry Wastes **25**, 1065–1071 (1953)

Thiel, G.: Die Wirkungen des Luft- und Winddruckes auf den Wasserstand in der Ostsee. Dt. Hydrogr. Z. **6**, 107–123 (1953)

Wyrtki, K.: Die Dynamik der Wasserbewegungen im Fehmarnbelt I. Kieler Meeresforsch. **9**, 155–170 (1952)

Wyrtki, K.: Der große Salzeinbruch in die Ostsee im November und Dezember 1951. Kieler Meeresforsch. **10**, 19–25 (1954)

4. Oxygen and Some Inorganic Nutrients

G. RHEINHEIMER

In connection with the biological investigations in the Kiel Fjord and Kiel Bight, regular determinations of the oxygen content and concentration of the most important nutrients were carried out. Thus at each station on all cruises the concentrations of inorganic nitrogen compounds such as ammonia, nitrite and nitrate, as well as orthophosphate, were measured. These investigations are related to earlier observations which were carried out in the years 1964 to 1973 in the entire Kiel Bight area and its fjords (see Rheinheimer, 1967, 1970a, b), so that comparisons with the conditions in the time from January 1974 to March 1975 can be made.

4.1 Material and Methods

Water samples for the chemical analyses were taken on 15 monthly cruises at all five stations from the inner Kiel Fjord to the central Kiel Bight as well as on two additional cruises on 14.2. and 24.6.1974 at three stations (1, 4, and 5) in 2-, 10-, and—if present—in 18-m depth (see Chap.2). The sampling took place by means of hydrographic samplers from the Hydrobios Company, Kiel. Immediately after filling, the water samples were stored in a cool place and later analyzed in the laboratory of the Marine Microbiology Department at the Institut für Meereskunde, Kiel. The determinations of the various compounds were made according to the following methods: oxygen according to Winkler, (see Grasshoff, 1976); ammonia according to Grasshoff, 1968; nitrite and nitrate according to Grasshoff, 1964; orthophosphate according to Murphy and Riley, 1962.

4.2 Oxygen

The oxygen content of the water was relatively high at all stations during the entire period of investigation (see Table 4.1). The average values varied between 8.19 and 10.64 mg O_2 l^{-1}. Of 195 samples investigated, 81 had more than 10 and only 4 less than 5 mg O_2 l^{-1}. The lowest oxygen content with 2.67 mg O_2 l^{-1} was found on 29.8.74 at Station 1 in the inner Kiel Fjord at 10-m depth—the highest with 13.26 mg O_2 l^{-1} on 10.3.75 at Station 5 in the middle of the Kiel Bight at 2-m depth. While during the winter months only relatively small differences could be determined at the various depths, the oxygen concentration, especially in the summer and autumn at Stations 1 and 2 (Kiel Fjord) in 10-m depth and at Stations 3 and 5 (Kiel Bight) in 18-m depth, was clearly lower than on the surface.

Table 4.1. Oxygen mg l^{-1}

Date	Station 1		Station 2		Station 3			Station 4		Station 5		
	2 m	10 m	2 m	10 m	2 m	10 m	18 m	2 m	10 m	2 m	10 m	18 m
Jan. 24, 1974	10.98	10.93	11.35	11.32	11.63	11.74	10.93	11.97	11.42	11.80	11.42	10.85
Feb. 14	7.97	7.19	—	—	—	—	—	11.74	11.92	11.14	8.90	6.69
Feb. 28	9.77	11.20	12.01	11.68	11.61	11.71	11.63	4.83	12.28	12.03	11.99	10.87
March 21	10.92	8.41	11.50	8.37	12.07	11.70	10.96	12.29	11.34	12.30	12.02	11.70
April 18	10.92	11.61	8.32	11.49	11.86	11.73	7.55	11.72	11.88	11.81	12.14	11.54
May 16	11.74	9.24	10.33	10.36	11.03	10.53	10.65	11.11	10.07	11.04	10.93	7.82
June 11	8.80	6.92	10.53	9.23	10.13	9.61	7.23	9.71	9.66	9.79	9.94	9.22
June 25	10.50	9.14	—	—	—	—	—	9.03	7.32	9.41	9.75	6.98
July 11	9.25	5.51	8.59	9.49	9.34	9.49	4.73	9.27	9.11	9.25	9.22	8.62
Aug. 7	8.00	5.85	—	—	—	—	—	—	—	—	—	—
Aug. 29	9.52	2.67	9.36	5.02	8.75	8.36	4.19	9.25	10.29	9.24	9.64	3.74
Sept. 12	8.54	7.27	9.52	6.72	9.42	6.91	5.32	9.76	7.92	9.66	6.19	5.96
Oct. 24	8.73	8.92	9.32	9.18	9.37	9.32	9.33	8.81	9.54	9.89	9.77	9.40
Nov. 21	8.99	7.11	7.78	9.15	9.07	8.97	7.32	9.05	8.38	8.00	8.02	6.67
Dec. 10	7.67	7.71	9.23	9.45	9.67	8.63	9.49	9.41	8.52	9.47	8.94	9.68
Jan. 23, 1975	8.06	9.66	10.76	10.76	9.01	8.81	9.87	9.38	9.42	10.98	10.54	10.55
Feb. 12	11.30	9.56	12.50	10.35	11.65	9.02	9.65	10.53	11.05	11.76	12.05	10.48
March 10	12.75	8.57	13.00	9.34	13.23	11.95	8.34	12.50	11.94	13.26	12.87	8.88

Table 4.2. Oxygen saturation %

Date	Station 1		Station 2		Station 3			Station 4		Station 5		
	2 m	10 m	2 m	10 m	2 m	10 m	18 m	2 m	10 m	2 m	10 m	18 m
Jan. 24, 1974	92.2	93.1	94.6	94.3	95.5	96.5	91.7	99.2	94.3	97.4	94.9	91.0
Feb. 14	85.9	78.5						98.8	100.0	93.1	74.8	57.3
Feb. 28	82.8	95.3	100.6	97.7	96.4	97.6	97.2		101.2	99.7	99.6	92.1
March 21	93.5	71.8	97.7	71.1	100.8	100.2	92.7	103.1	94.3	103.5	103.3	97.4
April 18	102.3	106.3	78.5	106.7	107.7	106.2	64.8	107.7	107.0	108.4	109.7	101.8
May 16	116.1	89.4	101.8	101.5	106.7	100.9	101.6	107.9	96.7	107.7	103.4	71.4
June 11	91.6	70.8	109.5	95.4	104.4	99.3	74.8	100.7	100.1	101.1	102.7	97.9
June 25	121.5	104.5						103.0	76.4	107.3	108.3	72.2
July 11	105.4	61.2	96.2	106.3	104.1	105.8	50.8	103.7	101.9	103.9	103.5	97.4
Aug. 29	109.8	30.6	107.6	58.3	92.7	97.4	48.3	105.0	119.9	103.2	109.9	42.7
Sept. 12	96.0	82.6	106.6	76.9	105.0	78.8	60.6	107.9	89.2	107.1	69.9	68.2
Oct. 24	87.3	89.9	93.0	91.6	94.6	93.4	93.6	87.5	95.6	98.7	97.5	96.4
Nov. 21	83.9	67.1	72.9	86.3	83.8	83.8	69.3	84.6	80.0	74.9	75.2	63.7
Dec. 10	70.2	70.9	84.4	89.9	88.2	78.8	86.8	85.8	78.7	86.3	81.4	89.8
Jan. 23, 1975	72.8	87.0	96.9	96.6	81.4	79.2	88.8	84.9	85.0	98.5	95.0	95.0
Feb. 12	94.4	85.3	105.2	91.2	95.9	78.6	85.8	86.3	97.1	96.4	98.1	93.6
March 10	110.5	73.4	109.2	80.0	109.3	100.0	73.8	103.5	98.0	109.1	105.5	76.3

The comparatively low values at this time, which were also observed during earlier investigations, result from the increased activity of the C-heterotrophic microorganisms in the water above the sea floor. An exception is Station 4, which lies above sandy sediment. Here the concentration of organic nutrients is evidently too low for such a strong oxygen consumption as at the other stations.

In Table 4.2 the oxgen saturation values are listed. These demonstrate very clearly the good oxygen supply in the study area. During the time from mid-February to September, values of over 100% were not infrequently registered. The over-saturation is the result of vigorous assimilation activity at this time. This occurs mostly in 2- and 10-m depth—but a slight oxygen over-saturation was also found at one station in 18-m depth both in April and in May 1974. A relatively low oxygen concentration was measured in the summer—particularly in the late summer above the sea floor at Stations 1, 2, 3, and 5 (see above). However, these were only on three occasions less than 50%.

While there was never a complete disappearance of the oxygen at the five stations investigated, in summer and autumn, however, more or less long periods of oxygen deficit can be measured in a few pits and depressions, above all in the area of the fjords. The presence of H_2S can then demonstrated here from time to time (see Bansemir and Rheinheimer, 1974). In warm and calm late summer periods, the H_2S concentration can increase to a rather high extent, so that in these areas by water mixing during the first storm the oxygen content of the overlaying water may be almost completely consumed. This has repeatedly caused the dying of fishes in recent years.

The oxygen supply in the muddy sediments at the investigated Stations 1, 2, 3, and 5 is less favorable than in the water. Frequently only a thin aerobic zone of often less than 1 cm above the oxygen-poor sediment is found here. This is at times completely anaerobic and colored black due to sulfide formation. During storms, the sediment may be more or less strongly stirred up, and the aerobic zone may thus temporarily be extended. The sandy sediment at Station 4, on the other hand, is always aerobic.

4.3 Inorganic Nutrients

The concentrations of the inorganic nitrogen compounds and also the phosphate content of the water are often greater in the Kiel Fjord than in the open Kiel Bight. On a few investigation cruises, however, the highest values for one or the other of these compounds were found at a station in the Kiel Bight (see Tables 4.3–4.6). Noteworthy is the occasional occurrence of very high values at a definite depht by a single station, or also at several adjacent depths and stations. In most of these cases, contaminations are most likely the cause—as, for example, due to the waste water outlet at Bülk.

4.3.1 Ammonia

The ammonia concentration of the water in the study area varies between 0.454 and 49.193 µg-at N l^{-1}. It undergoes relatively large fluctuations at nearly all stations throughout the year. Taken as a whole, however, during the winter months higher values are registered than in the spring and summer (see Table 4.3). This becomes especially clear when the occasional extremely high values are not taken into consideration. After the always relatively high winter values, a strong decrease in the ammonia content can be seen at the end of February 1974 and

Table 4.3. Ammonia µg-at NH_4-N l^{-1}

Date	Station 1		Station 2		Station 3			Station 4		Station 5		
	2 m	10 m	2 m	10 m	2 m	10 m	18 m	2 m	10 m	2 m	10 m	18 m
Jan. 24, 1974	14.143	14.064	8.171	42.429	10.607	4.243	5.971	2.986	3.457	4.007	5.186	4.793
Feb. 14	9.000	6.464						2.036	2.700	4.429	5.071	6.429
Feb. 28	2.393	2.293	1.957	1.714	0.900	0.929	1.279	1.086	1.164	0.900	1.136	1.164
March 21	4.071	5.714	4.143	4.143	3.429	1.857	1.357	1.786	3.286	3.571	5.143	4.000
April 18	1.493	2.064	0.611	0.543	1.289	0.611	1.693	0.814	0.454	0.651	1.737	1.791
May 16	3.143	3.829	3.771	1.714	17.857	13.929	1.714	1.371	1.943	1.507	1.543	2.914
June 11	2.343	2.286	4.000	1.229	2.629	1.200	1.429	0.971	1.314	1.400	0.971	1.259
June 25	0.629	4.007						0.786	0.707	1.257	0.864	7.700
July 11	11.029	2.400	3.057	3.429	3.371	3.314	2.743	5.657	2.971	2.286	49.143	9.714
Aug. 7	2.857	4.929										
Aug. 29	1.286	5.236	1.764	1.993	1.486	1.356	1.707	1.263	1.207	1.021	0.929	1.950
Sept. 12	2.918	2.171	2.138	2.239	5.632	0.679	0.882	1.154	2.850	21.239	1.391	1.629
Oct. 24	6.871	3.807	13.464	4.271	39.279	27.857	6.268	21.171	1.671	2.739	2.043	1.254
Nov. 21	2.714	4.004	4.139	2.850	2.348	2.511	1.873	1.221	1.059	1.466	1.561	1.873
Dec. 10	2.957	2.793	4.929	3.286	7.064	5.750	5.750	2.382	5.750	1.479	1.971	1.479
Jan. 23, 1975	2.714	3.714	39.143	7.357	2.714	3.000	1.714	1.750	1.786	2.429	1.971	6.000
Feb. 12	6.514	12.000	3.171	4.543	2.143	3.343	18.257	2.100	1.680	2.366	2.657	1.886
March 10	1.569	1.851	1.500	0.849	0.951	1.046	1.543	0.643	0.789	1.174	0.737	2.254

again in March 1975—although on March 21, 1974 a temporary increase may be noted. In the middle of April, however, very low values were measured again. This decrease in the ammonia concentration is associated with a vigorous phytoplankton development, which is shown by the high chlorophyll values (see Chap. 5) on 18.4.1974 and 10.3.1975. At most of the stations the lowest ammonia concentrations were found during this time. In the middle of May the values increase more or less strongly almost everywhere. This depends on the increase of zooplankton, which attains its maximum in May. At Station 3, the ammonia concentration in 2- and 10-m depth was even quite high, with 17.6 and 13.9 µg-at N l^{-1}. Still higher values were found at the end of October with 39.3 and 27.9 µg-at N l^{-1}. Corresponding to this is also the amount measured at the adjacent Station 4 in 2-m depth with 21.2 µg-at N l^{-1}. In these cases an influence of the waste water outlet at Bülk is suspected. Single extremely high ammonia values on July 11 in 10-m depth and on Sept. 12 in 2-m depth at the last Station 5 could not be explained, however. The few very high values found in the Kiel Fjord are due to local contaminations. At Laboe (St. 2) by corresponding wind conditions there may also be an influence from the waste water outlet at Bülk.

4.3.2 Nitrite

The nitrite concentrations are relatively low in the entire area of investigation. They vary between 0 and 2.286 µg-at N l^{-1}. The values in the inner Kiel Fjord at Station 1 are clearly greater than in the outer Fjord (St. 2) and Kiel Bight (St. 3–5; see Table 4.4). The nitrite content shows a distinct seasonal cycle with relatively high values in winter and low summer values. In the spring and especially in the summer, in spite of the very sensitive method of measurement, at times no nitrite could be found at several stations.

4.3.3 Nitrate

Of great interest is the course of the nitrate content, which likewise shows a pronounced yearly cycle with quite high winter values and very low summer values (see Table 4.5). Thus the nitrate concentrations vary over a wide range between 0 and 33.643 µg-at N l^{-1}. Thereby the values at both Kiel Fjord stations (1 and 2), especially in winter, are usually clearly higher than in the open Kiel Bight (St. 3–5). During the investigation year 1974 in the period from April to October, the nitrate concentrations at all stations were very low. They began to increase strongly in late autumn until January or February when the highest values were reached. Similar results were also obtained in previous years (see Rheinheimer, 1967). Depending on the given meteorological conditions, however, shifts in time up to several weeks have been found. The rapid decrease in the nitrate concentration in late winter or early spring is connected with the development of the phytoplankton spring bloom. The vigorous increase of the nitrate content again in the late autumn and winter is similarly correlated to the phytoplankton population, which, as seen in the falling chlorophyll values (see Chap. 5), strongly decrease at this time. The vertical mixing of the water and the liberation of nitrate from the sediment surface also has an important influence.

Table 4.4. Nitrite μg-at NO_2-Nl^{-1}

Date	Station 1		Station 2		Station 3			Station 4		Station 5		
	2 m	10 m	2 m	10 m	2 m	10 m	18 m	2 m	10 m	2 m	10 m	18 m
Jan. 24, 1974	1.286	1.125	1.179	1.071	0.857	0.857	0.964	1.125	0.911	0.964	0.964	0.857
Feb. 14	1.414	1.200						0.986	1.071	0.977	0.926	0.600
Feb. 28	1.029	1.121	0.907	0.943	0.843	0.864	0.907	0.807	0.936	0.907	0.907	0.986
March 21	0.969	0.969	0.600	0.814	0.583	0.600	1.100	0.471	0.686	0.771	0.771	0.600
April 18	0.589	0.279	0.364	0.054	0	0.050	0.225	0.054	0.161	0.043	0.054	0.161
May 16	0.913	0.254	0.236	0.121	0.050	0.101	0.101	0.050	0.031	0.050	0.050	0.152
June 11	0.400	0.350	0.200	0.100	0.050	0.050	0.150	0.050	0.050	0.100	0.050	0.050
June 25	0.250	0.429							0.054	0.054	0.054	0.050
July 11	0.150	0.150	0.100	0.050	0.100	0.050	0.080	0	0.040	0.050	0.050	0.107
Aug. 7	0.300	0.500										0
Aug. 29	0.400	0.250	0	0	0	0	0		0.250	0	0	0
Sept. 12	0.350	0.357	0.100	0.200	0.100	0.160	0.210	1.357	0.140	0.150	0.140	0.160
Oct. 24	0.482	0.214	0.246	0.279	0.107	0.129	0.107	0.161	0.064	0.064	0.054	0.107
Nov. 21	0.600	0.600	0.650	0.600	0.350	0.650	0.500	0.280	0.600	0.450	0.380	0.600
Dec. 10	2.286	2.057	2.286	2.229	1.829	1.829	1.600	1.657	1.657	1.429	1.429	1.600
Jan. 23, 1975	0.430	0.450	2.200	0.800	1.350	0.400	0.350	0.350	0.600	0.550	0.500	0.500
Feb. 12	0.920	0.800	0.600	0.750	0.350	0.680	0.500	0.200	0.150	0.200	0.300	0.700
March 10	1.500	1.232	0.461	1.061	0.214	0.632	0.354	0.096	0.343	0.096	0.471	0.386

Table 4.5. Nitrate µg-at $NO_3\text{-}N\ l^{-1}$

Date	Station 1		Station 2		Station 3			Station 4		Station 5		
	2 m	10 m	2 m	10 m	2 m	10 m	18 m	2 m	10 m	2 m	10 m	18 m
Jan. 24, 1974	33.643	26.893	29.571	23.464	7.179	4.714	12.964	7.179	6.482	5.893	7.179	11.679
Feb. 14	28.586	16.371						6.257	7.500	6.051	5.589	5.914
Feb. 28	18.550	19.064	13.193	10.214	5.450	7.657	4.271	3.757	4.636	6.807	5.743	8.757
March 21	13.343	17.886	8.743	13.371	3.964	4.543	3.614	2.829	4.500	3.957	3.957	4.071
April 18	2.325	2.636	0.093	0.346	0.400	0.807	0.072	0.152	0.285	0.243	0.175	1.039
May 16	4.687	2.671	1.879	0.164	1.414	0.356	0.447	0.304	0.541	0.293	0.293	3.048
June 11	0	0.964	0.257	0.414	0.396	0.373	1.336	0.396	0.430	0.529	0.407	0.613
June 25	0.550	1.057										
July 11	0.900	0.761	0.543	0.700	0.382	0.464	0.584	0.461	0.232	0.575	0.496	0.443
Aug. 7	0.191	1.050							0.174	0.411	0.625	0.321
Aug. 29	0.832	0.607	0.214	0.161	0.107	0.107	0.293	0.064	0	0.054	0.161	0.107
Sept. 12	1.414	1.786	0.400	1.943	0.361	0.161	0.326	0.839	0.342	0.182	0.342	0.297
Oct. 24	4.500	1.714	0.664	0.793	0.804	0.354	1.125	0.321	0.257	0.418	0.268	0.107
Nov. 21	3.021	1.471	5.114	1.329	1.757	2.457	1.407	1.488	1.168	0.836	1.013	1.329
Dec. 10	3.536	5.979	11.536	7.629	11.029	3.421	3.971	3.379	3.164	3.929	3.821	2.364
Jan. 23, 1975	11.250	12.086	12.432	17.414	7.543	8.171	8.757	7.364	7.543	6.629	6.893	10.000
Feb. 12	30.879	23.457	10.329	20.393	12.789	9.264	13.106	5.811	5.134	5.155	4.727	13.944
March 10	23.946	16.821	2.700	13.125	0.557	4.500	15.129	0.393	3.675	0.257	2.507	15.621

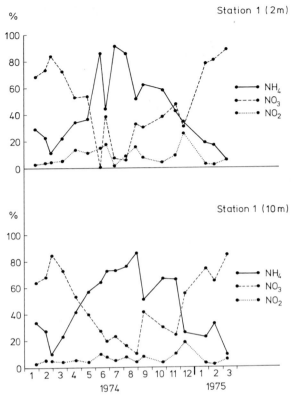

Fig.4.1. Percentage of the inorganic nitrogen compounds in the inner Kiel Fjord

The concentrations of all three inorganic nitrogen compounds in the Kiel Fjord and Kiel Bight are therefore higher in the winter than in the other seasons, and have their minima always in the spring or summer. Accordingly the total concentration of inorganic bound nitrogen is also considerably greater in the winter than during the rest of the year. The summer decrease in nitrite and nitrate, however, is much greater than that of ammonia. Therefore its percentage of the inorganic bound nitrogen increases greatly in the summer (see Figs.4.1 and 4.2). This is mainly an effect of phytoplankton grazing and excretion by zooplankton and zoobenthos. The inorganic bound nitrogen in the spring and summer is for the most part in the form of ammonia—in late autumn and winter, on the other hand, mostly as nitrate. This also confirms the results of earlier investigations in the Kiel Bight area (see Rheinheimer, 1967). During the year of investigation, however, the nitrate values in the winter were somewhat higher than in 1965/66.

4.3.4 Orthophosphate

The phosphate concentrations vary between 0.142 and 12.432 μg-at P l^{-1} and, taken, as a whole, are higher in winter than in the summer (see Table4.6). Very

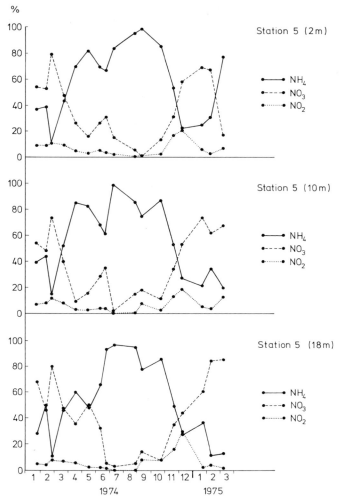

Fig. 4.2. Percentage of the inorganic nitrogen compounds in the central Kiel Bight

strong fluctuations are found at most stations, however. The phosphate content of
the water in the Kiel Fjord is generally not greater than in the open Kiel Bight.
On the various cruises of investigation, the maxima were repeatedly found at
different locations. If the individual depths are compared separately, however, a
different picture results. In water near the surface (2 m) in the inner Kiel Fjord,
usually much higher values are found than at the stations in the Kiel Bight. At a
depth of 10 m this is no longer so pronounced. While at the Fjord stations—
particularly in the inner Kiel Fjord—in most cases higher values were measured
at the surface, the opposite is true for the three stations in the Kiel Bight. Here the
higher values are more often found above the sea floor. This is especially clear at
Station 5 (KBM II), where at times anaerobic muddy sediment is found, and

Table 4.6. Orthophosphate µg-at PO_4-Pl^{-1}

Date	Station 1 2 m	Station 1 10 m	Station 2 2 m	Station 2 10 m	Station 3 2 m	Station 3 10 m	Station 3 18 m	Station 4 2 m	Station 4 10 m	Station 5 2 m	Station 5 10 m	Station 5 18 m
Jan. 24, 1974	1.947	1.603	1.489	1.283	0.687	0.641	1.099	0.916	0.802	1.374	1.031	3.321
Feb. 14	1.871	2.010						0.874	0.971	1.179	0.790	1.040
Feb. 28	3.803	1.732	2.781	1.477	0.881	0.455	0.771	0.839	2.810	0.881	3.577	3.632
March 21	3.135	1.239	1.694	0.948	0.968	1.026	2.242	0.929	2.903	2.710	2.710	2.090
April 18	0.794	0.358	0.487	0.139	1.316	0.655	0.787	0.171	0.119	0.206	0.171	0.258
May 16	5.216	0.984	0.910	0.606	0.455	0.758	0.425	0.787	0.682	0.485	0.713	1.174
June 11	1.061	2.123	0.455	0.455	0.303	0.273	0.758	12.432	0.652	0.379	0.303	0.652
June 25	1.000	1.600						0.258	1.900	0.610	0.240	0.700
July 11	1.423	1.219	0.960	0.916	0.406	2.439	3.048	1.116	0.406	1.016	0.864	0.610
Aug. 7	2.823	1.806										
Aug. 29	0.650	3.148	0.305	0.975	0.142	0.244	1.016	1.423	2.337	0.203	0.590	1.019
Sept. 12	1.539	1.539	0.940	1.675	0.342	0.684	2.565	0.171	0.564	0.431	0.332	0.513
Oct. 24	2.040	1.118	0.798	0.798	0.532	0.444	0.763	0.266	4.081	2.342	2.306	1.419
Nov. 21	1.729	1.513	1.513	1.405	2.810	3.998	2.702	1.362	1.513	1.189	1.189	1.405
Dec. 10	3.282	1.508	1.863	2.040	1.118	1.331	1.331	1.198	1.198	1.020	0.020	1.952
Jan. 23, 1975	1.755	1.755	1.652	1.652	1.631	1.362	1.652	1.858	0.867	1.507	1.445	2.209
Feb. 12	1.530	1.563	0.938	1.201	0.658	0.411	1.069	1.892	3.126	0.625	0.609	1.135
March 10	6.865	11.584	10284	6.055	3.555	2.942	2.316	3.310	3.212	2.574	3.555	2.966

phosphate from the sediment is then released into the water. Thereby it should also be considered that in the spring and autumn often less phytoplankton is present in the depths and therefore less phosphate is used up.

4.4 The Annual Cycle of Nutrients

A comparison of the concentrations of inorganic bound nitrogen and ortho-phosphate measured throughout the course of the year shows that both these substances are always present at all stations in all depths. It also shows further that after an accumulation of N in the winter, almost a complete assimilation of this takes place in the spring, so that the input and consumption are approximately in balance. At various stations in the spring and summer, however, the complete disappearance of nitrite, and on two locations also that of nitrate, was repeatedly observed. In previous years similar cases could also be found. From this can be seen that normally inorganic nutrients can hardly have a limiting effect on the phytoplankton development—and that such an effect, should it occur at all, would more likely be due to a deficiency of nitrogen rather than of phosphorus. The pronounced decrease of the ammonia values in the spring at the time of the phytoplankton spring bloom makes it evident that ammonia serves as a source of nitrogen for a part of the plankton algae, even though nitrate may still be present in the water. For a more complete understanding of the yearly cycles of the ammonia, nitrite and nitrate content, it is necessary to know the preferences of various plankton algae for the particular nitrogen compounds.

The annual cycle of nutrients in the Kiel Bight as it could be shown in this chapter is characteristic of coastal waters of the boreal-temperate climatic zone. Depending on the local conditions, however, there is a more or less important influence by nutrient inputs from land-side. The increase of nitrite and nitrate in the winter may be at least partially an effect of nitrification (see Chap. 17).

References

Bansemir, K., Rheinheimer, G.: Bakteriologische Untersuchungen über die Bildung von Schwefelwasserstoff in einer Vertiefung der inneren Kieler Förde. Kieler Meeresforsch. **30**, 91–98 (1974)

Grasshoff, K.: Zur Bestimmung von Nitrat in Meer- und Trinkwasser. Kieler Meeresforsch. **20**, 5–11 (1968)

Grasshoff, K.: Über eine empfindliche direkte Methode zur automatischen und manuellen Bestimmung von Ammoniak im Meerwasser. Z. anal. Chem. **234**, 13–22 (1964)

Grasshoff, K.: Methods of sea water analysis. Weinheim, New York: Verlag Chemie, 1976

Murphy, J., Riley, J. P.: A modified single solution method for the determination of phosphate in natural waters. Anal. Chim. Acta **27**, 31–36 (1962)

Rheinheimer, G.: Ökologische Untersuchungen zur Nitrifikation in Nord- und Ostsee. Helgoländer wiss. Meeresunters. **15**, 243–252 (1967)

Rheinheimer, G.: Mikrobiologische und chemische Untersuchungen in der Flensburger Förde. Ber. Deutsche wiss. Komm. Meeresforsch. **21**, 420–429 (1970a)

Rheinheimer, G.: Ammoniak-, Nitrit-, Nitrat- und Phosphatgehalt. In: Chemische, mikrobiologische und planktologische Untersuchungen in der Schlei im Hinblick auf deren Abwasserbelastung. Kieler Meeresforsch. **26**, 130–132 (1970b)

5. Seston and Its Main Components

J. LENZ

The data here presented will be better understood if a few words be first said on seston and its ecological role. The term seston covers all particles suspended in water regardless of their nature or origin. Depending on the aspect being dealt with, the particles can be classified under different headings, for instance according to particle size or chemical composition. The biologist will naturally want to divide seston into a living and a nonliving fraction, plankton and detritus, respectively. These may be further subdivided according to the nature and origin of the plankton organisms and detritus particles (see Table 5.1).

Especially with the various types of detritus, it is difficult to maintain consistency in classification, since some types belong to several categories at the same time. Thus resuspended bottom sediment often contains biogenous elements, just as soot is both aerogenous as well as anthropogenous. In addition, the terms autochthonous and allochthonous specify origin and offer yet another criterion. The first term may for instance be applied to biogenous detritus consisting of the remains of plankton formerly populating the investigation site, while the second term can be used to characterize the other three detritus types.

The amount of seston in an aquatic environment is first and foremost an indicator of the degree of eutrophication and the extent of terrestrial influence.

Table 5.1. Components of seston

A. Plankton

1	2	3	4	5
Phytoplankton (Autotrophic unicellular organisms)	Zooplankton (Heterotrophic protista and metazoa)	Bacterioplankton (Bacteria and fungi, both free-living and attached to particles)	Pseudoplankton (Organisms washed in from other biotopes)	Paraplankton (Epiphytes and epizoa on plankton organisms)

B. Detritus

1	2	3	4
Biogenous Detritus (Remains of organisms, feces)	Terrigenous Detritus (Suspended matter washed in by erosion, resuspended sediment)	Aerogenous Detritus (Dust, soot particles, volcanic ash)	Anthropogenous Detritus (Suspended matter discharged from municipal and industrial waste disposal)

Eutrophication is linked to plankton growth, which in turn produces an increased amount of biogenous detritus. The same positive correlation is true of terrestrial influence. The highest seston concentrations are found in the estuaries of large rivers and in shallow ocean areas with strong tidal currents, for which wide stretches of coast along the North Sea afford a typical example.

Apart from the specific role of plankton, it is the seston level that is of prominent ecological significance for a water body. Together with the content of "gelbstoff" (Kalle, 1966), it determines the depth of light penetration and therewith the distribution of the submersal plant world, as well as the rate of primary production in the benthic and pelagic zones. It moreover constitutes the staple diet of planktic and benthic filter-feeders. It also offers the bacterial populations a substratum to settle on and enhanced growth conditions. Finally, seston settling down through the water column affects the living conditions of the benthos fauna in a decisive way.

An index for the seston level in a water body is the secchi depth. In some places, such as the Elbe estuary and the mud-flats of the North Sea, this does not exceed a few dm. However, the Baltic Sea with its comparatively clear water possesses a much greater secchi depth, ranging from 5 to 11 m in the Kiel Bight according to season (Schinkowski, 1971). In the mid-Baltic, which is less exposed to inshore influences, the water is even more transparent.

Various authors such as Manheim et al. (1970), who studied the North American Atlantic coast, have derived a negative linear regression between seston content, expressed as dry weight per l, and the secchi depth in m. Expressed in orders of magnitude, a seston content of 0.1 mg l^{-1} roughly corresponds to a secchi depth of 10 m and 10 mg l^{-1} to a secchi depth of 1 m.

The seston amount actually measured in ecological studies (the term originally denotes that which has been strained or sieved off), generally diverges somewhat from the theoretical seston quantity, since the investigation methods normally used cover only part of the entire particle size spectrum. This limitation applies most particularly to the smaller size groups. The lower limit is here imposed by the pore size of the filters used, usually lying around 1 μm. The upper size limit, though, is frequently left to chance, i.e., samples are filtered as taken. A more precise method is to first pass the sample through a sieve with a fixed mesh size in order to eliminate any odd larger particles likely to contaminate the analysis result.

A size analysis of seston particles generally reveals a predominance of small particles with regard to both numbers and weight. An example is provided by Table 5.2, which shows the mean values for two different annual cycles, one at buoy A at the entrance to the Kiel Fjord and the other for the mixed surface layer in the western part of the Kiel Bight.

An attempt at an exact identification of the particles composing seston is beset with practical difficulties. Only in exceptional cases is it possible to determine the precise quantity of each of the components listed in Table 5.1. Microscopic analysis, while permitting the various plankton organisms to be fairly well distinguished from the detritus particles, does not allow the latter to be satisfactorily categorized. Similar problems are encountered in the chemical analysis of seston. What makes quantitative classification so difficult is the fact that all the compo-

Table 5.2. Mean particle size distribution for seston and some of its components (%)

A. Outer Kiel Fjord (after Speer, 1972)

Size class	1.5–55 µm	55–100 µm	100–300 µm	>300 µm
Seston	79.2	6.2	10.4	4.2
Protein	42.9	12.4	24.8	19.9
Chlorophyll a	61.3	22.8	15.9	—

B. Kiel Bight (after Lenz, 1974b)

Size class	1–150 µm	150–300 µm	300–600 µm	>600 µm
Seston	89.2	4.0	3.3	3.5
Organic matter	84.3	6.3	4.9	4.5

nents listed are made up of both organic and inorganic elements. Only few chemical parameters such as chlorophyll and adenosine triphosphate (ATP) are of a nature so specific as to justify their being used as the basis for a quantitative assessment of single components or groups of components.

We shall now turn our attention to the analyses carried out during the observation period 1974/75. Four Stations (Nos. 1, 2, 4, 5) covering a section from the inner part of the Kiel Fjord to the central part of the Kiel Bight in the Western Baltic (see Chap. 2) were visited once monthly from January 1974 to March 1975. Station 3 (Kiel lighthouse) could not be occupied. The results are listed in Tables 5.9–5.16. Sampling was conducted throughout with 5-l water samplers by Hydrobios Kiel, 0.5 l being used for each analysis.

To enable subsequent comparison of the results, the same filter type was used for all analyses. In accordance with the requirements for the determination of particulate carbon and nitrogen (C/N), Whatman GF/C glass-fiber filters of 2.5 cm diameter were chosen. These possess a mean pore size of 1 µm. The entire water volume sampled was first passed through a 300-µm sieve. Thus the seston under study ranges in particle size from 1–300 µm.

5.1 Seston

The gravimetric determination of seston content was carried out according to the method by Krey (1950). Glass-fiber filters achieve a precision of ±0.15 mg (Lenz, 1971), although parallel samples often tend to show a considerably wider scattering. For this reason duplicate measurements were carried out and the mean value taken as analysis result (Table 5.3).

Figure 5.1 shows the seasonal cycles for the four stations. Apart from the major deviations in spring 1974 at Station 1 (inner Kiel Fjord), the curves for both sampling depths 2 and 10 m run more or less parallel. At first sight, one is led to assume thorough mixing of the surface layer down to at least 10 m, although this is not always corroborated by the temperature and salinity distribution (cf.

Table 5.3. Seston $\mu g\ l^{-1}$

Date	Station 1		Station 2		Station 4		Station 5		
	2 m	10 m	2 m	10 m	2 m	10 m	2 m	10 m	18 m
Jan. 6, 1974	(5,310)	(5,740)	2,430	1,770	1,180	1,440	1,230	1,230	1,510
Feb. 28	3,800	4,200	2,640	2,740	1,130	1,200	2,850	1,360	(7,700)
March 21	3,960	(7,620)	2,750	2,860	1,320	2,350	1,690	1,930	2,940
April 18	(5,210)	3,080	3,230	2,710	1,330	1,240	1,380	1,200	1,510
May 16	(7,480)	3,090	2,710	2,670	1,600	1,750	1,560	2,150	1,690
June 11	(7,580)	(6,660)	4,330	3,070	1,930	1,810	2,050	2,680	2,190
July 11	(6,110)	(5,700)	3,230	2,990	2,130	1,460	1,970	1,390	1,480
Aug. 7	2,790	2,300	—	—	—	—	—	—	—
Aug. 29	4,170	2,250	2,730	2,180	1,540	2,130	3,300	3,420	1,820
Sept. 12	2,970	2,020	1,820	2,060	1,510	1,790	1,620	1,850	3,840
Oct. 24	3,150	3,030	(6,510)	(6,500)	2,310	2,250	3,820	3,160	1,750
Nov. 21	2,470	1,920	1,900	3,210	1,040	1,560	1,820	1,840	1,620
Dec. 10	1,920	1,610	2,400	2,440	2,410	—	1,600	1,590	3,520
Jan. 23, 1975	2,860	2,110	3,420	3,030	1,290	1,530	3,240	2,990	(5,060)
Feb. 12	2,390	2,520	1,950	2,260	1,180	1,520	1,280	1,080	3,830
March 10	3,700	3,110	4,220	3,040	2,270	1,270	1,920	2,250	2,010

Fig. 3.2). The higher seston values at 18-m depth at Station 5 (central Kiel Bight) seem rather to point to an overlayering by water bodies of different origins. It is conceivable that the inflowing, more saline bottom water stirs up and bears along sediment particles at times of high current speeds. All divers, for instance, know that the slightest water movement will stir up suspended matter newly settled to the bottom as long as its density is still very close to that of the surrounding water.

The high seston values during the first half of 1974 at Station 1 in the inner Kiel Fjord are probably at least partly attributable to the dredging operations that were being carried out in Kiel Harbor at the time. The exceptionally seston-rich water found in October at Station 2 (outer Kiel Fjord) revealed a maximal concentration of detritus particles when examined under the microscope. As expected, Stations 1 and 2 lying close to shore show a higher seston level than the stations farther out in the Kiel Bight. Curiously enough, the clearest water and therewith lowest seston level was not encountered at Station 5, lying farthest out, but at Station 4. The following mean values were calculated for the 2-m depth during the observation period, expressed in mg l^{-1}:4.1 (St. 1), 3.1 (St. 2), 1.6 (St. 4), and 2.1 (St. 5).

As mentioned before, the Kiel Bight is richer in seston than the Baltic proper. Banse (1957) surveyed the seston distribution along a longitudinal section from the Kiel Bight up to the Gulf of Finland in summer. East of Bornholm Island, seston in the surface layer decreased to an average of only 0.1–0.3 mg l^{-1}. However, it must be considered that in those days paper filters were used for the measurements and that particle retention on paper filters is lower than on the glass-fiber filters now in use.

Only at Station 1 (Fig. 5.1) does a marked seasonal cycle of seston content occur, recognizable by a summer maximum of plankton indicated by the other

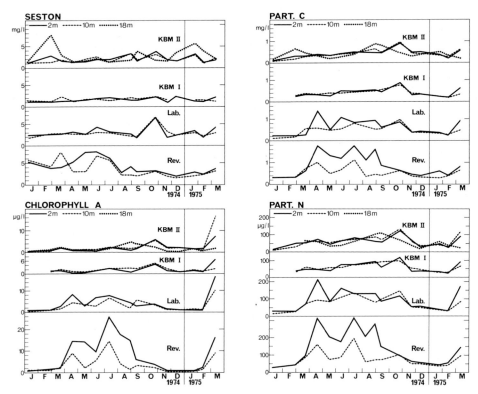

Fig. 5.1. Seasonal variation of seston, chlorophyll a, particulate carbon and particulate nitrogen at Station 1 *(Rev.)* and Station 2 *(Lab.)* in the Kiel Fjord and Station 4 *(KBM I)* and
Station 5 *(KBM II)* in the Kiel Bight (cf. Fig. 2.1)

parameters. In contrast to the observations by Krey (1961), who during a three-
year investigation period at the permanent station Boknis Eck (see Fig. 2.1) found
a significant seston peak in spring caused by the vernal bloom of phytoplankton,
we found this phenomenon missing at all our stations. It cannot be decided
whether a discernible spring bloom of plankton was absent altogether in the open
Kiel Bight in 1974, or whether we missed it on account of the four-week sampling
interval from mid-March to mid-April. Possible reasons for an absence of the
bloom will be discussed in the next section.

5.2 Chlorophyll a

The chlorophyll a content is taken by the planktologist as an index for the
amount of phytoplankton, i.e., primary producers, in the pelagic zone. This
method is based on the observation that chlorophyll a occurs virtually only in
living cells, loose chloroplasts from broken cells included. Chlorophyll, once set
free, is easily destroyed by sunlight. Degradation products of chlorophyll such as

pheophytine and pheophorbide are found in the fecal pellets of filter-feeders and in sediment. Their absorption spectrum overlaps partly with that of chlorophyll. In shallow areas with a great deal of biogenous detritus and stirred-up sediment in the water, this so-called "dead chlorophyll" may be present and disturb the photometric measurement of chlorophyll a (Gillbricht, 1952). A typical area where such conditions prevail is the Schlei Fjord with its shallow depths.

As said above, the chlorophyll a content is often used to calculate the biomass of phytoplankton. A commonly used factor for the conversion of chlorophyll into phytoplankton carbon is 40 (see Lenz, 1974a). Smetacek (1975) has, on the basis of his own investigations in the Kiel Bight, proposed the use of a variable conversion factor between 30 and 100, which is more appropriate considering the changing phytoplankton composition from season to season. Recently, Banse (1977) has critically examined the use of such conversion factors.

The chlorophyll filters are kept in deep-freeze until analyzed. The homogenization of the filters and of seston, as well as the simultaneous extraction of chlorophyll a in a 90% acetone solution, was carried out with the help of a homogenizer by Bühler, Tübingen. The photometric determination was performed according to the UNESCO method (1966). The precision achieved was $0.1 \, \mu g \, l^{-1}$.

When we regard the depth distribution of chlorophyll (Fig. 5.1), we discover that the 2-m level agrees almost perfectly with the 10-m level at Stations 4 and 5 throughout the year and at the two other stations during the cold season, with the exception of the spring increase in 1975. This agreement is contradicted by the distinctly higher values for the near-surface level during the summer season in the inner Kiel Fjord. This obviously reflects the better growth conditions for phytoplankton near the surface and is also very effectively demonstrated by the data on primary production (cf. Chap. 7). At 6-m depth, productivity is only a fraction of what it is in the surface zone. The weak stratification exhibited by the outlying stations can be explained by the greater depth of the euphotic zone as a result of the clearer water. In addition, the more even distribution of phytoplankton in the upper 10 m is a consequence of the more thorough mixing in the surface layer of the outer Kiel Bight through wind and currents.

At the end of August and the first half of September (cf. Table 5.4), we find higher chlorophyll values at the lower depth levels of the two outer Stations 4 and 5, and later of Station 2 than in the surface zone. An inversion of this type is evidently due to changes in water stratification. Less saline water with a lower chlorophyll and phytoplankton content has overlayered or displaced the surface layer (cf. Fig. 3.2 and Table 3.5). At Station 5, these water masses extend down to the 10-m level. During this time of year the chlorophyll concentration at the 18-m depth is at its highest, again ascribable to the prevailing hydrographic conditions. The outflow of Baltic water of low salinity at the surface is compensated for by the inflow of high-salinity water in the depths (cf. Chap. 3). What is now deep water with a higher salt content was, however, originally surface water from the northern part of the Belt Sea or the Kattegat, bearing along with it a relatively abundant plankton population.

Let us now look at the seasonal cycle of chlorophyll concentration. This shows interesting variations. Limiting our attention first to 1974, we notice how

Table 5.4. Chlorophyll a μg l^{-1}

Date	Station 1		Station 2		Station 4		Station 5		
	2 m	10 m	2 m	10 m	2 m	10 m	2 m	10 m	18 m
Jan. 6, 1974	0.9	1.2	0.9	0.4	—	—	0.4	0.5	0.7
Feb. 28	1.7	1.2	1.0	1.0	1.5	1.0	0.9	0.7	1.1
March 21	2.1	2.3	2.7	1.7	1.7	2.3	2.2	1.9	2.1
April 18	14.4	8.9	8.4	4.5	0.6	1.3	0.9	1.1	1.3
May 16	14.2	2.3	3.0	3.6	0.8	1.1	0.9	1.4	1.4
June 11	9.5	5.6	6.8	2.9	1.6	1.8	0.7	1.4	0.8
July 11	25.8	14.7	7.8	6.7	2.7	2.5	2.4	2.3	1.9
Aug. 7	17.7	4.0	—	—	—	—	—	—	—
Aug. 29	14.8	1.5	4.4	2.0	1.0	2.9	1.1	1.9	4.8
Sept. 12	6.0	3.4	2.9	5.7	1.8	2.6	1.9	2.2	4.0
Oct. 24	3.7	2.4	3.7	3.5	4.7	5.2	6.1	5.6	2.5
Nov. 21	0.9	0.5	1.6	1.3	1.7	2.5	2.4	2.1	0.6
Dec. 10	0.9	0.6	1.1	1.2	1.1	1.2	2.4	2.4	0.5
Jan. 23, 1975	0.8	0.7	1.1	1.6	1.7	2.0	1.7	1.8	1.9
Feb. 12	2.3	1.5	1.1	1.4	1.1	1.3	1.9	1.0	1.0
March 10	16.1	9.0	16.8	10.5	6.9	2.5	7.6	16.6	1.9

diverse the patterns of seasonal change are. The amplitude of seasonal extremes decreases from the inner to the outer stations and may be illustrated as follows by the quotient between maximum and minimum for the surface layer (2-m depth) of each station: 28.7 (St. 1), 9.3 (St. 2), 7.8 (St. 4), 15.3 (St. 5). At Station 5 the quotient is again greater, because the winter minimum of 0.4 μm l^{-1} is lowest here.

The growth period of phytoplankton in our area lasts from March to November. At the two inner stations in the Kiel Fjord we find the spring bloom followed by a more or less stable phytoplankton population right into autumn. Making allowance for the fact that samples were taken only once a month, we find three peaks for the phytoplankton in spring, summer and autumn. Three peaks are also discernible for the two outer stations in the Kiel Bight.

An intensive study of the phytoplankton seasonal cycle at the permanent station Boknis Eck in 1972/73 also revealed several peaks between spring and autumn (v. Bodungen, 1975). Each peak could be ascribed to mass development of certain phytoplankton species at the time (Smetacek, 1975). This means that in the Western Baltic we do not encounter the classical distribution pattern typical of temperate zones, i.e., a spring maximum and a less pronounced autumn peak, with a summer minimum interposed. Water exchange in this area is so intensive that, notwithstanding the strongly marked density stratification, water masses rich in inorganic nutrients are repeatedly brought to the surface. One good example can be picked out from our observation data. On 11.7.1974, the phosphate content at the surface suddenly shoots up at both Kiel Bight stations, so does the salt content (cf. Tables 4.6 and 3.5). As early as 1959 and again in 1961, attention was drawn by Krey to the frequent coupling in the Kiel Fjord and the Kiel Bight of nutrient concentration and salinity as a characteristic of upwelling deep water.

The spring bloom at the two outer stations in 1974 is conspicuous by its absence. As mentioned in the previous section, it was probably missed on account of the long intervals between sampling dates, for the actual spring bloom often lasts only a little longer than a fortnight (cf. v. Bröckel, 1973; Smetacek, 1975).

The onset of the spring bloom depends essentially on the light conditions and the stabilization of water stratification. The date for our investigation area usually lies somewhere between the beginning and end of March. The magnitude of the spring bloom, i.e., the accumulation of the phytoplankton biomass, is regulated by grazing pressure from the herbivorous zooplankton present. In mild winters with sustained vertical mixing leading to a delayed onset of the spring bloom, it happens that in the meanwhile a zooplankton stock of some proportions has been built up, which is then able to keep pace with the phytoplankton development. The heavier grazing pressure prevents the phytoplankton algae from accumulating too thickly, thus suppressing the spring bloom to some extent. Suppressed spring blooms of this kind have been described for 1971 (Lenz, 1974a) and for 1973 (Smetacek, 1975).

The absence of a spring maximum does not necessarily entail a fall in primary productivity. On the contrary, the closer phytoplankton is linked to herbivorous zooplankton, the better for the efficiency of the food chain in the pelagic zone, since in this case less food is lost through sedimentation. For the benthic zone, though, the absence of a well-developed phytoplankton bloom is disadvantageous.

In contrast to 1974, our observation data for 1975 show the onset of a classical spring bloom. As one glance at the salinity distribution will show (Fig. 3.2, Table 3.5), the development of the bloom is favored by the exceptionally well-defined density stratification for the season. As is to be expected, growth is faster at the surface than in the depths. The sole exception is Station 5, where the growth rate at the 10-m depth exceeds that at the 2-m level. No plausible explanation can be found for this. An error in analysis is not involved, since the same inverse relationship recurs with some other parameters (cf. Fig. 5.2).

Comparing the stations with each other, we see that the differences between the Kiel Fjord and the Kiel Bight are far more striking with the chlorophyll than with the seston concentration. For example, the summer maximum in July along the 2-m depth level shows the following decline as compared to Station 1 : 100% (St. 1), 30% (St. 2), 10% (St. 4), 9% (St. 5). In the autumn and winter of 1974/75, though, we find the highest concentration at Station 5. The lesser, but yet well-marked autumn maximum in October, often to be met with as late as November, is a typical feature in our area. The more intensive mixing in the water column commencing from the end of September onwards replenishes the nutrient supply in the surface layer and light conditions are still favorable enough to maintain a positive balance of primary production. This late resurgence of the phytoplankton bloom is moreover favored by the almost complete absence of herbivorous copepods, which by this time have been severely decimated by the two ctenophore species *Bolinopsis infundibulum* and *Pleurobrachia pileus*. These occur in great numbers in our area from late autumn to spring (cf. Lenz, 1974a).

5.3 Particulate Carbon and Nitrogen

Particulate carbon and nitrogen concentration are measured on the same filter in the method used. Moreover, since the curves for both parameters are also very similar (Fig. 5.1), it appears appropriate to discuss them under one heading.

As mentioned in the introduction, a comparative analysis requires that the same filter be used for all parameters. For this reason the otherwise customary pre-combustion of glass-fiber filters at 550° C to eliminate organic contaminants from the filter material was omitted. In the furnace, where the high temperatures elude accurate regulation, there is the risk of the glass-fiber mesh beginning to sinter, causing changes in the filtering properties. Instead several blank filters from each batch were analyzed along with the others and the mean blank filter value thus obtained subtracted from the analysis results (cf. Lenz, 1974a). The analyses were carried out with the help of a C-H-N-Analyzer by Hewlett and Packard, Model 185 B (see Ehrhardt, 1976). The accuracy obtained is ± 37 µg C l^{-1} and ± 5.6 µg N l^{-1} (Lenz, 1974a).

In the Western Baltic, where there are practically no plankton organisms or seston components containing calcium carbonate, the carbon content thus measured may be looked upon as identical with the organic carbon present (Table 5.5). Particulate organic carbon is made up of a planktic and a detrital component. Since most organic compounds contain a carbon constituent of approximately 50% by weight, doubling the carbon content gives us the organic matter present.

Whereas particulate organic matter in water plays an important role as food source for all filter-feeders, dissolved organic matter forms the basic diet of bacteria. The ratio between dissolved and particulate—the demarcation line being

Table 5.5. Particulate Carbon µg l^{-1}

Date	Station 1		Station 2		Station 4		Station 5		
	2 m	10 m	2 m	10 m	2 m	10 m	2 m	10 m	18 m
Jan. 6, 1974	322	—	246	123	—	—	111	91	173
Feb. 28	332	343	236	189	259	291	326	195	655
March 21	635	732	280	573	345	390	335	337	481
April 18	1,785	1,000	1,368	599	331	332	402	378	369
May 16	1,318	508	518	504	284	412	364	364	229
June 11	1,182	670	1,093	553	506	412	442	419	285
July 11	1,774	1,134	846	811	491	482	507	453	403
Aug. 7	1,108	372	—	—	—	—	—	—	—
Aug. 29	1,612	464	930	527	647	637	476	650	888
Sept. 12	859	412	615	552	449	555	466	473	815
Oct. 24	628	630	861	965	867	780	917	957	463
Nov. 21	433	368	391	391	310	368	485	453	298
Dec. 10	380	327	431	377	330	335	505	431	380
Jan. 23, 1975	590	285	366	328	228	220	368	338	495
Feb. 12	399	382	251	277	190	183	210	260	319
March 10	805	646	930	486	618	373	583	632	207

Table 5.6. Particulate Nitrogen μg l^{-1}

Date	Station 1		Station 2		Station 4		Station 5		
	2 m	10 m	2 m	10 m	2 m	10 m	2 m	10 m	18 m
Jan. 6, 1974	27	—	29	14	—	—	15	11	20
Feb. 28	43	43	28	26	40	34	53	30	—
March 21	94	87	73	76	51	64	55	58	66
April 18	313	163	213	94	49	49	74	60	59
May 16	206	76	87	88	42	60	47	55	36
June 11	178	87	164	111	78	60	66	65	39
July 11	315	199	132	135	77	78	82	74	62
Aug. 7	207	66	—	—	—	—	—	—	—
Aug. 29	280	76	132	81	94	89	62	87	104
Sept. 12	151	76	90	100	62	95	59	72	110
Oct. 24	99	104	119	147	120	101	126	134	71
Nov. 21	64	52	58	55	38	54	67	65	38
Dec. 10	58	53	61	53	39	47	56	63	46
Jan. 23, 1975	46	37	42	40	33	29	49	43	62
Feb. 12	55	43	32	33	24	28	28	30	41
March 10	143	97	172	85	91	64	93	116	26

variable according to the pore size of the filter used—generally lies between 10–20:1 (cf. Riley and Chester, 1971).

A study of the carbon content from February to May 1964 in the Eckernförde Bight yielded an average ratio of 9:1 between both fractions. The concentration of dissolved organic carbon was of the order of 2–5 mg l^{-1} (Krey et al., 1965).

Particulate nitrogen is often used as a basis for the determination of protein, the values obtained from the measurements being multiplied by the factor 6.25 in accordance with the average nitrogen content of protein. Since the greater proportion of nitrogen in particulate matter is bound to protein compounds, this conversion yields a fairly close approximation. We were able to dispense with the conversion here, because we additionally conducted a specific protein analysis, the results of which will be presently discussed. The nitrogen values (Table 5.6) can be used to check these.

A glance at Figure 5.1 shows us not only the almost identical curves for both parameters already mentioned, but also a striking parallelism with the chlorophyll content. We discover the same maxima in summer and autumn, the depth inversion in August/September and finally the ascent in the spring of the following year. From this we may conclude that a large part of the particulate carbon and nitrogen originates from phytoplankton. On the other hand, we notice that, compared with the chlorophyll values, the differences in concentration from station to station are slighter. If we compare the summer maxima in July at 2-m depth as we did with the chlorophyll values in the preceding section, we arrive at the following percentages for the carbon and nitrogen content respectively, related to Station 1:100/100 (St. 1), 48/42 (St. 2), 28/24 (St. 4), 29/26 (St. 5). The fact that the decrease from the inner to the outer stations is far slighter than with chlorophyll betrays the simultaneous presence of the other two C-N-containing

Table 5.7. Seasonal changes in the C:N ratio. (Mean values for all stations and sampling depths)

1974		1974		1975	
Jan.	9.18	July	5.98	Jan.	8.44
Feb.	7.30	Aug.	6.79	Feb.	7.86
March	6.58	Sept.	6.37	March	5.95
April	6.12	Oct.	6.92		
May	6.45	Nov.	7.12		
June	6.55	Dec.	7.34		

Table 5.8. Regression and correlation coefficients for the C:N ratio at stations 1, 2, 4, 5

Station	Slope m	Intercept b	Correlation coefficient r	Coefficient of determination r^2 (%)	Number of samples
1	5.28	120.65	0.985	97.0	31
2	5.89	49.39	0.970	94.1	30
4	6.63	14.78	0.973	94.7	28
5	6.39	27.49	0.957	91.6	30

seston components, heterotrophic plankton and organic detritus. Their fraction is often considerable.

The C:N ratio supplies some general information on the composition of suspended organic matter. The more protein compounds present, the smaller the C:N ratio will be as a result of the higher nitrogen content. Since protein compounds are more rapidly decomposed in water than higher molecular carbohydrates and lipids (cf. Rheinheimer, 1975), the C:N ratio accordingly shifts from plankton to detritus. The following values have been stated: 3–6 for phytoplankton, 3–8 for zooplankton and 10 and above for detritus (Parsons and Takahashi, 1973).

In view of the varying ratio between the planktic and detrital fraction in seston, we may expect seasonal changes in the C:N ratio (cf. Table 5.7).

In January we encounter the highest values for the C:N ratio. Organic matter in winter shows a nitrogen minimum in keeping with the reduced plankton fraction. Conversely, the C:N ratio is smallest in July 1974 and March 1975. Both these months are characterized by the highest chlorophyll concentration of all the stations and therewith by maxima in the phytoplankton biomass.

We can test by regression analysis whether differences exist between the stations in the C:N ratio and consequently in the composition of organic matter. The following Table 5.8 contains the parameters for the linear relationship $y = mx + b$, the variable x representing the nitrogen content.

What we notice first is the highly significant correlation between the two parameters at all the stations. This is further stressed by the coefficient of determination, which indicates the extent (in %) to which fluctuations in carbon content are explicable by fluctuations in the nitrogen content. What further catches our

Table 5.9. C/N ratio and theoretical protein content in
          particulate organic matter

C/N	Protein (%)	C/N	Protein (%)
3.1	100	7	44.6
4	78.1	8	39.1
5	62.5	9	34.7
6	52.1	10	31.3

interest in the regression equations is the order in which the Stations 1–5 appear. The slope representing the C:N ratios rises and there is a fall in the values for the intercept with the y axis, these values standing for the remaining "nitrogen-free" fraction of the organic matter. At Station 5 there is a reversal in this trend, which places this station between Station 2 and 4.

Proceeding from the assumption that the predominant fraction of particulate nitrogen is present in the form of protein compounds—for example, in July the mean quotient between the protein values as computed and the values actually measured for all four stations is 1.006—the conversion factors mentioned ($N \times 6.25$ = protein, $C \times 2$ = organic matter) can be used to calculate the percentage of protein compounds in organic matter by means of the C:N ratio. The ratios listed in Table 5.9 are offered as a guide here.

Applied to our case (cf. Table 5.8), the average percentual protein fraction of organic matter is seen to decline from the inner Fjord (59.2%) via the outer Fjord (53.1%) to the Kiel Bight at Station 4 (47.1%). Station 5 shows a slightly higher value (49,0%). Presuming that the plankton at all stations has the same protein percentage, it may be concluded that the Fjord stations are characterized by a higher plankton content in relation to organic matter. This hypothesis is confirmed by the ratio of chlorophyll a content to particulate carbon, for here the stations emerge in exactly the same numerical order as for the ratio carbon to nitrogen.

What may, of course, also be inferred from the above findings is that the plankton of the Kiel Fjord possesses a higher average protein and chlorophyll content than the plankton of the Kiel Bight. Should this be the case, two explanations may be offered: either the phytoplankton fraction of the total plankton concentration is greater in the Kiel Fjord or the phytoplankton here is richer in chlorophyll and protein because of differences in species composition. A qualitative difference of this kind exists, for instance, between diatoms and dinoflagellates, the former containing more chlorophyll and protein (cf. Strickland, 1965).

5.4 Protein

Since higher molecular protein compounds in dead plankton organisms are very rapidly hydrolyzed and decomposed by microorganisms on account of their small size, the protein fraction of seston can to a certain extent serve as a measure for the plankton biomass including bacteria (Krey, 1961). With a view to an analytical estimate of the higher molecular protein compounds, Krey et al. (1957)

Table 5.10. Protein $\mu g\ l^{-1}$

Date	Station 1		Station 2		Station 4		Station 5		
	2 m	10 m	2 m	10 m	2 m	10 m	2 m	10 m	18 m
Jan. 6, 1974	222	(1,270)	226	100	264	96	108	74	124
Feb. 28	—	—	—	128	236	214	328	152	700
March 21	642	526	440	544	468	410	316	324	464
April 18	1,584	1,000	1,324	652	262	260	434	360	362
May 16	1,200	516	534	554	244	358	304	358	260
June 11	1,078	538	766	700	416	374	408	390	242
July 11	1,974	1,290	768	842	494	492	464	440	412
Aug. 7	1.012	400	—	—	—	—	—	—	—
Aug. 29	1,776	468	818	504	560	564	294	490	586
Sept. 12	772	390	572	—	382	572	366	468	686
Oct. 24	656	662	738	838	756	622	754	840	464
Nov. 21	404	298	358	330	254	292	342	366	238
Dec. 10	292	223	280	214	240	298	316	328	286
Jan. 23, 1975	254	282	261	222	210	170	279	285	392
Feb. 12	320	231	149	137	112	121	168	126	233
March 10	800	592	—	504	400	348	524	692	125

therefore introduced to planktology the biuret method, based on a reaction with the peptide bond.

Compared to the biuret method, the Lowry method (Lowry et al., 1951) has the disadvantage of measuring the amino acids at a later stage in the decomposition process, but the advantage of possessing the greater sensitivity. Large-scale comparative measurements with seston samples from the Kiel Bight have shown, however, that the differences in results between both methods are negligible (Devulder, 1969; Lenz, 1974a). We thus chose the Lowry method for our protein determination. The precision achieved is $\pm 15\ \mu g\ l^{-1}$.

A glance at the seasonal cycle of protein (Table 5.10, Fig. 5.2) will confirm its close correspondence with the curve for particulate nitrogen, as pointed out in the foregoing section. Major deviations occur only where certain single values were omitted from either the protein or the nitrogen determination. The strikingly high value for the lower depth at Station 1 in January 1974 corresponds to a similarly high lipid content (Table 5.12), which on account of its exceptional character was regarded as untypical and excluded from the seasonal curve. Although the salinity distribution (Fig. 3.2., Table 3.5) shows a higher value for the 10-m depth as compared with the surface, it must be left undecided whether or not a higher concentration of small zooplankters suggested by this protein and lipid peak may be inferred here.

On the whole, the annual curve for the protein content closely parallels that for chlorophyll. A winter minimum is offset by a summer maximum manifesting itself in several peaks from April to October. Only the extremes are attenuated by the presence of heterotrophic plankton. The quotient between maximum and minimum during the observation period, calculated separately for each station and depth, ranges from 5.6 to 11.4. The corresponding figures for the chlorophyll content are 5.2 and 33.2.

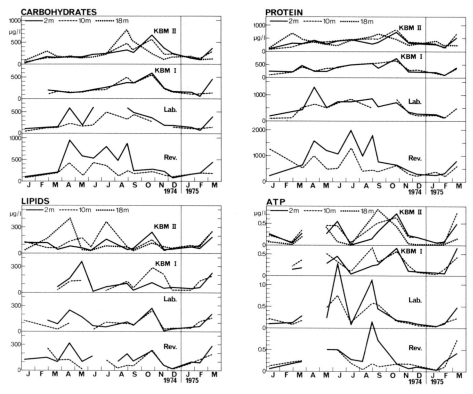

Fig. 5.2. Seasonal variation of carbohydrates, lipids, protein and ATP in particulate matter at Station 1 *(Rev.)* and Station 2 *(Lab.)* in the Kiel Fjord and at Station 4 *(KBM I)* and Station 5 *(KBM II)* in the Kiel Bight (cf. Fig. 2.1)

5.5 Carbohydrates

Where autochthonous seston particles are concerned, the carbohydrates contained in them originate primarily from phytoplankton. Depending on the algae species, they account for 20–40% of the organic matter in the cells, whereas only a small percentage can be measured in zooplankton (cf. Parsons and Takahashi, 1973).

The analyses (Table 5.11) were conducted, with slight modifications, according to the so-called phenol-sulfuric acid method as described by Handa (1966, 1967). The glass-fiber filters were homogenized in a cell homogenizer by Bühler, Tübingen. Glucose was used as reference standard. The precision achieved was $\pm 20 \, \mu g \, l^{-1}$.

Here again, the seasonal curve in Figure 5.2 is on the whole very similar to that of protein, carbon and nitrogen, thus pointing to their common origin, the phytoplankton. Only the two peaks in late summer and autumn at the outer stations in the Kiel Bight are more conspicuous here than with the other parameters. Partic-

Table 5.11. Carbohydrates µg l^{-1}

Date	Station 1		Station 2		Station 4		Station 5		
	2 m	10 m	2 m	10 m	2 m	10 m	2 m	10 m	18 m
Jan. 6, 1974	103	81	117	53	—	—	32	39	75
Feb. 28	164	160	152	128	211	108	178	146	296
March 21	206	212	161	127	183	163	157	157	187
April 18	953	431	596	237	146	158	176	185	157
May 16	594	150	199	168	164	156	170	142	151
June 11	533	433	612	203	215	199	232	235	167
July 11	800	365	—	493	269	217	246	235	232
Aug. 7	477	138	—	—	—	—	—	—	—
Aug. 29	866	237	604	330	376	502	335	480	770
Sept. 12	245	175	490	435	371	364	280	341	534
Okt. 24	281	225	370	274	602	551	675	576	239
Nov. 21	230	145	200	—	251	229	376	227	116
Dec. 10	77	101	196	152	174	152	255	233	166
Jan. 23, 1975	166	162	155	117	153	108	146	150	174
Feb. 12	186	191	91	125	70	—	108	135	120
March 10	439	184	396	156	466	137	371	289	122

ularly marked is the inversion in the two lower depths at Station 5 in August/ September. The hydrographic circumstances responsible for this have been discussed in Section 5.2.

When we compare the average contents of carbohydrate and chlorophyll a for the two depth levels at all the stations throughout the observation period, we arrive at the following ratios: 52.7 (St. 1), 70.3 (St. 2), 115.3 (St. 4), 97.6 (St. 5). Once again the stations appear in the same numerical order, a possible interpretation being as follows: either the phytoplankton in the inner Fjord is poorer in carbohydrates or richer in chlorophyll than in the open Kiel Bight. The lower content of carbohydrates at Stations 1 and 2 would conform well with the higher protein content deduced from the carbon : nitrogen ratio.

However, this hypothesis of a varying biochemical composition of phytoplankton suffers from a serious drawback: we do not exactly know how much of the protein content is accounted for by heterotrophic organisms and how much of the carbohydrate content is made up of organic detritus. Some higher molecular carbohydrates take very long to decompose in water and thus accumulate to some extent in organic detritus.

An interesting feature of the annual carbohydrate curve is the pronounced difference observed between the two depths at the onset of the spring bloom in 1975. Unlike all the parameters discussed so far, we find the noticeable increase (St. 5 excepted) only at the 2-m depth level, the 10-m level remaining unchanged. An interpretation of this would be that at the inception of the growth period, the phytoplankton cells tend first to build up protein compounds. The subsequent storing of carbohydrates is evidently begun earlier at the surface than in the depths, on account of the better growth conditions.

5.6 Lipids

Along with proteins and carbohydrates, lipids form one of the chief components of particulate organic matter. As an energy reserve they play a major part in the metabolism of both phytoplankton and zooplankton.

The determination of the lipid content, here understood as the total amount of fats and lipids, was carried out on the basis of the sulfo-phospho-vanillin reaction after Zöllner and Kirsch (1962). This photometric measurement has proved successful as a micro-method in hospital laboratories and was adapted for our purpose by P. Hendrikson and P. Fritsche (Hendrikson, 1975). Instead of the originally specified reference standard (Triolein), linoleic acid was used, which is more suitable for plankton samples. The precision achieved was $\pm 6.5\,\mu g\,l^{-1}$. The analysis results (Table 5.12) employed are almost exclusively mean values from duplicate determinations.

Some samples, especially for the first two months, were unfortunately lost during the analysis process or yielded such extreme values that they had to be disqualified from inclusion in the annual curve (Fig. 5.2). Examining the latter, we notice that the summer maximum regularly encountered so far, at least at the two first stations, is missing. An exception is the 10-m depth level at Station 5. Instead we meet with higher values in April/May and then again in October. Spring and autumn are the seasons at which a number of the more common zooplankton organisms attain their maximum abundance, especially copepods (Lohmann, 1908; Hillebrandt, 1972; Schnack, 1975).

The parallelism here observed points with some probability to a causality between zooplankton abundance and lipid content. Since the water sample volume was only 0.5 l and these were pre-filtered through a 300 µ gauze, the lipid content measured can only have been derived from small zooplankton organisms.

Table 5.12. Lipids $\mu g\,l^{-1}$

Date	Station 1		Station 2		Station 4		Station 5		
	2 m	10 m	2 m	10 m	2 m	10 m	2 m	10 m	18 m
Jan. 6, 1974	125	(663)	(923)	131	—	—	127	134	35
Feb. 28	151	262	134	—	—	—	122	62	176
March 21	100	119	92	28	68	25	48	61	63
April 18	312	130	253	100	167	132	83	141	397
May 16	103	21	175	—	362	143	64	171	43
June 11	170	—	72	23	22	—	38	73	42
July 11	—	126	55	117	76	27	166	365	85
Aug. 7	104	32	—	—	—	—	—	—	—
Aug. 29	194	64	116	95	101	134	46	70	75
Sept. 12	111	56	76	83	34	54	61	40	29
Oct. 24	230	244	269	247	119	284	247	154	121
Nov. 21	63	67	13	35	56	212	44	33	77
Dec. 10	22	27	35	43	67	31	50	50	59
Jan. 23, 1975	100	91	55	42	52	33	79	90	73
Feb. 12	90	130	67	119	66	137	58	82	96
March 10	288	191	210	163	231	193	190	247	250

The lipid content differs in yet another respect from the previous parameters: the values for the lower depths often exceed those for the near-surface zone, especially at Station 5. This may be taken as a further indication of the presence of zoo-plankton, which in contrast to phytoplankton prefers the deeper water layer, although thermoclines and haloclines sometimes serve as effective boundary lay-ers in confining vertical expansion in our area (Banse, 1955, 1959).

5.7 Adenosine Triphosphate (ATP)

What is known so far of ATP justifies the assumption that this compound occurs only in living organisms. Hence the ATP content can be used as a measure for the living fraction of seston (Holm-Hansen and Booth, 1966; Holm-Hansen and Pearl, 1972). The determination was carried out as specified by the authors, an ATP Photometer (Model IRB—La Jolla) being used. The luciferine-luciferase preparation used here was by Serva, Heidelberg. It was later found that the preparation by Boehringer (Mannheim) is better purified. Duplicate determina-tions were nearly always carried out and the mean value taken (Table 5.13). The precision calculated from the duplicate determinations was only $\pm 20\%$. The April values are unfortunately missing, as the samples could not be immediately deep-frozen on board.

Our first impression of the ATP values in Figure 5.2 is the extremely erratic course of the curves and the abrupt changes in concentration when compared with the other parameters. Most conspicuous are the low values for July, which do not at all agree with the other parameter values. Thus one is tempted to believe in an error in determination here. On consulting the microbiological data,

Table 5.13. ATP $\mu g \, l^{-1}$

Date	Station 1		Station 2		Station 4		Station 5		
	2 m	10 m	2 m	10 m	2 m	10 m	2 m	10 m	18 m
Jan. 6, 1974	0.057	0.131	0.107	0.226	—	—	0.266	0.240	0.086
Feb. 28	0.179	0.221	0.129	0.092	0.153	0.221	0.064	0.080	0.027
March 21	0.226	0.245	0.289	0.183	0.189	0.372	0.289	0.365	0.204
April 18	—	—	—	—	—	—	—	—	—
May 16	0.498	0.502	0.237	0.471	0.290	0.522	0.275	0.467	0.426
June 11	0.496	0.499	1.491	0.763	0.463	0.325	0.559	0.451	0.087
July 11	0.273	0.190	0.080	0.137	0.052	0.106	0.037	0.072	0.037
Aug. 7	0.230	0.051	—	—	—	—	—	—	—
Aug. 29	1.164	0.185	1.128	0.582	0.239	0.664	0.164	0.438	0.646
Sept. 12	0.730	0.116	0.454	0.558	0.267	0.317	0.320	0.520	0.823
Oct. 24	0.183	0.182	0.179	0.160	0.653	0.572	0.744	0.648	0.441
Nov. 21	0.074	0.179	0.151	0.125	0.120	0.245	0.233	0.190	0.045
Dec. 10	0.109	0.136	0.102	0.068	0.094	0.090	0.191	0.200	0.230
Jan. 23, 1975	0.033	0.040	0.048	0.040	0.071	0.047	0.067	0.058	0.028
Feb. 12	0.235	0.111	0.108	0.131	0.050	0.161	0.092	0.071	0.041
March 10	0.427	0.736	0.470	0.243	0.622	0.431	0.503	0.760	0.162

Table 5.14. Ratio between maximum and minimum values for ATP and protein during the study period

Station	1		2		3		5	
Depth	2 m	10 m	2 m	10 m	2 m	10 m	2 m	10 m
ATP	35.3	18.4	31.1	19.1	13.1	14.1	11.6	13.1
Protein	8.9	5.8	8.9	8.4	6.8	6.5	7.0	11.4

though, we discover a surprising parallelism to the saprophyte counts, these having been determined on nutrient agar and ZoBell tap-water mediums (Tables 11.3 and 11.4). Here, too, values abnormally low for the season were observed in July. This parallelism, though, is restricted to these saprophyte counts. It need only be added here that the surface water in July was also hydrographically exceptional in that the highest salinity for the summer months was recorded here (cf. Fig. 3.2, Table 3.5).

In all other points, however, there is a fairly good accord between the seasonal ATP curve and those of the other parameters, especially in the first quarter of 1974 and then again in the latter half of the year and in the following spring. The same late summer maximum at Station 1 occurs here as for protein, except that the ATP peak is maintained virtually undiminished up to Station 2. Further, we also find the October peak at the two outer stations and later, common to all parameters, the ascent induced by the spring bloom of 1975.

On the whole, the ATP curve is subject to far stronger oscillations than the protein values, which under certain conditions can likewise be regarded as representative of the living matter present. How much stronger the ATP fluctuations are may be illustrated by comparing the extremes for both parameters (Table 5.14). Only in a single instance are the above-mentioned, unusually low July values identical with the lowest value encountered; this value was excluded as aberrant.

It follows that ATP content is evidently a more sensitive indicator of living matter than protein content, since the latter probably does after all incorporate a certain amount of detrital matter. The protein contained in detritus probably varies with season, considering that the decomposition rate of dead protein is also a function of temperature.

5.8 Organic and Inorganic Matter

Having considered the individual organic components of seston singly, we shall now view our subject in another perspective and divide seston into an organic and inorganic constituent. These are distinguished from each other solely in terms of their chemical definitions and are, as has already been pointed out, by no means synonymous with plankton and detritus respectively. Diatoms, for example, may possess an inorganic fraction of 40–50% on account of their shells.

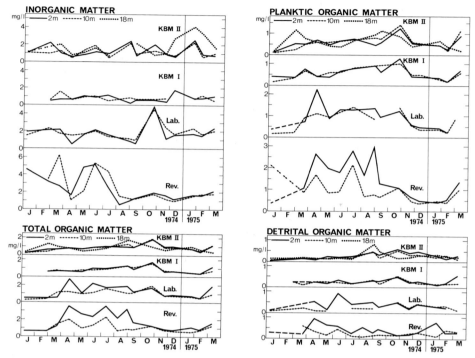

Fig. 5.3. Seasonal variation of the inorganic and organic fraction in particulate matter and of the planktic and detrital fraction in organic matter at Station 1 *(Rev.)* and Station 2 *(Lab.)* in the Kiel Fjord and at Station 4 *(KBM I)* and Station 5 *(KBM II)* in the Kiel Bight (cf. Fig. 2.1)

Figure 5.3 shows the annual curve for both constituents to enable direct comparison. Organic matter was obtained from particulate carbon by multiplication by the factor 2, the inorganic fraction being the difference between the value thus computed and seston weight.

The annual curves for the inorganic fraction require some correction. All values higher than approximately 2 mg/l must be looked upon as untypical for our area. The extraordinarily high values at Station 1 in the inner Kiel Fjord during the first half-year were plainly caused by dredging operations in Kiel Harbor. No explanation can be found for the precipitous increase indicated by the high October value at Station 2. The high winter values for the 18-m depth level at Station 5 in the central Kiel Bight are probably caused by stirred-up sediment. Discounting these extremes, the inorganic fraction of seston as a whole shows no major fluctuations. A more or less steady level is maintained throughout the year.

The differences between the stations are slight, only Station 4 exhibiting lower values. What is interesting is the fairly close agreement between the two upper depth levels. Taking the average for these two depth levels over the total study period (the extremes mentioned being omitted), we obtain the following average concentrations in mg/l for the individual stations: 1489 (St. 1), 1686 (St. 2), 806 (St. 4), 1186 (St. 5). The difference between Station 1 and 2 is not significant, since the average value for Station 1 probably proved too low on account of the omitted values.

5.9 Fraction of Plankton and Detritus in Organic Matter

Total particulate organic matter may be divided into two categories: the living part made up of plankton organisms, bacteria and fungi, and the non-living part or detritus.

It is practically impossible to separate these two components. All we have is an indirect method by which to determine the living fraction. This method is based on the determination of a chemical component specific to all living organisms, followed by calculating the corresponding amount of organic matter by means of a conversion factor. The components themselves pose problems on account of their specificity. What is more, the conversion ratio is not always constant, so that we are forced to operate with averages of greater or lesser reliability. The two components common to all organisms and available to us were ATP and protein. Since the values for the former are incomplete (Fig. 5.2), we chose protein content. We proceeded from the very general assumption that the mean value for protein content in the organic matter of plankton is 60%. In phytoplankton the protein fraction is frequently lower, in heterotrophic organisms generally higher than our assumed percentage.

The organic matter of living organisms thus calculated may show too high values at certain seasons, leading to an underestimation of detritus as the complementary constituent of total organic matter. What further complicates matters is that it is not yet exactly known how much of the protein content measured is incorporated in detritus. For this reason the values for the detrital fraction of organic matter must be regarded as minimal. Indeed, it must be admitted that our method of calculation at times yielded detritus values of nil.

The annual curves in Figure 5.3 show the universal predominance of the living fraction of organic matter over the detrital fraction. Only in a few exceptional cases is the detrital fraction greater than the planktic. The former never anywhere exceeds 1 mg l^{-1}, while the latter, especially at the first two stations, shows considerably higher values. The detrital fraction to some extent reflects the course followed by the plankton curve. This may be seen from the higher summer values and also from the differences in depth distribution. The seasonal variations for detritus, though, are altogether far less pronounced than for plankton. The fol-

Table 5.15. Average planktic and detrital fractions of total organic matter in µg l^{-1} (percentages in brackets)

Station	Planktic fraction	Detrital fraction	Total
1	1,176 (78.3)	325 (21.7)	1,501
2	824 (73.2)	301 (26.8)	1,125
4	596 (71.0)	243 (29.0)	839
5	617 (71.6)	245 (28.4)	862

lowing Table 5.15 compares both fractions (average values) for the two upper depth layers over the investigation period.

The detrital fraction of total organic matter averages roughly 20–30%. The ratio shifts from the inner to the outer stations in favor of detritus, since the actual decrease is here considerably less than with the planktic fraction. As with the other parameters, Station 4 is here again characterized by the lowest values.

5.10 Percentual Composition of Seston

In conclusion we may review the analyzed seston components in the light of general seasonal changes and discrepancies, where present, between the results from the Kiel Fjord and the open Kiel Bight.

It appeared best to arrange the results in table form, with all parameters expressed as % values of the seston content (Table 5.16). The accompanying seston values make it easy to derive the actual concentrations for each single parameter. For simplicity's sake, the first two stations (Kiel Fjord) and the two outer stations (Kiel Bight) were combined and reduced to one. Similarly, the data for two successive months were pooled throughout, so were the two upper sampling depths (2-m and 10-m). Thus one mean value, as given in the table, in the majority of cases represents eight separate observation data. The unusually high seston values ($>5 \, mg \, l^{-1}$) at Stations 1 and 2 (cf. Table 5.3) were discarded as untypical.

Table 5.16 shows us that the average total seston content in the Kiel Fjord is approximately one and a half times that of the Kiel Bight. The ratio varies with season, being greater in spring than in summer and autumn. The reason is that seston abundance in the Kiel Fjord culminates in spring and farther out in the Bight in summer and autumn. However, this ratio must be regarded with reservation, since we probably missed the spring bloom in the Kiel Bight in 1974, as mentioned in the chlorophyll section.

The majority of seston components (Tables 5.4–5.6 and 5.10–5.13) faithfully mirror the seasonal changes from the low-productivity months as shown by the January/February value to the growth period from March to October. This changing ratio is best reflected in the organic fraction of seston, which ranges from approximately 28% in winter to nearly 70% as maximum in summer. Only the lipid content, especially in the Kiel Fjord, does not conform to this pattern, implying that it is less closely linked to the other components (cf. Chap. 19). A few exceptions are also found with chlorophyll and ATP.

Regarding seasonal change, we find that the two areas frequently show surprisingly slight differences in the composition of particulate matter. The same is true of the total average values. From this we may infer as follows: although the Kiel Fjord exhibits a considerably greater degree of eutrophication than the Kiel Bight (the averaging of values unfortunately does not do full justice to the gradient from the inner to the outer stations), this eutrophication apparently hardly affects the chemical composition of seston.

Five factors combine in causing eutrophication in the Kiel Fjord. The first is terrestrial influence through the influx of nutrients from the shore, the second the

Table 5.16. Seasonal changes in the composition of seston in %

Season	Area	Seston mg/l	Inorganic matter	Organic matter	Protein	Carbo-hydrates	Lipids	C	N	Chloro-phyll a	ATP
1974 Jan./Feb.	KF	2.9	82.3	17.7	5.8	4.1	5.5	8.8	1.0	0.03	0.005
	KB	1.5	71.7	28.3	13.7	7.9	7.4	14.1	2.1	0.05	0.011
March/April	KF	3.1	43.7	56.3	27.1	11.8	4.6	28.1	4.5	0.18	0.008
	KB	1.6	55.5	44.5	22.1	10.4	5.7	22.3	3.6	0.09	0.019
May/June	KF	3.2	50.4	49.6	23.0	11.3	2.9	24.8	3.9	0.19	0.019
	KB	1.9	57.9	42.1	18.8	9.9	6.6	21.1	3.1	0.06	0.022
July/Aug.	KF	2.8	31.6	68.4	35.2	17.1	3.6	34.2	7.3	0.35	0.014
	KB	2.2	50.6	49.4	21.6	15.1	5.6	24.7	3.6	0.10	0.010
Sept./Oct.	KF	2.5	44.8	55.2	26.4	12.5	6.6	27.6	4.4	0.16	0.013
	KB	2.3	40.6	59.4	25.9	20.4	5.4	29.7	4.2	0.17	0.022
Nov./Dec.	KF	2.2	64.8	35.2	13.6	7.1	1.7	17.6	2.6	0.05	0.005
	KB	1.7	52.7	47.3	17.9	13.9	4.0	23.6	3.2	0.12	0.010
1975 Jan./Feb.	KF	2.6	72.3	27.7	8.9	5.7	3.3	13.8	1.6	0.05	0.004
	KB	1.8	72.2	27.8	10.2	6.9	4.2	13.9	1.8	0.09	0.004
March	KF	3.5	59.0	41.0	18.1	8.4	6.1	20.5	3.5	0.37	0.013
	KB	1.9	41.9	58.1	25.8	16.6	11.3	29.1	4.8	0.44	0.030
Average	KF	2.85	56.1	43.9	19.8	9.8	4.3	21.9	3.6	0.17	0.010
	KB	1.86	55.4	44.6	19.5	12.6	6.3	22.3	3.3	0.15	0.016

Seston content: 100%;   KF: Kiel Fjord: Stations 1 and 2; KB: Kiel Bight: Stations 4 and 5

emptying of the Schwentine, a small though sewage-laden river, into the inner Fjord. The third factor was until recently the discharge into the Kiel Fjord of domestic sewage from several outlying suburbs situated on its eastern side. Most of these have now been connected to the municipal sewage disposal system terminating at Bülk outside the Fjord. The fourth factor is the ship traffic both associated with and independent of the shipyards located here. The drainage into the sea of rain water from the streets of Kiel municipality constitutes the fifth and presumably least significant factor. Luckily, the comparatively brisk rate of water exchange between the Kiel Fjord and the Kiel Bight, in turn governed by the hydrographic regime of the Western Baltic (cf. Chap. 3), has so far kept eutrophication within bounds. However, in the deeper parts of the inner Fjord, as in other areas of Kiel Bight, anoxic conditions frequently occur in late summer and autumn, leading at times of wind-induced upwelling to fish mortality (see Chap. 18).

As already mentioned, the amount and composition of seston in conjunction with a knowledge of the prevailing hydrographic conditions may serve as an index for eutrophication processes. However, we must not lose sight of the fact that the method by which we have here investigated the seston concentration does not afford more than a few random glimpses into a dynamic process, since seston in its composition is largely ruled by the interlocking of building-up and breaking-down processes. The ratios of the components among each other are subject to continuous change within the complex interactions of biotic and abiotic factors. Since our analysis methods to date lack specificity, our presentation here cannot pretend to be more than a rough sketch of the actual picture.

References

Banse, K.: Über das Verhalten von meroplanktischen Larven in geschichtetem Wasser. Kieler Meeresforsch. **11**, 188–200 (1955)

Banse, K.: Ergebnisse eines hydrographisch-produktionsbiologischen Längsschnittes durch die Ostsee im Sommer 1956. II. Die Verteilung von Sauerstoff, Phosphat und suspendierter Substanz. Kieler Meeresforsch. **13**, 186–201 (1957)

Banse, K.: Die Vertikalverteilung planktischer Copepoden in der Kieler Bucht. Ber. Dt. Wiss. Kommn. Meeresforschung **15**, 357–390 (1959)

Banse, K.: Determining the carbon-to-chlorophyll ratio of natural phytoplankton. (In press) (1977)

Bodungen, v., B.: Der Jahresgang der Nährsalze und der Primärproduktion des Planktons in der Kieler Bucht unter Berücksichtigung der Hydrographie. Thesis Univ. Kiel (1975)

Bröckel, v., K.: Eine Methode zur Bestimmung des Kaloriengehaltes von Seston. Kieler Meeresforsch. **29**, 34–49 (1973)

Devulder, K.: Jahreszeitliche, tiefenabhängige und örtliche Veränderungen im wechselseitigen Verhältnis von Nukleinsäuren, Eiweiß und Chlorophyll in Netzplankton. Ber. Dt. Wiss. Kommn. Meeresforsch. **20**, 216–255 (1969)

Ehrhardt, M.: Determination of particulate organic carbon and nitrogen, 215–220. In: Grasshoff, K. (ed.), Methods of Seawater Analysis. Weinheim-New York: Verlag Chemie, 1976

Gillbricht, M.: Untersuchungen zur Produktionsbiologie des Planktons in der Kieler Bucht I. Kieler Meeresforsch. **8**, 173–191 (1952)

Handa, N.: Examination on the applicability of the phenolsulfuric acid method to the determination of dissolved carbohydrates in sea water. J. Oceanogr. Soc. Japan **22**, 79–86 (1966)

Handa, N.: The distribution of the dissolved and the particulate carbohydrates in the Kuroshio and its adjacent areas. J. Oceanogr. Soc. Japan **23**, 115–123 (1967)

Hendrikson, P.: Auf- und Abbauprozesse partikulärer organischer Substanz anhand von Seston- und Sinkstoffanalysen. Thesis Univ. Kiel (1975)

Hillebrandt, M.: Untersuchungen über die qualitative und quantitative Zusammensetzung des Zooplanktons in der Kieler Bucht während der Jahre 1966–1968. Thesis Univ. Kiel (1972)

Holm-Hansen, O., Booth, C. R.: The measurement of adenosine triphosphate in the ocean and its ecological significance. Limnol. Oceanogr. **11**, 510–519 (1966)

Holm-Hansen, O., Paerl, H. W.: The applicability of ATP determination for estimation of microbial biomass and metabolic activity, 149–168. In: Melchiorri-Santolini, U., Hopton, J. W. (eds.) Detritus and Its Role in Aquatic Ecosystems. Mem. Ist. Ital. Idrobiol. **29**, Suppl. (1972)

Kalle, K.: The problem of Gelbstoff in the sea. Oceanogr. Mar. Biol. Ann. Rev. **4**, 91–104 (1966)

Krey, J.: Eine neue Methode zur quantitativen Bestimmung des Planktons. Kieler Meeresforsch. **7**, 58–75 (1950)

Krey, J.: Über den Gehalt an gelöstem anorganischem Phosphor in der Kieler Förde 1952–1957. Kieler Meeresforsch. **15**, 17–28 (1959)

Krey, J.: Beobachtungen über den Gehalt an Mikrobiomasse und Detritus in der Kieler Bucht 1958–1960. Kieler Meeresforsch. **17**, 163–175 (1961)

Krey, J., Banse, K., Hagmeier, E.: Über die Bestimmung von Eiweiß im Plankton mittels der Biuretreaktion. Kieler Meeresforsch. **13**, 35–40 (1957)

Krey, J., Koske, P. H., Szekielda, K.-H.: Produktionsbiologische und hydrographische Untersuchungen in der Eckernförder Bucht. Kieler Meeresforsch. **21**, 135–143 (1965)

Lenz, J.: Zur Methode der Sestonbestimmung. Kieler Meeresforsch. **27**, 180–193 (1971)

Lenz, J.: Untersuchung zum Nahrungsgefüge im Pelagial der Kieler Bucht. Der Gehalt an Phytoplankton, Zooplankton und organischem Detritus in Abhängigkeit von Wasserschichtung, Tiefe und Jahreszeit. Habilitationsschrift Univ. Kiel (1974 a)

Lenz, J.: On the amount and size distribution of suspended organic matter in the Kiel Bight. Ber. Dt. Wiss. Kommn. Meeresforsch. **23**, 209–225 (1974 b)

Lohmann, H.: Untersuchung zur Feststellung des vollständigen Gehaltes des Meeres an Plankton. Wiss. Meeresunters. Abt. Kiel N.F. **10**, 131–370 (1908)

Lowry, O. H., Rosebrough, N. J., Farr, A. L., Randall, R. J.: Protein measurement with the folinphenol reagent. J. Biol. Chem. **193**, 265–275 (1951)

Manheim, F. T., Meade, R. H., Bond, G. C.: Suspended matter in surface waters of the Atlantic Continental Margin from Cape Cod to the Florida Keys. Science **167**, 371–376 (1970)

Parsons, T., Takahashi, M.: Biological Oceanographic Processes. Oxford: Pergamon Press, 1973

Rheinheimer, G.: Mikrobiologie der Gewässer. 2nd ed. Jena: G. Fischer, 1975

Riley, J. P., Chester, R.: Introduction to Marine Chemistry. London: Academic Press, 1971

Schinkowski, H.: Untersuchung über den Einfluß einiger produktionsbiologischer Parameter auf die Sichttiefe im Meere. Kieler Meeresforsch. **27**, 4–19 (1971)

Schnack, S.: Untersuchungen zur Nahrungsbiologie der Copepoden (Crustacea) in der Kieler Bucht. Thesis Univ. Kiel (1975)

Smetacek, V.: Die Sukzession des Phytoplanktons in der Kieler Bucht. Thesis Univ. Kiel (1975)

Speer, A.: Ein Jahresüberblick produktionsbiologischer Untersuchungen an verschiedenen Planktongrößengruppen unter besonderer Berücksichtigung der Energieverteilung und abwasserbiologischer Fragen in der Kieler Außenförde. Thesis Univ. Kiel (1972)

Strickland, J. D. H.: Production of organic matter in the primary stages of the marine food chain, 477–610. In: Riley, J. P., Skirrow, G. (eds.), Chemical Oceanography. Vol. I. London: Academic Press, 1965

UNESCO: Determination of photosynthetic pigments in sea water. Monographs on oceanographic methodology I. Paris: UNESCO (1966)

Zöllner, N., Kirsch, K.: Über die quantitative Bestimmung von Lipoiden (Mikromethode) mittels der vielen Lipoiden (allen bekannten Plasma-Lipoiden) gemeinsamen Sulfo-Phospho-Vanillin-Reaktion. Z. ges. exp. Med. **135**, 545–561 (1962)

6. Determination of Organic Substances and Respiration Potential

K. GOCKE and H.-G. HOPPE

Development and activity of heterotrophic microorganisms are governed by the availability of organic substances. Organic material is composed of different fractions in respect to microbial utilization. The larger fraction consists of material which is refractory to bacterial attack. Because most of the microorganisms do not have the necessary enzymatic properties to decompose this material, it tends to accumulate in the aquatic ecosystem. Only a small number of highly specialized bacteria are able of breaking down these substances. The smaller fraction is characterized by rapid rates of utilization.

In order to determine the total amount of organic carbon, the COD method was used. This technique gives only limited information because (1) only a fraction of the organic material is oxidized and (2) the conversion factor (conversion of COD to organic C) varies according to the composition of the organic material. For the measurement of the fraction of labile organic substances the BOD method was chosen. Since the size relation between the labile and the refractory fraction depends to a certain extent on the length of the incubation time, the distinction between the two fractions is arbitrary. Estimation of the heterotrophic respiration potential of the fraction of labile organic carbon content was made by means of dehydrogenase activity measurement. This method provides information on the maximal respiration rate of a model substrate (succinate) and should be related to the biomass of microorganisms with corresponding heterotrophic uptake properties.

6.1 Description and Application of the Chemical Oxygen Demand (COD) Method

Chemical oxygen demand is applied as an estimate of dissolved organic material in fresh water areas. Standard methods have been admitted to laboratory manuals such as American Standard Methods (1955) or Deutsche Einheitsverfahren (1968). As such determination of chemical oxygen demand is applied for freshwater and sewage, it has its disadvantages in brackish water and sea water. This is caused by the oxydation of chloride by strong oxidizers such as chromate ions which will falsify the results significantly.

On the other hand, chemical oxygen demand will provide an acceptable relative measurement of dissolved organic matter if investigations are performed in a definite water body with little alteration in substrate composition. Because microbes are able to decompose organic compounds according to a typical pattern, this condition may be approximated in the brackish water research area of the Kiel Bight. The method we used to determine the chemical oxygen demand is a modification of the standard method as suggested by Williams (pers. comm. 1972). It does not require any specialized chemical equipment and is therefore applicable also in small biological laboratories.

The procedure runs as follows: 50 ml of sample water is pipetted into a 250-ml conical flask and an exact volume of 0.01 N potassium permanganate solution (5 ml or more depending on the carbon content of the brackish water) and 5 ml of 16% NaOH solution is added. Subsequently the sample is treated on a boiling water bath for 30 min and cooled. Then 5 ml of 4 N H_2SO_4 is added to make acid and about 250 mg of potassium iodide. If a precipitate remains after acidification, a little more acid is added. The iodine liberated is titrated by 0.01 N thiosulfate solution, using starch as indicator. The procedure is repeated, omiting the brackish water and boiling. The difference between the two titers will give the amount of permanganate reduced by the sample water. All titrations should be done in duplicate.

The procedure can be standardized by repeating with a known amount of glucose (1 ml of a 10 mg/100 ml glucose solution) instead of sample water. The results are expressed as mg organic $C\,l^{-1}$ sample water and calculated by the following formula:

$$\text{mg C}\,l^{-1} = \frac{a \cdot 20 \cdot 0.04}{b}$$

where a = titer of the $KMnO_4$ solution minus titer of the water sample
        b = titer of 0.1 mg glucose
    0.04 = carbon content of 0.1 mg glucose.

COD was determined on all stations and depths during the Kiel Bight program on brackish water 1974/75. The values obtained by this method exhibited little relation towards other parameters. Thus COD belongs to those parameters which show relatively small seasonal and regional fluctuations. The same observation was made with other parameters related to the dissolved nutrient content of brackish water, such as BOD and $K_t + S_n$ (see Chap. 15). The mean values of COD registered, as well as the extremes, are demonstrated in Table 6.1.

Table 6.1. Mean values of COD

	Station 1		Station 2		Station 3			Station 4		Station 5		
	2 m	10 m	2 m	10 m	2 m	10 m	18 m	2 m	10 m	2 m	10 m	18 m
mean value mg C l^{-1}	0.70	0.62	0.56	0.63	0.57	0.53	0.52	0.57	0.52	0.58	0.55	0.54
Maximum	1.00	0.85	0.93	0.91	0.79	0.72	0.75	0.68	0.66	0.86	0.79	0.77
Minimum mg C l^{-1}	0.50	0.53	0.39	0.54	0.41	0.41	0.22	0.31	0.33	0.50	0.41	0.35

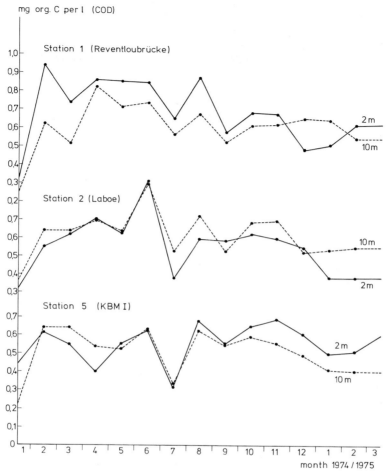

Fig.6.1. Seasonal and regional fluctuations of COD in the Kiel Bight 1974/75

From offshore Station 5 to the mouth of the Kiel Fjord Station 2, surface water mean values of COD differed insignificantly. Only in the polluted inner Kiel Fjord (St. 1) could a significant increase of COD be determined. Of course, these values provide little information as to fluctuations of substrate supply in the different regions. The fact that seasonal COD in the brackish water area remains fairly constant can theoretically be explained by the metabolic activity of bacteria and other living organisms on chemically oxidizable substances. Especially bacteria are able to metabolize organic nutrients down to a very low threshold concentration. Rapidity of growth rates enables heterotrophic bacteria to adapt their activity, number and biomass to fluctuations in the nutrimental supply. Only in inshore eutrophicated brackish water areas such as the inner Kiel Fjord can a higher concentration of oxidizable substances be maintained because microorganisms introduced into the brackish water by terrestrial runoff and pollution are partly eliminated by the new environment, and autochthoneous bacterial populations need a certain lag phase to adapt to the increasing nutrient concentration. Of course also autochthoneous substrate formation by phytoplankton is much stronger in the inner Kiel Fjord (see Chap. 7), than in offshore regions. As expected from these considerations, differences between COD minima and maxima are greatest in near-shore surface water. Similar findings at the 18-m sample from Station 3 may be attributed to a temporary increase of sediment particles.

Vertical distribution of COD measurements is demonstrated in Figure 6.1. As can be seen also from Table 6.1, mean COD values decrease slightly from the surface to the depth at most of the stations. The same observation was made with other measurements of organic substrates ($K_t + S_n$). Lower COD values in greater depth should be attributed to an increasing degree of remineralization by planktonic organisms in these water layers. There is a remarkable parallel in the seasonal changes of COD at various water depths. This observation indicates that COD distribution is governed by the location of main organic matter production in the euphotic zone. Exceptions may be explained by the hydrographic conditions at sampling date, or rapid sedimentation of planktonic cells after plankton has bloomed.

6.2 Description and Application
of the Biochemical Oxygen Demand (BOD) Method

Basically the method used in this study resembles the well-known technique for the determination of the biochemical oxygen demand. However, since previous studies often produced incorrect results, some modifications were introduced. Therefore the method will be briefly described here. Samples from 2-m depth were taken by means of clean 5-l or 2-l samplers at Station 1 (inner Kiel Fjord) and Station 5 (central Kiel Bight). The samples were processed not later than 2–3 h after sampling. During transport to the laboratory they were stored at in situ temperature.

To remove larger zooplankton and detritus particles 1 l of each sample is filtered through a stainless steel net (75 µm mesh size) into a clean 1-l glass-stoppered bottle. Afterwards, the filtered samples are warmed to 20° C, and after transferring to special glass vessels (see Fig. 6.2) saturated with oxygen by bubbling with air. Subsequently three thoroughly cleaned BOD bottles (about 120-ml capacity) are filled to overflowing. The initial oxygen content of one bottle is determined immediately, using the Winkler technique. The two other BOD bottles are placed in a water bath and incubated at 20° C in the dark. After seven days, the oxygen content of these bottles is measured. The BOD is the difference between the values before and after incubation. The precision of the technique is good; concentration differences between the two incubated bottles seldom amount to more than 0.1 mg O_2 l^{-1}.

Some additional remarks should be made regarding the saturation of the water with oxygen. This step was not performed to increase the oxygen content of the samples. The biochemical oxygen demand of the water samples in the area

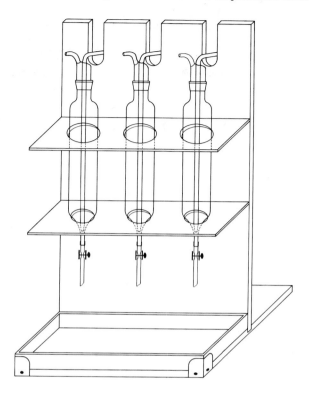

Fig.6.2. Special glass vessels used for oxygen saturating of the samples by air bubbling

studied is usually quite low. Thus the original oxygen content is sufficiently high to allow a total oxydation of the organic matter present in the sample. On the contrary, the bubbling with air should prevent over-saturation. Over-saturation would occur if a cold oxygen-saturated water sample were filled in a BOD bottle and incubated at 20° C. The bubble thus formed due to over-saturation will escape determination. Therefore, especially when studying BOD during the cold season, serious errors can occur due to losses of oxygen by physical causes.

The results of the BOD measurements are demonstrated in Table 6.2. Despite the significant differences in the degree of eutrophication between Station 1 (inner Kiel Fjord) and Station 5 (central Kiel Bight), the differences between the BOD values are relatively small. The annual average values were found to be 1.64 mg $O_2 l^{-1}$ at Station 1 and 1.14 mg $O_2 l^{-1}$ at Station 5. The total range was from 0.35–2.85 mg $O_2 l^{-1}$.

Thus, compared with other areas (rivers, lakes) exposed to human activities, the area studied seems to be less polluted. To convert BOD values into concentrations of labile organic material, one has to multiply by the R_Q factor (ratio of the CO_2 produced to the O_2 consumed). This factor obviously is related to the composition of the labile organic material. The extreme values could be ca. 0.7 if fat and 1.0 if carbohydrates are subjected to oxidation. R_Q factors which have

Table 6.2. Biochemical oxygen demand (BOD$_7$) in the inner Kiel Fjord (St. 1) and in the central Kiel Bight (St. 5)

Date	Station 1 (inner Kiel Fjord) mg O$_2$ l^{-1}	Station 5 (central Kiel Bight) mg O$_2$ l^{-1}
Feb. 28, 1974	0.93	0.45
March 21	1.72	1.16
April 18	—	0.96
May 16	2.84	1.70
June 11	2.14	0.96
July 11	1.65	0.35
Aug. 29	—	—
Sept. 12	1.43	0.95
Oct. 24	2.13	1.95
Nov. 21	0.96	1.33
Dec. 10	0.97	0.84
Jan. 23, 1975	1.35	1.14
Feb. 12	1.18	1.10
March 10	2.32	1.93

been employed for this calculation in the literature vary between 0.75 (Zsolnay, 1975) and 0.85 (Ogura, 1972). Bryan et al. (1976) assumed the value to be 0.8. In our study the latter value was taken. Thus, the average values for the BOD found in the inner Kiel Fjord (1.64 mg O$_2$ l^{-1}) and in the central Kiel Bight (1.14 mg O$_2$ l^{-1}) would be equivalent to the oxidation of 0.44 or 0.30 mg C l^{-1} respectively. Since no data are available for the total organic carbon in the studied area, the percentage of labile organic carbon cannot be calculated. However, investigations performed in other coastel areas of the western Baltic Sea revealed a percentage of labile DOC to be 8–12% of the total DOC (concentrations of DOC used for these calculations were obtained by Dr. R. Dawson).

If this value were valid for conditions in the area studied, then it would be much lower than the 20% found by Ogura (1972) in the North Pacific, the 29% obtained by Zsolnay (1975) in the central Baltic and the 50% found in New England waters by Barber (1968). However, the results are difficult to compare because of the different methods used. The incubation period chosen in this study is much shorter than that of the above authors. Nevertheless, it can be stated that the amount of easily degradable substances represent only a small fraction of the total amount of organic substances. Such low values are surprising in view of the eutrophic status and relatively high bacterial activity of the area (especially the Kiel Fjord). However, the bacterial activity can be high in the presence of low concentrations of degradable material when the uptake of these substances is balanced by more or less instantaneous input.

When the concentrations of labile organic substances are compared with the COD values, it is obvious that they represent a much higher percentage of this group of material. It amounts to 63% at Station 1 and 56% at Station 5. It is well known that only a fraction of the total amount of organic material is oxidized by potassium permanganate. Whether the fraction of organic material oxidized by

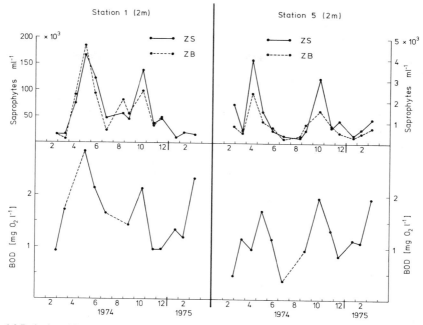

Fig. 6.3 Relationship between BOD and numbers of saprophytic bacteria (*ZS*: bacteria growing on ZoBell Medium 2216 with 25‰ salinity; *ZB*: bacteria growing on ZoBell medium
2216 with 8‰ salinity)

heterotrophic organisms is about the same as that oxidized by permanganate is
unknown.

The seasonal variations of the BOD are shown in Figure 6.3. The curves both
at Station 1 and Station 5 exhibit two major peaks in May and October. The
graph also demonstrates the relationship between the numbers of saprophytic
bacteria growing on medium with 25‰ and 8‰ salinity and the amount of BOD.
The saprophytic bacteria seem to react very quickly when provided with greater
amounts of labile substances (cf. Chap. 11). Despite its simplicity, the BOD seems
to be a very valuable parameter. However, it might be necessary to separate the
BOD due to labile dissolved organic substances from the BOD due to labile
particulate organic matter. This can be achieved by filtration.

6.3 Description and Application
of Dehydrogenase Activity (DHA) Determination
as a Measure for Potential Respiration

Respiration is the basic parameter for the determination of substrate mineralization and energy transfer in aquatic as well as terrestrial microbial populations.
Measurements of oxygen consumption are normally carried out by means of
manometry, oxygen electrode or iodometry (Winkler method). These methods

may be advantageous in respiration measurements of soils, sediment or activated sludge, but with natural water samples from brackish water and other biotopes or even „Sinkstoff" from sediment traps they do not provide sufficient results. Samples with comparatively low respiratory activity have to be incubated for at least one day to obtain measurable oxygen consumption rates. For actively metabolizing microorganisms with generation times as short as 18 h during this period of measurement, changes in the composition of the microbial population cannot be excluded, especially when natural conditons are altered by the use of small glass bottles for incubation.

Another methodical approach to the estimation of respiratory potential in biological material is the measurement of the activity of enzymes interposed between substrate oxidation and consumption of oxygen. This can be done either by the measurement of dehydrogenase activity (DHA) or the activity of the electron transport system (ETS). As hydrogen acceptors instead of oxygen different agents, especially tetrazolium salts (TTC, INT) are used. The first technique has been widely and successfully employed in sediment, sludge and soil microbiology, and marine organisms (Lenhard, 1956, 1966; Curl and Sandberg, 1961; Rühle 1966; Kalbe, 1968; Jones and Prasad, 1969; Skuyins, 1973; Malicky-Schlatte, 1973; Bremner and Tabatabai, 1973). Electrochemical instead of ascorbic acid standardization of the DHA assay was described by Packard and Healy (1968). The second technique requires supplementation of water samples with coenzymes, and was applied with different variations to measure potential respiration in marine planktonic populations (Packard et al., 1971, 1974; Hobbie et al., 1972; Owens and King, 1975; Kenner and Ahmed, 1975a, b).

The DHA method used in our brackish water investigations in 1974/75 for the measurement of succinate dehydrogenase activity of planktonic organisms was based on Curl and Sandberg's description. Our version will be described here briefly.

500 ml of sample water is filtered gently through a 0.2 μm membrane filter (Sartorius). The filter is cut into small pieces and introduced into a Winkler bottle. After addition of 6 ml freshly prepared standard reaction mixture, consisting of 2 ml Tris-HCl buffer (pH 7.7), 2 ml Na-succinate solution (0.4 M sodium succinate stock solution, diluted three times with water before use) and 2 ml INT solution (100 mg INT per 50 ml sterile distilled water, pH adjusted to 7.5 with 3 N Na_2CO_3 solution), the samples are incubated for exactly 30 min at 35° C on a laboratory shaker. A blank without INT is run for each sample, three parallels for each measurement are required. The reaction is stopped by addition of 1 ml 1 N HCl. 12 ml of a 1:5 mixture of tetrachlorethylene and acetone are added to extract non-water-soluble INT-formazan from the actively respiring cells. After 1.5 h extraction on a laboratory shaker at 35° C, samples are filtered through glass fiber filters and washed with 5 ml extraction mixture. Water phase is separated from the organic phase by means of a funnel tube. The red-colored formazan-containing phase is adjusted to a standard volume with extraction mixture and the extinction is measured in a photospectrometer at 492 nm. DHA values are given as extinction at 492 nm h^{-1} incubation time and l^{-1} sample volume.

In our respiratory potential measurement, the respiratory activity of all living organisms, as well as free enzymes in a water sample is estimated. The values obtained therefore must not necessarily correlate with one of the other biological parameters measured in our Baltic Sea experiments in 1974/75. They will depend mainly on the biomass composition, which is influenced by the varying proportion of phytoplankton, zooplankton and microbes at different seasons.

In the polluted inner Kiel Fjord (St. 1), maximum values of DHA were obtained during the spring. During the rest of the year values declined. They showed considerable variability from month to month. This observation is also valid for the values estimated on the other stations (2.5). We attribute this finding to rapid variations in algae, zooplankton and bacteria development. The difficulty in finding explanations for DHA values may correspond to those of ATP measurements (see Chap. 5). Mean values of DHA were 0.182 in the inner Kiel Fjord (St. 1), 0.186 at Laboe (St. 2) and 0.078 in the middle of the Kiel Bight (St. 5). The ratio of 1 : 2.33 between polluted inner Kiel Fjord and the offshore station is surprisingly low. Similar ratios were only observed in total bacteria counts and the number of actively metabolizing bacteria. This may lead to the conclusion that these microorganisms are mainly responsible for respiration potential as determined by our DHA method.

References

Barber, R.R.: Dissolved organic carbon from deep water resists microbial oxidation. Nature (London) **220**, 274–275 (1968)

Bremner, J.M., Tabatabai, M.A.: Effect of some inorganic substances on TTC assay of dehydrogenase activity in soils. Soil Biol. Biochem., Vol. **5**, 385–386 (1973)

Bryan, J.R., Riley, J.P., Williams, P.J. LeB: A Winkler procedure for making precise measurements of oxygen concentration for productivity and related studies. J. Exptl. Mar. Biol. Ecol. **21**, 191–197 (1976)

Curl, H.J., Sandberg, J.: The measurement of dehydrogenase activity in marine organisms. J. Mar. Res. **19**, 123–138 (1961)

Deutsche Einheitsverfahren zur Wasser-, Abwasser- und Schlammuntersuchung, Weinheim: Verlag Chemie 1968

Halász, A.: Zusammenhang zwischen Dehydrogenase-aktivität und Wachstumsrate des Belebtschlammes. Schweiz. Zeitschr. f. Hydrolog., **34**, 94–104 (1972)

Hobbie, J.E., Holm-Hansen, O., Packard, T.T., Pomeroy, L.R., Sheldon, R.W., Thomas, J.P., Wiebe, W.J.: A study of the distribution and activity of microorganisms in ocean water. Limnol. Oceanogr. **17**, 544–555 (1972)

Jones, P.H., Prasad, D.: The use of Tetrazolium salts as a measure of sludge activity. J. Water Pollution Control Federation, Washington, 441–449 (1969)

Kalbe, L.: Untersuchungen zur Bestimmung der Sedimentaktivität mit 2,3,5-Triphenyltetrazoliumchlorid (TTC). Limnologia **6**, 37–44 (1968)

Kenner, R.A., Ahmed. S.J.: Measurements of electron transport activities in marine phytoplankton. Mar. Biol. **33**, 119–127 (1975a)

Kenner, R.A., Ahmed, S.J.: Correlation between oxygen utilization and electron transport activity in marine phytoplankton. Mar. Biol. **33**, 129–133 (1975b)

Lenhard, G.: Die Dehydrogenaseaktivität des Bodens als Maß für die Menge an mikrobiell abbaubaren Humusstoffen. Zeitschrift für Pflanzenernährung, Düngung, Bodenkunde **77**, 193–198 (1956)

Lenhard, G.: The dehydrogenase activity for the study of soils and river deposits. Soil. Sci., **101**, 400–402 (1966)

Malicky-Schlatte, G.: Über die Dehydrogenaseaktivität im Sediment des Lunzer Untersees. Arch. Hydrobiol. **72**, 525–532 (1973)

Ogura, N.: Rate and extent of decomposition of dissolved organic matter in surface seawater. Mar. Biol. **13**, 89–93 (1972)

Owens, T. G., King, F. D.: The measurement of respiratory electron-transport-system activity in marine zooplankton. Mar. Biol. **30**, 27–36 (1975)

Packard, T. T., Harmon, D., Boucher, J.: Respiratory electron transport activity in plankton from upwelling waters. Tethys **6**, 213–222 (1974)

Packard, T. T., Healy, M. L.: Electrochemical standardization of the dehydrogenase assay used in the estimation of respiration rates. J. Mar. Res. **26**, 66–74 (1968)

Packard, T. T., Healy, M. L., Richards, F. A.: Vertical distribution of the activity of the respiratory electron transport system in marine plankton. Limnol. Oceanogr. **16**, 60–70 (1971)

Rühle, E.: Sedimentaktivität. Limnologica **4**, 323–332 (1966)

Skujins, J.: Dehydrogenase: An indicator of biological activities in arid solis. Bull. Ecol. Res. Comm. **17**, 235–241 (1973)

Standard Methods for the examinations of water, sewage, and industrial wastes. (1955)

Zsolnay, A.: Total labile carbon in the euphotic zone of the Baltic Sea as measured by BOD. Mar. Biol. **29**, 125–128 (1975)

7. Primary Production

B. PROBST

In addition to light, primary production is dependent upon the availability of inorganic nutrients limiting phytoplanktion growth in the euphotic zone. The availability of nutrient is, to a large extent, dependent upon remineralization processes in the water column and in the upper sediment layers and overlying water. It is further dependent upon the mechanisms supplying the euphotic zone with nutrients.

The western Baltic includes a number of particularly shallow areas in which remineralization processes in the bottom layers have an immediate influence on the algae production in the upper water layers. In comparison to the open areas of the Baltic where long-term remineralization processes are of less significance when compared to the short-term turnover, the turnover of nutrients from remineralization processes at the bottom in shallow waters makes a more significant contribution.

This leads to a high sequence of phytoplankton blooms during the summer period, and to an extended production period especially in the eutrophicated areas of the western Baltic, when light is not a limiting factor.

Krey and Sarma (1970) undertook the first extensive primary productivity investigations in the Kiel Bight. Further measurements with a high sampling sequence were undertaken by von Bodungen (1975) at Station A (Boknis Eck; see Fig. 2.1). The production data in the Flensburg Fjord (Horstmann et al., 1975) and our own data from Station 1 (Reventlou-Brücke) in the inner Kiel Fjord have also been included in the discussion. Primary productivity measurements in this brackish water area cannot be directly compared with data obtained from marine areas. The methodology of ^{14}C-measurements in brackish waters is not entirely standardized, and factors such as alkalinity, incubation time, and incubation depth, together with the evaluation and interpretation of data, can cause considerable variations in the results of primary productivity measurements. The variation between measurements largely arise from variations in the duration of incubation and from the difficulty in defining whether the result represents gross or net production. In this article the differences between the two terms are neglected when the term primary production is used.

7.1 Material and Methods

Primary productivity measurements were carried out using the ^{14}C-method as described by Steemann-Nielsen (1952) with inclusion of the modifications recom-

mended by Gargas (1975). Samples were taken at Station 1 (Reventlou-Brücke) at
the depths: surface, 2, 4, and 6 m. The bottom depth at the sampling station was
recorded as 7 m.

For in situ incubation, 100-ml bottles (light and dark) were incubated at the
same depth from which the samples were taken. In order to avoid light damage to
the phytoplankton, speciel care was taken to shield the samples from open sunlight. Incubation took place around noon with a duration time of incubation of
around 6 h (see Table 7.1). The samples were filtered through membrane filters
(Sartorius, pore width 0.2 μm) and stored in a desiccator.

Measurements of the sample activities were carried out using the liquid scintillation method as described by Gargas (1975).

Alkalinity of the samples was determined according to Buch (1945) utilizing
the parameters pH, temperature, and salinity. The counting efficiency of the liquid
scintillation was estimated by analyzing an external standard and no correction
factors were applied when the values lay above 95%. Because of the uncertainties
in extrapolating the production values for the incubation time to a daily production figure, the results have been expressed here in terms of mg $C\,m^{-2}\,h^{-1}$
respectively in mg $C\,m^{-3}\,h^{-1}$.

The measurements were undertaken from March 1974 to February 1975.
From July to December 1975 some of the primary production measurements
were repeated at Station 1 (Reventlou-Brücke) using the method described above,
however incubation extended from sunrise to true noon. Twice this value was
considered as representing the daily production. Possible higher rates of photosynthesis during the first half of the day were not taken into account.

7.2 Primary Production in the Kiel Fjord and Different Areas
of the Kiel Bight

The nutrient concentration in the rather heavily eutrophicated waters of the
inner Kiel Fjord almost never reaches production-limiting concentrations, which
is apparently the main reason for the high production at this station. During the
summer period, when remineralization of organic substances is high, nutrient
concentrations seem to be sufficient to maintain high primary productivity in the
Kiel Fjord. With the exception of a decrease in primary production immediately
after the spring bloom (see Fig. 7.1), the production values are highest during the
time of highest solar radiation, i.e., July, resulting in an extremely high value of
603 mg $C\,m^{-2}\,h^{-1}$. It is remarkable that, at this time, (Table 7.1) a production of
84 mg $C\,m^{-3}\,h^{-1}$ could still be measured at a depth of 6 m (see Fig. 7.3), though
the 10% light depth was already at 4 m. This high production leads to a strong
depletion of dissolved nitrogen in the water column, though considerable
amounts of nitrogen are still available (see Chap. 4).

Comparing the production isopleths of Figure 7.2 with primary production
measurements at Station A (Boknis Eck) in the northern part of the mouth of the
Eckenförder Bucht (Fig. 7.4, after von Bodungen, 1975), the same tendency can be
observed especially in the summer, however, the production in 1.5 h in the heavily

Table 7.1. Primary production in mg C m^{-3} h^{-1} and the integrated primary production in mg C m^{-2} h^{-1} at Station 1 (Reventlou Brücke)

Date	Primary production (mg C m^{-3} h^{-1}) ($\bar{x}$)				Incubation time	Integrated value (mg C m^{-2} h^{-1})
	0 m	2 m	4 m	6 m		
March 21, 1974	3.00	3.34	1.53	0.81	9.30–15.30 h	13.54
April 18	64.29	23.10	6.81	1.15	9.30–15.30 h	125.25
May 16	18.40	7.54	2.29	0.22	10.00–15.00 h	38.30
June 11	38.45	16.85	3.15	0.55	9.30–15.30 h	78.99
July 11	91.56	122.63	91.36	83.84	9.15–15.15 h	603.39
Aug. 29	63.31	55.46	22.25	5.47	9.30–16.00 h	224.19
Sept. 12	22.37	23.89	19.17	7.48	9.00–14.45 h	114.00
Oct. 24	4.07	13.65	4.49	0.35	9.30–15.30 h	40.70
Nov. 21	0.80	0.70	0.70	0.60	9.45–15.45 h	4.20
Dec. 10	1.00	0.80	0.60	0.20	9.30–15.30 h	4.00
Jan. 23, 1975	0.85	0.81	0.54	0.23	9.15–15.45 h	3.78
Feb. 20	2.13	1.02	0.50	0.16	9.00–16.15 h	5.33

eutrophicated waters at Station 1 in the Kiel Fjord almost equals the daily production at Station A (Boknis Eck).

If we compare production values from the Flensburg Fjord (an area almost as eutrophicated as the Kiel Fjord), we can conclude that primary production measured in 1974 at Station 1 is extremely high even for a heavily eutrophicated area. The investigations in the Flensburg Fjord were undertaken from May to September 1972. The comparison of the daily (or total) production of this period with the production at Station 1 in the inner Kiel Fjord during the same period in 1975 shows that in the latter area, primary productivity is on average twice as high. It should, however, be taken into consideration, that in 1975 there was a summer period of high solar radiation. Data from the Flensburg Fjord were obtained from Horstmann et al. (1975). Table 7.2 shows the total primary production for the period from May to September 1972. The stations were chosen to range from the heavily eutrophicated inner Flensburg Fjord towards the less polluted outer area of this fjord (see Fig. 5). Station 1 (Reventlou-Brücke) in the Kiel Fjord is also comparable with Station a (Flensburg Kollund) in terms of the nutrient values as well as the stage of eutrophication (Gemeinsames Komitee Flensburger Förde, 1974).

The repeated measurements of the 1974 investigations in 1975 at Station 1 shows that in 1974 in July, production was as high in less than 2 h as that from a whole day in 1975 (1008 mg C m^{-2} d^{-1}, see Table 7.3). However, in September the average production per h is similar in both years.

If we omit the extremely high values of July 1974, the production curves of the period of investigation of 1974 and 1975 show similar tendencies. If we take into consideration the relatively symmetric curves during the summer months, we can conclude an annual production of 200 g C m^{-2} y^{-1} for 1975 at Station 1 (Reventlou-Brücke). Von Bodungen (1975) obtained a figure for annual production of 158 g C m^{-2} y^{-1} at Station A (Boknis Eck) which is only slightly eutrophicated.

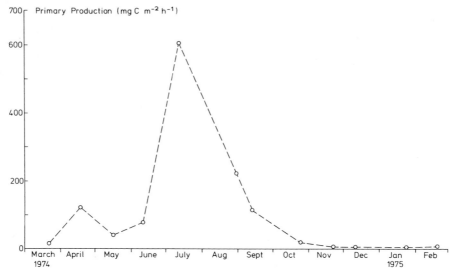

Fig. 7.1. Primary production (mg C m^{-2} h^{-1}) at Station 1 (Reventlou Brücke) in the inner Kiel Fjord

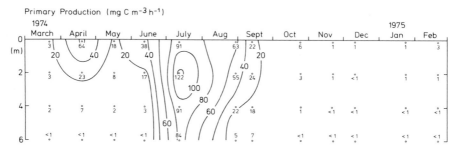

Fig. 7.2. Isopleths of primary production (mg C m^{-3} h^{-1}) at Station 1

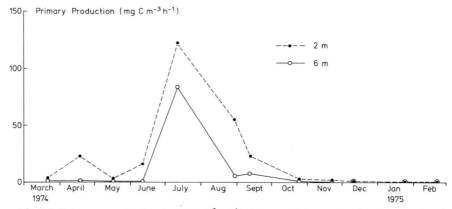

Fig. 7.3. Primary production (mg C m^{-3} h^{-1}) at 2-m and 6-m water depth at Station 1

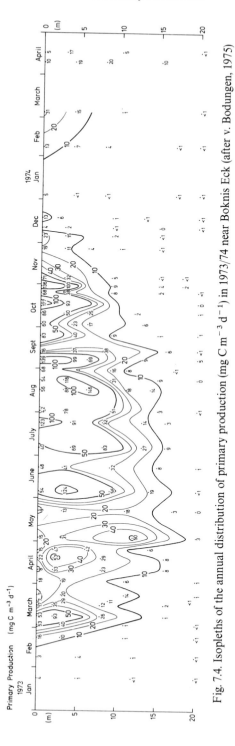

Fig. 7.4. Isopleths of the annual distribution of primary production (mg C m^{-3} d^{-1}) in 1973/74 near Boknis Eck (after v. Bodungen, 1975)

Table 7.2. Primary production in the Flensburg Fjord from May
to September 1972 (t) (after Horstmann et al., 1975)

Station (see Fig. 7.5)	Primary production $(\text{g C m}^{-2} \text{t}^{-1})$
(a) Flensburg-Kollund	255
(b) Innenförde	181
(c) Holnis	115
(d) Mittlere Förde	78
(e) Außenförde	98
(f) Geltinger Bucht	101
(g) Sonderburg (Alssund Süd)	130
(h) Alssund Nord	165
(i) Vemmingbund	77
(j) Horup Hav	85
(k) Fördemündung	87
(l) Sildekule-Nybol Noor	394

Table 7.3. Integrated values of hourly and diurnal primary
production in 1975 at Station 1 (Reventlou Brücke).
(Incubation time: sunrise to true noon)

Date	$\text{mg C m}^{-2} \text{h}^{-1} (\bar{x})$	$\text{mg C m}^{-2} \text{d}^{-1}$
July 7, 1975	68.74	1,008.42
Aug. 5	72.26	1,011.74
Aug. 12	33.20	448.20
Aug. 22	38.71	522.59
Aug. 29	81.73	1,062.49
Sept. 5	66.92	803.04
Sept. 9	102.48	1,229.76
Oct. 1	1.98	23.76
Oct. 23	2.81	26.70
Oct. 31	2.03	18.27
Nov. 27	2.96	17.76
Dec. 23	0.76	5.07

Table 7.4. Annual primary production values for some other areas
of the Baltic

	Primary production $(\text{g C m}^{-2} \text{y}^{-1})$	
Proper Baltic	30–78	Fonselius, 1971; Sen Gupta, 1972
Arkona Sea	65–73	Kaiser and Schulz, 1973;
Bornholm Sea	63–78	Renk, 1974
Danzig Deep	117,5	Renk, 1974
Danzig Bight	104,1	

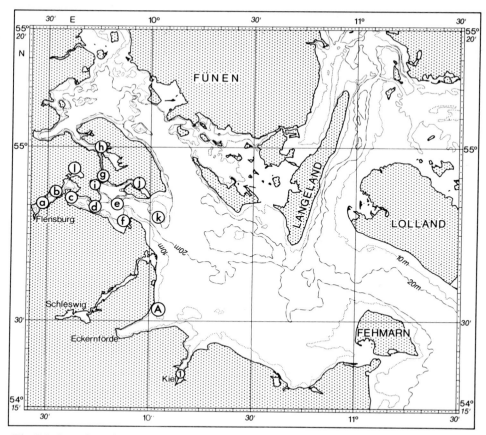

Fig. 7.5. Location of stations in the Flensburg Fjord of primary production measurements form May to Sept. 1972 (explanation see Table 7.2)

The author states that 1.5% of the production at Boknis Eck arises from pollution. Horstmann (1972) obtained primary production data of 60 g C m^{-2} y^{-1} for the Kiel Bight, of which 4% were considered to be generated from pollution. The production values for the open water of the Baltic (see Table 7.4) suggests that the Baltic is in general an oligotrophic system with slow mineral cycling and low production (Jansson, 1976). This is also true for the middle of the Kiel Bight as shown by Horstmann et al. (1975).

References

Bodungen, v. B.: Der Jahresgang der Nährsalze und der Primärproduktion des Planktons in der Kieler Bucht unter Berücksichtigung der Hydrographie. Thesis Univ. Kiel (1975)

Buch, K.: Kolsyrejämnvikten i. Baltiska Havet. Fenia 68, No. 5 (1945)

Fonselius, S. H.: On primary production in the Baltic. ICES; Statutory meeting CM 1971/L: 16 (1971)

Gargas, E.: A manual for phytoplankton primary production studies in the Baltic. The Baltic Marine Biol. Publ. No. **2**, 4–88 (1975)

Gemeinsames Komitee Flensburger Förde: Untersuchungen der Flensburger Förde. Gemeinsames Kom. Flensburger Förde. Amtshuset, Aabenraa: Selbstverlag. 1974

Horstmann, U.: Über den Einfluß von häuslichem Abwasser auf das Plankton in der Kieler Bucht. Kieler Meeresforsch. **28**, 178–179 (1972)

Horstmann, U., Schiemann, S., Martens, P., Hansen, E., Weigel, P.: Untersuchungen über den Einfluß von Abwasser auf das Plankton in der Kieler Bucht. BMFT Forsch. Ber. M 75-08. Meeresforsch. 1–41 (1975)

Jansson, B.-O.: The Baltic—A Systems Analysis of a Semienclosed Sea. Joint Oceanogr. Ass. 1976. Gen. Symposia, Charnock a. Deacon. Plenum Press

Kaiser, W., Schulz, S.: Biologische Untersuchungen während des internationalen Ostseejahres (IBY) 1969/70. II. Untersuchungen zur Primärproduktion. Beiträge zur Meereskunde, **32**, 9–31 (1973)

Krey, J., Sarma, A. H. V.: Primary production and seasonal cycle of phytoplankton in Kiel Bight during 1967 and 1968 and its relation to environmental factors, ICES; Statutory meeting, CM 1970/L:8, Plankton Committee, (1970)

Renk, H.: Primary production and chlorophyll content of the Baltic Sea. Part III. Primary production in the southern part of the Baltic. Pol. Arch. Hydrobiol. **21**, 191–209 (1974)

Sen Gupta, R.: A study on nitrogen and phosphorus and their interrelationship in the Baltic. Thesis Univ. Göteborg (1973)

Steemann-Nielsen, E.: The use of radio-active (^{14} C) for measuring organic production in the sea. J. Cons. Perm. Intern Explor. Mer. **18**, 117–140 (1952)

8. Plankton Populations

J. LENZ

Many processes in the pelagic ecosystem involve a close interaction between bacteria and plankton, among these the regeneration of inorganic nutrients for phytoplankton growth (see Parsons and Takahashi, 1973; Rheinheimer, 1975), the heterotrophic utilization of photo-assimilated organic compounds released by phytoplankton (e.g., Williams and Yentsch, 1976; Iturriaga and Hoppe, 1977) and the significance of bacteria as a food source for planktic filter-feeders (see Jørgensen, 1966). In this context, it appears appropriate to add some general information on plankton populations inhabiting brackish waters in order to supplement the present studies on bacteria and fungi in this environment.

Remane and Schlieper (1971) have described three ways in which brackish water populations are affected by their particular environment, as compared with those living in marine habitats. Firstly, there is a fall in species abundance with decreasing salinity, a minimum being reached at about 6‰; below this limit there is a sharp rise in the number of halo-tolerant freshwater species. Secondly, brackish water organisms generally show a reduction both in body size and thickness of their calcareous parts. Thirdly, we have the so-called "brackish water submergence" (Remane, 1955), by which is meant the change in depth distribution of many marine organisms with increasing distance from their original environment. They tend to descend into the depths, since in stratified water bodies, salinity decrease in the deep is slower than at the surface.

All three features of brackish water environments are recognizable in the plankton of the Baltic. Many examples can be found to illustrate the first and third characteristics (Remane, 1951, 1955; Gessner, 1957; Arndt, 1964), whereas the second, pertaining to size reduction, is less evident in planktic than in benthic communities. A good example for reduction in organism size with falling salinity is the common jellyfish *Aurelia aurita*. This phenomenon is more difficult to demonstrate, though, with small plankters such as copepods, since their body size is often subject to changes controlled by factors other than salinity, for instance temperature or nutrition. The same difficulties are encountered with phytoplankton. However, comparing phytoplankton, especially diatoms, from a marine environment such as the North Sea with those from the brackish waters of the Western Baltic does give one the impression that the latter is often smaller and of a more delicate habitus.

This reduction in size, though, does not necessarily lessen vitality, since there are quite a number of species that thrive under brackish water conditions. The main reason here is probably the absence of competition in this extreme environment.

As far as we know, there are no genuine brackish water species existing in plankton. Brackish waters form an environment of a transient nature as demonstrated by the changing history of the Baltic (cf. Gessner, 1957; Dietrich and Köster, 1974). For this reason, it is thought that the periods of stable conditions in the past were not long-lasting enough to allow distinct species to evolve. All organisms inhabiting brackish waters are either of thalassogenous or limnogenous origin (Remane and Schlieper, 1971). Thus wherever a changing environment of this kind is established through mixing of fresh and salt waters, it will be colonized from both adjacent habitats, limnic and marine, through the infiltration of euryhaline species.

8.1 Plankton Populations of the Kiel Bight

The Kiel Bight, being part of the transition zone between North Sea and Baltic Sea, undergoes marked fluctuations in salinity from 10 to 30‰ as a result of the prevailing current pattern (see Chap. 3). In the classification of brackish water zones given below (Table 8.1), the Kiel Bight encompasses the α mesohaline and the polyhaline zones. On the whole, these correspond to the upper and lower half of the water column in our study area.

Quite a number of zooplankton groups characteristic of the marine environment do not enter the mixohaline zone at all, such as radiolarians and foraminifera, siphonophores, pelagic mollusks, ostracods, euphausids and salps. Other groups are either represented only by a few species, e.g., scyphozoa, ctenophores and chaetognaths, or exhibit a gradual decline in species abundance. Copepods and many meroplanktic larvae are among the latter. The meso- and oligohaline zones are, on the other hand, populated by rotifers and cladocera, which belong to fresh water plankton.

As regards phytoplankton, the situation is very much the same. Marine diatoms and dinoflagellates inhabit brackish waters in reduced numbers, some genera being more euryhaline than others, whereas the third important group among the larger phytoplankton, the blue-green algae, are indigenous to fresh water regions.

It is therefore fairly easy to allocate to each brackish water zone its typical plankton population. The Baltic with its large expanse lends itself well to an attempt of this kind (see Arndt, 1964). However, we must bear in mind that in our

Table 8.1. Brackish water zones with reference to the "Venice System 1958" (see Remane and Schlieper, 1971)

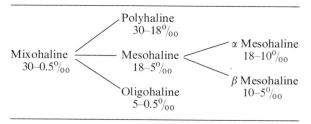

study area, the plankton populations are an intrinsic part of the structure of the water masses (Kändler, 1950, 1961; Banse, 1955, 1956, 1959).

In the surface layer, especially during prolonged periods of outflow from the east, we may encounter the planktic flora and fauna of the Baltic proper. One such occasion occurred at the end of August during our joint investigation program, when a large brownish-yellow patch of the blue-green alga *Nodularia spumigena* was observed in the Kiel Bight. During summer, this species dominates in the central Baltic along with other blue-green algae. The low salinity of 10.7‰ measured at the surface bore proof to its having originated from that region.

In contrast, halo-tolerant marine species enter the Kiel Bight in the deep. The copepod *Calanus helgolandicus*, for instance, acts as an indicator species for salt water intrusions. The regular inflow of more saline water from the north into the deeper part of the Kiel Bight in summer is probably responsible for the proliferation of various dinoflagellate species in late summer and autumn.

Most of the zooplankters in our area belong to the ecological group of filter-feeders. These are tintinnids and naked ciliates, both of which were detected in most of the samples taken for phytoplankton analysis (Sect. 8.2), rotifers, meroplanktic larvae, the tunicate *Oicopleura dioica* and about ten copepod species.

Besides the seasonal occurrence of ichthyoplankton, there are only few purely carnivorous zooplankters present, among these several hydromedusae, *Aurelia*, two ctenophores and one or two chaetognaths. For more detailed information, the reader is referred to the doctoral theses of Hillebrandt, 1972 and Schnack, 1975.

8.2 Phytoplankton Populations During the Study Period 1974/75

From the same water samples employed for seston analysis (see Chap. 5), 200 ml subsamples were drawn off for phytoplankton species analysis for the Kiel Fjord (Sts. 1 and 2) and the Kiel Bight (Sts. 4 and 5) during the joint investigation program from January 1974 to March 1975. At all stations, samples were regularly collected from the 2-m and 10-m depth levels and additionally from the 18-m depth level (see Chap. 2) at the more outlying stations. Immediately after collection, the water samples were preserved in 1% hexamin-buffered formalin and stored in brown glass bottles.

For lack of time and manpower, the subsequent microscopic analysis had to be restricted to one depth level only. Our choice of the 2-m depth samples for analysis was based on the assumption that, since the surface layer was generally more or less well-mixed (cf. Chap. 3), no major differences were to be expected between the 2-m and 10-m depth levels.

Cell counting—in colonial forms each cell singly—was performed according to the Utermöhl technique (Utermöhl, 1958). In most cases a 5- or 10-ml counting chamber was sufficient. The works of Brandt and Apstein (1908), Hendey (1964) and Drebes (1974) served as our basis for species identification. Especially with some diatom genera such as *Coscinodiscus*, *Thalassiosira* and *Chaetoceros*, identification was often not possible beyond the genus level. The so-called μ-flagellates, although always present, were not counted because the Utermöhl technique does not permit the use of very high magnifications, e.g., oil immersion objectives,

Table 8.2. Phytoplankton cell numbers for the surface layer (2 m) in the Kiel Fjord
(Sts. 1 and 2) and in the Kiel Bight (Sts. 4 and 5)

Date	Station 1 (Reventlou Brücke)			Station 2 (Laboe)			Station 4 (KBM I)			Station 5 (KBM II)		
	A	B	C	A	B	C	A	B	C	A	B	C
Jan. 6, 1974	15	97	3	26	98	0	—	—	—	7	98	0
Feb. 28	2	100	0	12	100	0	9	98	1	12	100	0
March 21	183	100	0	668	100	0	511	100	0	183	100	0
April 18	4,640	100	0	11,700	100	0	47	100	0	77	100	0
May 16	2,850	0	77	115	99	1	1	100	0	83	34	66
June 11	21,000	100	0	21,950	100	0	7,100	100	0	244	99	1
July 11	5,090	9	39	6,290	10	7	1,630	18	0	1,640	29	0
Aug. 7	2,300	85	13	—	—	—	—	—	—	—	—	—
Aug. 29	754	44	56	577	74	23	114	95	2	167	17	8
Sept. 12	72	43	57	331	95	5	327	98	2	1,280	25	1
Oct. 24	557	98	2	315	92	8	158	84	16	195	23	77
Nov. 21	195	23	4	20	53	47	26	69	30	39	46	54
Dec. 10	25	79	21	—	—	—	27	64	36	49	73	27
Jan. 23, 1975	131	99	1	113	99	1	326	100	0	181	100	0
Feb. 12	969	97	0	20	98	0	164	0	0	402	0	0
March 10	2,130	96	0	2,290	99	0	2,006	96	0	1,910	97	0

A: cells ml^{-1} = 10^3 cells l^{-1}; B: % diatoms; C: % dinoflagellates.

which are necessary if these tiny flagellates, mostly distorted by preservation, are
to be reliably distinguished from cell remnants such as loose chloroplasts.

The changes occuring from season to season in the total number of phytoplankton cells are depicted in Table 8.2. The high figures recorded from March to
June 1974 (excepting the May value at St. 1), and then again from October to
March 1975 are caused by the dominance of the small diatom *Skeletonema costatum*, whereas the similar-sized cells of the blue-green alga *Anabaena baltica* are
responsible for the high values found at all stations in July. In early August we
again have a mass development at Station 1 in the inner Kiel Fjord, this time due
to a bloom of the diatom *Thalassiosira gravida*. Three weeks later, we find a high
concentration of the dinoflagellate *Prorocentrum micans* at Stations 1 and 2 in the
inner and outer Kiel Fjord.

In evaluating the great differences encountered in cell number per volume
water, the range covering four to five orders of magnitude, we must take into
account the immensely wide spectrum of cell size within a phytoplankton community. It is therefore obvious that cell counts will not correlate well with phytoplankton biomass as estimated, for instance, by chlorophyll measurements (see
Chap. 5).

Since we are here mainly concerned with species composition, it was not
attempted to compute phytoplankton cell volume or carbon content from the cell
counts. This would have entailed the additional effort of measuring cell sizes
which, especially with many diatom species, are extremely variable. In our case,
high cell counts were due to mass occurrences of very small forms which at other
observation dates often played only a minor role.

As may also be seen from Table 8.2, diatoms and dinoflagellates account for the highest cell numbers among the larger phytoplankton species in our area. These are superceded only during the summer months by a third group, the blue-green algae. In July, these were found to preponderate at all four stations from the inner Kiel Fjord to the central Kiel Bight, remaining dominant in this region (St. 5) until September. Another exception was noted in the inner Kiel Fjord in November and in the Bight in February of the following year, when the diatoms or dinoflagellates otherwise most abundant were outnumbered by unidentified small flagellates.

On the whole, we observe a numerical predominance of diatoms among the larger phytoplankton during the greater part of the year. This predominance is virtually undisputed during the colder season from January to April, and also occasionally later in the year, as demonstrated in June and to a slightly lesser extent in August/September at Station 4 in the Kiel Bight. Dinoflagellates, on the other hand, play their major role during the warmer season from May to December.

To all appearances, a complete displacement of diatoms by dinoflagellates and other species is rare in our area (Fig. 8.1). On one such occasion, the small dinoflagellate *Exuviella baltica* dominated the phytoplankton in the inner Kiel Fjord (St. 1) in May. From Table 8.2 we see that dinoflagellates normally account for 30–60% of the total cell number in the warmer season. This percentage is very much higher from the viewpoint of the biomass fraction taken up by dinoflagellates in the summer phytoplankton population (see Smetacek, 1975), since many species, especially those of the genus *Ceratium*, have a considerably larger cell size than most diatom species common in our area.

The next Table 8.3 provides an impression of the species abundance found at the various sampling dates and sites. A note of caution is required here, since the table incorporates only those species that could be identified under the inverted microscope in the course of routine analysis of 5- to 10-ml water volume. The figures must therefore be regarded as minimum values. From this table with all its limitations, we see that diversity is quite low, sometimes even very low. During summer, we generally encounter a greater diversity, with the exception of May and part of June. At this time of year there is a considerable admixture of passing water masses from the Baltic proper into the surface layer of the Kiel Bight, these waters being characterized by low species abundance (cf. Chap. 3).

As regards the species abundance of diatoms and dinoflagellates over the year, Table 8.3 shows a corresponding seasonal distribution to Table 8.2. The species abundance of diatoms tends to be highest in spring and autumn, whereas that of dinoflagellates attains its maximum in late summer and autumn. As already mentioned in the previous section, the high incidence of the latter may be explained by the incursion of water from the Kattegat or northern part of the Belt Sea, where dinoflagellates flourish in August. The gradual salinity increase generally observed in the upper layer from August onwards up to the end of the year indicates that water from the north regularly contributes to the surface layer of the Kiel Bight in autumn (see Chap. 3).

In the following, we shall examine the differences between the four stations, two representative of the Kiel Fjord and two of the Kiel Bight. From Table 8.4 we

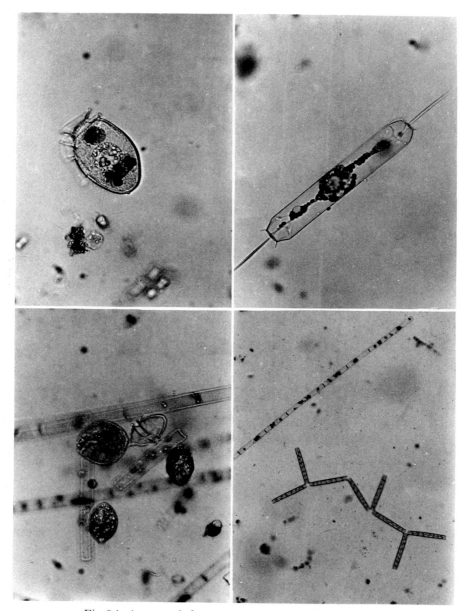

Fig. 8.1. An example for summer plankton in the Kiel Fjord

note a significant decline in the mean cell number and a less pronounced decrease in species abundance from the Fjord to the Bight. The highest figures are not found at Station 1 in the inner Kiel Fjord, as could be expected from the seston parameters analyzed (Chap. 5), but at Station 2 in the outer Kiel Fjord. This disparity, however, is not great enough to affect the main picture significantly,

Table 8.3. Number of phytoplankton species found in the upper layer (2 m) in the Kiel Fjord (Sts. 1 and 2) and in the Kiel Bight (Sts. 4 and 5)

Date	Station 1 (Reventlou Brücke)			Station 2 (Laboe)			Station 4 (KBM I)			Station 5 (KBM II)		
	Total	Diat.	Dino.	Total	Diat.	Dino.	Total	Diat.	Dino.	Total	Diat.	Dino.
Jan. 6, 1974	7	6	1	11	10	0	—	—	—	6	5	0
Feb. 28	5	5	0	13	11	0	9	7	1	3	3	0
March 21	13	13	0	11	11	0	8	8	0	6	6	0
April 18	13	12	0	15	12	2	9	8	1	8	7	1
May 16	5	1	1	4	1	2	1	1	0	2	1	1
June 11	4	3	1	12	6	5	8	5	1	5	3	1
July 11	20	10	6	16	10	4	9	5	3	9	7	1
Aug. 7	16	10	4	—	—	—	—	—	—	—	—	—
Aug. 29	16	10	5	14	8	4	10	7	2	6	3	2
Sept. 12	10	6	4	10	5	4	11	6	4	11	5	4
Oct. 24	12	6	6	9	5	4	16	9	6	18	10	7
Nov. 21	16	9	6	14	8	5	18	12	4	13	9	4
Dec. 10	11	7	4	—	—	—	11	7	3	12	9	3
Jan. 23, 1975	4	12	2	11	9	2	14	13	1	13	10	3
Feb. 12	8	7	0	12	10	0	4	1	1	9	5	2
March 10	13	11	0	19	15	1	11	8	0	7	5	0

Total: total number; Diat.: diatoms; Dino.: dinoflagellates

Table 8.4. Mean values for phytoplankton cell numbers, number of species per sample and total number of diatom species recorded in the surface layer (2 m) of the Kiel Fjord (Sts. 1 and 2) and Kiel Bight (Sts. 4 and 5) during the observation period

Station	1	2	4	5
Cell number ml^{-1}	3,370	4,020	1,110	540
Species per sample	12.3	13.1	11.2	9.0
Total number of diatom species	30	35	29	23

The following sampling dates were excluded from averaging because of incompleteness: 6.1., 16.5., 7.8., 10.12., 12.2.

that is, the general decline from the Kiel Fjord to the Kiel Bight which was also characteristic of total seston, as well as of most of its components. With regard to species abundance, however, one is tempted to believe that this is purely a matter of cell concentration and therefore dependent on the number of cells examined in this case.

An intercomparison of the stations in respect of species composition shows a great deal of irregularity in the distribution pattern, for there are instances of the same population type being encountered at all sampling sites and others where different populations inhabit the Fjord and Bight or even two adjacent stations. An example of the former is the pronounced bloom of *Skeletonema costatum* encompassing the entire investigation area in June and again in March of the following year, and then the mass occurrence of *Anabaena* in July. An example of

Table 8.5. Seasonal occurrence of common phytoplankton species (diatoms and dinoflagellates) observed in Kiel Fjord and Kiel Bight

Species (Genus)	Seasons (Quarters)			
A. Diatoms				
Actinoptychus undulatus (Bail.) Ralfs[a]	I	II	III	IV
Asterionella bleakeleyi W. Smith[a, b]	I	II		IV
Biddulphia sp.[a]	I	II	III	IV
Cerataulina bergonii Peragallo[a, b]	I		III	IV
Chaetoceros atlanticum Cleve[a]		II		
Chaetoceros breve Schütt[a]	I			
Chaetoceros curvisetum Cleve[b]	I			IV
Chaetoceros danicum Cleve[a, b]	I	II	III	IV
Chaetoceros debile Cleve[b]	I	II		IV
Chaetoceros decipiens Cleve[b]	I	II		
Chaetoceros didymum Ehrenberg[a, b]	I	II		IV
Chaetoceros gracile Schütt[a]	I	II		IV
Chaetoceros laciniosum Schütt[b]	I	II		
Chaetoceros radians Schütt[a]	I	II	III	IV
Chaetoceros perpusillum Cleve[a]	I	II		IV
Chaetoceros subtile Cleve[a]	I	II		IV
Chaetoceros sp.[a, b]	I	II	III	IV
Coscinodiscus concinnus W. Smith[a]	I	II		
Coscinodiscus granii Gough[a]			III	
Coscinodiscus sp.[a, b]	I	II	III	IV
Detonula confervacea (Cleve) Gran[b]	I	II		
Ditylum brightwellii (West) Grunow[a, b]			III	IV
Fragillaria sp.[a, b]	I	II	III	IV
Guinardia flaccida (Castr.) Peragallo[a, b]	I	II	III	IV
Leptocylindrus danicus Cleve[a, b]	I	II	III	IV
Licmophora sp[a, b]	I	II	III	IV
Melosira juergensii Agardh[a]	I	II	III	IV
Melosira moniliformis (Müller) Agardh[a, b]	I	II	III	IV
Melosira sulcata (Ehrenb.) Kützing[a]	I	II	III	IV
Melosira sp.[a]	I			
Nitzschia closterium (Ehrenb.) W. Smith[a, b]	I	II	III	IV
Nitzschia delicatissima Cleve[b]	I			
Nitzschia longissima (Brébisson) Ralfs[a, b]	I	II	III	IV
Nitzschia seriata Cleve[a, b]	I	II	III	IV
Rhizosolenia alata Brightwell[a, b]	I	II	III	IV
Rhizosolenia fragillissima Bergon[a, b]	I	II	III	IV
Rhizosolenia hebetata Bailey[a, b]	I	II	III	IV
Rhizosolenia setigera Brightwell[a, b]	I	II	III	IV
Skeletonema costatum (Grev.) Cleve[a, b]	I	II	III	IV
Thalassionema nitzschioides Grunow[a, b]	I	II	III	IV
Thalassiosira baltica (Grunow) Ostenfeld[a, b]	I	II	III	IV
Thalassiosira decipiens (Grunow) Jörgensen[b]		II		
Thalassiosira gravida Cleve[b]	I		III	IV
Thalassiosira nana Lohmann[a]	I	II	III	IV
Thalassiosira nordenskiöldii Cleve[b]	I	II	III	
Thalassiosira polychorda (Gran) Pr.-Lavrenko[b]	I			
Thalassiosira saturni Lohmann[a]	I	II	III	IV
Thalassiosira sp.[b]	I			

[a] Lohmann 1908; [b] present study.

Table 8.5 (continued)

Species (Genus)	Seasons (Quarters)			
B. Dinoflagellates (autrophic forms only)				
Amphidinium sp.	I	II	III	IV
Ceratium furca (Ehrenb.) Claparède and Lachmann[a, b]	I	II	III	IV
Ceratium fusus (Ehrenb.) Dujard. [a, b]	I	II	III	IV
Ceratium longipes (Bail.) Gran[a]	I	II	III	IV
Ceratium tripos (O.F. Müller) Nitzsch[a, b]	I	II	III	IV
Dinophysis acuminata Claparède and Lachmann[a, b]	I	II	III	IV
Dinophysis acuta Ehrenberg[a, b]	I	II	III	IV
Dinophysis norvegica Claparède and Lachmann[b]				IV
Dinophysis rotundata Claparède and Lachmann[a]	I	II	III	IV
Exuviella baltica Lohmann[a, b]	I	II	III	IV
Gonyaulax grindleyi Reinecke[a]	I	II	III	IV
Gonyaulax spinifera (Clap. and Lachm.) Diesing[a]	I	II	III	IV
Gymnodinium sp.[a]		II	III	
Heterocapsa triquetra (Ehrenb.) Stein[a, b]	I	II	III	IV
Peridinium pallidum Ostenfeld[a]	I	II	III	IV
Peridinium trochoideum (Stein) Lemmermann[a]	I	II	III	IV
Peridinium sp.[b]		II	III	IV
Prorocentrum micans Ehrenberg[a, b]	I	II	III	IV

the latter situation is found in April. The fjord water population is dominated by *Skeletonema costatum*, other diatom species such as *Chaetoceros didymis* and *Chaetoceros decipiens*, together with *Rhizosolenia hebetata* f. *semispina* being greatly outnumbered; these, on the contrary, are the main species in the Bight, *Skeletonema* being totally absent here.

Differences in species composition occur not only between the Kiel Fjord and the Kiel Bight, where they could be attributable to different environmental conditions, but also within the compass of one of these areas alone. The February samples for 1975 are an example. In the inner fjord the diatom population, consisting of six species, is dominated by *Skeletonema* (99% of cell number); in the outer fjord, however, *Skeletonema* is of comparatively minor importance, comprising 18% of the ten diatom species present. The chief species in this outer sector of the fjord (39%), a member of the genus *Melosira*, was not recorded at all in the inner part of the fjord. It should be mentioned that fresh water species such as *Scenedesmus*, *Pediastrum* and *Coelaster* are occasionally found in the Kiel Fjord, having been carried in by the Schwentine river discharge.

Table 8.5 gives a list of the diatom and dinoflagellate species observed. For comparison, the observations by Lohmann (1908) have been included, who investigated the annual cycle of plankton abundance in the outer fjord. His study is remarkable for its comprehensiveness; four depths between 0 and 15 m were sampled from a fixed station at weekly intervals over the period of one year. Like us, he dispensed with species identification in some genera, or listed only the more common ones.

Although our table is by no means complete, we may compare it with the check-list for the southeastern North Sea compiled by Drebes and Elbrächter (1976) on the basis of long-term records from the islands of Heligoland and Sylt (List) in the German Bight. Species number is reduced by about two-thirds in our area, dinoflagellates being apparently more affected than diatoms. A comparison with the check-list for the Oslo Fjord (Heimdal et al., 1973) shows very much the same results.

Since our area is characterized by a high degree of seasonal variability resulting from the prevalence of advection processes (see Chap. 3), it is difficult to distinguish between regular and random occurrences of the species from season to season. Therefore all observations have incorporated in Table 8.5 without further discrimination. Thus a distribution pattern of I, II, IV is often found for a winter species when this was observed to maintain itself until April, and I, III, IV for a warm water species preponderating in summer and autumn, with some individuals surviving until January.

Overbeck (1962) and Schiemann (1974) have shown that very small phytoplankton species are the main contributors to the extremely high primary production found in some shallow low-salinity fjords of the Western Baltic. Comparable investigations on their role in the less eutrophic open waters of the Baltic Sea are so far lacking. Although the above-cited study by Lohmann (1908) was one of the first to stress the importance of minute autotrophic and heterotrophic algae composing the nanoplankton, to this day little is known of their systematical position. Their identification and quantitative assessement require a great deal of effort. Most of them are possibly physiologically less susceptible to changes in salinity than larger cells on account of their small size; thus they may be better adapted to thrive in both marine and brackish water environments. As far as we can judge by our present state of knowledge, these nanoplankters appear to have certain features in common with bacteria. Among these we may count the low standing stock expressed as biomass per unit volume as opposed to the high reproduction rate (Malone, 1971), which apparently counterbalances the grazing pressure to which they are subjected by a large variety of filter-feeders.

References

Arndt, E. A.: Tiere der Ostsee. Die neue Brehm-Bücherei Nr. 328. Wittenberg Lutherstadt: A. Ziemsen 1964
Banse, K.: Über das Verhalten von meroplanktischen Larven in geschichtetem Wasser. Kieler Meeresforsch. **11**, 188–200 (1955)
Banse, K.: Über den Transport von meroplanktischen Larven aus dem Kattegat in die Kieler Bucht. Ber. Dt. Wiss. Kommn. Meeresforsch. **14**, 147–164 (1956)
Banse, K.: Die Vertikalverteilung planktischer Copepoden in der Kieler Bucht. Ber. Dt. Wiss. Kommn. Meeresforsch. **15**, 357–390 (1959)
Brandt, K., Apstein, C. (eds.): Nordisches Plankton. Botanischer Teil. Kiel-Leipzig: Lipsius and Tischer, 1908
Dietrich, G., Köster, R.: Geschichte der Ostsee, 11–18. In: Magaard, L., Rheinheimer, G. (eds.), Meereskunde der Ostsee. Berlin-Heidelberg-New York: Springer 1974
Drebes, G.: Marines Phytoplankton. Stuttgart: Georg Thieme, 1974

Drebes, G., Elbrächter, M.: A checklist of planktonic diatoms and dinoflagellates from Helgoland and List (Sylt), German Bight. Botan. Mar. **19**, 75–83 (1976)

Gessner, F.: Meer und Strand. Berlin: VEB Deutscher Verlag der Wissenschaften, 1957

Heimdal, B. R., Hasle, G. R., Throndsen, J.: An annotated check-list of plankton algae from the Oslofjord, Norway (1951–1972). Norw. J. Botan. **20**, 13–19 (1973)

Hendey, N. I.: An Introductory Account of the Smaller Algae of British Coastal Waters. Part V: Bacillariophycea (Diatoms). London: HMSO (1964)

Hillebrandt, M.: Untersuchungen über die qualitative und quantitative Zusammensetzung des Zooplanktons in der Kieler Bucht während der Jahre 1966–1968. Thesis Univ. Kiel (1972)

Iturriaga, R., Hoppe, H.-G.: Observations of heterotrophic activity on photoassimilated organic matter. Mar. Biol. **40**, 101–108 (1977)

Jørgensen, C. B.: Biology of Suspension Feeding. Oxford: Pergamon Press, 1966

Kändler, R.: Jahreszeitliches Vorkommen und unperiodisches Auftreten von Fischbrut, Medusen und Dekapodenlarven im Fehmarnbelt in den Jahren 1934–43. Ber. Dt. Wiss. Kommn. Meeresforsch. **12**, 49–85 (1950)

Kändler, R.: Über das Vorkommen von Fischbrut, Dekapodenlarven und Medusen in der Kieler Förde. Kieler Meeresforsch. **17**, 48–64 (1961)

Lohmann, H.: Untersuchung zur Feststellung des vollständigen Gehaltes des Meeres an Plankton. Wiss. Meeresunters. Abt. Kiel, N. F. **10**, 131–370 (1908)

Malone, T. C.: The relative importance of nannoplankton and netplankton as primary producers in tropical oceanic and neritic phytoplankton communities. Limnol. Oceanogr. **16**, 633–639 (1971)

Overbeck, J.: Das Nannoplankton (μ-Algen) der Rügenschen Brackwässer als Hauptproduzent in Abhängigkeit vom Salzgehalt. Kieler Meeresforsch. **18**, 157–171 (1962)

Parsons, T., Takahashi, M.: Biological Oceanographic Processes. 186 pp. Oxford: Pergamon Press, 1973

Remane, A.: Einführung in die Zoologische Ökologie der Nord- und Ostsee, 1–238. In: Grimpe, G., Wagler, E. (eds.). Die Tierwelt der Nord- und Ostsee. Leipzig: Wiss. Verlagsbuchhandlung, 1941

Remane, A.: Die Brackwasser-Submergenz und die Umkomposition der Coenosen in Belt- und Ostsee. Kieler Meeresforsch. **11**, 59–73 (1955)

Remane, A., Schlieper, C.: Biology of Brackish Water. In: Elster, H.-J., Ohle, W. (eds). Die Binnengewässer Vol. 25. Stuttgart: E. Schweizbart'sche Verlagsbuchhandlung, 1971

Rheinheimer, G.: Mikrobiologie der Gewässer. 2nd ed. Jena: G. Fischer, 1975

Schiemann, S.: Die Primärproduktion des Phytoplanktons der Schlei und des Windebyer Noors im Jahre 1972. Thesis Univ. Kiel 1974

Schnack, S.: Untersuchungen zur Nahrungsbiologie der Copepoden (Crustacea) in der Kieler Bucht. Thesis Univ. Kiel 1975

Smetacek, V.: Die Sukzession des Phytoplanktons in der Kieler Bucht. Thesis Univ. Kiel 1975

Utermöhl, H.: Zur Vervollkommnung der quantitativen Phytoplankton-Methodik. Mitt. Intern. Verb. Limnol. **9**, 1–38 (1958)

Williams, P. J. Le B., Yentsch, C. S.: An examination of photosynthetic production, excretion of photosynthetic products, and heterotrophic utilization of dissolved organic compounds with reference to results from a coastal subtropical sea. Mar. Biol. **35**, 31–40 (1976)

9. Fungi

J.SCHNEIDER

For a long time the existence of fungi in the sea and their active role in marine and brackish water biotopes was seriously doubted by most scientists. This opinion was probably the reason for an unjustified negative appreciation of the conditions of life in the sea in regard to fungi, apart from methodical difficulties.

Thus some mycologists believed even as late as the forties of this century that decay resulting from fungal activity could not occur in wood saturated with sea water as a consequence of insufficient oxygen supply. Furthermore salt water was generally considered as a fungistatic medium.

During the last decades, however, increasing evidence could be established that sea water is not unfavorable for fungal organisms. It could not only be demonstrated that fungi from nearly all higher taxa occur in the sea, but that they play an active part there in the cycle of life processes. Like fungi in terrestrial and limnetic habitats, they most probably contribute—as heterotrophic organisms— to the degradation and mineralization of organic substrates, as saprophytes or parasites. Fungi are therefore found predominantly in those parts of the sea where organic material is present in sufficient quantities, e.g., in estuarine or inshore waters, in the cast-off at the surf zone with its remnants of animals and plants. However, they could also be isolated from sand grains and from water with a poor detritus content. On the other hand, numerous parasitic fungi have been found living primarily in marine algae and animals. Representatives of the Lower Fungi are *Eurychasmidium* sp., *Ectrogella* sp., occurring in red algae (Johnson and Sparrow, 1961), and *Lagenidium* sp., which is reported from a marine diatom (Drebes, 1966). Among the Higher Fungi Ascomycetes have been observed almost exclusively as parasites, e.g., *Haloguignardia* sp., *Lulworthia kniepii*, *Spathulospora adelpha*, *Chadefaudia* sp. in red and brown algae (Kohlmeyer, 1974). Very recently the first Deuteromycete *(Fungus imperfectus)* could be added to this list *(Sphaceloma cecidii)* (Kohlmeyer, 1972). Marine animals, like fish, mollusks and crustaceans are often infected by fungi or fungus-like organisms (Alderman, 1976). Economically important are *Ostracoblabe implexa*, a mycelial fungus, causing the oyster disease, and *Saprolegnia parasitica* which infects Salmonidae when reaching coastal waters (for literature see next paragraph).

During the last decades, fungi in marine habitats have attracted the interest of an increasing number of scientists, especially in Europe and the USA. However, the investigations have been concentrated mainly on taxonomical, floristic and physiological studies. Ecological problems regarding salinity and temperature responses have generally been investigated quantitatively solely in laboratory experiments. Field studies, on the other hand, were performed only in a qualitative or semi-quantitative way (exception: yeasts). A method for the estimation of Lower Fungi in water samples (Gaertner, 1968a) remained unsatisfactory, even when applied in an extensive and laborious way (Bremer, 1976). Even in cases where obviously wide-spread and easily demonstrated fungi—like Thraustochytriaceae, the lignicolous Ascomycetes and the yeasts—are involved, the activities of these organisms are not clearly understood. Furthermore the taxonomy of the Thraustochytriales, which are typical representatives of saline aquatic habitats, is doubtful and provisional, with the consequence that field ecological studies are seriously hampered (Ascomycetes and Deuteromycetes, however, are easy to identify in most cases in regard to their spores).

The present knowledge of marine and brackish water fungi has been accumulated by Jones (1976) and Hughes (1975). An older, but still very valuable publication is that of Johnson and Sparrow (1961). Studies on brackish water fungi have been performed almost exclusively in European and North American regions. The results of these investigations will be presented here in three groups according to the groups of fungi on which scientists have concentrated, namely Lower Fungi, Ascomycetes including Yeasts, and Deuteromycetes *(Fungi imperfecti)*.

9.1 Lower Fungi (Mastigomycotina) [1]

A clear separation of forms occurring only in brackish water from those which can only live in constant high saline oceanic waters (35‰ S) is not possible at present. Apparently, the presence of many Lower Fungi in inshore water, estuaries etc. is more dependent on the availability of certain substrates (algal detritus, host organisms, etc.) than on salinity or temperature. Furthermore, there have been increasingly found species of Chytridiomycetes from brackish water, which have been supposed to be terrestrial and limnetic forms.

Harder and Uebelmesser (1955) for example could find no difference (regarding the species composition) between water samples from the Baltic, the North Sea and the Mediterranean Sea (which are very different as to salinity and hydrographic conditions) and they could isolate "terrestrial species" such as *Rhizophydium spaerotheca*, *R. carpophilum*, *Olpidium* sp., *Phlyctochytrium* sp., from brackish samples as well as from dune sand, free of NaCl; Johnson (1967) found *Rhizophydium pollinis-pini* and *Phlyctochytrium biporosum* in limnetic as well as in marine biotopes. Field ecological investigations (Booth, 1969, 1971) and laboratory studies on Lower Fungi (Jones and Harrison, 1976) had similar results. It seems well established at present that species of *Thraustochytrium* (cf. Fig. 9.1 a–d) *Schizochytrium*, *Dermocystidium*, *Haliphthoros*, *Althornia*, and *Ostracoblabe* are halophilic, euryhaline and partly parasitic fungi. Numerous Chytridiomycetes can live in fresh as well as in salt water; however, they are observed in saline habitats only in small quantities. Species of *Saprolegnia* and other nonidentified organisms are reported to infect salmonides when reaching inshore waters of the British Isles (Stuart and Fuller, 1968; Willoughby 1968, 1969; Munro 1970).

---

[1] Including Chytridiomycetes, Hyphochytridiomycetes, Oomycetes (according to Sparrow, 1973). The older expression is used here for convenience.

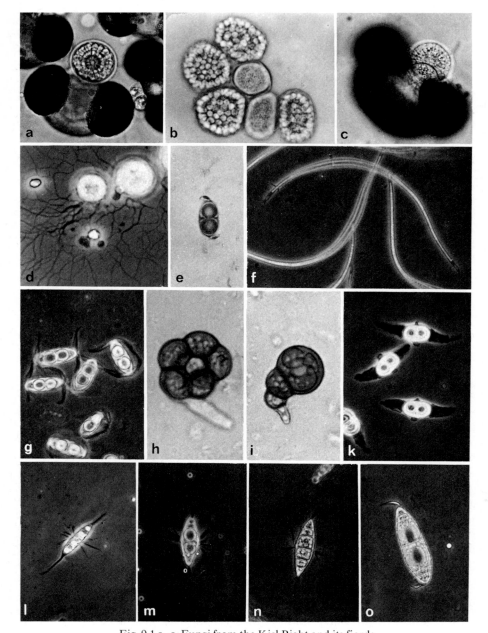

Fig. 9.1 a–o. Fungi from the Kiel Bight and its fjords

(a) *Thraustochytrium striatum* (Mastigomycotina, Saprolegniales). Sporangium with beginning formation of zoospores; on pollen bait. ca. × 450

(b) *Thraustochytrium* sp.. Sporangia in different stages of development; on agar. ca. × 450

(c) *Thraustochytrium kinnei*. Sporangium with deliminated basal rudiment; on pollen bait. ca. × 450

(d) *Thraustochytrium striatum*. Sporangia with rhizoids; on agar. ca. × 530

Since the mid-sixties several investigations of the occurrence and especially the quantities of Lower Fungi in the German Bay, the Weser estuary (North Sea) and the Western Baltic (including the Kiel Fjord and the Schlei Fjord) have been performed (Gaertner, 1968b; Schneider, 1968, 1969; Ulken, 1974).

The investigations in the German Bay-Weser region had the following results: the number of Lower Fungi—as they are demonstrable by the method of Gaertner 1968a—is generally higher in sediments than in the water (muddy sediments harbouring more fungi than sandy ones), and is higher in inshore waters than at some distance from land. Seasonal fluctuations could hardly be observed. The numbers of "infectious entities"[2] at two stations in the outer Weser are within a range from 0 to $1500 \, l^{-1}$ (in water) or 230 to $24,000 \, l^{-1}$ (in sediment). Among the determinable fungi, the following species were regularily observed: *Schizochytrium aggregatum*, *Thraustochytrium kinnei* (Fig. 9.1c), *Thr. multirudimentale*, *Thr. pachydermum*, *Thr. visurgense*, and *Thr. aggregatum*. Special studies regarding the occurrence of chytrids in the Weser estuary revealed a maximum of fungi in spring (Ulken, 1974).

Schneider (1970) investigated the Schlei Fjord, a brackish inlet to the Western Baltic. Going up to the inner part of the Schlei, e.g., into waters of decreasing salinity, the number of halophilic marine species, such as *Thraustochytrium* and *Schizochytrium*, decreased. Thus, at the mouth of the Schlei (13–20‰ S approx.) the following fungi could regularly be observed: *Schizochytrium aggregatum*, *Thr. kinnei*, *Thr. pachydermum*, and *Thr. striatum* (Fig. 9.1a, d); *Labyrinthula* (not belonging to the fungi). At the innermost station (Schleswig; 2.2–10‰ S) only *Schizochytrium aggregatum* and a *Thraustochytrium* sp. could be demonstrated. An increase of limnetic or terrestrial fungi did not take place, and only one species of *Rhizophydium* and *Olipidium* have been found in the Schlei occasionally (Harder and Uebelmesser, 1955, reported three species).

Quantitative investigations (by the method according to Gaertner, 1968a) revealed on the other hand an increasing number of "infectious entities" per l of sample water in direction to the inner part of the Schlei Fjord.

In the course of the year the number fluctuated markedly, with maxima mainly from July to October. A certain correlation exists to high water temperatures, high phosphore concentrations, and to low bacterial counts and nitrate

---

[2] This expression is introduced by Gaertner (pers. comm.) to emphasize the fact that thraustochytriaceous fungi may be present in the sample in different developmental stages (sporangia, zoospores or aplanospores) which may directly or indirectly cause the infection of the pollen bait (which is indispensible for the demonstration of these fungi).

(e) *Halosphaeria hamata* (Ascomycotina, Sphaeriales). Ascospore. ca. × 450
(f) *Lulworthia* sp. (Ascomycotina, Sphaeriales). Ascospores. ca. × 450
(g) *Halosphaeria quadriremis*. Ascospores ca. × 450
(h) *Zalerion maritimum* (Deuteromycotina). Conidium. ca. × 770
(i) *Cirrenalia macrocephala* (Deuteromycotina). Conidium. ca. × 770
(k) *Halosphaeria tubulifera*. Ascospores ca. × 450
(l) *Corollospora maritima* (Ascomycotina, Sphaeriales). Ascospore. ca. × 450
(m) *Corollospora cristata*. Ascospore. ca. × 450
(n) *Corollospora comata*. Ascospore. ca. × 450
(o) *Haligena spartinae* (Ascomycotina, Sphaeriales) Ascospore. ca. × 340

Table 9.1. Average and maximal numbers (per l) of Lower
Fungi at different stations of the Schlei Fjord (according to
Schneider, 1970)

Station	Average numbers	Maximal values
Tonne Schlei-Olpenitz	178	470
Rabelsund	270	480
Lindaunis	223	500
Große Breite	414	1,000

content of the water. The numbers of Lower Fungi which could be demonstrated
at four stations of the Schlei Fjord are compiled in Table 9.1. In the Kiel Fjord on
the other hand numbers between 135 and 64, and in the Flensburg Fjord 190–46
"infectious entities" have been detected.

Here also some correlation of high fungi numbers to higher water temperatures could be observed.

9.2 Yeasts[3]

Studies of yeasts in brackish waters have been performed mainly in two re-
spects: taxonomy and correlation with pollution. A number of investigations in
estuaries and related waters with changing salinity provide quantitative data,
especially from North America and Europe (Roth et al., 1962; Rheinheimer, 1970;
Combs et al., 1971; Hoppe, 1972a; Meyers and Ahearn, 1974; Fell, 1976).

At present no definite answer can be offered as to the role of yeasts in brackish
waters. The majority of them are supposed to be saprophytes. Temperature and
salinity are probably not the main factors determining distribution, since most
yeasts found in marine habitats are eurytherm and euryhaline. Since the greatest
numbers of yeasts occur in inshore waters, they probably depend primarily on the
level and the quality of nutrients (Fell, 1967; Hoppe 1972a). Also the patchy
distribution of these fungi in open oceanic waters may be an expression of the
differences in nutrient levels (apart from hydrographic influences). In the case of
Metschnikowia, the role of yeasts occurring in near-shore, brackish and estuarine
waters (Seki and Fulton, 1969) seems somewhat better elucidated. This organism
is pathogen or parasitic to marine copepods.

Van Uden (1967) investigated the yeast flora of estuaries and demonstrated
that some species occurred in open oceanic regions and in estuaries *(Debaryomyces hansenii)* while others could be found almost exclusively in brackish
inshore waters with strong terrestrial influence *(Candida* sp.). The latter species
are supposed, according to the author, to be pollution indicators, having their
origin in terrestrial runoff or pollution (see also Combs et al., 1971; Spencer et al.,
1970).

Fell (1976) states in his summarizing publication that "the distribution of the
individual species varies from those that appear ubiquitous to those that appear

---

[3] These organisms are generally classified among the Ascomycotina (Hemiascomycetes). For
methodical reasons they are, as in most publications, considered separately.

limited by geographic or hydrographic conditions". According to Fell *Debaryomyces hansenii* and *Torulopsis candida* have been found in all regions investigated. *Cryptococcus albidus*, *Candida polymorpha*, and *Rhodotorula glutinis* appear to be widely distributed but less frequent. Meyers et al. (1967) examined water samples from the German Bay (North Sea) and found yeast population densities from less than $10\,l^{-1}$ to more than $3000\,l^{-1}$. The prevalent species they found was *Debaryomyces hansenii*. In the innermost part of the German Bay, southeast of Heligoland, which is strongly influenced by the river Elbe, species such as *Candida lipolytica*, *C. silvicola*, *C. tenuis*, *Cryptococcus infirmo-miniatus*, *Rhodotorula graminis*, *Sporobolomyces roseus*, and *Hansenula californica* were predominant. During two summer periods the occurrence of *Debaryomyces* was probably correlated with blooms of the dinoflagellate *Noctiluca*.

Schaumann (1976) reports on the occurrence of hyphomycetes and yeasts in the Wester estuary (German Bay, North Sea). He states a certain correlation between the quantity of fungal propagules and the turbidity of the water and the fresh water inflow. The absolute numbers of both yeasts and hyphomycetes (mycelial forms) were estimated at about $140,000\,l^{-1}$ (for each group). A strong seasonal variation was observed, with high numbers in the winter and lower numbers in the summer. An antagonism between the (supposed) allochthonous fungi and the autochthonous bacteria seems doubtful according to Schaumann. Norkrans (1966a) studied yeasts from the Kungsbacka Fjord, a brackish water on the west coast of Sweden with considerably changing hydrographic conditions and a consequent mixing of three water bodies: North Sea water with salinities of approx. 30‰ S, water from the Baltic (approx. 20‰ S at the Belt Sea outlets) and fresh water from rivers. She also found yeast species of the already cited genera, and additional *Pichia*, *Torulopsis* and *Saccharomyces* sp.

The yeasts isolated from samples could be divided into two groups in respect to salinity response: *Debaryomyces hansenii*, *Rhodotorula glutinis* and *Rh. rubra* survived cultivation in sea water for 120 days, whereas species of *Saccharomyces*, *Candida*, *Pichia* and *Cryptococcus* were either unable to survive or had only very few survivors in the tests (Norkrans, 1966b).

The region of the western Baltic, e.g., the Kiel Bight and some of its fjords, was investigated by Rheinheimer (1970) and Hoppe (1972a,b). In his study of the river-like brackish Schlei Fjord Rheinheimer found especially *Debaryomyces*, *Rhodotorula*, *Cryptococcus* sp., e.g., halo-tolerant fungi of terrestrial origin. As to the number of yeasts, they were generally higher in the Schlei than in the Baltic Sea immediately off the mouth of the Schlei. Maximal numbers were found during the autumn and winter months. In the inner parts of the Schlei, the numbers varied between several 1000 and 10,000 cells l^{-1}, thus being considerably higher than in the outer parts. In summer the numbers decreased to approximately 100 cells l^{-1}. There was a correlation between the number of yeasts, the number of coliform bacteria and viable bacterial counts: this is strong evidence that the yeasts originate from pollution or terrestrial runoff. According to the author, the winter maxima are due to a prolonged time of survival in colder winter water and, possibly, to a greater availability of nutrients during the autumn and winter months as a consequence of dying phytoplankton, and the sewage runoff from refineries processing sugar beets and potatoes in late fall.

Hoppe (1972, a, b) examined the occurrence and distribution of yeasts in the western Baltic. In the innermost parts of the Kiel Fjord he found yeast numbers of 24,000 to 900 cells l^{-1} in water samples. The numbers decreased considerably to the outer stations (ca. $100 l^{-1}$). This decrease was stronger than that of the numbers of fresh water bacteria. Maximal development in spring and autumn preceded that of the bacteria. Furthermore the yeast numbers (along the fjord profile) in water samples from 10-m depth, decreased faster than in 1-m samples, which is possibly due to the inflow of Kattegat-Belt sea water (with higher salinity) near the bottom with a smaller content of microorganisms. The respective numbers for the Arkona and Bornholm basins (mid-Baltic; with a salinity of only 10–6‰ S) were 70–10 cells l^{-1} in all water depths investigated. Very high numbers were found at the sewage inlet at the mouth of the Kiel Fjord (ca. 10^6 cells l^{-1} decreasing to 10^3 cells l^{-1} at 1 km distance from the inlet).

In the course of the investigations of the Kiel Fjord and Kiel Bight which led to this publication, yeast counts were also performed. In addition to the estimation of the total number of viable cells, the number of red yeast colonies was counted separately. The method applied was that of Hoppe's (1972 a, b) study and may be described here. From the stations 1 and 5 (Reventlou Brücke, 2, 10 m and KBM II, 2, 10, 18 m) 10 or 100 ml samples of water were filtered through Millipore filters (pore size 0.6 μm). The filter discs were subsequently incubated at $+ 10°$ C on a medium of the following composition:

Difco-Peptone	5.0 g
Meat extract	2.4 g
Glucose	20.0 g
Yeast extract	1.0 g
$FePO_4 \cdot 4H_2O$	0.01 g
Agar	15.0 g
Aged seawater	500 ml
Distilled water	500 ml.

After sterilization the pH was adjusted with lactic acid (10%) to 4–4.5, and streptomycine sulfate and Binotal (a penicillin derivative)—0.25 g l^{-1} each— added to the solution.

Although only two stations were investigated in regard to yeasts, the following conclusions can be extracted from the results given in the Tables 9.2 and 9.4.

The total number of viable yeasts (including the red yeasts) at Station 1 in the inner Kiel Fjord was generally much higher (in 2-m as well as in 10-m depth) than at Station 5 in the central Kiel Bight (Tables 9.2, 9.3). Thus, the average total number of viable yeasts at Station 5 was only 4.1% (at 2 m) and 15.5% (at 10 m) of that of Station 1. As to the red yeasts, the average percentages were 4.9% (2 m) and 5.5% (10 m). At Station 1 generally the higher counts occurred in the 2-m samples, while at Station 5 most yeasts were found in the 10- (18-) m samples.

Three peaks of maximal development of the yeasts were observed in the course of the investigation period: in January, May (June) and August/October. The red yeasts had the third maximum already in July, and no prominent peak in the fall. For comparison: the peaks for the saprophytic bacteria growing on sea or tap water media (Chap. 11) were in April/May and October. The tendency of the

Table 9.2. Total numbers of viable yeasts per l, after 14 days of incubation and % red yeasts

Date	Station 1				Station 5					
	2 m		10 m		2 m		10 m		18 m	
	N	%	N	%	N	%	N	%	N	%
Jan. 24, 1974	4,150	8.4	19,900	49.5	130	23.1	365	2.7	225	8.9
Feb. 14	3,100	6.5	1,450	6.9	10	50.0	10	0	25	0
Feb. 28	—	—	—	—	—	—	—	—	—	—
March 21	3,150	11.1	3,550	9.9	5	100.0	20	50.0	20	25.0
April 18	1,300[a]	3.8	0[a]	0	0[a]	0	0[a]	0	0[a]	0
May 16	5,350[a]	9.3	100[a]	0	500[a]	12.0	930[a]	1.1	0[a]	0
June 11	3,100	12.9	800	18.8	0	0	160	18.8	25	0
June 25	400	12.5	100	0	20	50.0	45	22.2	15	0
July 11	1,000	25.0	750	6.7	155	38.7	145	55.2	165	39.4
Aug. 7	14,300[a]	0	6,550[a]	0	—	—	—	—	—	—
Aug. 29	1,100[a]	13.6	200[a]	25.0	110[a]	0	100[a]	0	10[a]	0
Sept. 12	100	50.0	200	50.0	225	0	520	0	30	0
Oct. 24	5,200	21.2	2,750	21.8	0	0	495	3.0	40	0
Nov. 21	2,000	17.5	2,550	11.8	10	50.0	10	0	10	0
Dec. 10	—	—	—	—	—	—	—	—	—	—
Jan. 23, 1975	1,400	21.4	2,850	29.8	40	50.0	40[a]	0	60[a]	0
Feb. 12	1,150	0	800	0	40	0	0	0	40	0
March 10	2,200	20.5	1,950	35.9	95	15.8	155	19.4	0	0
Average numbers:	2,182	14.6	1,289	17.7	89	32.5	200	12.3	46	5

[a] After seven days.

yeasts to show their maximal development before that of the bacteria—as already observed by Hoppe (1972a)—seems to be confirmed by this investigation, although one should not neglect the influence of the hydrography of the investigation area (Chap. 3); for example, the correlation of yeast and bacterial development might be simulated by the unpredictable mixing of water masses.

Table 9.4 demonstrates how the numbers of yeasts and saprophytic bacteria are influenced by the distance from land and by the water temperature. At both depths there is a clear decrease of the numbers of both groups of organism to be observed at Station 5 in comparison to Station 1.

However, the percentage of yeasts counted at Station 5 is generally higher than that of the saprophytic bacteria, in January as well as in July. The high counts of yeasts in July in comparison to the very low percentages of the bacteria at this time are remarkable. These observations may be interpreted by the different sensibility of yeasts and saprophytic bacteria to water temperature and nutrient content.

According to the statistical evaluation (Chap. 19) a correlation was demonstrable only between total number of yeasts and particular lipids, and turnover time of glucose respectively, in 10-m samples. No correlation was found, however, between total number of yeasts, red yeasts, chlorophyll and primary production, respectively.

Table 9.3. Numbers of red yeasts per l, after 14 days of incubation

Date	Station 1		Station 5		
	2 m	10 m	2 m	10 m	18 m
Jan. 24, 1974	350	9,850	30	10	20
Feb. 14	200	100	5	0	0
Feb. 28	—	—	—	—	—
March 21	350	350	5	10	5
April 18	50[a]	0[a]	0[a]	0[a]	0[a]
May 16	500[a]	0[a]	60[a]	10[a]	0[a]
June 11	400	150	0	30	0
June 25	50	0	10	10	0
July 11	250	50	60	80	65
Aug. 7	—	—	—	—	—
Aug. 29	150[a]	50[a]	0[a]	0[a]	0[a]
Sept. 12	50	100	0	0	0
Oct. 24	1,100	600	15	15	0
Nov. 21	350	300	5	0	0
Dec. 10	—	—	—	—	—
Jan. 23, 1975	300	850	20	0[a]	0[a]
Feb. 12	0	0	0	0	0
March 10	450	700	15	30	0
Average numbers:	300	232	15	13	—

[a] After seven days.

Table 9.4. Percentages of yeasts and saprophytic bacteria found at Station 5 in comparison to Station 1 (=100%) at two times of the investigation period, and at two water depths. Additionally the average percentages basing on the numbers of all sampling times of the investigation period

	Watertemperature °C		Yeasts, total	Red yeasts	Saprophytic bacteria	
	St. 1	St. 5			On ZS medium	On ZL medium
2 m						
Jan. 24, 1974	3.7	3.0	3.1	8.8	2.6	0.4%
July 11, 1974	16.7	15.5	15.5	24.0	0.7	0.02%
Average percentage (2 m)		4.1	4.9	2.2	0.4%
10 m						
Jan. 24, 1974	3.6	2.9	1.8	0.1	2.3	9.4%
July 11, 1974	15.4	15.5	19.3	—	1.5	0.5%
Average percentage (10 m)		15.5	5.5	2.0	1.6%

9.3 Lignicolous Fungi (Ascomycotina[4], Deuteromycotina)

The third group of fungi which has been fairly well investigated comprises Ascomycetes and Deuteromycetes *(Fungi imperfecti)* which occur mainly in wood submerged in saline water. These fungi are in most cases easily determined by their typical ascospores or conidia. The greatest part of the marine and brackish water Ascomycetes belong to the Halosphaeriaceae, a taxon including only salt water fungi characterized by early deliquescing asci, and spores with conspicuous appendages or sheaths (cf. Fig. 9.1 e–o).

In Europe three regions have been more intensively investigated in regard to brackish water Asco- and Deuteromycetes (lignicolous as well as nonlignicolous fungi): estuaries of the British Isles (Jones, 1968, 1971; Byrne and Jones, 1974), the SE part of the North Sea (German Bay) including the Weser estuary (Höhnk, 1954, 1955, 1956; Siepmann, 1959; Schaumann, 1975), and the Baltic (Henningsson, 1974; Schneider, 1976). Numerous studies on brackish water fungi have been performed in the United States as well, some of which may be cited here: Meyers and Reynolds (1960), Johnson (1967), Kohlmeyer (1969, 1971), Neish (1970), Gessner et al. (1972), Shearer (1972), Meyers (1974); see also Hughes (1975) who summarizes the knowledge on lignicolous fungi. Two methods have been applied in general: (1) samples from wooden constructions, such as harbor pilings, or from driftwood; (2) exposure of sterilized panels to the water under observation. Both kinds of sample are incubated in the laboratory after collection in order to enhance the development of "fruiting stages" (fruitbodies, conidia, etc.), which are indispensible for the determination of species. These investigations delivered not only lists of species, but also ecological information about the range of occurrence of the different species and the influence of salinity and the trophic status of the water.

For one year, sterilized panels of five species of wood, e.g., *Fagus silvatica* (Beech), *Pinus silvestris* (Pine) *Lophira procera* (Bongossi), *Discorynia* sp. (Basralocus), and *Ocotea rodiaei* (Demerara Greenheart), were exposed at four stations of the fjords. Every six weeks samples were collected, superficially cleaned of algal growth and subsequently studied under the binocular for fruitbodies. In order to allow further species of water fungi not fruiting at the time of sampling to form reproductive stages, the panels were incubated in sterilized damp chambers for a further year at room temperature in the dark. Further scrutinizing of the wood surfaces led in nearly all cases to a considerable increase of the number of fungi. Twentythree species of Asco- and Deuteromycetes could be definitely determined, most of them occurring on beech wood, where the development was fastest. Fungi predominantly found were *Ceriosporopsis halima, Halosphaeria appendiculata, H. mediosetigera, Monodictys pelagica, Zalerion maritimum* (Fig. 9.1 h), *Lulworthia* sp. (Fig. 9.1 f), and *Naïs inornata*.

On pine wood, the development was already markedly reduced, although to a less degree than expected from the content of resins. The minimal time for the formation of fruiting stages on these two European wood species remained below ten weeks. This was in contrast to the results obtained with the tropical wood

---

[4] Excl. Hemiascomycetes p.p. (Yeasts).

species: there the development time was considerably greater and the number of fungi was reduced. Salinity was of less influence on the occurrence of fungi. Few species were regularly found on panels exposed to oligohaline waters (at Schleswig), namely *Halosphaeria mediosetigera, H. hamata* (Fig. 9.1 e), *Naïs inornata* and *Monodictys pelagica.* The time of exposition and the water temperature, however, influenced the mycological pattern more markedly at the four places. In addition, the duration of incubation played a considerable role in regard to the number of species obtained.

Fungi new for the Western Baltic were *Halosphaeria stellata, Corollospora cristata* (Fig. 9.1 m), and *Naïs inornata.*

The following grew only on beech wood: *Ceriosporopsis longissima, Halosphaeria tubulifera* (Fig. 9.1 k), and *H. hamata* (Fig. 9.1 e); on pine only *Corollospora comata* (Fig. 9.1 n), *Halosphaeria stellata*, and *H. maritima.*

A second series of investigations, with fresh panels exchanged every six weeks, revealed nearly the same number of species, while the composition of species had altered. This might be an indicator of a change in the water condition.

References

Alderman, D. J.: Fungal diseases of marine animals. In: Recent Advances in Aquatic Mycology. 223–260, Jones, E. G. B. (ed.) London: Elek Science, 1976

Booth, T.: Marine fungi from British Columbia: Monocentric chytrids and chytridiacious species from coastal and interior halomorphic soils. Syesis **2**, 141–161 (1969)

Booth, T.: Occurrence and distribution of zoosporic fungi and some Actinomycetales in coastal soils of southwestern British Columbia and the San Juan Islands. Syesis **4**, 197–208 (1971)

Bremer, G. B.: The ecology of marine lower fungi. In: Recent Advances in Aquatic Mycology. Jones, E. G. B. (ed.) London: Elek Science, 313–334 (1976)

Byrne, P. J., Jones, E. G. B.: Lignicolous marine fungi. Veröff. Inst. Meeresforsch. Bremerh. Suppl **5**, 301–320 (1974)

Combs, T. J., Murchelano, R. A., Jurgen, F.: Yeasts from Long Island Sound. Mycologia **63**, 178–181 (1971)

Drebes, G.: Ein parasitischer Phycomycet (Lagenidiales) in *Coscinodiscus.* Helgoländer wiss. Meeresunters. **13**, 426–435 (1966)

Fell, J. W.: Distribution of yeasts in the Indian Ocean. Bull. Mar. Sci. **17**, 454–470 (1967)

Fell, J. W.: Yeasts in oceanic regions. In: Recent Advances in Aquatic Mycology. Jones, E. G. B. (ed.) London: Elek Science, 93–124 (1976)

Gaertner, A.: Eine Methode des quantitativen Nachweises niederer, mit Pollen köderbarer Pilze im Meerwasser und im Sediment. Veröff. Inst. Meeresforsch. Bremerh. **3**, 75–92 (1968 a)

Gaertner, A.: Die Fluktuationen mariner niederer Pilze in der Deutschen Bucht 1965 und 1966. Veröff. Inst. Meeresforsch. Bremerh. Sonderbd. **3**, 105–120 (1968 b)

Gessner, R. V., Goos, R. D., Sieburth, J. McN.: The fungal microcosm of the internodes of *Spartina alterniflora.* Mar. Biol. **16**, 269–273 (1972)

Harder, R., Uebelmesser, E.: Über marine saprophytische Chytridiales und einige andere Pilze vom Meeresboden und Meeresstrand. Arch. Mikrobiol. **22**, 87–144 (1955)

Henningsson, M.: Aquatic lignicolous fungi in the Baltic along the West coast of Sweden. Svensk Botan. Tidskrift **68**, 401–425 (1974)

Höhnk, W.: Studien zur Brack- u. Seewassermycologie IV. Ascomyceten des Küstensandes. Veröff. Inst. Meeresforsch. Bremerh. **3**, 27–33 (1954)

Höhnk,W.: Studien zur Brack- und Seewassermycologie V. Höhere Pilze des submersen Holzes. Veröff. Inst. Meeresforsch, Bremerh. **3**, 199–227 (1955)

Höhnk,W.: Studien zur Brack- und Seewassermycologie VI. Über die pilzliche Besiedelung verschiedener salziger submerser Standorte. Veröff. Inst. Meeresforsch. Bremerh. **4**, 195–213 (1956)

Hoppe,H.-G.: Untersuchungen zur Ökologie der Hefen im Bereich der westlichen Ostsee. Kieler Meeresforsch. **28**, 54–77 (1972a)

Hoppe,H.-G.: Taxonomische Untersuchungen an Hefen aus der westlichen Ostsee. Kieler Meeresforsch. **28**, 219–226 (1972b)

Hughes,G.C.: Intertidal lignicolous fungi from Newfoundland. Can. J. Botan. **49**, 1–11 (1971)

Hughes,G.C.: Studies of Fungi in Oceans and Estuaries since 1961. I. Lignicolous, caulicolous and folicolous species. Oceanogr. Mar. Biol. Ann. Rev. **13**, 69–180 (1975)

Johnson,T.W.: The estuarine mycoflora. In: Estuaries. Lauff,G.H. (ed.) Am. Assoc. Advan. Sci. Publ. **83**, 303–305 (1967)

Johnson,T.W., Sparrow,F.K.: Fungi in Oceans and Estuaries. Weinheim: J.Cramer, 1961

Jones,E.B.G.: The distribution of marine fungi on wood submerged in the sea. In: Biodeterioration of Materials. Proc. 1st. Intern. Biodet. Symp. Southampton, 460–485 (1968)

Jones,E.B.G.: The ecology and rotting ability of marine fungi. In: Marine Borers, Fungi and Fouling Organisms of Wood. Jones,E.B.G., Eltringham,S.K. (eds.) Paris: O.E.C.D., 237–258 (1971)

Jones,E.B.G. (ed.): Recent Advances in Aquatic Mycology. London: Elek Science, 1976

Jones,E.B.G., Harrison,J.L.: Physiology of marine phycomycetes. In: Recent Advances in Aquatic Mycology. Jones,E.B.G. (ed.) London: Elek Science, 261–278, 1976

Kohlmeyer,J.: Ecological notes on fungi in mangrove forests. Trans. Brit. Mycol. Soc. **53**, 237–250 (1969)

Kohlmeyer,J.: Annotated check-list of New England marine fungi. Trans. Brit. Mycol. Soc. **57**, 473–492 (1971)

Kohlmeyer,J.: Parasitic *Haloguignardia oceanica* (Ascomycetes) and hyperparasitic *Sphaceloma cedidii* sp. nov. (Deuteromycetes) in drift Sargassum in North Carolina. J. Elish. Mitch. Sci. Soc. **88**, 255–259 (1972)

Kohlmeyer,J.: Higher fungi as parasites and symbionts of algae. Veröff. Inst. Meeresforsch. Bremerh. Suppl. **5**, 339–356 (1974)

Meyers,S.P.: Contribution of fungi to biodegradation of *Spartina* and other brackish marshland vegetation. Veröff. Inst. Meeresforsch. Bremerh. Suppl. **5**, 357–376 (1974)

Meyers,S.P., Ahearn,D.G.: Implication of yeasts and yeast-like fungi in marine processes. Veröff. Inst. Meeresforsch. Bremerh. Suppl. **5**, 321–338 (1974)

Meyers,S.P., Ahearn,D.G., Gunkel,W., Roth,F.J.: Yeasts from the North Sea. Mar. Biol. **1**, 118–123 (1967)

Meyers,S.P., Reynolds,E.S.: Occurrence of lignicolous fungi in Northern Atlantic and Pacific marine localities. Can. J. Botan. **38**, 217–226 (1960)

Munro,A.L.S.: Ulcerative Dermal Necrosis, a disease of migratory salmonid fishes in the rivers of the British Isles. Biological Conservation, **2**, 129–132 (1970)

Neish,G.A.: Ligincolous marine fungi from Nova Scotia. Can. J. Botan. **48**, 2319–2322 (1970)

Norkrans,B.: On the occurrence of yeasts in an estuary off the Swedish west coast. Svensk Bot. Tidskrift, **60**, 463–482 (1966a)

Norkrans,B.: Studies on marine-occurring yeasts: Growth related to pH, NaCl concentration and temperature. Arch. Mikrobiol. **54**, 374–392 (1966b)

Rheinheimer,G.: Hefen. In: Chemische, mikrobiologische und planktologische Untersuchungen in der Schlei im Hinblick auf deren Abwasserbelastung. Kieler Meeresforsch. **26**, (2), 179 (1970)

Roth,I.F., Ahearn,D.G., Fell,J.W., Meyers,S.P., Meyer,S.A.: Ecology and taxonomy of yeasts isolated from various marine substrates. Limnol. Oceanogr. **7**, 178–185 (1962)

Schaumann,K.: Ökologische Untersuchungen über höhere Pilze im Meer- und Brackwasser der Deutschen Bucht unter besonderer Berücksichtigung der holzbesiedelnden Arten. Veröff. Inst. Meeresforsch. Bremerh. **15** (13), 79–182 (1975)

Schaumann,K.: Pilzkeime im Wasser des Weser-Ästuars (Deutsche Bucht). I. Quantitative Ergebnisse 1974. ibid. **16** (1), 63–82 (1976)

Schneider, J.: Über niedere Phycomyceten der westlichen Ostsee. Veröff. Inst. Meeresforsch. Bremerh. Sonderbd. **3**, 93–104 (1968)

Schneider, J.: Zur Taxonomie, Verbreitung und Ökologie einiger mariner Phycomyceten. Kieler Meeresforsch. **25**, 316–327 (1969)

Schneider, J.: Niedere Pilze. In: Chemische, mikrobiologische und planktologische Untersuchungen in der Schlei im Hinblick auf deren Abwasserbelastung. Kieler Meeresforsch. **26** (2), 173–178 (1970)

Schneider, J.: Lignicole marine Pilze (Ascomyceten und Deuteromyceten) aus zwei Ostseeförden. Botanica Marina **19**, 295–307 (1976)

Shearer, G. A.: Fungi of the Chesapeake Bay and its tributaries. III. The distribution of wood inhabiting Ascomycetes and *Fungi imperfecti* of the Patuxent river. Am. J. Botan. **59**, 961–969 (1972)

Seki, H., Fulton, J.: Infection of marine copepods by *Metschnikowia* sp. Mycopath. Mycol. appl. **38**, 61–70 (1969)

Siepmann, R.: Ein Beitrag zur saprophytischen Pilzflora des Watts der Wesermündung. Veröff. Inst. Meeresforsch. Bremerh. **6**, 213–281 (1959)

Sparrow, F. K.: Mastigomycotina (Zoosporic Fungi). In: The Fungi. Ainsworth, G., Sussman, A. S. (eds.) **4 B**, 61–73, 1973

Spencer, J. F. T., Gorin, P. A. J., Gardner, N. R.: Yeasts isolated from the South Saskatchewan, a polluted river. Can. J. Microbiol. **16**, 1051–1057 (1970)

Stuart, M. R., Fuller, H. T.: Mycological aspects of diseased Atlantic Salmon. Nature (London) **217**, 90–92 (1968)

Uden, N. van: Occurrence and origin of yeasts in estuaries. In: Estuaries. Lauff, G. H. (ed.) AAAS Wash. Publ. **83**, 306–310 (1967)

Ulken, A.: Chytridineen im Küstenbereich. Veröff. Inst. Meeresforsch. Bremerh. Suppl. **5**, 83–104 (1974)

Willoughby, L. G.: Atlantic Salmon disease fungus. Nature (London) **217**, 872–873 (1968)

Willoughby, L. G.: Salmon disease in Windermere and the river Leven; the fungal aspect. Salmon and Trout Magazine **186**, 124–130 (1969)

10. Estimation of Bacterial Number and Biomass by Epifluorescence Microscopy and Scanning Electron Microscopy

R. ZIMMERMANN

In order to help understand the microbial ecology of an aquatic biotope, it is necessary to know the total bacterial numbers and the bacterial biomass. However, only a few methods are available today which reflect the quantity and form-diversity of the bacterial flora. The small size of the bacterial cell as well as the heterogeneity of the habitat restrict the choice of methods.

One of the few applicable methods, the direct count technique, renders it possible to estimate the bacterial standing stock of a water body, which is of prime importance because it provides the basis for assessing further parameters of aquatic microbiology. In contrast to the microscopic count, so-called indirect methods, such as the estimation of ATP or ETS activity, are inadequate to determine the bacterial biomass within the euphotic zone (Jassby, 1975; Watson, 1976). Difficulties arise owing to the limited specificity when applying these indirect methods to quantify bacteria in the presence of phytoplankton. Also below the euphotic zone, the interpretation of data obtained by indirect measurement, may be rather difficult due to the presence of microzooplankton. Because of the presence of bacterial aggregates and attachment to particles, pretreatment of the water sample by fractionated filtration, which in principle should enhance methodological specificity, seems to be relatively unpromising. In addition, the dependence of indirect methods on conversion factors, the choice of which is usually somewhat of a compromise, gives rise to further inaccuracies. If bacterial biomass and number is to be calculated, the conversion factor is based on the physiological properties of an "average-sized" aquatic bacterium. The average size of an aquatic bacterium, however, has been grossly overestimated in the literature owing to insufficient optical presentation of small-sized bacteria.

This problem of optical presentation is also a point which leads to discrepancies in the direct count methods used to date. Attempts to apply the direct count method, which nowadays means a quantification of stained bacteria on a membrane filter, have been performed for many years (Razumov, 1932). However, with the exception of its routine use mainly in East-European countries (Ivatin, 1973; Oláh, 1974; Overbeck, 1974; Sorokin, 1973; Tronova, 1974) this technique has not been widely adopted in the field of aquatic microbiology. The microscopic differentiation between small bacteria and unspecific particles of similar size was almost impossible and thus led to dubious results. Subjectivity concerning optical identification of bacteria prevented comparison of data obtained by different authors.

In comparison to the use of bright-field microscopy and diachromes, the application of epifluorescence microscopic techniques (Bell and Dutka, 1972) and black membrane filters to minimize interfering background fluorescence (Francisco et al., 1973) signified a step forward. Little reliability can, however, be placed on the detection of cells smaller than 0.4 μm, whose numbers are a significant portion of the total number of cells in almost all natural waters. The determination of cell sizes, which is a basic requirement for biomass calculation, is made especially inaccurate due to unfavorable surface properties of the membrane filters. The use of polycarbonate filters (Zimmermann and Meyer-Reil, 1974) instead of filter materials based on cellulose nitrate or other cellulose derivatives essentially overcame the difficulties associated with direct counting, and the merits of the former (Nuclepore) could be demonstrated using epifluorescence microscopy and scanning electron microscopy (Zimmermann, 1975).

The new direct count technique was applied in order to obtain data on number, biomass and size distribution of bacteria during the microbiological investigations in the Kiel Fjord, the Kiel Bight and other brackish areas, together with considerations of regional and seasonal alterations. Besides the registration of attached bacteria and the quantification of particle area, an attempt was made to differentiate detritus according to morphological criteria.

10.1 Staining Technique for the Epifluorescence Microscopic Count

The staining recipe for polycarbonate filters is essentially the same as that given by Zimmermann and Meyer-Reil (1974) as a preliminary technique. In order to obtain uniform contrast, however, the method was slightly modified and should therefore be briefly explained. After filtration (0.15 bar) of 1–3 ml of a formalin fixed water sample (final concentration of formaldehyde 0.8–1.2%) water sample through a polycarbonate filter (25 mm $\emptyset$, 0.2 μm pore size), 0.5 ml of an aqueous fluorochrome solution (Acridine Orange or Euchrysine 2 GNX, $1:10^4$) is pipetted onto the filter and removed by vacuum after 1 min. In order to destain the filter, 1 ml of iso-propyl alcohol is added and immediately removed. Without releasing the vacuum, the filter is taken off the filter support, air-dried, cut into wedges and mounted on a slide covered with a mixture of cinnamic aldehyde and eugenol 2:1). The preparation is then examined by means of epifluorescence microscopy (magnification × 1560), using blue light excitation (KP 490, KP 500, dichroic beam splitting filter 510, LP 520).

Unbound dye, however, may gradually be released by detritus and thus cause an interfering background fluorescence which reduces the contrast. Some drops of the mounting mixture should therefore be added, in order to replace contaminated mounting medium (Fig. 10.1). By this treatment, bacteria are not removed from the filter surface and fluorescence intensity is not reduced. Using a 10×10 graticulated eye piece, bacteria within 50 fields (grid areas) are counted.

Even distribution of bacteria on the filter is a characteristic of the apparatus employed, e.g., the porosity of the filter support and the shape of the filtration reservoir. The ground glass joints of the cylindrical reservoir and of the filter support holder should preferably have exactly the same inside diameter, other-

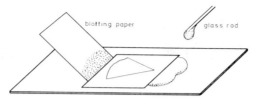

Fig. 10.1. Exchange of mounting medium

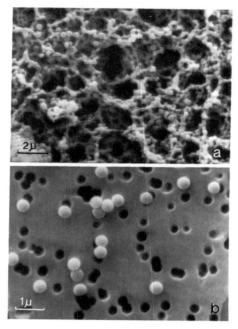

Fig. 10.2a and b. Scanning electron micrograph of the surface (a) of a cellulose nitrate filter (pore size 0.2 μm, × 4750, and (b) of a polycarbonate filter (pore size 0.2 μm, × 9500. On both filters are spherical latex particles (0.32 μm ∅)

wise rim effects will interfere with the count. Because the polycarbonate filter is very thin (10 μm), the effective filter area may not be well bordered by the ground glass joints, which clamp the rim of the filter. A silver filter (Selas Flotronics) which serves as a solvent resistant underlay for multiple use, should therefore be positioned between polycarbonate filter and filter support. A fine-meshed Teflon-ized steel net or a porous steel plate may be used instead of a sintered glass frit, which is prone to clogging and thus leads to variations in flow rates.

When using a cellulose nitrate filter to count bacteria, the particles are trapped in the "spongy" structure in different focal plains (Fig. 10.2) and small bacteria may even be retained, to some degree, within the filter material. This effect may be the reason for numerical discrepancies between the direct count obtained with cellulose nitrate filters and polycarbonate filters (Jones and Simon, 1975). Due to the horizontal position of cells on the surface of the polycarbonate filter, however, it is possible to identify bacteria not only by their fluorescence intensity but also by their distinct form and sharp outline.

10.2 Preparation of Specimens for Scanning Electron Microscopy

In addition to favorable conditions for the epifluorescence microscopic count, the displaying of cells on the plane surfaces of polycarbonate filters (Fig. 10.2) is also a basic requirement for the estimation of bacterial biomass using scanning electron microscopy. For control counts and biomass estimation of water samples, particularly from the Kiel Fjord and the Kiel Bight, a Cambridge S 600 scanning electron microscope has been adopted. Specimen preparation was performed by treating bacteria on the polycarbonate filter with increasing percentages of alcohol and Frigen 113. Subsequently, 0.5 ml of each dilution was pipetted into the filtration vessel and removed by vacuum after 3–5 min. The filter was then air-dried or critical-point dried, cut to convenient size and mounted with silver paint onto a specimen stub. The specimen were sputtered with gold an viewed under the microscope at 15 kV.

Only slight differences in the preservation of bacterial shape could be detected between samples air-dried or critical-point dried. Similar observations have been reported also by Weise (pers. comm.). Because critical-point drying does not necessarily guarantee that no cells will be lost, air drying after dehydration with alcohol and Frigen 113 was applied for routine use. Shape and size of bacterial cells are sufficiently preserved by this treatment in order to count and estimate cell lengths. Preliminary experiments to investigate the possible effects of shrinkage, caused by the treatment of cells with alcohols and with Frigen (Boyde, pers. comm.) showed that cells within the representative range of cell sizes of marine

Table 10.1. Mean volume of bacteria according to different classes of cell length

	Mean cell length or cell diameter (μm)	Range of length (μm)	Mean cell width (μm)	Mean volume (μm^3)
Cocci	0.3	→0.4	—	0.014
	0.5	0.4–0.6	—	0.065
	0.7	0.6–0.8	—	0.180
Rods	0.4	→0.6	0.32	0.023
	0.8	0.6–1.0	0.43	0.095
	1.2	1.0–1.4	0.475	0.185
	1.7	1.4–2.0	0.51	0.292
	2.4	2.0–2.8	0.54	0.508
	>2.8[a]	—	—[c]	—
Filaments	—[b]	—	—[c]	—

[a] The length of cells over 2.8 μm were measured separately.
[b] The length of filaments is measured by means of an ocular net micrometer.
[c] In any case the width of the cells was measured.

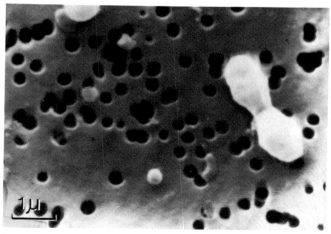

Fig. 10.3. Marked differences of bacterial volumes in the Kiel Fjord. Scanning electron micrograph, × 3670

and brackish bacteria (p. 114), which generally are much smaller than soil bacteria or cultured bacteria, will not undergo any significant alteration in size due to their favorable surface-to-volume proportions.

About 150 cells per sample have been differentiated by epifluorescence microscopy according to their length without applying a shrinkage factor. For each cell-length class an average bacterial volume was estimated by scanning electron microscopy (Table 10.1). Biomass calculation was based on data for bacterial number and classification with regard to cell lengths. This scheme of calculation is convenient only for bacterial populations which are characterized by a small range of size distribution and form variation. In bacterial habitats which are rich in nutrients, however, spirilli or filamentous forms may account for a significant part of the population, and vol/vol ratios of 1:500 are common (Fig. 10.3). In this case stereoscopic analysis of micrographs (Boyde and Williams, 1971) or the use of an automatic particle analyzer would be more suitable methods.

10.3 Preliminary Examinations

The use of the direct count method, or its different technical versions, was restricted for marine research mostly to the analysis of single water samples, in order to prove its applicability and reliability by statistical methods (Oppenheimer, 1952; Jannasch and Jones 1959; Brisou et al., 1963). Regular studies, however, dealing with the horizontal and vertical distribution of the total bacterial number and biomass of a certain marine or brackish area have rarely been performed (Konovalova, 1973; Taga and Matsuda, 1974; Väätänen, 1976).

Since the counting of bacteria on polycarbonate filters proved to be relatively accurate during preliminary experiments, it offered the possibility of obtaining

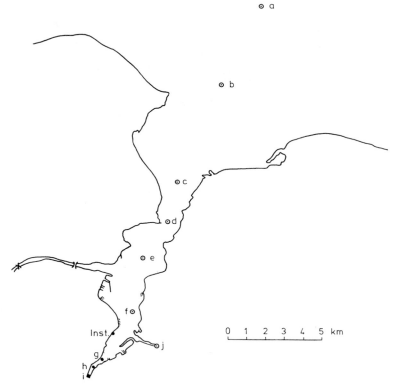

Fig. 10.4. Position of sampling stations for preliminary examinations. *Inst.:* institute's pier

information on the distribution pattern of bacteria and its correlation to a variety of biotic and abiotic parameters during the large-scale investigations of the Kiel Fjord and the Kiel Bight in 1974. Before the start of this program, however, some problems concerning the determination of local succession and temporal frequency of sampling had to be elucidated.

Figure 10.4 shows the location of ten stations of a preliminary examination of the Kiel Fjord, and its transition towards the Kiel Bight (see also Gocke, 1975). During fall 1973 and winter 1973/74 about 30 water samples from a depth of 2 m were collected and examined microscopically. With the exception of Station j, which is situated near a main tributary discharging waste water, all the stations were located approximately along the axis of the fjord. Due to relatively small distances between the stations, especially in the inner part of the fjord, the data followed the overall trend. The bacterial number decreased moderately towards the Bight after Station i (Fig. 10.5). The ratios of the counts obtained from samples of the transition area (Stations a and b) compared with counts obtained from samples of the inner fjord (Stations g, h, and i) amounted to only about 1:3, whereas saprophytic bacteria show corresponding ratios of 1:20 up to 1:400 (Gocke, 1975). There was little variation in the count over the four-month period, even though there was a marked decrease of temperature during this time.

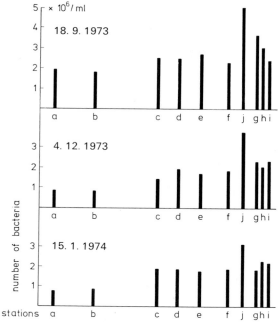

Fig. 10.5. Horizontal distribution of bacteria on three sections through the Kiel area

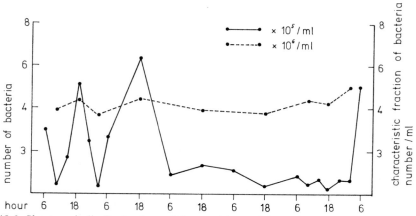

Fig. 10.6. Short periodic fluctuation of the total bacterial number and of a characteristic bacterial population at the institute's pier

In a further experiment, short term fluctuations of the bacterial number were studied. Samples were taken every 12 h from 1-m depth at a station near the institute's pier (Fig. 10.4). Although the number of saprophytic bacteria (Gocke, 1975), as well as the number of a certain bacterial population, which could be clearly identified under the microscope by its characteristic fluorescence and morphology, was variable, the total number of bacteria remained relatively constant (Fig. 10.6).

Taking into account that the ecological significance of time-dependent biological data has been considered dubious because of the hydrographic instability of the research area (Dietrich, 1961), the constancy of the total number of bacteria is somewhat astonishing. As opposed to the distinct changes of the number of certain fractions of bacteria (for instance the saprophytes), the constancy of the total population seems to represent a very even distribution of bacteria over a wide range. The small degree of fluctuation of the total numbers over the four-month period (Fig. 10.5) reflects to a certain extent integration of the short term competitive selectivities, arising from different uptake rates of a substrate by different populations.

10.4 Examination of the Kiel Fjord and Kiel Bight 1974/75

10.4.1 Regional and Seasonal Distribution of Bacteria

By analysis of the data obtained from the investigations in the Kiel Fjord and Kiel Bight 1974/75, only small differences were noted throughout the whole year between the total bacterial numbers in the Fjord (Sts. 1, and 2) and in the Bight (Sts. 3, 4, and 5; Table 10.2). With regard to the water samples from 2-m depth, maximal and minimal ratios were 1:4.3 (18.4.1974), and 1:1.3 (10.12.1974; Table 10.3).

Figure 10.7 shows some examples of local bacterial distribution at different seasons. These instantaneous images may serve to elucidate some of the effects of water exchange upon local distribution of bacteria. Owing to the action of easterly winds, for example, water from the Bight, which consistently showed a homogenous horizontal and vertical distribution of bacteria throughout the year (Fig. 10.9) was pushed into the Fjord. This influx of Bight water was especially apparent at Station 2, where the bacterial numbers were then similar to those of the Kiel Bight (Aug. 29, 1974). During winter, the permanent action of strong wind created an extensive mixing of waters from different origins and therefore the relative differences of the bacterial numbers between Bight and Fjord were small (Feb. 28, 1974; Nov. 21, 1974). During spring (April 18, 1974), the situation was characterized by a distinct difference between those areas, due to a multiplication of the bacterial numbers in the Fjord, promoted by the preceding stagnation period. Except for the samples collected in June 1974 (Table 10.3) and in November 1974 (Fig. 10.7), Station 1 consistently showed maximal numbers of bacteria. The two discrepancies may possibly be explained by the upwelling of bottom water at the very end of the Fjord (Amann and Boje, 1975). Salinity measurements, however, do not support this finding (Table 3.5).

Taking into account that a distinct stratification of the water prevailed over a substantial period of the year, the collection of only two samples at each station may just suffice to give a very rough idea of the vertical bacterial distribution. Slightly lower numbers of bacteria in bottom water samples of the Kiel Fjord, as indicated by the mean values of a one-year period (Table 10.2), may reflect influx of water from the Bight.

Table 10.2. Mean values ($\times 10^6$ ml^{-1}) of bacterial numbers of the year 1974

Station	1	2	3	4	5
2-m depth	3.10	2.58	1.43	1.32	1.46
over ground	2.47	2.31	1.32	1.37	1.58

Table 10.3. Total bacterial numbers ($\times 10^6$ ml^{-1}) at the Kiel Fjord (Station 1 and 2) and Kiel Bight (Station 3, 4, and 5) in the investigation period 1974/75

Date	Jan. 24	Feb. 28	March 21	April 18	May 16	June 11	July 11	Aug. 29	Sept. 12	Oct. 24	Nov. 21	Dec. 10	Jan. 23	Feb. 12	March 10
Station 1; 2 m	2.01	1.93	1.55	5.34	5.26	5.25	3.95	3.90	1.97	2.72	1.73	1.51	0.96	1.69	1.32
Station 1; 10 m	1.29	1.34	1.89	3.90	2.58	3.59	4.19	2.52	2.65	1.70	(5.68)	1.57			
Station 2; 2 m	1.47	1.53	0.74	4.89	3.14	5.98	2.98	2.19	1.05	2.36	2.22	2.41			
Station 2; 10 m	1.22	1.24	1.15	4.17	3.06	1.89	4.28	2.05	2.52	2.46	1.23	2.46			
Station 3; 2 m	0.80	0.81	0.57	1.82	1.57	1.56	2.70	1.99	1.14	1.75	1.24	1.16			
Station 3; 18 m	0.97	0.86	0.49	5.24	1.48	1.68	2.31	5.67	1.19	1.79	1.12	1.34			
Station 4; 2 m	0.96	1.08	0.54	1.23	1.14	1.49	2.30	2.16	1.30	1.38	1.02	1.20			
Station 4; 10 m	0.84	1.28	0.45	1.42	1.57	1.91	1.79	1.49	1.47	1.81	1.07	1.34			
Station 5; 2 m	0.83	1.09	0.61	1.60	1.81	1.78	2.22	2.22	1.10	1.82	1.21	1.24	0.67	0.64	(1.72)
Station 5; 18 m	0.70	0.80	0.52	2.05	1.79	1.89	2.99	1.97	1.47	2.74	1.06	0.99			

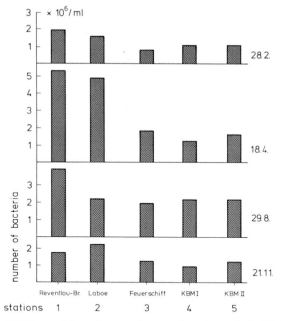

Fig. 10.7. Bacterial numbers on four sections through the Kiel area

Monthly fluctuations of the bacterial numbers in the Fjord differed considerably from those of the Bight (Fig. 10.8). At Station 1 (2 m) high values appeared during spring (April 18, 1974, May 16, 1974, June 11, 1974), whereas in the Bight (2 m) maximal numbers occurred in summer (July 11, 1974, Aug. 29, 1974). A second maximum in fall (Oct. 24, 1974) was common to nearly all stations and also at both depths. Except during May 1974, when influx of water from the Kiel Bight reduced the bacterial number at Station 2 (2 m), bacterial fluctuations at the 2-m depth showed equal tendency at both stations of the Kiel Fjord (Table 10.3).

Bacterial numbers of the Kiel Bight (2 m) fluctuated monthly to a small extent (Fig. 10.9). There is also a good conformity of the bacterial numbers at all three stations with respect to their seasonal tendency. These findings give rise to the assumption that monthly intervals of sampling may be sufficient to depict the seasonal fluctuation of the bacterial standing stock in the Kiel Bight.

Deviations of the general range of values, as occasionally occurs in the sample taken at bottom depth (St. 3, April 18, 1974, and Aug. 29, 1974), signified the presence of a certain patchiness, which may be credited to resuspension of sedimented material. There was, however, no hint of the occurrence of short-term changes in the bacterial number due to bacterial growth or a major exchange of the water. The probability of a marked, short-term changes seemed to be more likely in the Kiel Fjord and therefore, closer-spaced sampling would have been more desirable for following the pronounced increase of bacterial number between March and April 1974 (500% increase). In the Kiel Bight, however, where a corresponding rise in temperature was also recorded at this time, the increase of

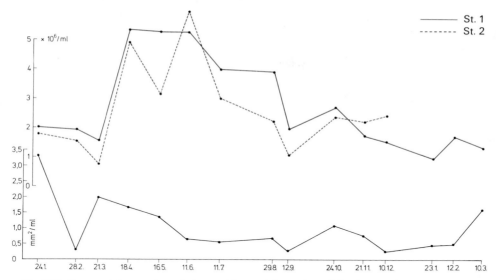

Fig. 10.8. Seasonal fluctuation of the total bacterial number of Stations 1 (2 m) and 2 (2 m). Seasonal fluctuation of the particle area of Station 1 (2 m)

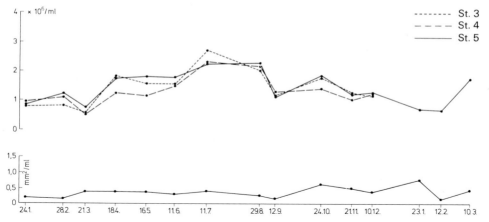

Fig. 10.9. Seasonal fluctuation of the total bacterial number of Station 3, 4, and 5 (always 2-m depth). Seasonal fluctuation of the particle area of Station 5 (2 m)

the bacterial number was relatively small (270% increase), perhaps signifying a deficiency in rapidly decomposable nutrients.

10.4.2 Estimation of Bacterial Cell Sizes and Biomass

Regional and seasonal variations of the bacterial quantity are described here on the basis of the term "number of bacteria". The reliability of these counts is confirmed by the good correspondence with parallel counts performed (Chap. 16). Since the size distribution of bacteria is rather similar in nearly all water samples

Table 10.4. Size distribution of bacteria for a one year period. (Mean values of 1974) Percentage of different classes of cell length and volume on total number and biomass of bacteria

	Number (%)				Biomass (%)			
Diameter μm Cocci	−0.3				−0.3			
Length μm Rods	−0.4	−0.8	−1.2	>1.2	−0.4	−0.8	−1.2	>1.2
Volume μm³	−0.018	−0.095	−0.185	>0.185	−0.018	−0.095	−0.185	>0.185
Station 1 (2 m)	70.4	21.2	5.0	3.9	28.9	42.5	17.2	11.3
Station 1 (10 m)	74.1	17.9	4.4	3.4	31.6	37.4	17.7	13.3
Station 5 (2 m)	72.3	18.4	3.9	3.7	33.4	39.1	16.0	11.5
Station 5 (18 m)	76.5	16.1	3.4	3.9	37.0	36.3	14.2	12.5

(Table 10.4), the fluctuations in both bacterial number and "total biomass of bacteria" (Table 10.5) do not change substantially. However, as long as methodology is restricted to the application of epifluorescence microscopy, subjectivity may be the reason for under- or over-estimations of the actual bacterial volume.

A remarkable point connceted with size distribution is the constantly high percentage of very small cells (cocci and short rods up to 0.4 μm diamter, or length). Owing to the limited optical resolution of light microscopy, the precise form of these cells could not be identified accurately. Therefore, rods and cocci belonging to this size range were treated as one fraction when using fluorescence microscopy. Only by the use of the scanning electron microscopy was it possible to demonstrate, that most of these extremely small bacteria are short rods rather than cocci. As shown by the scanning electron microscope, a certain part of this small fraction does pass the pores of a 0.2 μm pore-size filter (Fig. 10.10), and this renders the exact estimation of the bacterial number within this size range somewhat inaccurate. Application of polycarbonate filters with a pore size of 0.1 μm (which cannot be used for routine filtration due to low flow rates) showed that the above-mentioned proportion amounts to approximately 15% of the fraction, which is 10% of the total number of bacteria. This error, however, is negligible when expressed in terms of volume or biomass since this fraction of small-sized cells contributes only 5% (overall mean) to the total bacterial mass.

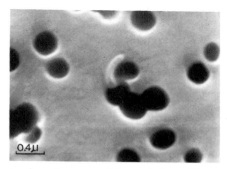

Fig. 10.10. Unsufficient retention of very small bacteria by a 0.2 μm pore size polycarbonate filter. Scanning electron micrograph, ×20,000

Table 10.5. Bacterial biomass ($\times 10^4$ μm^3 ml^{-1} or mg C m^{-3}) in the inner Kiel Fjord (Station 1) and the central Kiel Bight (Station 5) in 1974/75

Date		Jan. 24	Feb. 28	March 21	April 18	May 16	June 11	July 11	Aug. 29	Sept. 12	Oct. 24	Nov. 21	Dec. 10	Jan. 23	Feb. 12	March 10
Station	Depth															
1	2 m	12.8	7.3	6.9	21.7	22.5	24.0	19.4	24.2	10.2	11.4	7.6	6.1	5.0	8.6	7.8
1	10 m	7.6	5.1	9.9	19.7	10.6	13.3	17.5	9.8	11.5	10.1	(25.0)	6.2			
5	2 m	4.9	4.8	2.0	6.2	8.7	4.6	11.0	10.7	5.9	6.9	5.0	4.6	3.3	3.6	(8.5)
5	18 m	3.4	2.8	1.5	11.1	9.4	8.4	8.8	11.3	6.1	10.1	3.9	3.3			

Table 10.6. Average cell volume of marine bacteria as calculated by different authors

Reference		Average volume (μm^3)
Zobell (1963)	Seawater	0.2
Sorokin (1964)	Central Pacific Ocean	0.15
Konovalowa (1973)	Amur bay	0.4–0.7
Ferguson and Rublee (1975)	Coastal water	0.09
Zimmermann (1975)	Kiel area	0.06

Table 10.7. Proportion of bacterial biomass in % of total biomass based on protein content, Chapter 5, in 2-m depth

Date	March 21	April 18	May 16	June 11	July 11	Aug. 29	Sept. 12	Oct. 24	Nov. 21	Dec. 10	Jan. 23	Feb. 12	March 10
Station 1 (2 m)	1.3	1.7	2.3	2.7	1.2	1.6	1.6	2.1	2.3	2.5	2.4	3.2	1.2
Station 5 (2 m)	0.8	1.7	3.5	1.4	2.9	4.4	1.9	1.1	1.8	1.8	1.4	2.6	1.9

With regard to the compositions within the bacterial size ranges at different depths at Station 1 and 5 over the year, there appears to be no marked tendency to deviation from the general pattern (Table 10.4). In the course of microscopic analysis of water samples, however, it is possible to register significant fluctuations of certain bacteria (in particular the large cells), which can easily be identified because of their typical morphology. Numerically the contribution from these forms will be of little significance in relation to the total number.

Although an "average-sized" marine or brackish water bacterium is subject to idealization, its volume serves to calculate total bacterial biomass or number when indirect methods are applied. There is, however, considerable discrepancy in the published values for the mean size of a marine bacterium (Table 10.6). The mean bacterial volume from samples from the Kiel Fjord and Kiel Bight was found to be 0.06 μm^3, a magnitude which is in agreement with the findings of Ferguson and Rublee (1976). The slight discrepancy between the mean volume measured by these authors and that found in the present work in the Kiel area may well not only be due to the different sampling location, but more likely to the use of different filters (see p. 105). Bacterial biomass was found to contribute significantly to the planktonic microbial standing stock of marine upwelling areas, which are rich in nutrients (Watson, 1976). In the Kiel area the bacterial biomass represents only a small proportion of the standing stock (Table 10.7).

10.4.3 Bacteria Attached to Detritus

Detritus has been previously regarded as the typical habitat for a marine bacterium (Wood, 1953; Seki, 1972). This conception served to interpret effects in the food chain, especially the filter-feeding activity of zooplankton. By microscopic observations of water samples from different marine areas, Wiebe and Pomeroy (1972) showed, however, that the amount of bacteria attached to detritus is relatively small in comparison to free cells. Similar findings were noticed from samples from the Kiel area. The overall mean of attached bacteria was found to be 62,000 ml^{-1} (2 m) and 90,000 ml^{-1} (bottom sample), which is only 3.1% and 5.2% respectively of the corresponding total numbers. The maximum and minimum percentages found were 23% and 1% respectively. There appeared to be no correlation between frequency of attachment and, for example, temporal continuity and horizontal distribution of the total number of bacteria. A trend was apparent, however, between the number of attached bacteria and the depth of sampling (Table 10.8). Because the number of bacteria-containing detritus varied only slightly throughout the water column (cf. the ratio between 2 m and bottom water: 1:1.1), the increase of attached bacteria may be attributed to further bac-

Table 10.8. Proportion of attached bacteria in % of the total number (mean values 1974)

Station	1	2	3	4	5
2-m depth	2.9	3.4	2.8	2.8	3.8%
Above ground	3.7	4.2	5.5	4.4	8.1%

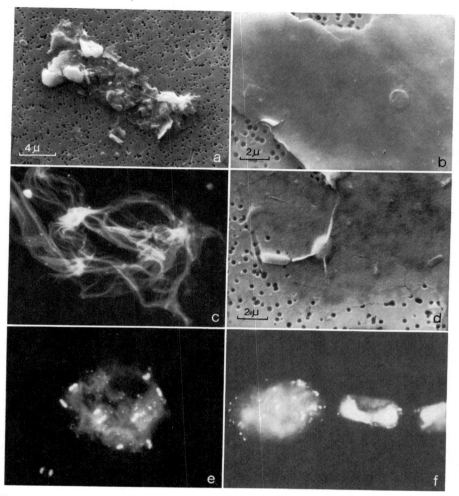

Fig. 10.11. (a) Conglomeratic particle, SEM-micrograph, ×2500. (b) Chitinous particle with a discus-like bacterium, SEM-micrograph, ×5000. (c) Membranous particle, epi-fluorescence micrograph, ×740. (d) Membranous particle and bacteria, SEM-micrograph, ×5000. (e) Light, transparent detritus with dense bacterial colonisation, epi-fluorescence micrograph, ×1850. (f) Detritus formation at the end of a Sceletonema chain. epi-fluorescence micrograph, ×1850

terial colonization of particles, which had already previously colonized in the near-surface layers. This increase of the number of cells within one particle is evident when the numbers of "densely colonized particles" (more than five bacteria within 20 µm² of the particle area) are compared. The ratio of the above-mentioned parameter between the 2-m and the bottom sample is then 1:2.7. In the light of the above, initial bacterial attack on an easily degradable particle appears to occur very soon after the particle has been formed. Initial particle formation, or the transformation of necrotic plasma of a planktonic organism, is considered to be a rapid process. Gradual bacterial decomposition of the cell contents within an apparently intact algal cell has rarely been noted in the Kiel area. A frequent observation was one of discharged plasma, resulting from cell lysis, being initially invaded by bacteria (Fig. 10.11 f).

Bacterial cells within detritus are somewhat larger than free bacteria and thus make a slightly larger contribution to the total biomass. Mean cell size of attached bacteria, however, cannot be accurately estimated owing to unfavorable positioning of the cells on the detrital particles. The low number of attached bacteria seems to be of no significance; however, enzymatic analysis of attached bacteria showed that in this respect, attachment may play a more important role than is suggested by the low numbers (Hendricks, 1974).

In comparison to the total amount of detritus, the number of particles containing bacteria is small (20% of the total number of particles). The particles, which appear to have varying amounts of substrate affinity towards bacteria, show also quite different structures under the fluorescence microscope. Classifications of detritus according to a rough pattern have already been carried out by Nishizawa et al. (1954), Kane (1964), and Wiebe and Pomeroy (1972). Their descriptions were restricted to particles of relatively dense structure, which could therefore be optically represented by phase-contrast microscopy. A characteristic type of particle has been described as a "floc" or a "flocculent aggregate" (Wiebe and Pomeroy, 1972). These are conglomerate structures, possessing an organic matrix with mineral inclusions (Fig. 10.11 a). This type of particle seldom occurred in samples from the area under investigation. Epifluorescence microscopy reveals that bacteria are densely colonized within these particles. Particle formation may be due to adsorptive aggregation, however, production from fecal pellets should also be considered as a possible source of these forms. Chitinous plate-like fragments with sharp outlines form another type of particle, which is seldom encountered (Fig. 10.11 b). These plates are only sparsely colonized by bacteria. Eventually the particles show bacterial "food prints", which are produced through the action of chitinoclastic bacteria. Frequently large membranous particles void of attachment (Fig. 10.11 c and d) comprise a significant part of the total measured area of the detritus. The majority of all particles, however, is formed from a light, transparent and voluminous detritus (Fig. 10.11 e). This kind of particle, which can only be seen by fluorochromation, is the favored substrate for bacterial attachment. Colloidal aggregation may contribute to its formation; however, plasma released from phytoplankton may also generate these particles (Fig. 10.11 f).

References

Amann, V., Boje, R.: Contribution to: Jahresbericht für das Jahr 1974, Inst. Meereskunde, Kiel, p. 47 (1975)

Bell, J. B., Dutka, B. J.: Bacterial densities by fluorescent microscopy. Proc. 15th Conf. Great Lakes Res. 15–20 (1972)

Boyde, A., Williams, R. A. D.: Estimation of the volumes of bacterial cells by scanning electron microscopy. Archs. oral Biol. **16**, 259–267 (1971)

Brisou, J., de Rautlin de la Roy, Y., Curcier, R., Campello, F.: Numération comparative des bactéries marines par culture et lecture directe sur membranes. C. R. Soc. Biol. CL VII (3), 635–638 (1963)

Dietrich, G.: Eine Forschungsfahrt zur Untersuchung der kurzfristigen Schwankungen in der Schichtung und Bewegung der Ostsee im Sommer 1960. Kieler Meeresforsch. **17**, 135–136 (1961)

Ferguson, R. L., Rublee, P.: Contribution of bacteria to standing crop of coastal plankton. Limnol. Oceanogr. **21 (1)**, 141–145 (1976)

Francisco, D. E., Mah, R. A., Rabin, A. C.: Acridine Orange-Epifluorescence technique for counting Bacteria in natural waters. Trans. Am. Microsc. Soc. **92**, 416–421 (1973)

Gocke, K.: Studies on short-term variations of heterotrophic activity in the Kiel Fjord. Marine Biol. **33**, 49–55 (1975)

Hendricks, C. W.: Sorption of heterotrophic and enteric bacteria to glass surfaces in the continuous culture of river water. Appl. Microbiol. **28 (4)**, 572–578 (1974)

Ivatin, A. W.: Number of bacteria in the water of the Kuibyshev Revervoir and its correlation with the amount of organo-mineral suspended matter. Microbiology **42 (3)**, 465–468 (1973)

Jannasch, H. W., Jones, G. E.: Bacterial populations in sea water as determined by different methods of enumeration. Limnol. Oceanogr. **4**, 128–139 (1959)

Jassby, A. D.: An evaluation of ATP estimations of bacterial biomass in the presence of phytoplankton. Limnol. Oceanogr. **20 (4)**, 646–648 (1975)

Jones, J. G., Simon, B. M.: An investigation of errors in direct counts of aquatic bacteria by epifluorescence microscopy with reference to a new method for dyeing membrane filters. J. Appl. Bact. **39** (1975)

Kane, J. E.: Organic aggregates in surface waters of the Ligurian Sea. Limnol. Oceanogr. **9**, 287–294 (1964)

Konovalova, G. V.: Productivity of bacterioplankton in Amur Bay in the Sea of Japan. Microbiology **42 (6)**, 974–979 (1973)

Nishizawa, S., Fukuda, M., Inoue, N.: Photographic study of suspended matter and plankton in the sea. Bull. Fac. Fisk. Hokkaido Univ. **5**, 36–40 (1954)

Olah, J.: Number, biomass, and production of planktonic bacteria in the shallow Lake Balaton. Arch. Hydrobiol. **73 (2)**, 193–217 (1974)

Oppenheimer, C. H.: The membrane filter in marine microbiology. J. Bacteriol. **64**, 783–786 (1952)

Overbeck, J.: Microbiology and biochemistry. Mitt. intern. Verein. Limnol. **20**, 200–228 (1974)

Razumov, A. S.: Direct method for counting water bacteria (in Russian). Microbiologija **1**, 131–146 (1932).

Seki, H.: The role of microorganisms in the marine food chain with reference to organic aggregate. Mem. Ist. Ital. Idrobiol. **29 Suppl.**, 245–259 (1972)

Sorokin, Y. I.: A quantitative study of the microflora in the Central Pacific Ocean. J. Conseil **29**, 25–40 (1964)

Sorokin, Y. I.: Productivity of coastal tropical waters of the western Pacific. Oceanology **13 (4)**, 551–558 (1973)

Taga, N., Matsuda, O.: Bacterial populations attached to plankton and detritus in seawater. In: Effect of the Ocean Environment on Microbial Activities. 433–448 Colwell, R. R., and Morita, R. Y., (eds.) Baltimore-London-Tokyo University Park Press (1974)

Tronova, T. M.: The microflora of different types of mineral waters in the south eastern part of western Siberia. Microbiology **43 (1)**, 108–111 (1974)

Väätänen, P. Microbial studies in coastal waters of the Northern Baltic Sea. I Distribution and abundance of bacteria and yeasts in the Tvärminne area. Walter and Andrée de Nottbeck Foundation, Scientific Reports **No. 1** (1976)

Watson, S. W.: Concentration, distribution and role of bacteria in the ocean. Res. proposal submitted to the National Science Foundation W.H.O.I. Proposal Serial Nr. 290 (1975)

Wiebe, W. J., Pomeroy, L. R.: Microorganisms and their association with aggregates and detritus in the sea: a microscopic study. Mem. Ist. Ital. Idrobiol., **29 Suppl.** 325–352 (1972)

Wood, E. J. F.: Heterotrophic bacteria in marine environments of eastern Australia, Australian J. Mar. Freshwater Res., **4 (1)** 160–200 (1953)

Zimmermann, R.: Entwicklung und Anwendung von fluoreszenz- und rasterelektronenmikroskopischen Methoden zur Ermittlung der Bakterienmenge in Wasserproben. Thesis Univ. Kiel (1975)

Zimmermann, R., Meyer-Reil, L. A.: A new method for fluorescence staining of bacterial populations on membrane filters. Kieler Meeresforsch. **30 (1)**, 24–27 (1974)

Zobell, C. E.: Domain of the marine microbiologist. In: Oppenheimer, C. H. (ed.): Symp. Mar. Microbiol. Springfield (1963)

11. Regional and Seasonal Distribution of Saprophytic and Coliform Bacteria

G. RHEINHEIMER

The amount of saprophytic and coliform bacteria gives important information on the biological and hygienic condition of the water. The term saprophyte is applied to all heterotrophic bacteria which are able to develop on agar media and which can be counted by means of the plate method (see Rheinheimer, 1975a). Since the concentrations of nutrients in the media used are relatively high (see below), the bacteria which develop are above all those with high nutrient requirements. These are forms which have a high metabolic activity and, as a rule, are able to break down proteins and carbohydrates very quickly. After a supply of such nutrients, a rapid development of these bacteria especially at summer water temperatures takes place. Experiments in which yeast extract (1 g per 10 l) was added to water from the Kiel Fjord showed that the saprophyte numbers increased very rapidly and, after the nutrients were used up, dropped off again almost as quickly (see Rheinheimer, 1975b). The saprophytes thus react more quickly to changes in their environment than the rest of the bacteria, and reflect the content of easily degradable organic substances in the water. Accordingly, the saprophytes are a good indicator of the pollution load of the water at a given time, although the proportion of saprophytes amounts at the most to only a few % of the total bacteria numbers (Rheinheimer, 1975a). Since saprophytes usually have relatively large cells, however, their proportion in the bacteria biomass is greater than their proportion in the total bacteria numbers. The coliform count as a supplement gives an indication of the fecal contamination of the water, for example that caused by municipal sewage or by shipping.

11.1 Material and Methods

On 15 monthly cruises, samples of water were taken at all the stations in the Kiel Fjord and Kiel Bight (see Chap. 2), and also on two additional voyages (February 14 and June 25, 74) at Stations 1, 4, and 5. Altogether 12 samples could be analyzed at a given time, which were divided among the stations investigated as follows:

1. Reventlou Brücke (inner Kiel Fjord)	2 m,	10 m	
2. Laboe (outer Kiel Fjord)	2 m,	10 m	
3. Kiel Bight (Ls Kiel)	2 m,	10 m,	18 m
4. Central Kiel Bight, KBM I	2 m,	10 m	
5. Central Kiel Bight, KBM II	2 m,	10 m,	18 m

All samples were processed immediately on board. For determination of the saprophyte numbers, three yeast extract-peptone media with different salinities and one medium consisting of meat extract-peptone were used. These had the following composition:

1. ZS   Yeast extract-peptone agar with sea water mixture S 24‰
        (ZoBell Medium 2216E)

yeast extract (Difco)	5.0
peptone (Difco)	1.0 g
$FePO_4$	0.01 g
agar (Difco)	15.0 g
aged sea water	750 ml
distilled water	250 ml
pH 7.6	

2. ZB   Yeast extract-peptone agar with sea water mixture S 8‰
        Same composition as (1), however with 250 ml aged sea water and 750 ml distilled water.

3. ZL   Yeast extract-peptone agar with fresh water
        Same composition as (1), however prepared with tap water.

4. N   Meat extract-peptone agar with fresh water (nutrient agar)

meat extract (Oxoid)	5 g
peptone (Brunnengräber)	5 g
NaCl	2 g
$K_2HPO_4 \cdot 3H_2O$	1 g
agar	20 g
tap water	1000 ml
pH 7.5	

The nutrient media were sterilized for 20 min at 120° in an autoclave.

The sample water was diluted with a 3:1 mixture of sea water and distilled water; the dilution for Station 1 was 1:200, for all other stations 1:10. Initially (January to March 1974) two parallels were prepared at a time, and later three. The plates were incubated at 20° C. Counting of the colonies were carried out after 7 and 14 days by means of a counting apparatus, and the average value of the parallels was determined. For details see Schlieper, 1968. If not otherwise indicated, the evaluations are based on the counts obtained after 14 days incubation, since then higher numbers were usually found than after 7 days.

The highest colony count (average value) of a given sample is referred to as the total saprophyte number. As a rule, this was found on ZS or ZB agar medium.

The determination of the coliform numbers was made using the tricolored agar method according to Gassner (Gassner, 1918). Three parallels were prepared at a time and the plates incubated at 37° C. The counting took place after 24 and 48 h, whereby the latter values were used for the final evaluation. In addition, water samples from Stations 1 and 5 were filtered through a membrane filter (0.2 μm pore size) and the filters incubated at 37° C on Endo nutrient pads manufactured by the Sartorius Company, Göttingen, Germany. Counting of the positive colonies (those with a metallic shimmer) was carried out after 24 and 48 h.

Samples from the uppermost sediment layer (0–2 cm) were also taken at Stations 1, 4, and 5. The removal of the sediment took place by means of a well-cleaned Van Veen grab. Great care was taken so that the sediment surface was not disturbed, both in lifting and opening the grab on board ship. The sample material was removed from the grab with a sterilized syringe, which had been cut off and polished evenly at one end (see Schlieper, 1968), placed immediately into the dilution water (seawater–distilled water mixture 1:1) and then shaken vigorously. For determination of the colony counts on the nutrient media 1 to 4, dilutions of 1:10,000 were used. In this way, the most suitable degree of dilution could be chosen for the evaluations, at which about 50–300 colonies were found on the plates. For determining the coliform numbers, a dilution of 1:100 was used. The results were calculated each time both for 1 cm³ fresh (wet) sediment and for 1 g dry sediment.

11.2 Distribution of Marine, Brackish Water and Fresh Water Bacteria in the Water

The saprophyte and coliform numbers given in Tables 11.1–11.4 and 11.7 are, as would be expected, nearly always highest at Station 1 in the inner Kiel Fjord, which carries the greatest waste load; the numbers then decrease sharply in the outer Kiel Fjord (St. 2) and especially in the Kiel Bight (Sts. 3 to 5). This is clearly demonstrated by the average values, which are listed together with the maxima and minima in Table 11.5.

The average total saprophyte numbers decrease already in the outer Kiel Fjord at Laboe (St. 2) down to one fifth, and going out toward the middle of the Kiel Bight (Sts. 4 and 5) drop further to only a few % of the values found at Station 1. Similar results have been found for the average colony counts on the different nutrient media as well as the average coliform number (see Tables 11.1–11.7). The colony counts determined on nutrient media prepared with fresh water (ZL and N) showed an even greater decrease than those on media with sea water mixtures (ZS and ZB)—to less than 1%.

These are mainly non-native bacteria which mostly reach the sea by way of rivers, drainage channels and land erosion. Their optimal development is generally on fresh water media, and they are more or less strongly suppressed by brackish and sea water. Accordingly most of them are soon overcome by the competition with the halophilic Baltic Sea bacteria, which are better adapted to this milieu (see Rheinheimer, 1968, 1975a). Therefore the proportion of bacteria growing on fresh water media, of the total saprophyte number, is significantly greater at Stations 1 and 2 in the Kiel Fjord than at the Stations 3 to 5 lying farther out in the open Kiel Bight. At 2-m depth, the proportion of the colonies counted on the agar medium ZL decreases from 17.7% of the total saprophyte number at Station 1, to 4% at Station 5, and on medium N from 10.4% to 3.0% (see Table 11.6). The proportion of the coliforms along the same profile also showed a clear decrease from 0.05% to 0.01% of the total saprophyte number.

From the rapid decrease of the bacteria which are able to develop on fresh water media, as well as the coliforms it may be concluded that these bacteria can

Table 11.1. Colony counts per ml on medium 1 (ZS) (yeast extract-peptone agar with sea water mixture S 24‰)

Date	Station 1		Station 2		Station 3			Station 4		Station 5		
	2 m	10 m	2 m	10 m	2 m	10 m	18 m	2 m	10 m	2 m	10 m	18 m
Jan. 24, 1974	13,600	7,200	7,700	1,685	890	1,240	3,945	298	572	351	167	680
Feb. 14	4,600	62,500						473	542	1,017	688	157
Feb. 28	16,800	15,500	700	4,490	200	390	1,115	600	136	1,875	775	299
March 21	15,900	22,300	2,485	3,400	1,000	2,065	660	794	385	531	227	428
April 18	74,600	56,734	10,330		1,977	2,537	7,773	2,464	2,591	3,959	2,860	2,280
May 16	166,866	30,400	22,447	15,480	3,413	3,823	6,540	1,900	2,140	1,436	1,261	915
June 11	122,667	48,267	28,533	6,787	1,547	1,297	677	856	518	602	857	449
June 25	15,134	79,800						362	211	209	273	301
July 11	47,066	24,600	3,956	9,687	2,273	1,690	663	694	235	336	380	246
Aug. 7	39,600	19,934										
Aug. 29	55,000	25,000	5,653	4,686	733	393	14,460	243	92	263	107	174
Sept. 12	45,734	62,066	7,426	5,470	9,373	5,613	7,856	689	514	604	443	377
Oct. 24	138,134	43,134	6,837	6,133	6,157	6,147	7,557	1,331	1,469	3,070	1,895	419
Nov. 21	37,000	49,200	13,466	5,330	4,203	8,230	4,573	483	1,295	751	629	637
Dec. 10	46,066	33,200	10,280	14,000	5,853	3,877	5,957	530	4,130	1,108	403	188
Jan. 23, 1975	11,667	9,067	2,733	3,883	687	1,133	1,223	305	456	≈400	367	337
Feb. 12	19,333	19,200	7,300		1,300	1,763	3,220	98	236	660	667	1,297
March 10	18,000	17,000	6,386	3,016	4,327	1,893	910	1,400	1,075	1,240	379	700

Table 11.2. Colony counts per ml on medium 2 (ZB) (yeast extract-peptone agar with sea water mixture S 8‰)

Date	Station 1		Station 2		Station 3			Station 4		Station 5		
	2 m	10 m	2 m	10 m	2 m	10 m	18 m	2 m	10 m	2 m	10 m	18 m
Jan. 24, 1974	5,900	1,100	5,180	3,150	1,650	1,560	3,030	172	277	434	221	206
Feb. 14	3,700	31,500		10,990	145	670	1,300	441	386	1,098	720	409
Feb. 28	27,600	21,300	7,450	2,045	1,065	2,145	810	801	720	488	680	368
March 21	6,000	7,600	2,385					482	415	309	189	366
April 18	91,600	58,800	23,347	26,933	3,113	4,217	7,640	2,368	2,888	3,120	2,791	3,612
May 16	184,266	30,600	17,053	5,803	2,850	3,853	3,433	1,029	1,048	1,627	800	1,360
June 11	93,400	44,600	33,400		797	993	610	729	1,104	812	720	529
June 25	19,934	95,334						303	383	228	337	292
July11	23,600	8,466	1,083	1,227	423	633	183	176	181	150	220	114
Aug. 7	6,134	15,466										
Aug. 29	82,266	4,600	3,490	1,043	510	460	7,903	371	109	243	95	155
Sept. 12	54,200	65,200	3,833	5,776	4,733	11,900	5,423	888	529	75	579	227
Oct. 24	98,666	59,600	8,487	6,713	9,573	5,173	12,143	1,534	1,187	2,933	1,591	2,944
Nov. 21	32,400	47,466	6,110	5,873	7,250	6,960	4,133	813	1,373	1,207	1,132	687
Dec. 10	48,066	42,534	14,533	14,680	5,683	5,347	5,360	514	2,762	1,257	1,523	790
Jan. 23, 1975	10,200	10,467	3,177	1,573	1,177	1,647	1,347	335	375	333	307	283
Feb. 12	19,667	23,867	7,473		1,610	1,397	3,686	483	1,964	460	761	1,255
March 10	17,000	12,134	2,560	1,450	1,197	520	117	743	743	468	271	—

Table 11.3. Colony counts per ml on medium 3 (ZL) (yeast extract-peptone agar with fresh water)

Date	Station 1		Station 2		Station 3			Station 4		Station 5		
	2 m	10 m	2 m	10 m	2 m	10 m	18 m	2 m	10 m	2 m	10 m	18 m
Jan. 24, 1974	7,200	800	1,715	1,275	275	230	455	300	57	26	75	54
Feb. 14	2,400	2,700						76	38	24	18	25
Feb. 28	400	100	145	205	10	50	25	21	43	82	36	16
March 21	2,200	2,000	2,850	2,050	15	70	40	48	23	14	29	14
April 18	19,934	8,866	6,600		433	470	597	314	262	185	170	122
May 16	29,466	532	1,027	1,057	293	220	30	103	130	16	26	26
June 11	11,400	1,533	3,937	300	7	20	57	11	9	4	116	9
June 25	334	22,266						45	18	18	2	10
July 11	6,066	666	403	253	3	3	40	2	2	1	3	7
Aug. 7	1,734	5,394										
Aug. 29	18,000	400	1,633	403	20	263	20	48	19	23	36	34
Sept. 12	38,600	2,000	1,106	1,133	296	213	23	69	93	18	11	38
Oct. 24	12,534	3,400	810	887	97	153	90	15	16	36	144	ca. 120
Nov. 21	7,934	1,866	976	980	380	153	540	72	5	23	43	44
Dec. 10	2,334	1,934	2,513	3,893	90	153	410	27	20	26	14	15
Jan. 23, 1975	1,266	3,267	373	453	30	93	83	29	35	20	20	27
Feb. 12	1,466	1,800	760		30	30	255	24	31	51	22	52
March 10	4,134	534	1,163	107	737	63	267	460	199	147	84	7

Table 11.4. Colony counts per ml on medium 4 (N) (meat extract-peptone agar with fresh water)

Date	Station 1		Station 2		Station 3			Station 4		Station 5		
	2 m	10 m	2 m	10 m	2 m	10 m	18 m	2 m	10 m	2 m	10 m	18 m
Jan. 24, 1974	3,500	800	1,795	2,090	385	190	710	54	67	37	78	46
Feb. 14	1,800	1,300						42	32	30	31	24
Feb. 28	200	2,400	165	160	245	30	10	30	6	5	18	5
March 21	2,900	1,100	400	270	30	75	45	17	10	15	8	7
April 18	5,734	2,334	2,540		740	147	550	27	124	98	165	121
May 16	5,532	666	683	467	37	190	120	30	33	8	7	18
June 11	4,600	1,200	597	137	20	3	77	8	6	5	126	6
June 25	500	1,066						31	5	15	1	28
July 11	8,000	2,000	683	397	10	13	40	7	9	5	2	18
Aug. 7	1,734	3,200										
Aug. 29	31,800	1,000	1,073	320	213	43	230	86	26	69	32	43
Sept. 12	13,334	7,466	1,328	3,386	243	283	40	29	153	15	26	75
Oct. 24	9,466	2,600	2,367	3,127	670	703	677	16	24	30	30	79
Nov. 21	2,400	1,934	1,573	1,930	890	916	2,536	333	14	116	141	310
Dec. 10	2,934	2,934	3,570	3,727	520	500	787	114	104	64	75	39
Jan. 23, 1975	933	1,267	400	353	60	73	47	29	42	9	11	18
Feb. 12	1,800	533	317		27	20	143	23	17	54	16	66
March 10	2,334	400	593	27	27	20	0	19	3	11	104	8

Table 11.5. Average total saprophyte numbers and average colony counts on the different media with maxima and minima

Station	1		2		3			4		5		
Depth	2 m	10 m	2 m	10 m	2 m	10 m	18 m	2 m	10 m	2 m	10 m	18 m
Av. tot. no.	55,061	39,045	11,159	8,121	3,544	3,521	4,843	882	1,183	1,152	846	896 Bact./ml
Max	166,866	79,800	28,533	15,480	9,373	8,230	14,460	2,464	4,130	3,959	2,860	2,280
Av. ZS	49,892	35,598	9,082	6,465	2,929	2,806	4,475	619	976	1,083	728	581 Bact./ml
Min	4,600	7,200	700	1,685	200	390	660	98	92	209	107	157
Max	184,266	95,334	33,400	26,933	9,573	11,900	12,143	2,368	2,888	3,120	2,791	3,612
Av. ZB	48,133	33,245	9,304	6,712	2,785	3,165	3,808	717	967	897	761	850 Bact./ml
Min	3,700	1,100	1,083	1,227	145	460	117	172	109	75	95	114
Max	38,600	22,266	6,600	3,893	737	470	597	460	262	185	170	122
Av. ZL	9,745	3,216	1,734	1,009	181	146	195	98	59	42	50	36 Bact./ml
Min	334	100	145	107	3	3	23	2	2	1	2	7
Max	31,800	7,466	3,570	3,727	890	916	2,536	333	153	116	165	310
Av. N	5,751	1,824	1,206	1,261	274	214	401	53	40	34	51	54 Bact./ml
Min	200	400	165	27	10	3	0	7	3	5	1	5
Max	96,333	30,000	45,500	39,000	4,000	5,667	15,333	9,333	1,000	1,000	17,333	3,000
Av. Colif.	27,823	9,312	8,022	8,630	967	1,367	3,267	755	196	157	1,206	274 Bact./ml
Min	2,000	0	0	0	0	0	0	0	0	0	0	0
No. of samples	17	17	15	15	15	15	15	17	17	17	17	17

Table 11.6. Percentage of average colony counts of freshwater growing bacteria (media ZL and N) on total saprophyte numbers in water

Station	1		2		3			4		5		
Depth	2	10	2	10	2	10	18	2	10	2	10	18 m
ZL av.	17.7	8.2	15.5	12.4	5.1	4.2	4.0	11.1	5.0	3.7	5.9	4.0%
N av.	10.4	4.7	10.8	15.5	7.7	6.1	8.3	6.0	3.4	3.0	6.0	6.0%

scarcely play a mentionable role in the turn-over of matter in the western Baltic Sea.

The breakdown processes occurring here are almost exclusively caused by halophilic forms. In the Kiel Bight, these are genuine marine bacteria with salinity optima between 30 and 40‰, as well as brackish water bacteria with salinity optima between 10 and 25‰ (see Rheinheimer, 1971, 1975a). This is doubtless due to the lively exchange of water of the Kiel Bight with that of the bordering sea areas. In an often repeated exchange, either water with a high salinity content flows in from the North Sea, or low salinity water from the Baltic Sea proper, influencing the composition of the microflora. This is brought about by the bacteria population which is carried along at a given time, as well as by the resulting fluctuation in the salinity of the water. Similar conditions also prevail in the North Sea at the areas around the river mouths, for example that of the Elbe and Weser. In the middle Baltic Sea, on the other hand, with decreasing salinity the proportion of brackish water bacteria increases clearly at the expense of the genuine marine bacteria (see Rheinheimer, 1968).

Also of interest is the vertical distribution of the saprophytic bacteria at the various stations investigated. In the Kiel Fjord (Sts. 1 and 2), the total saprophyte numbers as well as the colony counts on the separate nutrient media are at 2-m depth—i.e., in water near the surface—as a rule distinctly greater than above the sea bed at 10-m depth. At Station 4 at a depth of 10 m, higher average values are found on the media ZS and ZB—lower, however, on ZL and N, and much smaller coliform numbers than in the surface water (see Table 11.5). At the deeper Stations 3 and 5, most values decrease at 10-m depth, and above the sea bed at 18-m depth begin to increase again. Doubtless here the influence of the sediment becomes perceptible, which consists of relatively nutrient-rich mud in this area. At the stations in the Fjord, on the other hand, the amount of easily degradable organic substrates in the water is usually greater at the surface than in the deeper parts. This is due to the rather heavy pollution load here caused by waste water and refuse.

The curves of the total saprophyte numbers represented in Figures 11.1 and 11.2 show at all five stations distinct seasonal fluctuations, with maxima in the spring (generally in April) and in the autumn (October to December), while the minima occur during the summer and winter months. This is therefore of special interest, since the absolute numbers at the various stations show at times considerable differences (see above). Observations which are in complete agreement with these have also been made during previous years. The only exception is the

Bact./ml   Bact./ml

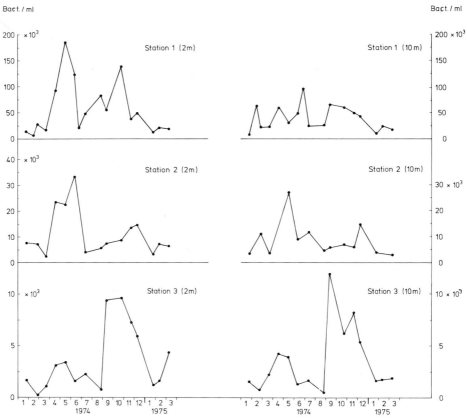

Fig. 11.1. Total numbers of saprophytes in the Kiel Fjord (Sts. 1, 2) and the Kiel Bight (St. 3) in 2- and 10-m depth

sample series from 10-m depth at Station 1 (Reventlou Brücke) in the inner Kiel Fjord. Here, especially during the first half of the investigation period, the sapro-phyte curve more often shows fluctuations, which are possibly due to occasional disturbance of the sediments. Strong spring and fall peaks, however, may occur at all depths. These indicate a correlation between saprophyte and phytoplankton development. The spring peak follows the strong increase in the spring plankton, which as a rule begins in March—and the fall peak follows, although at a some-what longer time interval, the late summer maximum of the phytoplankton. While the spring peak of the total saprophyte number in the Kiel Fjord coincides with the high primary production values (see Chap. 7), the autumn maximum occurs only after this has clearly already begun to decrease. The same is true for chlorophyll, particulate carbon, nitrogen, protein and carbohydrates (see Chap. 5). These relations are not so clear at the other stations. Thus quite high values for all these parameters could be found in October—during the other autumn months, however, they were also low. From this it would appear that the autumn maximum of the saprophytic bacteria only occurs when the phytoplank-

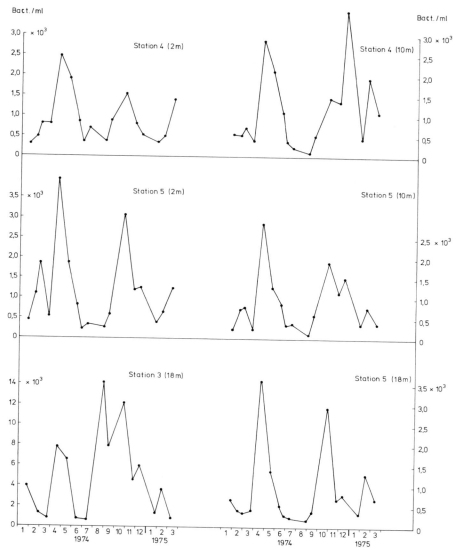

Fig. 11.2. Total numbers of saprophytes in the Kiel Bight (Sts. 3, 4, and 5)

ton population is already decreasing. With the death of the plankton cells, the saprophytic bacteria receive abundant nutrients so that they can multiply vigorously. In the spring the number of saprophytes increases at about the same time as the amount of phytoplankton, but decreases more strongly in May or June. During the summer maximum of phytoplankton production, the saprophyte number even drops to a minimum. The relatively high water temperature certainly plays a role in this reciprocal development during the summer months. The turn-over of materials occurs so rapidly that a vigorous development of the heterotrophic microorganisms is hardly possible. At the same time the zooplankton greatly increases during the warm seasons, whereby the phytoplankton crop is consumed to a high extent. Since many zooplankters use also bacteria and fungi as food, the summer increase of zooplankton can also have a direct negative influence on the amount of saprophytic bacteria. This should not be overestimated, however, since the total bacteria numbers determined for the months of July and August by means of fluorescent microscopy were relatively high (see Chap. 10). Accordingly the main reason for the summer decrease of the saprophyte numbers is most likely the less favorable nutritive conditions for this group of bacteria.

A comparison of the saprophyte numbers found in the water of the Kiel Fjord and Kiel Bight with the total bacteria numbers determined by the method of fluorescence microscopy (see Chap. 10) shows that the former undergo much greater regional and seasonal fluctuations. Thus in 1974 in the yearly averages of the investigated profile from Stations 1 to 5, there was a decrease in the total saprophyte number down to 1/50, and in the total number of bacteria of 1/2. The seasonal fluctuations in the saprophyte number are also greater than in the total number of bacteria, even if the differences here are not quite as great as the regional. A similar situation was also found in the brackish water area of the Elbe estuary. From this it can be concluded that the saprophytic bacteria react especially rapidly to changes in the environment—particularly in the concentration of easily degradable organic substances. This is confirmed in an investigation by Gocke (1975) on the short-term variations of the heterotrophic activity in the considerably polluted Kiel Fjord, in which a good correlation between the saprophyte numbers and the maximal uptake velocity of glucose and acetate could be determined (see Chap. 15).

In the inner Kiel Fjord the saprophyte numbers are, as a rule, somewhat higher than in the Elbe estuary between Brunsbüttel and Cuxhaven, where comparable salinities have at times been measured. The percentages of the colonies growing on the fresh water media ZL and N of the total saprophyte numbers are quite similar in these otherwise two very different brackish water areas. The total saprophyte numbers are generally higher in the Kiel Bight (Sts. 3–5) than in the middle and eastern Baltic Sea—but lower, however, than in the brackish water area of the German Bay (North Sea).

The coliform numbers (see Table 11.7) were highest, as a rule, at Station 1 in the inner Kiel Fjord and, except on two occasions, were greater at 2-m depth than at 10 m. On the tricolored agar according to Gassner, the numbers in the surface water varied between 3 and 96 per ml. Only on January 24 and December 10, 1974 were more coliform bacteria found at Station 2 in the outer Kiel Fjord than at Station 1 in the inner Fjord. In the Kiel Bight the values were always considerably lower. At Station 3 these were mostly less than five, and further out at Stations 4 and 5, below one colony per ml. In many cases no colonies could be demonstrated in 10 ml of water. The average values can be seen in Table 11.5. A stronger fecal contamination is thus confined to the Kiel Fjord, and, outside the investigated profile area, to a relatively narrow zone of waste water outlets. Before the purification plant of the Kiel city was erected at Bülk, at times very high coliform

Table 11.7. Coliforms per 1 on Gassner-medium after 48 h

Date	Station 1		Station 2		Station 3			Station 4		Station 5		
	2 m	10 m	2 m	10 m	2 m	10 m	18 m	2 m	10 m	2 m	10 m	18 m
Jan. 24, 1974	35,000	26,000	45,500	39,000	4,000	5,500	14,000	0	0	500	500	3,000
Feb. 14	71,000	15,000	1,000	500	0	0	0	1,000	1,000	0	0	0
Feb. 28	4,000	2,000	3,500	6,000	500	1,000	0	0	0	500	0	0
March 21	16,000	12,000	0	330	0	0	330	0	0	0	0	0
April 18	10,000	0	660	3,660	0	0	330	0	0	0	0	330
May 16	64,660	660	3,000	0	0	667	667	330	0	670	0	0
June 11	13,333	3,333	0	300	0	0	0	0	333	0	0	333
June 25	2,000	670				333		1,500				
July 11	5,330	300			3,333		333					
Aug. 7	3,333	333										
Aug. 29	29,000	333	3,670	0		333	333	0	0	0	0	0
Sept. 12	15,000	10,667	4,333	7,000	3,333	1,000	333	0	0	0	0	0
Oct. 24[a]	96,333	30,000	8,000	15,333	677	1,000	677	0	0	0	0	333
Nov. 21	25,333	8,667	8,000	5,333	1,000	1,333	15,333	0	667	1,000	17,333	333
Dec. 10	13,000	15,666	30,000	36,666	1,333	3,666	3,333		333	0	0	0
Jan. 23, 1975	20,667	22,333	333	12,667	3,666	5,667	2,000	667	1,000	0	0	333
Feb. 12	16,667	7,000	2,000	1,333	0	333	1,667	0	0	0	333	0
March 10	35,667	3,667	10,333	1,333		0	10,000	9,333		0	2,333	0

[a] After 24 h.

Table 11.8. Coliforms per l on Endo-pads after 48 h

Date	Station 1		Station 5		
	2 m	10 m	2 m	10 m	18 m
Jan. 24, 1974	9,500	2,500	10	230	200
Feb. 14	14,000	1,000	0	0	0
Feb. 28	0	0	0	0	0
March 21	25,000	7,500	0	0	0
April 18	3,000	0	0	0	0
May 16	0	0	0	10	0
June 11	13,000	2,000	0	0	0
June 25	3,500	0	560	0	0
July 11	14.500	2,500	0	0	0
Aug. 7	500	0			
Aug. 29	25,000	1,000	13	0	0
Sept. 12	6,500	14,500	10	110	10
Oct. 24	190,000	7,000	40	510	540
Nov. 21	23,000	15,000	310	620	690
Dec. 10	23,000	24,500	90	70	20
Jan. 23, 1975	13,000	12,500	40	80	180
Feb. 12	17,500	5,000	30	10	50
March 10	100,000	4,500	0	10,000	60

numbers could be found, although at a distance of 1–2 km away higher values were only seldom measured (see Sadjedi, 1971; Rheinheimer, 1975a). It could be shown that the coliforms die off very quickly in the brackish water of the Baltic Sea. For this reason, the coliform numbers in the coastal areas should be evaluated differently than in inland bodies of water, and the values measured in the Kiel Fjord show that there is still a relatively heavy load of pollution here.

The coliform counts are greater in the winter than in the summer (see Table 11.5). They show therefore a different seasonal cycle than the saprophyte numbers. The higher values in the winter are due to the longer survival time of allochthonous bacteria at lower water temperatures (see Rheinheimer, 1975a).

For samples form Stations 1 and 5, coliform counts were also determined with the aid of Endo nutrient pads (see Sect. 11.1). The number of colonies with a metallic shine (see Table 11.8) often deviates from those found on the tricolored agar according to Gassner, since with this method a somewhat different spectrum of endobacteria is included—but on the whole, a similar picture is presented with regard to both their regional and seasonal distribution.

In spite of relatively heavy pollution load in the Kiel Fjord, the microflora in this area is, on the whole, likewise influenced more indirectly by the contamination, whereby the phytoplankton plays an important role as supplier of organic nutrients. Because of this, the curves representing the saprophyte numbers at stations in the Kiel Fjord have a shape similar to those in the much less polluted Kiel Bight—the expected large variations are shown only by the absolute values.

11.3 Distribution of Marine, Brackish Water
and Fresh Water Bacteria in the Sediments

The saprophyte numbers of the uppermost sediment zone show quite large differences at Stations 1, 4, and 5 which were investigated. The total saprophyte numbers which were found on the agar media ZS or ZB prepared with sea water mixtures (see Sect. 11.1), as well as the colony counts determined on the medium ZL prepared with fresh water, are listed in Table 11.9. Next to the values counted directly for 1 cm^3 wet sediment, the values calculated for 1 g dry sediment are also included. The latter is always considerably higher for muddy sediments and lower for sandy sediments, than the former.

The highest total saprophyte numbers were found with one exception (25.6.74) at Station 1 in the inner Kiel Fjord. Here they were between 340,000 and 65,500,000 per cm^3 wet sediment, and between 850,000 and 327,500,000 per g dry sediment respectively. The sediment is a nutrient-rich muddy material, which is anaerobic beneath the surface and contains hydrogen sulfide.

The sandy sediment at Station 4 in the Kiel Bight has—again with one exception (24.1.74)—the lowest total saprophyte numbers. These vary between 34,000 and 1,613,000 per cm^3 wet sediment or 21,000 and 1,015,000 per g dry sediment.

The values determined for Station 5 lie generally between those for the first two stations. They vary between 195,000 and 3,122,000 per cm^3 wet sediment or 390,000 and 6,937,000 per g dry sediment. At this station there is also muddy sediment which is, however, less nutrient-rich than in the comparatively strongly polluted inner Kiel Fjord.

The proportions of bacteria growing on the fresh water medium ZL of the total saprophyte numbers differ in the sediment only very little from those in the water, and lie almost always under 30%. The lowest is from the sandy sediment of Station 4 (see Table 11.10). The percentages are 6.9% for Station 1, 4.3% for Station 4 and 8.9% for Station 5. The rather low proportion of terrestrial bacteria, even for the relatively heavily polluted Station 1 in the inner Kiel Fjord, shows that these bacteria, along with those allochthonous forms carried in with the sewage, mostly have only a limited time of survival also in the sediments (see Rheinheimer, 1975a). Therefore the breakdown of organic matter in the sediments is also mainly due to the halophilic marine and brackish water bacteria. Accordingly, the proportion of the bacteria growing on the fresh-water medium ZL (and similarly on N) in the muddy sediments at Stations 1 and 5, is distinctly higher in the winter months than during the summer (see Table 11.10). In the relatively nutrient-poor sandy sediment at Station 4, on the other hand, the proportion of these bacteria shows stronger fluctuations throughout the entire year.

The seasonal variations in the saprophyte numbers (see Table 11.9) is also of great interest, although in the sediments these are not as distinct as in the water. In the nutrient-rich mud of the most strongly polluted Station 1, the highest values are found in August and September with smaller peaks in May–June as well as on 12.2.1975. The lowest total saprophyte numbers were found in the winter. At Stations 4 and 5 in the Kiel Bight, the maxima of the total saprophyte

Table 11.9. Total saprophyte counts and numbers of fresh water-growing bacteria of the uppermost sediment zone at Stations 1, 4 and 5 for 1 cm³ fresh sediment and 1 g dry sediment

| | Total saprophyte number | | | | | | Bacteria number on fresh water medium ZL | | | | | |
| | Station 1 | | Station 4 | | Station 5 | | Station 1 | | Station 4 | | Station 5 | |
	1 cm³	1 g	1 cm³	1 g	1 cm³	1 g	1 cm³	1 g	1 cm³	1 g	1 cm³	1 g
Jan. 24, 1974	913	3,042	610	381	490	980	353	1,175	4	2	70	140
Feb. 14	1,070	3,566	34	21	555	1,388	178	592	5	3	128	319
Feb. 28	1,371	4,571	100	59	256	427	214	713	9	5	64	106
March 21	1,838	6,125	135	90	325	756	453	1,508	6	4	90	209
April 18	1,393	4,976	50	31	563	1,024	337	1,202	6	4	28	51
May 16	23,242	70,429	96	62	3,122	6,937	1,875	5,682	10	6	43	96
June 11	20,033	74,198	120	78	968	2,306	1,967	7,284	17	11	100	238
June 25	1,985	7,352	1,613	1,015	2,665	6,500	442	1,636	11	6	38	93
July 11	17,433	51,275	117	113	985	2,189	550	1,618	18	12	45	100
Aug. 29	65,500	327,500	57	47	1,313	2,625	2,083	10,417	6	5	54	88
Sept. 12	38,333	127,778	86	58	870	967	567	1,889	7	5	83	93
Oct. 24	15,500	51,667	299	199	475	950	500	1,667	33	22	107	213
Nov. 21	28,150	93,833	262	174	1,445	2,408	633	2,111	13	9	48	81
Dec. 10	7,470	24,900	160	100	230	575	283	945	9	5	40	100
Jan. 23, 1975	4,998	9,997	63	49	745	1,490	263	527	10	8	170	340
Feb. 12	22,933	114,667	603	335	1,067	2,667	6,500	32,500	25	14	223	558
March 10	340	850	153	95	195	390	103	258	6	4	112	223

Table 11.10. Percentage of fresh water medium ZL growing bacteria on total saprophyte numbers in sediment

Date	Station 1	Station 4	Station 5
Jan. 24, 1974	38.7%	0.7%	14.3%
Feb. 14	16.6	14.7	23.1
Feb. 28	15.6	9.0	25.0
March 21	24.6	4.4	27.7
April 18	24.2	12,0	5.0
May 16	8.1	10,4	1.4
June 11	9.8	14.2	10.3
June 25	22.3	0.7	1.4
July 11	3.2	15.4	4.6
Aug. 29	3.2	10.5	4.1
Sept. 12	1.5	8.1	9.5
Oct. 24	3.2	11.0	22.5
Nov. 21	2.2	5.0	3.3
Dec. 10	3.8	5.6	17.4
Jan. 23, 1975	5.3	15.9	22.8
Feb. 12	28.3	4.1	20.9
March 10	30.3	3.9	57.4

numbers occurred in May or June and the minima again in winter. After a decrease beginning in the late summer, the values then rise again in the fall. These observations agree completely with those on the seasonal distribution of saprophytes in the water column. Occasional rather high and particularly low values found in the winter are probably related to changes in the sediment surface due to stirring up and displacement by strong deep currents caused by storms.

The amount of bacteria rapidly decreases with increasing depth of the sediment. The total saprophyte number in a 5-cm horizon is mostly only a fraction of that on the surface, and continues to decrease further. Saprophytic bacteria have still been found, however, even in the deeper horizons.

References

Gassner, G.: Ein neuer Dreifarbennährboden zur Typhus-Ruhr-Diagnose. Zblt. Bakt. Abt. I. **80**, 219–222 (1918)

Gocke, K.: Short-term variations of heterotrophic activity in the Kiel Fjord. Mar. Biol. **33**, 127–135 (1975)

Rheinheimer, G.: Beobachtungen über den Einfluß von Salzgehaltsschwankungen auf die Bakterienflora der westlichen Ostsee. Sarsia **34**, 253–262 (1968)

Rheinheimer, G.: Über das Vorkommen von Brackwasserbakterien in der Ostsee. Vie et Milieu, Suppl. **22**, 281–291 (1971)

Rheinheimer, G.: Mikrobiologie der Gewässer. 2nd ed. Jena, Stuttgart: Fischer, 1975a

Rheinheimer, G.: Beziehungen zwischen Bakterienzahl und bakterieller Aktivität im Wasser. Mitt. Slowak, Akad. Wiss. (in press, 1975b)

Sadjedi, F.: Qualitative und quantitative Untersuchungen zum Vorkommen der coliformen Bakterien im Bereich der westlichen Ostsee. Thesis Univ. Kiel (1971)

Schlieper, C. (ed.): Methoden der meeresbiologischen Forschung. Jena: Fischer, 1968

12. Distribution of Special Physiological Bacteria Groups

M. BÖLTER

The bacteriological properties of a water mass may be studied by different methods in order to determine physiological bacteria groups quantitatively and qualitatively. One possibility is to use solid and fluid media. These may give sufficient data by using the plate or MPN (Most Probable Number) technique (Schlieper, 1968). Thus one may follow the fluctuations of bacteria populations in correlation to the salt content of the water by using yeast extract media with different salt concentrations (Rheinheimer, 1968). Such methods are also suitable for detecting specific bacteria groups such as chitin and cellulose-digesting bacteria (Kadota, 1956; Lehnberg, 1972). This chapter deals with the colony-forming units (cfu) on different peptone media, the spore-forming, chitinoclastic, and cellulolytic bacteria, their regional and seasonal distribution.

12.1 Material and Methods

The poured-plate method was used to determine the number of colony-forming bacteria. The following media were used:

1. Medium for counting saprophytic bacteria (S 16‰) (cf Chap. 11)
peptone (Difco)	5.0 g
yeast extract (Difco)	1.0 g
aged sea water	500 ml
distilled water	500 ml
pH after sterilisation	
(120° C/15 min)	7.6

2. Medium with diluted nutrients
peptone	0.5 g
yeast extract	0.1 g
aged sea water	500 ml
distilled water	500 ml
pH after sterilization	
(120° C/15 min)	7.6

3. Medium for counting spore-forming bacteria
   Prior to plate, the water sample was treated for 20 min at 80° C to kill the vegetative cells. For composition of the medium see (1).

4. Medium for counting chitinoclastic bacteria

Chitin (no. CH 051, Schuchardt) was used as sole carbon source in the medium (Skerman, 1967, modified). The chitin suspension and the water sample were mixed aseptically in a petri dish.

5. Medium for counting cellulolytic bacteria

The determination of cellulolytic bacteria was carried out using a simplified MPN technique. One ml of the undiluted and diluted sample (1:10, 1:100) was added to 25 ml of a sterile basal medium in an Erlenmeyer flask. In addition to this, 10 and 100 ml of the water sample were filtered through 0.2 μm cellulose acetate membrane filters (Sartorius). These filters were also added to sterile basal medium.

Beside this medium the flasks contain a strip of chromatography paper (no. 2043 b, Schleicher and Schüll). The basal medium contains (according to Lehnberg, 1972, modified):

peptone	0.5 g
NaCl	15.0 g
$Na_2HPO_4 \cdot 2H_2O$	0.5 g
NH_4NO_3	0.5 g
KNO_3	0.5 g
$FePO_4$	0.01 g
distilled water	1000 ml
pH after sterilization	
(120° C/15 min)	7.6

In most instances cellulolytic bacteria can be detected by colored colonies on the chromatography paper and by mazeration of the paper.

The determination of colony-forming bacteria on medium (1) was carried out with five parallels. The determination on medium (2) took place with ten parallels for the water samples from the surface (2 m).

The examination of the peptone media was carried out after two weeks' incubation at 20° C. The examinations for chitinoclastic and cellulolytic bacteria were carried out after a maximum incubation at 20° C of four weeks.

12.2 Results and Discussion

The results of the determination of saprophytic bacteria in the Kiel Fjord and Kiel Bight counted on medium (1) are summarized in Table 12.1 column (1). By using five parallels and optimal dilutions, their confidence range of the average runs up to 9%.

The numbers in column (1) were compared with those in columns (2)–(4) by using correlation coefficients, which are presented in the matrix (Table 12.2).

The colony numbers in column (1) show the highest values. This can be reduced to more favorable dilutions. The colonies per plate were in the range that is required for statistical analysis (v. Soestbergen and Lee, 1969).

Less colony counts were obtained by Meyer-Reil (pers. comm.) who was using a medium with filter-sterilized natural sea water.

Table 12.1. Results of the determination of colony-forming bacteria

Date	Station 1						Station 5					
	Delut.	(1) Colony number	±S (%)	(2) Colony number	(3) Colony number	(4) Colony number	Delut.	(1) Colony number	±S (%)	(2) Colony number	(3) Colony number	(4) Colony number
Sept. 12, 1974	1:200	81,000	7.5	54,000	3,200	21,030	1:100	23,500	7.7	75	28	78
Oct. 24	1:2,000	162,000	2.1	98,666	17,970	39,730	1:100	6,700	18.4	2,933	19	65
Nov. 21	1:200	36,100	4.5	32,400	1,130	3,330	1:100	5,500	5.2	1,207	34	120
Dec. 10	1:200	93,300	18.0	48,066	1,300	60,570	1:10	3,000	9.8	1,257	15	125
Jan. 23, 1975	1:100	10,400	1.1	10,200	1,600	4,800	1:10	500	11.6	333	13	42
Feb. 12	1:100	16,100	4.8	19,667	2,100	4,130	1:10	1,000	13.5	460		
March 10	1:200	17,900	13.1	17,000			1:10	700	9.2	468		

Column (1) contains the averages of five parallels with their standard deviations of the average in percent.
Column (2) contains the numbers of saprophytic bacteria on brackish water medium (S 8‰) after Rheinheimer (pers. comm.).
Column (3) contains the colony-forming units on the medium which was set up with water of Station 1 and 5, respectively.
Column (4) contains the colony-forming units on medium (3) with an addition of 0.5 g peptone/l.
The last two columns are data of Meyer-Reil (pers. comm.)

Table 12.2. Correlation matrix of the colony numbers on different media (listed in Table 12.1)

Station 1 Colony number in column	2	3	4
1	0.9848[a]	0.8211[a]	0.7581
2		0.8683[a]	0.6331
3			0.3499

Station 5 Colony number in column	2	3	4
1	0.8988[a]	0.5799	0.3257
2		0.1004	−0.1868
3			0.3571

[a] Correlation coefficients indicate a correlation by 1 or 5% error, respectively. The correlation analysis at Station 5 was performed by omitting the data Sept. 12.

Nevertheless significant correlations could be shown between columns (1), (2), and (3) (St. 1) and between columns (1) and (2) (St. 5). A medium prepared with one tenth of the normal nutrient concentrations was used to determine colony numbers from water samples of 2, 10, and 18 m, respectively. According to Buck (1974) such medium may give better results in coastal areas. The counts are presented in Table 12.3. Generally, a smaller colony size was obtained on this medium. This fact is obviously due to the lower nutrient concentration. The results show a clear decrease in the number of saprophytic bacteria from the Kiel Fjord to the Kiel Bight (cf. Chap. 11), though the number of cfu are not always higher or lower than those on the medium used by Rheinheimer (see Chap. 11). Using this medium, it was impossible to show an evident tendency for a different fraction of bacteria to grow on the agar medium (2). Bissonnette et al. (1975) and Buck (1974) found such fractionation in their investigation. Results of Ishida and Kadota (1974), who also used media with different nutrient concentrations, show considerably different numbers of bacteria counted by using diluted media.

An increase of the ratio of bacteria growing on diluted media and bacteria growing on media with normal strength of nutrient concentration parallel to the distance from the mouth of a river, which may be regarded as an inlet of organic material, was stated by Ishida and Kadota (1974). Table 12.3 shows such increase of the ratio of colony numbers column (1)/colony numbers column (2) in less magnitude for the data of 11.6., and 29.8.1974, the ratio becomes 0.2 at Station 1 up to 10.0 at Station 4 (29.8.74).

The data of 16.5.1974 yield no clear slope. Perhaps other influences, such as stress or adaptation to the given nutrient concentration, overlap a detectable fractionation. The splitting of the population is evident by the media used by Meyer-Reil [cf. columns (3) and (4), Table 12.1]. Significant correlation coeffi-

Table 12.3. Results of the determination of colonyforming bacteria on medium (2) (tenth nutrient concentration) in comparison with results of other media [column (1)]

Date	16. 5. 1974				11. 6. 1974						29. 8. 1974					
Station/ depth	Delut.	(1) Colony number	±S (%)	(2) Colony number	Delut.	(1) Colony number	±S (%)	(2) Colony number	(3) Colony number	(4) Colony number	Delut.	(1) Colony number	±S (%)	(2) Colony number	(3) Colony number	(4) Colony number
1/2 m	1:200	67,900	8.0	30,600	1:200	83,900	22.9	93,400	8,000	12,630	1:2,000	17,000	64.1	82,260	54,970	193,870
1/8 m	1:10	3,300	10.5	17,053	1:200	12,800	3.6	44,600			1:200	550	18.2	4,600		
2/2 m	1:10	3,300	3.9	26,933	1:100	57,000	14.3	33,400			1:10	3,600	25.4	3,490		
2/10 m	1:2	600	2.2	2,850	1:100	11,500	35.7	5,803			1:100	4,100	21.4	1,043		
3/2 m	1:2	700	4.5	3,433	1:10	4,300	9.9	797			1:10	2,800	23.7	510		
3/18 m	1:2	2,000	9.4	1,029	1:10	3,700	15.9	610			1:10	2,300	59.5	7,903		
4/2 m	1:2	2,100	5.6	1,048	1:10	2,500	32.7	729			1:10	3,700	15.9	371		
4/10 m	1:2	1,200	16.3	1,627	1:10	2,800	31.4	1,104			1:10	500	14.0	109		
5/2 m	1:2	1,200	13.8	1,360	1:100	7,900	54.1	812	5	55	1:10	480	34.2	243	25	41
5/18 m					1:100	4,600	26.8	529			1:10	450	52.9	155		

Legend for columns 2–4 see Table 1

cients were found between the numbers of colonies growing on agar plates prepared with the normally used strength and one tenth of nutrient concentrations. This shows that the methods used give comparable dates within their confidence limits.

At Station 1 correlations were found between the numbers of colonies obtained by the medium (1) and the numbers of colonies listed in columns (2) and (3), Table 12.1. This is obviously due to the fact that there exists a spectrum of omnipotent bacteria.

No correlation was found between the plate counts and the direct counts (Chap. 10). Such a correlation was not expected, because only a limited spectrum of naturally occurring bacteria is able to grow on agar plates.

Spore-forming bacteria show an unregular fluctuation in their numbers. It is evident that this group has its main distribution in the sediments. The highest number of spore-forming bacteria was found in the sediment at Station 1 (average 4000 cfu ml^{-1} wet sediment). Less numbers of spore-forming bacteria were found at Stations 4 and 5 (430 cfu ml^{-1} and 2000 cfu ml^{-1} on average, respectively). This obviously depends on the properties of the different stations: at Station 1 we find mainly mud, rich in nutrients, at Station 4 gravel sediment (average grain size 0.238–0.410 mm, Weise 1975), and at Station 5 a less nutrient-rich mud sediment.

Investigations of Rüger (1975) in the Skagerrak show a similar fluctuation of the number of spore-forming bacteria. The data are in relation to the properties of the sediments, i.e., on average ten-fold higher numbers were found on many sediments with high nutrient concentration, 2.8–4.9% organic material in dry weight (Rüger, pers. comm.). No noticeable fluctuations of spore-forming bacteria were found in the water (average: 10 cfu ml^{-1}). An influence of the sediments on the water column above was not demonstrable.

Chitinoclastic bacteria show no marked seasonal fluctuations. A slight maximum was found in the inner Kiel Fjord at Station 1 in the period from 11.7.–12.9.1974. However, the numbers of these bacteria in the central Kiel Bight at Station 5 were lower. The data show maxima in the numbers of chitinoclastic bacteria in the sediments and the water column above. This may be explained by streams near the bottom which whirl the mud layer or prevent the sedimentation of planktonic material (cf. Chap. 3). The surface water samples represent the maximum of activity of chitinoclastic bacteria for only 16% of all samples (see Fig. 12.1).

The cellulolytic bacteria also show only small fluctuation (Fig. 12.2). The reciprocal value of the highest dilution with a positive result was defined as the MPN. Because the highest dilution was overgrown in some cases, the number of cellulolytic bacteria must be considered to be higher.

Over the investigation period, cellulolytic bacteria were found in the Kiel Fjord at Stations 1 and 2 in the water and sediments. However, only very little or even no cellulolytic activity was found in the Kiel Bight at Stations 3, 4, and 5. The numbers found at Stations 1 and 2 may be due to the influence of land and drainages, whose effect is less at the outer stations. A correlation between the cellulolytic activity determined by tensile strength of an exposed rope and the water temperature, as found by Lehnberg (1972) in the Kiel Fjord, was not noticed.

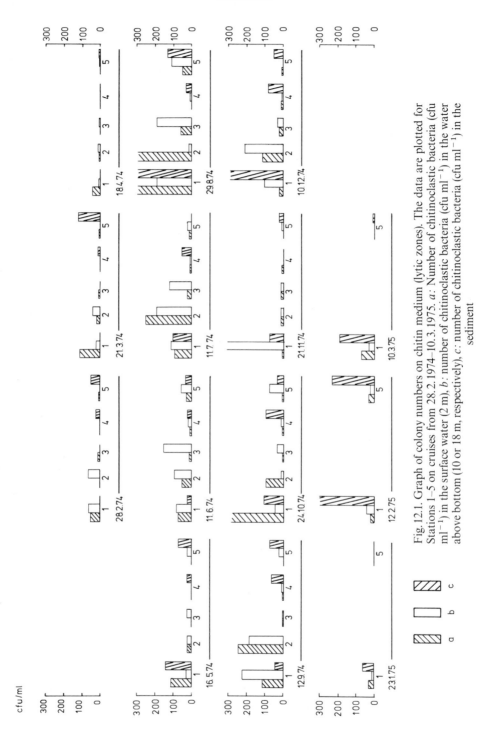

Fig. 12.1. Graph of colony numbers on chitin medium (lytic zones). The data are plotted for Stations 1–5 on cruises from 28.2.1974–10.3.1975. *a*: Number of chitinoclastic bacteria (cfu ml^{-1}) in the surface water (2 m), *b*: number of chitinoclastic bacteria (cfu ml^{-1}) in the water above bottom (10 or 18 m, respectively), *c*: number of chitinoclastic bacteria (cfu ml^{-1}) in the sediment

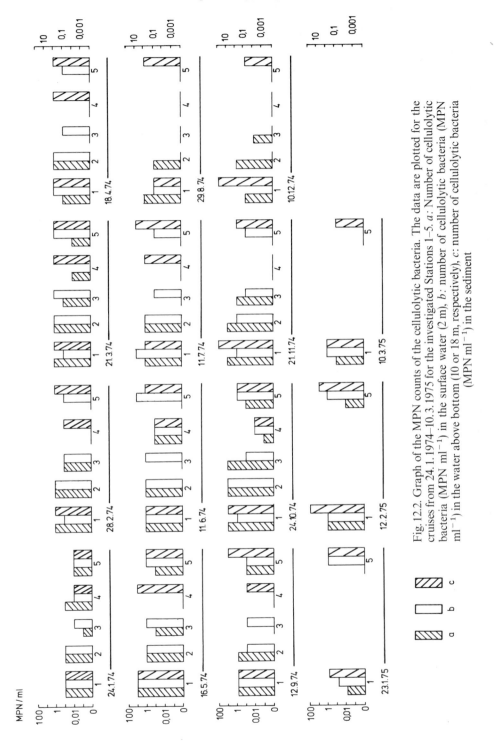

Fig. 12.2. Graph of the MPN counts of the cellulolytic bacteria. The data are plotted for the cruises from 24.1.1974–10.3.1975 for the investigated Stations 1–5. a: Number of cellulolytic bacteria (MPN ml^{-1}) in the surface water (2 m), b: number of cellulolytic bacteria (MPN ml^{-1}) in the water above bottom (10 or 18 m, respectively), c: number of cellulolytic bacteria (MPN ml^{-1}) in the sediment

There is no significant correlation between the number of cellulolytic and chitinoclastic bacteria and other parameters, such as phytoplankton data, as was noticed by Lear (1961), Seki and Taga (1963) and others. Data of zooplankton were not determined in this study. However, one may expect relations to the phyto-plankton data (see Chap. 5), because these are closely related to zooplankton.

On the other hand, the variety of chitinoclastic bacteria is very large (see Campbell and Williams, 1951; Clarke and Tracy, 1956). One has also to consider that chitin digestion is only one property of those bacteria which normally grow on agar plates enriched with chitin. Maxima in the number of chitinoclastic bacteria correspond with the maxima in the the number of the saprophytic bacteria (29.8.1974). A correlation at the confidence level of 95% between chitino-clastic saprophytes and bacteria growing on chitin plates exists only at Station 5 (for further data see Chap. 13). It is not possible to give a clear explanation on the extreme values of chitinoclastic bacteria in the water of Stations 1 and 2 in August and at Station 1 in November. Although one can find high values of some plankton data (see Chap. 5), these data do not correspond with the plankton data at all. Different populations as described for water, plankton and detritus („Aufwuchs") (Seki and Taga 1963, Shimuda et al., 1971, Taga and Matsuda, 1974) may be a reason that no correlation with plankton data were found. Nevertheless, according to Zimmermann (Chap. 10), only few bacteria are attached to detritus. At those times, when high numbers of chitinoclastic bacteria existed, no remarkable increase in detritus was established (Zimmermann, pers. comm.).

The represented results of seasonal fluctuation of various bacteria groups may show many relationships to other parameters. Further investigations are needed and other comparisons have to be effected (see Chap. 19).

References

Bissonnette, G. K., Jezeski, J. J., Macfeters, G. A., Stuart, D. G.: Influence of environmental stress on enumeration of indicator bacteria from natural waters. Appl. Microbiol. **29**, 186–194 (1975)

Buck, J. D.: Effect of medium composition on the recovery of bacteria from sea water. J. Exp. Mar. Biol. Ecol. **15**, 25–34 (1974)

Campbell, L. L., Williams, O. B.: A study of chitin-decomposing micro-organisms of marine origin. J. Gen. Microbiol. **5**, 894–905 (1951)

Clarke, P. H., Tracey, M. V.: The occurrence of chitinase in some bacteria. J. Gen. Microbiol. **14**, 188–196 (1956)

Ishida, Y., Kadota, H.: Ecological studies on the bacteria in the Sea and Lake waters polluted with organic substances. I. Responses of bacteria to different concentrations of organic substances. Bull. Jap. Soc. Sci. Fish. **40**, 999–1005 (1974)

Kadota, H.: A study of marine aerobic cellulose-decomposing bacteria. — Mem. Coll. Agric. Kyoto 74 (Fish. Ser. 6): 1–128 (1956)

Lear, D. W.: Occurrence and significance of chitinoclastic bacteria in pelagic waters and zooplankton. Bact. Proc. **61**, 47 (1961)

Lehnberg, B.: Ökologische Untersuchungen an agar- und zellulosezersetzenden Bakterien aus Nord- und Ostsee. Thesis Univ. Kiel (1972)

Rheinheimer, G.: Beobachtungen über den Einfluß von Salzgehaltschwankungen auf die Bakterienflora der westlichen Ostsee. Sarsia **34**, 253–262 (1968)

Rüger, H.-J.: Bakteriensporen in marinen Sedimenten (Nordatlantik, Skagerrak, Biskaya und Auftriebsgebiet vor Nordwestafrika) — quantitative Untersuchungen. Veröff. Inst. Meeresforsch. Bremerh. **15**, 227–236 (1975)

Schlieper, C. (ed): Methoden der meeresbiologischen Forschung. Jena: Fischer (1968)

Seki, H., Taga, N.: Microbial studies on the decomposition of chitin in the marine environment. I.–IV. J. Oceanogr. Soc. Jap. **19**, 101–108, 109–111, 143–151, 152–157 (1963)

Shimuda, U., Ashino, K., Kaneko, E.: Bacterial flora of phyto- and zooplankton in the inshore water of Japan. Can. J. Microbiol. **17**, 1157–1160 (1971)

Skerman, V. D. B.: A Guide to the Identification of the Genera of Bacteria. 2nd ed., Baltimore: Williams and Wilkins Co. (1967)

Soestbergen, A. A. van, Lee, C. H.: Pour plates or streak plates? Appl. Microbiol. **18**, 1092–1093 (1969)

Taga, N., Matsuda, O.: Bacterial populations attached to plankton and detritus in sea water. In: Colwell, R. R., Morita, R. Y. (eds.): Effect of the ocean environment on microbial activities. Baltimore-London-Tokyo, University Park Press, 1974

Weise, W.: Fluoreszenz- und rasterelektronenmikroskopische Untersuchungen über die Bakterienbesiedlung von marinen Sandsedimenten. Diplomarbeit, Univ. Kiel (1975)

13. Numerical Taxonomy and Character Analysis of Saprophytic Bacteria Isolated from the Kiel Fjord and the Kiel Bight

M. BÖLTER

Saprophytic bacteria represent only a small portion of the total number of bacteria in a body of water. This portion may be of great importance with regard to pollution, influences of land and other factors. Saprophytic bacteria may represent a major part of the active bacteria flora at least in coastal areas.

Investigations in the western Baltic Sea over a period of many years showed relationships between the number of saprophytic bacteria and other parameters, e.g., phytoplankton data (Rheinheimer, 1975). Isolations showed that most of the saprophytic bacteria are halophilic organisms adapted to the salinity of brackish water (Rheinheimer, 1971; Meyer-Reil, 1973). Ahrens (1969) pointed out that star-forming brackish water bacteria show a seasonal fluctuation in the Western Baltic Sea. These bacteria reach maximal numbers in late fall.

Therefore it was of interest to follow the fluctuation of the saprophytic bacteria flora to characterize their importance in the Kiel Fjord and Kiel Bight.

The knowledge of the properties of various saprophytic bacteria may be used in order to describe and characterize bodies of water. Such investigations were carried out in other areas with special reference to pathogen bacteria (Bonde, 1968; Kaneko and Colwell, 1974 and others), or physiological groups (Kadota, 1956; Lehnberg, 1972). Other investigators (e.g., Altschuler and Riley, 1967; Sieburth, 1967) followed the fluctuations of saprophytic bacteria populations.

The isolation of bacteria from yeast extract-pepton medium (cf. Chaps. 11, 12) yielded a wide spectrum of bacteria comprising many taxonomic groups (Zobell and Upham, 1944; Anderson, 1964). The determination of freshly isolated marine bacteria becomes a special problem. Mostly the determinations were carried out using key characteristics, e.g., Shewan et al. 1960a, b.

The numerical taxonomy (Sneath, 1957a, b; Sokal and Sneath, 1963) offers the possibility of a quick and comprehensive handling of large numbers of data, which permits following the fluctuation of great portions of bacteria. Oliver and Colwell (1974) employed a method which allows the following of fluctuations of bacterial populations by a special numerical analysis. In this investigation, the attempt was made to follow the fluctuations additionally by comparing the characteristics of the bacteria isolated. In this way it became possible to define adaptations, character complexes, and physiological groups among the saprophytes. Typical bacteria strains are described with special regard to the seasons and stations.

13.1 Material and Methods

13.1.1 Isolation of the Bacteria Strains

The isolation of the bacteria strains was carried out from agar plates which were used to determine the number of saprophytic bacteria (cf. Chap. 11). In the period between January and March 1974 the isolations were carried out according to colony morphological aspects. During April to August 1974 the isolation procedure was modified: sectors of the agar plates which contain approximately 50 colonies were chosen and all bacteria colonies isolated. In the period from September 1974 to March 1975 the following isolation method was used: the water samples were diluted to give an average of 50 colonies per plate, and the total bacteria colonies were isolated. These methods were used for surface samples. The bacteria from other samples (10 m, 18 m, sediments) were isolated under colony morphology aspects. Using these methods, up to 60 bacteria strains were brought in pure cultures for each cruise. By these procedures it became possible to isolate the most abundant saprophytic bacteria. Consequently, this made it possible to describe the saprophytic bacteria population (Altschuler and Riley, 1967; Rovira and Ridge, 1973).

13.1.2 Morphological, Physiological and Biochemical Tests

Many tests are necessary to classify bacteria strains by determination schemes and to compare them by numerical taxonomy. The characters used in this study refere to morphological, physiological, and biochemical aspects (see Table 13.1). Forty four characters were employed in the numerical study (listed in Table 13.2). The choice of the characters was carried out with special regard to the research area. Constant times were used in the examinations and all strains were tested under same conditions. It is very important to analyze the results by numerical taxonomy (Sneath, 1968; Holmberg and Nord, 1975).

13.1.3 Numerical Taxonomy

All characters may be coded as multistate characters (Proctor, 1966; Bölter and Meyer-Reil, 1974; Boeyé and Aerts, 1976). One example shows the coding procedure:

a) two-state character (e.g., indol formation)
not tested: 0
positive result: 1
negative result: 2

b) multistate character (e.g., pigmentation)
not tested: 0
white: 1
yellow: 2
brown: 3

violet:	4
red:	5
fluorescent:	6
ocher:	7
other:	8

In this way, the use of addidative coding was avoided, as this may give too much information and lead to an over-estimation of single characters (Sneath, 1962). The coding of all characters is presented in Table 13.2.

The calculation of the similarity index was carried out according to the equation

$$100 \times \frac{n_s}{n_s + n_d} = S\ (\%),$$

where n_s represents the number of characters shared by two strains, and n_d the number of characters differing between two strains.

The clustering method follows the "single linkage clustering" (Sokal and Sneath, 1963): two strains or two groups are linked together at the highest S values which is shared by two members of these groups.

This study defined that all members of a group must show a similarity of $S \geq 75\%$. The interspecific similarity must be at a level of $S \geq 85\%$. The calculation of the median strains (modoform, Sneath, 1957b) was carried out for each group which has three or more members.

Hypothetical median organisms (HMO) are calculated under the following presumptions: the number of characters of a group (for which the HMO will be calculated) must reach a defined level p. The characters are judged as positive, negative, or variable. These levels are:

$$p > 66\% \triangleq +$$

$$66 > p > 33\% \triangleq \pm$$

$$p < 33\% \triangleq -$$

p is calculated by the equation $p = n/N$, where n represents the number of strains in the group which are positive in the result of the character, and N represents the number of strains in the group. With different levels of p, HMOs have been calculated by many authors (Beers et al., 1962; Colwell, 1964, 1970; Bölter and Meyer-Reil, 1974). In this study, HMOs were calculated for "natural groups", i.e., bacteria strains which were isolated at *one* station or *one* water depth.

Frequency of characters may be determined for all parts of the isolated populations of saprophytic bacteria. These frequencies can be calculated by the equation $p = n/N$, as described above. Thus one may obtain curves of frequencies of characters. By means of correlation analyses, relationships between characters were noticeable, and character complexes able to describe the population, were obtained. The presentation of the results is given in a correlation matrix.

Table 13.1. Tests used for the taxonomic study

Cell morphology:	Size, shape, arrangement, motility. Liquid cultures (medium 2216 E), incubation 24 h, phase contrast microscopy (× 1250).
Gram-stain:	According to Drews (1968).
Colony form, spreading:	Cultures incubated on plates (medium 2216 E), room temperature, 2–4 weeks.
Pigment formation:	Media: 2216 E, 2216 E enriched with starch, alginate, or gelatine. Diffusible pigment: liquid medium 2216 E.
Indol formation:	Medium: 5.0 g Bacto-tryptone is dissolved in a mixture of aged sea water (500 ml), and distilled water (500 ml). Kovac's indol reagent was used to test for indol. Incubation: 5–7 days.
Reaction on Glucose:	MOF medium (Leifson, 1963), modified:

Bacto-peptone   1.0 g
Yeast-extract   0.1 g
Ammoniumsulfate 0.5 g
Tris buffer   0.5 g
Phenol red   0.01 g
Aged sea water   500 ml
Distilled water   500 ml

Glucose (10% in distilled water) was sterilized seperately and added aseptically to the medium to give a concentration of 1%. The tubes are inoculated in duplicate. One tube is overlayed with 3 ml paraffin to test anaerobic reaction. Observation time up to four weeks.

Starch hydrolysis:	Medium 2216 E enriched with 0.5% soluble starch. Incubation time: two weeks.
Chitin digestion:	According to Skerman (1967).
Agar digestion:	Basal medium for chitin digestion. Incubation time: four weeks.
Alginate digestion:	Liquid medium 2216 E enriched with 10% Na-alginate (Roth Co., No. 9180). Incubation time: 10–14 days, test reaction with Fehling solution I and II.
Nitrate reduction:	Medium 2216 E enriched with 0.1% KNO_3. Incubation time up to four weeks, test reaction with Lunge's and Nessler's reagents, gas production was tested with Durham vials.
Ammoniak formation from peptone:	Liquid medium 2216 E, incubation time seven days, test reaction with Nessler's reagent.
Gelatine liquefication:	15% gelatine is added to the sea water mixture (see above). Incubation time up to four weeks.
Catalase production:	Test reaction with 3% H_2O_2.
Oxydase production:	According to Steel (1961).
Salt requirements:	Liquid medium (2216 E) with different NaCl concentrations: 0%, 1.6%, 10%. KCl was used equimolar to 1.6% NaCl. Observations were carried out after incubation of 2 and 14 days, microscopically (see above).

All liquid media were inoculated with one drop of a freshly grown cell suspension (medium 2216 E). Incubation temperatures: 20° C. All chemicals from Merck Co., if not otherwise indicated. More detailed information of the tests is given by Bölter (1976).

Table 13.2. Coding of the characters

Two-state characters are coded as follows:

Positive reaction: 1
Negative reaction: 2
Weak reaction: 3

The codes of two-state characters are not listed.
"not tested" is coded by 0.
Characters which show more than one property are coded as multistate characters (see text).

No.	Character	Result	Code
1	shape of cell	coccus	1
		straight rod	2
		curved rod	3
		spiral	4
		pleomorphic	5
		"horseshoe roll"	6
		other	7
2	size of cell	0–1 μm	1
		1–3 μm	2
		>3 μm	3
3	cell arrangement (predominant form >75%)	single	1
		chains	2
		stars	3
		other	4
4	motility	nonmotile	1
		motile	2
		gliding	3
5	Gram-stain	negative	1
		positive	2
		variable	3
6	colony form	round	1
		other	2
		myceloid	3
7	colony size ∅	<1 cm	1
		∼1 cm	2
		>1 cm	3
8	swarming		
9	pigment formation (medium 2216 E)	white	1
		yellow	2
		brown	3
		violet	4
		red	5
		fluorescent	6
		ocher	7
		other	8

Different pigmentation on:

10	gelatine
11	alginate
12	starch
13	diffusible pigment (liquid medium 2216 E)
14	indol formation

Table 13.2 (continued)

No.	Character	Result	Code

Reaction on glucose (MOF-medium)

15	aerobic acid (oxidative reaction)		
16	anaerobic acid (fermentation)		
17	anaerobic gas		
18	reduction of phenol red (aerobic)		
19	reduction of phenol red (anaerobic)		

Polysaccharids

20	starch hydrolysis		
21	chitin digestion		
22	agar digestion		
23	alginate digestion		

Other tests

24	reduction of nitrate ($\rightarrow NO_2$)		
25	reduction of nitrate ($\rightarrow N_2$)		
26	reduction of nitrate ($\rightarrow NH_3$)		
27	formation of ammoniak from peptone		
28	growth on gelatine	no growth	1
		filamentous growth	2
		other	3
29	gelatine liquefication	no liquefication	1
		cylindrical liquefication	2
		other	3
30	oxydase		
31	catalase		

Growth in

32	0% NaCl		
33	1.6% NaCl		
34	10% NaCl		
35	KCl (equimolar to 1.6% NaCl)		

Changed cell morphology after incubation (14 days) in

36	0% NaCl		
37	10% NaCl		
38	KCl (equimolar to 1.6% NaCl)		

Growth within seven days in

39	0% NaCl		
40	10% NaCl		
41	KCl (equimolar to 1.6% NaCl)		

Positive reaction in MOF-medium within seven days

42	aerobic		
43	anaerobic		
44	reduction of nitrate ($\rightarrow NO_2$ or N_2) within seven days		

13.1.4 Classifying by Key Diagnostics

All bacteria strains are classified into systematic groups using the schemes of Shewan et al. (1960 a, b) and the key diagnostics in Bergey's Manual (Buchanan et al., 1974). These schemes were modified with special regard to the bacteria isolated from the Western Baltic Sea. The percentages of the bacteria in the different groups were calculated. Correlation calculations were carried out to describe their mutual relationships.

Summarizing, the taxonomic analysis was carried out in the following steps:

1. Calculation of the similarity indexes of the bacteria strains isolated during the time of investigation, clustering, calculation of the median strains of the groups, and calculation of the HMOs for the bacteria isolated at Stations 1 and 5, respectively.

2. Comparison of all HMOs with regard to their seasonal fluctuation.

3. Comparison of all median strains of all calculated groups and comparison of all ungrouped bacteria strains to follow their seasonal and regional distribution.

4. Determination of all bacteria strains and median strains by schemes to follow the fluctuation of the taxonomic groups.

5. Frequency of characters, correlations and complexes.

All cruises are coded by capital letters A–S (see Table 13.3).

13.2 Results

The analysis of 704 bacteria strains which were isolated during the different cruises yielded in 50 groups. 527 bacteria strains could be combined in these groups, i.e., 75% of all studied bacteria. The clustering could be done on the average at the 87.5% S level. This corresponds with a conformity of 32–39 from 37–44 characters studied. The results of this analysis are summarized in Table 13.3.

The table shows that isolates of one station or one horizon may already fulfill the qualification of a homogenous group (cf. also Table 13.4). Such "natural groups", as mentioned above, are not considered especially in the following discussion.

Some particularities of the isolated bacteria are described below.

On cruise C (Feb. 28, 1974) a rather homogenous population was isolated at both stations. Bacteria strains form Station 1 and Station 5 are grouped together in the cluster A. Even on the agar plates, from which they were isolated, their colony size and shape as well as their color were very similar. Those colonies represented the dominant part of the bacteria spectrum obtained on agar plates.

On cruise E (April 18, 1974) a curved nonmotile rod was isolated. Such a form was often observed by epifluorescence microscopy (Zimmermann, pers. comm.). On the YEP medium the colony of this bacterium shows a slight pink pigmentation.

Table 13.3. Data of the numerical taxonomic analysis (all strains isolated)

(1) Cruise	(2) Date	(3) Number of isolated bacteria	(4) Number of tested bacteria	(5) % (4) of (3)	(6) Minimal S_{int} of the analysis	(7) Number of clusters	(8) Number of ungrouped strains	(9) % (8) of (4)	(10) Clusters (and their S_{int})	(11) Number of strains per cluster	(12) Number of the median strain and its S_m	(13) S_{itr} of the clusters	(14) S_s of the value for S_{itr}	(15) $S_s/S_{itr} \times 100$
A	Jan. 24, 1974	26	23	88.5	70	3	4	17.4	1 (92)	4	5 91.7	89.17	4.40	4.82
									A (82)	9	8 87.6	81.82	5.96	7.28
									B (82)	6	17 87.0	82.50	6.01	7.28
B	Feb. 14	20	15	75.0	73	2	3	20.0	A (78)	5	1 82.8	78.53	8.15	10.37
									B (84)	7	6 87.5	83.89	6.53	7.78
C	Feb. 28	30	15	50.0	73	2	3	20.0	A (90)	8	11 93.4	89.26	4.39	4.92
									B (87)	4	10 89.5	86.90	4.48	5.15
D	March 21	38	23	60.5	77	3	7	21.2	A (85)	6	11 85.6	86.27	6.99	7.21
									B (88)	7	5 90.9	84.00	6.06	8.10
									3 (86)	3	14 86.2	86.13	0.95	1.10
E	April 18	34	27	79.4	68	1	8	29.6	A (84)	19	18 84.5	80.43	5.86	7.28
F	May 16	78	58	74.4	81	4	16	27.6	A (89)	23	34 90.0	86.77	4.99	5.75
									B (88)	9	51 88.6	86.29	4.83	5.59
									1 (87)	5	55 95.4	92.93	6.20	6.67
									5 (86)	5	20 87.4	82.32	4.79	8.82
G	June 11	53	36	67.9	65	2	11	30.1	A (89)	19	9 90.1	86.04	5.08	5.90
									3 (90)	6	17 91.7	89.74	4.72	5.27
H	June 25	48	29	60.4	79	2	5	17.2	1 (93)	8	18 92.3	90.23	4.08	4.52
									2 (90)	16	16 91.9	88.90	4.47	5.02
J	July 11	60	45	75.0	73	3	9	20.0	A (86)	23	35 82.6	76.90	7.70	10.00
									B (84)	9	42 84.1	80.80	5.44	6.73
									4 (88)	4	15 88.6	87.50	1.20	1.37
K	Aug. 7	32	28	87.5	81	2	11	35.3	A (86)	14	24 88.7	85.26	5.08	5.96
									2 (86)	3	21 86.4	84.97	2.49	2.93
L	Aug. 29	77	48	62.3	79	3	8	16.7	A (88)	19	1 90.5	86.05	5.80	6.74
									B (90)	18	22 94.0	91.15	5.09	5.58
									3 (90)	3	8 91.9	90.70	2.30	2.54

Table 13.3 (continued)

(1) Cruise	(2) Date	(3) Number of isolated bacteria	(4) Number of tested bacteria	(5) % (4) of (3)	(6) Minimal S_{int} of the analysis	(7) Number of clusters	(8) Number of ungrouped strains	(9) % (8) of (4)	(10) Clusters (and their S_{int})	(11) Number of strains per cluster	(12) Number of the median strain and its S_m	(13) S_{itr} of the clusters	(14) S_s of the value for S_{itr}	(15) $S_s/S_{itr} \times 100$
M	Sept. 12	71	39	54.9	77	2	15	38.5	A (89)	21	5 91.8	87.47	4.95	5.66
									3 (88)	3	33 88.7	86.37	4.45	5.15
N	Oct. 24	72	49	68.1	77	1	16	32.7	A (90)	33	14 92.2	89.46	4.30	4.81
O	Nov. 21	64	43	67.2	81	3	5	11.6	A (88)	25	3 92.5	89.29	4.59	5.14
									B (88)	8	18 89.0	85.72	6.33	7.62
									5 (93)	5	16 93.8	92.50	3.05	3.30
P	Dec. 10	62	43	69.4	75	5	7	16.3	A (90)	22	8 89.9	86.76	8.18	9.43
									3 (86)	4	30 85.6	84.10	4.06	4.83
									4 (86)	4	37 90.1	86.75	5.29	6.10
									5 (84)	3	41 90.9	87.87	8.54	9.72
									6 (87)	3	25 87.5	84.83	4.84	5.71
Q	Jan. 23, 1975	101	64	63.4	77	3	10	15.6	A (90)	37	29 91.8	90.23	4.20	4.65
									B (88)	13	52 83.4	80.81	6.45	7.98
									5 (93)	4	33 93.2	91.30	4.43	4.85
R	Feb. 12	76	50	65.8	79	3	18	36.0	A (90)	24	8 88.4	84.71	6.67	7.87
									3 (86)	5	2 85.8	82.29	6.75	8.20
									4 (81)	3	43 81.8	78.77	5.18	6.58
S	March 10	94	69	73.4	79	6	21	30.4	A (90)	28	5 86.8	82.80	5.80	7.00
									5 (90)	4	66 90.2	87.92	5.10	5.80
									6 (86)	6	50 88.8	84.00	5.90	7.02
									7 (88)	4	49 93.8	91.48	3.60	3.94
									8 (86)	3	45 85.9	83.83	8.84	10.54
									9 (87)	3	14 88.2	86.43	3.22	3.73
Sums or averages		1,036	704	68.0	74.5	50	177	22.5	87.5	527	10.2/87.2			

Abbreviations: S_{int}: interspecific S-value; S_{itr}: intraspecific S-value; S_s: standard deviation of the S_{itr}-value; S_m: S-value of the median-strain.

Table 13.4. Statistical data for the "natural groups" (cf. Table 13.3 and text)

Cruise	Date	Station 1 (2 m)				Station 1 (10 m)			
		Number of isolated bacteria	S_{itr}	S_s	$S_s/S_{itr} \times 100$	Number of isolated bacteria	S_{itr}	S_s	$S_s/S_{itr} \times 100$
A[a]	Jan. 24, 1974	3	61.03	13.18	21.6	4	69.58	9.09	4.3
B	Feb. 14	2	67.50			1			
C	Feb. 28	5	75.95	11.32	14.9	0			
D	March 21	4	85.98	6.42	7.2	5	71.78	7.43	10.4
E[b]	April 18	9	77.58	7.69	9.9	0			
F	May 16	14	74.02	9.19	12.4	16	78.69	8.90	11.3
G	June 11	6	80.45	9.87	12.3	5	91.07	3.42	3.8
H	June 25	7	87.42	4.83	5.5	2	88.60		
J	July 11	9	76.58	8.20	10.7	6	78.19	8.92	11.4
K	Aug. 7	11	68.13	12.07	17.7	9	82.59	8.68	10.5
L	Aug. 29	18	80.89	10.36	12.8	5	80.61	7.07	8.8
M	Sept. 12	17	80.50	10.95	13.6	2	56.40		
N[c]	Oct. 24	15	88.70	5.95	6.7	5	85.00	10.60	12.5
O	Nov. 21	14	84.23	10.54	12.5	4	84.85	7.10	8.4
P	Dec. 10	22	82.93	11.14	13.4	2	72.70		
Q[d]	Jan. 23, 1975	34	81.75	10.84	13.3	4	76.00	17.60	23.2
R[d]	Feb. 12	17	77.97	11.77	15.1	2	79.50		
S[d]	March 10	21	76.19	8.55	11.2	8	67.79	8.80	13.0

Table 13.4 (continued)

Cruise	Date	Station 1 (Sed.)				Station 5 (2 m)			
		Number of isolated bacteria	S_{itr}	S_s	$S_s/S_{itr} \times 100$	Number of isolated bacteria	S_{itr}	S_s	$S_s/S_{itr} \times 100$
A[a]	Jan. 24, 1974	3	83.90	7.33	8.7	6	68.13	8.82	12.9
B	Feb. 14	2	75.60			3	88.33	5.85	6.6
C	Feb. 28	4	67.53	7.18	10.6	5	92.68	2.83	3.1
D	March 21	3	81.83	4.64	5.7	5	70.87	9.80	13.8
E[b]	April 18	0				8	81.17	5.60	6.9
F	May 16	4	79.28	7.53	9.5	8	75.56	9.95	13.2
G	June 11	6	77.05	9.98	13.0	7	66.77	13.94	20.9
H	June 25	3	67.00	7.47	11.1	7	75.17	12.74	16.9
J	July 11	7	78.34	6.91	8.8	7	72.75	9.60	13.2
K	Aug. 7	8	80.03	5.79	7.2	0			
L	Aug. 29	2	69.80			16	82.72	15.40	18.6
M	Sept. 12	1				13	76.36	10.66	14.0
N[c]	Oct. 24	3	67.63	5.98	8.8	13	88.30	5.15	5.8
O	Nov. 21	3	84.07	3.82	4.5	12	84.16	8.90	10.6
P	Dec. 10	4	70.43	8.87	12.6	4	70.85	9.49	13.4
Q[d]	Jan. 23, 1975	5	86.36	3.86	4.5	14	77.03	13.86	17.8
R[d]	Feb. 12	5	68.68	5.08	7.4	16	80.77	7.28	9.0
S[d]	March 10	7	73.53	9.62	13.1	18	81.22	7.68	9.5

Table 13.4 (continued)

Cruise	Date	Station 5 (18 m)				Station 5 (Sed.)			
		Number of isolated bacteria	S_{itr}	S_s	$S_s/S_{itr} \times 100$	Number of isolated bacteria	S_{itr}	S_s	$S_s/S_{itr} \times 100$
A[a]	Jan 24, 1974	2	92.70			0			
B	Feb. 14	2	65.90			5	71.53	10.64	14.9
C	Feb. 28	0				1			
D	March 21	0				6			
E[b]	April 18	4	65.15	14.44	22.2	4	67.06	13.51	17.4
F	May 16	10	82.04	7.35	9.0	6	69.67	15.31	22.0
G	June 11	6	71.03	11.55		6	80.59	11.22	13.9
H	June 25	7	85.12	8.83	10.4	3	80.50	8.75	10.9
J	July 11	9	72.29	9.73	13.5	7	79.77	8.81	11.0
K	Aug. 7	0				0	68.66	10.45	15.2
L	Aug. 29	5	81.83	12.64	15.4	2	93.20		
M	Sept. 12	4	69.68	10.84	15.6	2	79.50		
N[c]	Oct. 24	5	75.91	7.37	9.7	6	74.36	11.43	15.4
O	Nov. 21	5	84.33	6.29	7.5	5	78.86	5.47	6.9
P	Dec. 10	5	77.73	12.36	15.9	6	76.69	8.30	9.8
Q[d]	Jan. 23, 1975	4	64.78	16.46	25.4	3	74.53	3.53	4.7
R[d]	Feb. 12	5	73.58	7.50	10.2	5	72.73	11.88	16.3
S[d]	March 10	6	74.91	6.04	8.1	9	79.18	7.07	8.9

[a] Strains 4, 5, 7 were isolated from other stations.
[b] Strains 26, 27 from other stations.
[c] Strains 48, 49 from other stations.
[d] Three strains (cruise Q, R) and four strains (cruise S) were isolated from membrane filters (nuclepore) which laid on an agar plate (medium 2216 E).

On cruise F (May 16, 1974) only little differentiation was found in the bacteria visible on agar plates. Nevertheless, it was possible to distinguish many cells of different morphological shape.

The bacteria isolated on cruise H (June 25, 1974) did not show morphological differences, but they did show differences in their biochemical properties. This gave the possibility of separating the bacterial flora of Stations 1 and 5.

A good differentiation was also possible for the bacteria isolated on cruise L (Aug. 29, 1974). Cluster A includes 22 bacteria strains (19 of them isolated at St. 1), cluster B includes 18 bacteria strains (17 of them isolated at St. 5). The last group may be represented by a median organism which was tentatively determined as *Vibrio parahaemolyticus*.

The bacteria isolated on cruise R (Feb. 12, 1975) form a rather homogeneous group. Using the S values which describe homogeneous populations in the definition used, one may conclude that very similar properties prevail.

More detailed information on the bacteria isolated is given by Bölter (1976).

13.2.1 Numerical Taxonomy of the HMOs

The condensed information included in the HMO may serve for the description of the fluctuations of bacterial populations. Differences in the frequencies of characters analyzed may be due to adaptations or special substrate affinities.

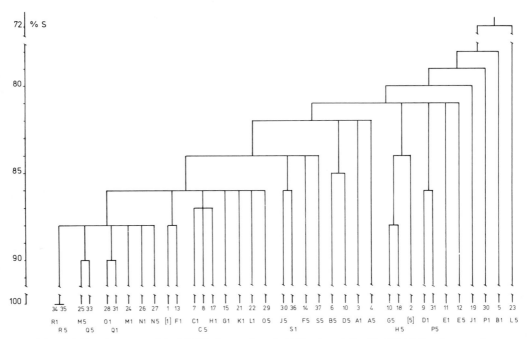

Fig. 13.1. Dendrogram of the HMOs for cruises A–S (Sts. 1 and 5). *A1*: HMO for the population isolated at Station 1 on cruise A (Jan. 24, 1974). [1] and [5]: HMO for all bacteria isolates at Stations 1 and 5, respectively

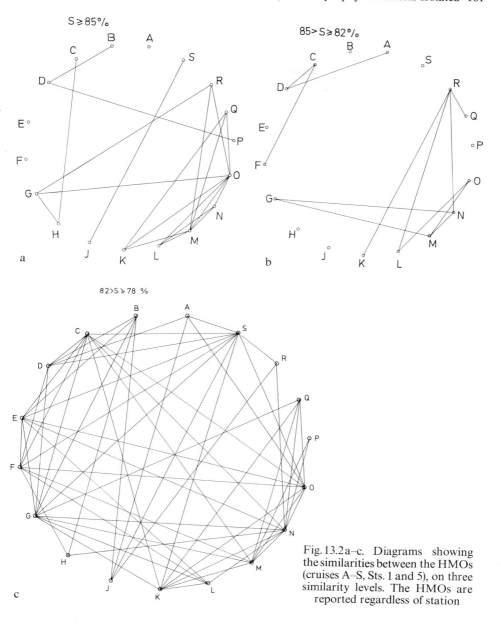

Fig. 13.2a–c. Diagrams showing the similarities between the HMOs (cruises A–S, Sts. 1 and 5), on three similarity levels. The HMOs are reported regardless of station

These characters become significant and are of special interest for determinations and descriptions of an ecological situation.

In the analysis described, 27 characters show such properties: the characters 2, 4, 5, 6, 7, 9, *14, 15, 16, 20, 21, 23, 24*, 26, 27, 28, 29, *31–35*, 38, *39, 41–44*, (for decoding see Table 13.2). Numbers in italics indicate characters which frequently show positive reactions by bacteria strains isolated at Station 5. This means that these bacteria possess a more extensive spectrum of degradation abilities. This fact is particularly of interest for the bacteria isolated at cruises A (Jan. 24, 1974), G (June 11), H (June 25), L (July 11), N (Oct. 24), O (Nov. 21), and P (Dec. 10). Especially during the summer period, such differentiation of the population becomes detectable.

By calculation of the S values, the comparison of the HMOs (Sts. 1 and 5, cruises A–S) results in the dendrogram shown in Figure 13.1. It becomes obvious that the populations isolated on the same cruises but at different stations may either be similar to or may differ from each other. To demonstrate these relationships, the points on the periphery of a circle represent the individual cruises (see Fig. 13.2). Relationships between two HMOs at a given niveau (S value) are represented by a line. The lower the S value is defined, the denser becomes the net of connections between the cruises. In spite of many special forms isolated during the investigation period, high similarities between the HMOs of various cruises are found.

13.2.2 Comparison of the Median Strains and Ungrouped
Strains by Numerical Taxonomy

The median strains represent a larger spectrum of bacteria than the HMOs. The taxonomic analysis of all strains isolated yielded 50 groups (see Table 13.3) and consequently 50 median strains for further analyzing. According to the given definition (see Sect. 13.1), each median strain represents at least two other bacteria of its group in their characters. Maximally, 32 strains were summarized in one group. Indeed, a loss of character complexes and special character combinations takes place regarding the whole populations. On the other hand, one obtains a surveyable spectrum and many incidental variations are eliminated.

The median strains may also be regarded as an information pool for the groups. The comparison of all median strains available may give more detailed information on the fluctuation of the population. If high similarities exist between median strains over a long period of time or for different stations, it may be suspected that similar types of bacteria populations prevail. Furthermore, in this case similar conditions must have favored the selection of these bacteria.

Figure 13.3 shows the dendrogram of the median strains analyzed. Four clusters are distinguishable at $S = 92\%$. These clusters may be termed homogeneous: the intraspecific S values are 90.97% (cluster 1), 88.78% (cluster 2), 89.53% (cluster 3), and 90.34% (cluster 4). The members of these groups indicate high similarities between the populations of quite different stations and seasons, respectively. For example, cluster 1 includes strains isolated at cruises G (June 11, 1974), K (Aug. 7, 1974), M (Sep. 12, 1974), O (Nov. 21, 1974), Q (Jan. 23, 1975), and R (Feb. 12, 1975). Noteworthy and of special interest are pairs of only two strains, which are not considered as groups (see Sect. 13.1). A similarity of $S = 90\%$ was proved between the median strains $A15 - D9$, $B1 - J56$, $L1 - O17$, and $O30 - P48$. If one plots the similarities of this calculation in a presentation such as Figure 13.2 (on the level of $S = 90\%$), at least one connection exists between the bacterial populations isolated on two different cruises. That means that no bacterial population may be regarded as a separate population.

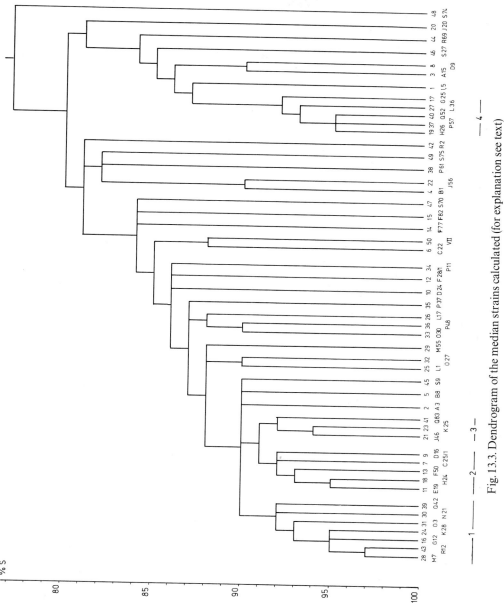

Fig. 13.3. Dendrogram of the median strains calculated (for explanation see text)

Further analysis, which describes not only seasonal fluctuation but also regional distribution, shows a wide spreading of similar bacteria strains and populations. This became obvious by using the similarity indices of the median strains and ungrouped strains. These connections between the median and ungrouped strains are demonstrated in Figures 13.4 and 13.5, respectively. If the limit of the S level is restricted to 5%, which means that two characters additionally may be regarded as variable, the net becomes more dense. Bacteria strains isolated in surface waters at Station 1 can be found at other times in the sediment of Station 5. This example is valid for many connections which can be found in the graphs and which shows the great complexity of the population.

The various bacteria strains show no special reference to their place of isolation (e.g., water or sediment). This fact may be due to the close relationships between the water and the sediment in the shallow water of the investigation area. It is obvious that Station 1 shows more connections between the different cruises than Station 5. This fact may be due to less exchange of water and, consequently, a more homogeneous level of nutrients together with higher pollution (cf. Chap. 19).

One has to presume that a diluted water sample represents the spectrum of bacteria occurring in the original water sample. Further analysis was carried out to include the ungrouped strains. Figure 13.5 demonstrates their relationships on a level of $S = 87\%$. This gives additional information as compared to Figure 13.4. It becomes obvious that no fundamental difference exists between the median strains and the ungrouped strains.

From the total number of bacteria isolated on each cruise, on the average six strains were found which show a similarity of $S \geq 90\%$. By restriction of the S level to 5%, on the average 19 strains were found. These numbers of "connection strains" still represent a minimum, because similarities between the median strains and ungrouped strains were not taken into consideration.

Seventy eight % of the median strains and 66% of the ungrouped strains show a similarity of $S \geq 85\%$ with other median strains or ungrouped strains isolated at different stations. This means that the bacteria populations isolated from 22 water samples show no similarity of $S \geq 85\%$ with another sample. On looking at these numbers, one has to take into consideration that the median strains of the clusters determined in most instances contain bacteria from different stations or water samples of one cruise. Considering these connections, only the populations of the samples of Station 5 (18 m) on cruise A (Jan. 24, 1974) and cruise N (Oct. 24, 1974) are of separate position.

The homogenity in the bacterial population may be due to rather stable hydrographic conditions. The separated position of the above two stations corresponded with fluctuations in the properties of the body of water: on cruise A (Jan. 24, 1974) North Sea water rich in salinity, phosphate and nitrate was observed (see Chaps. 3 and 4). In parallel fashion, the number of saprophytic bacteria growing on sea water medium showed an increase (see Chap. 11). On cruise N (Oct. 24, 1974) very low concentrations of inorganic nutrients such as phosphate, ammonium and nitrate were measured. Parallel low counts of saprophytic bacteria on sea water medium were obtained (see Chap. 3, 4, 11).

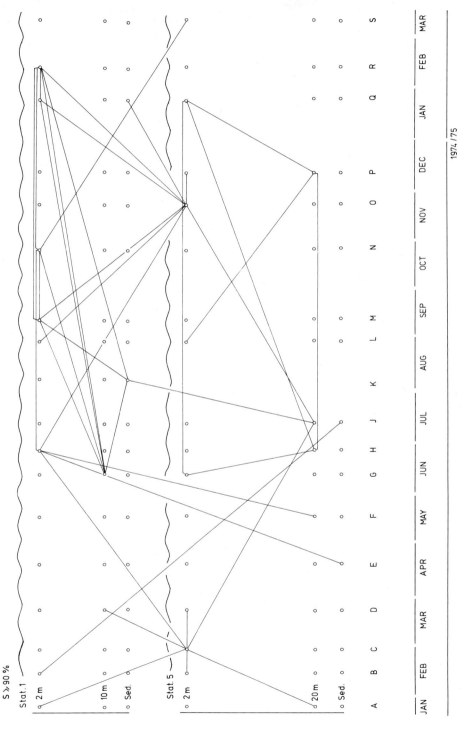

Fig. 13.4. Diagram showing the relationships between the median strains. A connection between two points (water samples represented by their population isolated) means that two median strains exist which represent a similarity of at least 90%

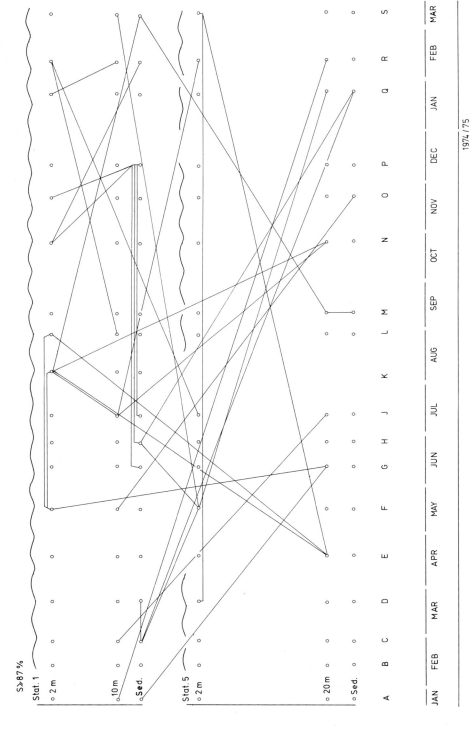

Fig. 13.5. Diagram demonstrating the relationships between the ungrouped strains (cf. Fig. 13.4). Strains representing a similarity of at least 87% are connected by a line, i.e., their station of isolation

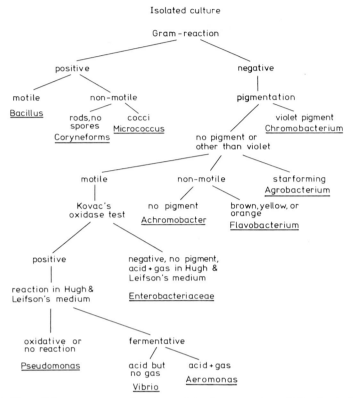

Fig. 13.6. Outline of the sequences of tests used in the screening of the bacteria isolated

13.2.3 Classifying of Bacterial Strains by Using Determination Schemes

The differentiation of the bacteria isolated by determination schemes may result only in higher taxa or groups. The schemes usually used in the literature were modified (see Fig. 13.6) with special regard to the saprophytic bacteria in the Western Baltic Sea. Among these, Agrobacteria are of special interest, as already mentioned by Ahrens (1969). However, many of the other colonies visually identified as *Agrobacterium* sp. (according to Ahrens, 1969), did not show typical star-forming in liquid media. Bacteria which did show ocher pigmentation on agar plates, but did not show typical aggregates are listed as "brown Flavobacteria". Although the Achromobacteriaceae (Breed et al., 1957) lost their separated taxonomic position (Hendrie et al., 1974; Buchanan and Gibbons, 1974), they will nevertheless be considered in the following discussion as a uniform taxonomic group, to allow a comparison with earlier investigations. Table 13.5 summarizes the determinations of the HMOs. Most of them are tentatively determined as *Achromobacter*.

All strains isolated were determined by the scheme in Figure 13.6. The percentages of the bacteria in the taxa are shown in Figure 13.7 and demonstrate the fluctuations of the groups. Correlations were calculated between the different

Table 13.5. Results of classification of the median strains and hypothetical median organism (HMO)

Cruise	Cluster	Median strain	Median strain related to the taxonomic group	Station	HMO related to the taxonomic group
A	1	1—5	Enterobacteriaceae	1	*Achromobacter*
	A	A 3	*Achromobacter*	5	*Achromobacter*
	B	A 15	*Vibrio*		
B	A	B 1	Bacillaceae	1	Bacillaceae
	B	B 8	Bacillaceae	5	Bacillaceae
C	A	C 25/1	*Achromobacter*	1	Pseudomonadaceae
	B	C 22	Pseudomonadaceae	5	*Achromobacter* Coryneforms
D	A	D 16	*Achromobacter*	1	*Achromobacter*
	B	D 9	Bacillaceae	5	*Achromobacter*
	3	D 24	*Flavobacterium*		
E	A	E 19	*Flavobacterium*	1	*Flavobacterium*
				5	*Flavobacterium*
F	A	F 50	*Achromobacter*	1	*Achromobacter*
	B	F 77	Pseudomonadaceae	5	*Achromobacter*
	1	F 82	Coryneforms		
	5	F 28/1	*Flavobacterium*		
G	A	G 12	*Flavobacterium*	1	*Flavobacterium*
	3	G 25	Enterobacteriaceae	5	*Achromobacter*
H	1	H 26	*Vibrio*	1	*Achromobacter*
	2	H 24	*Achromobacter*	5	Pseudomonadaceae/ *Vibrio*
J	A	J 46	*Achromobacter*	1	Pseudomonadaceae
	B	J 56	Coryneforms	5	*Achromobacter*/ Coryneforms
	4	J 20	Pseudomonadaceae		
K	A	K 28	*Achromobacter*	1	*Achromobacter*
	2	K 25	Bacillaceae		
L	A	L 1	*Achromobacter*	1	*Achromobacter*
	B	L 36	*Vibrio*	5	*Vibrio*
	3	L 17	*Achromobacter*		
M	A	M 7	*Achromobacter*	1	*Achromobacter*
	3	M 55	*Flavobacterium*	5	*Flavobacterium*/ Pseudomonadaceae
N	A	N 21	*Agrobacterium*	1	*Flavobacterium*
				5	*Flavobacterium*
O	A	O 3	*Achromobacter*	1	*Achromobacter*
	B	O 30	*Achromobacter*	5	*Achromobacter*
	5	O 27	*Achromobacter*		
P	A	P 11	*Flavobacterium*	1	*Achromobacter*
	3	P 48	*Achromobacter*	5	*Flavobacterium*
	4	P 57	*Vibrio*		
	5	P 61	Coryneforms		
	6	P 37	Coryneforms		
Q	A	Q 42	*Achromobacter*	1	*Achromobacter*/ Coryneforms
	3	Q 83	*Flavobacterium*	5	*Flavobacterium*
	5	Q 52	*Vibrio*		

Table 13.5 (continued)

Cruise	Cluster	Median strain	Median strain related to the taxonomic group	Station	HMO related to the taxonomic group
R	A	R 12	*Achromobacter*	1	*Achromobacter*
	3	R 2	*Achromobacter*	5	*Achromobacter*
	4	R 69	Bacillaceae		
S	A	S 9	*Agrobacterium*	1	*Achromobacter*
	5	S VII	Pseudomonadaceae	5	*Achromobacter*
	6	S 75	*Achromobacter*		
	7	S 74	*Flavobacterium*		
	8	S 70	*Agrobacterium*		
	9	S 27	*Vibrio*		

Table 13.6. Correlation coefficients calculated for the comparison of the curves presented in Figure 13.7

Group of bacteria (x)	Group of bacteria (y)	r	A	B	Confidence limit
Bacillus	Coryneforms	0.5344	1.7917	6.27	95%
Bacillus	*Achromobact.*	−0.4948	−1.8982	37.25	95%
Bacillus	*Agrobact.*	−0.5798	−0.4961	6.07	99%
Corynef.	*Achromob.*	−0.5376	−0.6097	37.78	95%
Achromob.	*Flavobact.*	−0.4667	−0.2451	17.34	95%

The table contents the correlation coefficients (r) and the parameters (A) and (B) of the equation: $y = Ax + B$, (confidence level at least 95%)

percentages of the groups. Table 13.6 presents the correlation coefficients on a confidence level of 1 or 5%, respectively.

It could be shown that positive correlations exist only between the Gram-positive taxa (*Bacillus*–Coryneforms). The Correlations between Gram-positive and Gram-negative taxa are negative. Another point of interest is the mutual relationship between *Achromobacter* and Flavobacteria.

Most of the bacteria isolated from sediments are Gram-positive, whereas most of the bacteria isolated from the overlayer of water show Gram-negative reaction. In most cases, the bacteria isolated from sediments were determined as Coryneforms. Thus, comparing all bacteria isolated from sediments, the following distribution of taxonomic groups was found: Coryneforms (21.9%), Flavobacteria (19.8%), *Achromobacter* (17.8%), "brown Flavobacteria" (10.9%), *Bacillus* (6.8%), *Pseudomonas* (6.8%), *Agrobacterium* (6.1%), *Micrococcus* (3.4%), *Vibrio* (2.0%), Enterobacteria (2.0%), others (2.5%).

As described by the determination of the HMO (see above), one of the dominating group is *Achromobacter*. This is valid also for all bacteria isolated. Generally, the genus *Achromobacter* cannot be considered as a typical marine bacterium, which is characterized by its motility and pigmentation (Zobell, 1946; Genovese, 1967).

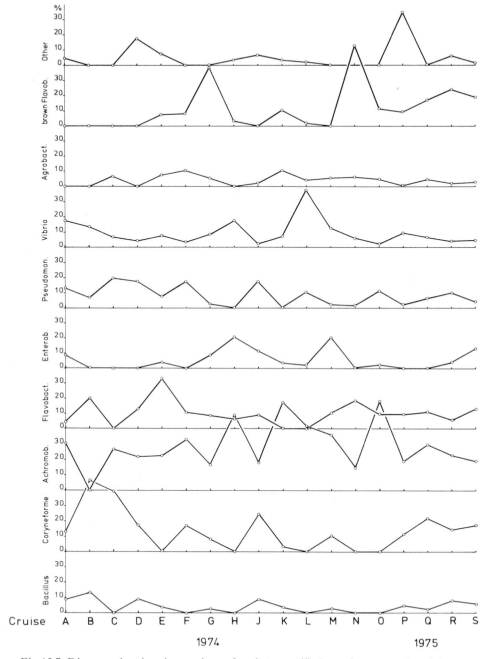

Fig. 13.7. Diagram showing the portions of various specific bacteria groups (% of the total population isolated on cruises A–S)

13.2.4 Analysis of the Frequency of Characters

The consideration of the frequency of characters allows further conclusions on the fluctuation of the bacteria population. By using the calculation of all correlations between the frequencies of characters of all populations, one realizes character complexes. These complexes may be related to other parameters. Figure 13.8 represents the frequency of all characters investigated for the populations of Stations 1 and 5 (to decode the numbers of the characters see Table 13.2).

Only for some characters could a typical seasonal rhythm be demonstrated. The characters of the different populations (St. 1 or 5) often show different fluctuations. Characters which can be observed sporadically are of special interest, e.g., indol formation, or chitin digestion. The fluctuations of such characters often show significant correlations, and changes in the populations may be concluded. The correlation coefficients are summarized in the correlation matrix (Fig. 13.9).

The populations of both Stations 1 and 5 are similar in their number of correlation coefficients (102 and 96, respectively). The populations show correlations between the same characters 29 times. This may be related to the high similarity of the population, as mentioned above. The following character complexes describing the whole population are important:

Character	Correlates with the following characters
4	29, 38, 41, 42
9	31
14	21
15	42
16	21, 41, 42
20	29
21	14, 16, 29, 35, 39, 44
24	44
26	29, 39
27	32, 39
28	29, 35, 38, 42, 43
29	4, 20, 21, 26, 28, 35, 38, 41, 42, 43
32	27, 36, 39
35	21, 28, 29, 38, 41, 43
36	32
38	4, 28, 29, 35, 41, 42
39	21, 26, 27, 32
41	29, 35, 38, 42, 43
42	4, 15, 16, 28, 29, 38, 43
43	16, 28, 29, 35, 41, 42
44	21, 24

The populations of Stations 1 and 5 can be characterized by some additional characters. At Station 1 characters 2, 3, 5, 6, 7, and 23, and at Station 5 characters 2, 3, 5, 7, 34, 37, and 40 play an important role.

Characters 1, 8, 10–13, 17–19, 22, 25, 30, and 33 may describe the whole population isolated. Because of the small fluctuations in their frequencies (see Fig. 13.8), they cannot be used for differentiating the isolated bacteria population.

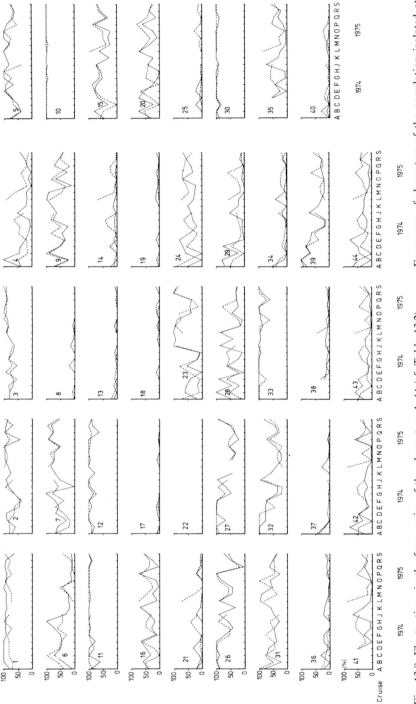

Fig. 13.8. Fluctuations in the frequencies of the characters *1–44* (cf. Table 13.2).————: Frequency of characters of the population isolated at Station 1. – – – – : Frequency of characters of the population isolated at Station 5. Represented are % positive results for the characters obtained for the population of Stations 1 and 5, respectively. For multistate characters only one property of the possible result is shown: For character 1, 2, 7, 28, 29 the code 2, for character 3, 4, 5, 6, 9 the code 1

Station 5

```
Nr.  2  3  4  5  6  7  9 14 15 16 20 21 23 24 26 27 28 29 31 32 34 35 36 37 38 39 40 41 42 43 44

 2   ×  +
 3      ×              +
 4         ×              +*  +  +*              +                  +           +  +        +
 5        −* ×                             +  −  −                  −
 6        −     ×
 7              +  ×
 9                 ×                                +*
14                    ×  +* + +*        − +        −      +*        + +       +* +* +* +*
15   −                 ×  +              + +        +        +        +       +  +  +  +
16                     ×  +* +     +            +                   +  +* +
20         +               +  ×         +* −*    +*                        +  +*
21                     +*  + +  ×       + +              +*        +*       +* +* +
23                              ×                                            −
24                                 ×         +*                          +      +*
26                     +* + +* +        ×     +                  +
27   −* +*                                 ×        +*     +      +
28      +*                          +*          ×  +        +*     +        +* +*
29      +*        +           + +        + + +* ×              +     +       +* +  +  +*
31   +*          +*    −                          ×
32      +*           + +*    +          +* +* + + +* ×        +*     +*
34                                                     ×  + +*    + +
35      +* +               + +          +* +*     +*    ×        +       +* +* +* +
36                                              +    + ×        +*
37                                                       ×
38      +               +*      + +*        +* +*   +    +*   ×        +* +
39   − +* +*                + + +     +* +* +* +* +*   +*   +* ×
40                                                              ×
41      +* +                     +* +        + +* +*   +*   +*  +* +*  × +* +* +*
42      +* +        +* +* +         +     + +* − +*   +    +* +*      × +* +*
43      +* +*                + + +       +* +* +*   +*   +*  +* +*  +* +* × +*
44                              +     +*                        +              ×
```

Station 1

Fig. 13.9. Correlation matrix for the comparison of the characters *1–44* (cf. Table 13.2). The matrix contains the correlations between the frequencies of characters for the populations of Station 1 *(left)* and Station 5 *(right)*. Only characters are listed which show at least one relation with another character. Symbols: + *: positive correlation, confidence level 1%, + : positive correlation, confidence level 5%, — *: negative correlation, confidence level 1%, —: negative correlation, confidence level 5%

By comparing the frequencies of the characters (1–44) of the population at Station 1 with those of Station 5, significant correlations are obvious for the characters 2, 3, 5, 6, 7, 9, 12, 15, 17, 23, 26, 27, 29, 32, 33, 37, and 39.

No difference exists between the salinity requirements of the populations isolated at Stations 1 and 5. The percentage of bacteria capable of growth in the liquid medium prepared with 10% NaCl (cf. Table 13.1) was highest for the population isolated from sediment of Station 1. At Station 5 the following distribution becomes obvious: with increasing water depth the percentage of cells capable of growth in the above-mentioned medium increases, at a water depth of 2 m, 6.2% of the bacteria are able to grow in the medium, 12.6% of the bacteria isolated from water samples of 10-m depth, and 33.3% of the bacteria isolated from water samples of 18-m depth. Especially Station 5 ist greatly influenced by fluctuations in the salinity of the water (cf. Chap. 3).

Motility (character 4) becomes of special interest because it correlates with 11 other parameters at Station 1 and with seven other parameters at Station 5. As mentioned above, the typical bacteria strain (HMO) was tentatively described as nonmotile *Achromobacter*. If motility occurs, it is strongly connected with the ability to degradate carbohydrates and proteins.

13.3 Discussion

It must be taken into consideration that the investigations were restricted to a small portion of bacteria which could be isolated on agar plates. However, at least at certain periods, saprophytic bacteria represent an active part of the total population.

The activity of the total population cannot be concluded from taxonomic differences in the composition of bacterial populations. This can be shown by the high similarities of the median strains and ungrouped strains, found independent in time and location. Nevertheless, numbers of saprophytic bacteria, controlled by quantity and quality of nutrients, can serve as an indicator for activities occurring in nature (see Chaps. 11, 12).

Sieburth (1967, 1968) showed that the spectrum of the bacteria populations are influenced by temperature. In the western Baltic Sea such relationships were not demonstrable, because short-term fluctuations in the hydrographic conditions are typical for this region (Siedler and Hatje, 1974; Dietrich, 1962; cf. Chaps. 3 and 19).

It was not possible to find a specific bacteria group chracteristic of sediments, although the spectrum of sediment bacteria presents more forms showing Gram-positive reaction than the bacteria isolated from water. The same was valid for the comparison of the populations isolated at Stations 1 and 5, respectively. No clear separation of the populations according to the stations and their pollution could be shown. This means that at least the bacteria populations from inshore and offshore do not differ as much as was expected. Seki (1966, 1967) and Sieburth (1967, 1968) showed that the fluctuation of the bacteria populations is strongly influenced by individual parameters, e. g., temperature. In the study presented, a co-operation of many parameters must be supposed, which led to a prevalence of a specific bacteria taxa as shown on cruise L (Aug. 29, 1974) for Station 5. No clear suppression or enhancement of any taxonomic group was observed at any other time. The fluctuations in the composition of the populations isolated show no direct connection to seasonal changes in the physical or chemical parameters.

The determined communities of bacteria populations show some general aspects which are in accordance with Altschuler and Riley (1967) and Murchelano and Brown (1970), who found a maximum of Flavobacteria in spring and winter, whereas in summer *Achromobacter* and *Vibrio* dominate.

According to Anderson (1962) and Bonde (1968) 31% and 23%, respectively, of the bacterial flora belonged to the genus *Micrococcus*. However, this high percentage could not be confirmed in the present study.

Simidu and Aiso (1962) and Ezura et al. (1974) found that 80% of the population isolated showed Gram-negative character. These results are in good agreement with the percentage of Gram-negative bacteria found in the western Baltic Sea. These authors determined the dominating part of the bacteria isolated as *Pseudomonas* (up to 30%), whereas in the western Baltic Sea only 8% of the bacteria isolated could be determined as *Pseudomonas*.

Bacteria isolated from the sediments obviously showed no seasonal fluctuation. This is in accordance with the results of Carney et al. (1975). In contrast, Bonde (1968) found fluctuations of the bacterial population in the Göteborg Bight.

The difference in bacteria populations isolated from water and sediments does not become obvious in the present study. However, Quigley and Colwell (1968) described differences in the populations for off shore regions. The high similarities of populations isolated from water or sediments found in the present study may depend on the shallow water of the investigation area. Surface waves may often cause the mixing of the upper sediment layer (Dietrich and Köster, 1974). Only few cruises indicate a differentiation between bacteria populations in water and sediment. At cruise A (Jan. 24, 1974), a high number of Micrococci and *Bacillus*-like bacteria were found in the sediment, whereas in the water the number of both was relatively low.

A significant correlation of a specific bacteria group to the phytoplankton blooms in Apr./May, Jul./Aug. 1974 and Mar. 1975 (Lenz, pers. comm.) cannot be shown in this study. These influences may be overlapped by other parameters. It must be taken into consideration that the activity of the total population occurring in the natural environment will be the result of inhibition and stimulation of the excreta or grazing by plankton cells (cf. Bell et al., 1974).

Between the frequencies of the characters tested and the chemical and physical properties of the water, no significant correlations could be demonstrated. As mentioned above, the hydrographic conditions may vary within extremely short times. Consequently, a correlation to biological parameters measured over such long periods of time are difficult to demonstrate (cf. Chap. 19). The salinity and its fluctuation does not show any noticeable influence on the saprophytic bacteria isolated from a media with a salt content similar to that of brackish water (S = 16‰). The population in general shows a relatively high salt tolerance. At nearly all times one is able to find bacteria strains which are capable of growing on media with different salt concentrations. It is supposed that most of the bacteria occurring in the Kiel Bight and Kiel Fjord are adapted to the salinity range of this area.

The fluctuations of the physiological groups become more important than the fluctuation of taxonomic groups. The physiological groups may be indicative of a heterotrophic activity (Genovese et al., 1968). The ability of bacteria to adapt to varying ecological situations must be regarded with special interest, e.g., on cruises J (July 11, 1974) and M (Sept. 12, 1974): very different and heterogeneous populations show an ability to decompose alginate. However, despite adaptation, the heterogeneous character of the bacteria populations occurring in the natural waters is normally preserved.

The homogeneity described for the total population during the time of the investigation will be demonstrated by the high similarities between the bacteria isolated at various stations and times. Oliver and Colwell (1974) suppose that similar bacteria groups exist throughout the seasons. Their results are based on the high similarities between the HMOs of the bacteria isolated.

According to Gauthier et al. (1975), specific bacteria groups show only very small fluctuation. The results obtained in the study presented justify the assumption that a very adaptable population of saprophytic bacteria exists. This population shows an omnipotent character. By using numerical taxonomy and character analysis, it became possible to describe the bacteria population of the western Baltic Sea in a general sense.

It could be shown that bacteria belonging to different taxonomic groups occur in the environment investigated. Despite these differences in the taxonomic groups isolated at different cruises and stations, a high similarity between the populations (HMOs, median strains, and ungrouped strains) exists. This underlines the above-mentioned omnipotent character of the saprophytic bacteria population isolated from the western Baltic Sea.

References

Ahrens, R.: Ökologische Untersuchungen an sternbildenden *Agrobacterium*-Arten aus der Ostsee. Kieler Meeresforsch. **25**, 190–204 (1969)

Altschuler, S. J., Riley, G. A.: Microbiological studies in Long Island Sound. Bull. Bingham oceanogr. Coll. **19**, 81–88 (1967)

Anderson, J. I. W.: Heterotrophic bacteria in North Sea water. Ph. D. Thesis, Glasgow University (1962). Cited by: Scholes, R. B., Shewan, J. M.: The present status of some aspects of marine microbiology. Advan. Mar. Biol. **2**, 133–169 (1964)

Beers, R. J., Fischer, J., Megraw, S., Lockhart, W. R.: A comparison of methods for computer taxonomy. J. Gen. Microbiol. **28**, 641–652 (1962)

Bell, W. H., Lang, J. M., Mitchell, R.: Selective stimulation of marine bacteria by algal extracellular products. Limnol. Oceanogr. **19**, 833–839 (1974)

Boeye, A., Aerts, M.: Numerical taxonomy of *Bacillus* isolates from North Sea sediments. Intern. J. Syst. Bact. **26**, 427–441 (1976)

Bölter, M.: Untersuchungen zur Fluktuation der Bakterienpopulation in der Kieler Förde und Kieler Bucht. Thesis Univ. Kiel (1976)

Bölter, M., Meyer-Reil, L.-A.: Untersuchungen an Bakterienstämmen aus dem Auftriebsgebiet vor der westafrikanischen Küste: Taxonomie und Nährstoffansprüche. Bot. Mar. **17**, 227–248 (1974)

Bonde, G. J.: Studies on the dispersion and disappearance phenomena of enteric bacteria in the marine environment. Rev. Intern. Océanogr. Méd. **9**, 17–44 (1968)

Breed, R. S., Murray, E. G. D., Smith, N. R.: Bergey's Manual of Determinative Bacteriology 7th ed. Baltimore: Williams and Wilkins Co., 1957

Buchanan, R. E., Gibbons, N. E. (eds.): Bergey's Manual of Determinative Bacteriology 8th ed. Baltimore: Williams and Wilkins Co., 1974

Colwell, R. R.: A study of features used in the diagnosis of *Pseudomonas aeruginosa*. J. Gen. Microbiol. **37**, 181–194 (1964)

Colwell, R. R.: Polyphasic taxonomy of the genus *Vibrio*: Numerical taxonomy of *Vibrio cholerae*, *Vibrio parahaemolyticus*, and related *Vibrio* species. J. Bact. **104**, 410–433 (1970)

Dietrich, G.: Eine Forschungsfahrt zur Untersuchung der kurzfristigen Schwankungen in der Schichtung und Bewegung der Ostsee im Sommer 1960. Kieler Meeresforsch. **17**, 135–136 (1961)

Dietrich, G., Köster, R.: Bodengestalt und Bodenbedeckung. In: Meereskunde der Ostsee, 11–18. Magaard, L., Rheinheimer, G. (eds.) Berlin-Heidelberg-New York: Springer, 1974

Drews, G.: Mikrobiologisches Praktikum für Naturwissenschaftler. Berlin-Heidelberg-New York: Springer, 1968

Ezura, Y., Katsunoba, D., Tajima, K., Kimura, T., Sakai, M.: Seasonal differences in bacterial counts and heterotrophic bacterial flora in Akkeshi Bay. In: Effect of the Ocean Environment on Microbial Activities. 112–123. Colwell, R. R., Morita, R. Y. (eds.) Baltimore-London-Tokyo: University Park Press, 1974

Gauthier, M. J., Shewan, J. M., Gibson, D. M., Lee, J. V.: Taxonomic position and seasonal variations in marine neritic environment of some Gram-negative antibiotic-producing bacteria. J. Gen. Microbiol. **87**, 211–218 (1975)

Genovese, S.: Sur quelques problèmes de bactériologie marine. Rev. Intern. Océanogr. Méd. **8**, 41–50 (1967)

Genovese, S., Bruni, V., Macri, G.: Activité microbienne endogène et bactéries contaminantes dans la mer. Rev. Intern. Océanogr. Méd. **9**, 73–81 (1968)

Hendrie, S., Holding, A. J., Shewan, J. M.: Emended description of the genus *Alcaligenes* and of *A. faecalis* and proposal that the genera named *Achromobacter* be rejected: Status of the named species of *Alcaligenes* and *Achromobacter*. Request for an opinion. Intern. J. Syst. Bact. **24**, 534–550 (1974)

Holmberg, K., Nord, C.-E.: Numerical taxonomy and laboratory identification of *Actinomyces* and *Arachnia* and some related bacteria. J. Gen. Microbiol. **91**, 17–44 (1975)

Kadota, H.: A study of marine aerobic cellulose-decomposing bacteria. — Mem. Coll. Agric. Kyoto **74** (Fish. Ser. 6): 1–128 (1956)

Kaneko, T., Colwell, R. R.: Ecology of *Vibrio parahaemolyticus* in Chesapeake Bay. J. Bact. **113**, 24–32 (1973)

Kaneko, T., Colwell, R. R.: Distribution of *Vibrio parahaemolyticus* and related organisms in the Atlantic Ocean of South Carolina and Georgia. Appl. Microbiol. **28**, 1009–1017 (1974)

Lehnberg, B.: Ökologische Untersuchungen an agar- und zellulosezersetzenden Bakterien aus der Nord- und Ostsee. Thesis Univ. Kiel (1972)

Leifson, E.: Determination of carbohydrate metabolism of marine bacteria. J. Bact. **85**, 1183–1184 (1963)

Meyer-Reil, L.-A.: Untersuchungen über die Salzansprüche von Ostseebakterien. Bot. Mar. **16**, 65–76 (1973)

Murchelano, R. A., Brown, C.: Heterotrophic bacteria in Long Island Sound. Mar. Biol. **7**, 1–6 (1970)

Oliver, J. D., Colwell, R. R.: Computer program designed to follow fluctuations in microbial populations to application in a study of Chesapeake Bay microflora. Appl. Microbiol. **28**, 185–192 (1974)

Oppenheimer, C. H., Zobell, C. E.: The growth and viability of sixty-three species of marine bacteria as influenced by hydrostatic pressure. J. Mar. Res. **11**, 10–18 (1952)

Proctor, J. R.: Some process of numerical taxonomy in terms of distance. Syst. Zool. **15**, 131–140 (1966)

Quigley, M. M., Colwell, R. R.: Properties of bacteria isolated from deep-sea sediments. J. Bact. **95**, 211–220 (1968)

Rheinheimer, G.: Über das Vorkommen von Brackwasserbakterien in der Ostsee. — Vie et Milieu, Troisième Symposium Européen de Biologie Marine, Suppl. **22**, 281–291 (1971)

Rheinheimer, G.: Mikrobiologie der Gewässer, 2. ed. Jena: Fischer, 1975

Rovira, A. D., Ridge, E. H.: The use of a selective medium to study the ecology of *Pseudomonas spp.* in soil. Bull. Ecol. Res. Comm. (Stockholm) **17**, 329–335 (1973)

Seki, H.: Seasonal fluctuation of heterotrophic bacteria in the sea of Aburatsubo Inlet. J. Ocenaogr. Soc. Jap. **22**, 93–104 (1966)

Seki, H.: Ecological studies on the lipolytic activity of microorganisms in the sea of Aburatsubo Inlet. Rec. Oceanogr. Works in Japan **9**, 75–113 (1967)

Shewan,J.M., Hobbs,G., Hodgkiss,W.: A determination scheme for the identification of Gram-negative bacteria, with special reference to the *Pseudomonadaceae*. — J. Appl. Bact. **23**, 379–390 (1960a)

Shewan,J.M., Hobbs,G., Hodgkiss,W.: The *Pseudomonas* and *Achromobacter* groups of bacteria in the spoilage of marine white fish. — J. Appl. Bact. **23**, 463–468 (1960b)

Sieburth,J.McN.: Seasonal selection of estuarine bacteria by water temperature. J. Exptl. Mar. Biol. Ecol. **1**, 98–121 (1967)

Sieburth,J.McN.: Observations on planktonic bacteria in Narragansett Bay, Rhode Island; A Résumé. Bull. Misaki Mar. Biol. 1st. Kyoto Univ. **12**, 49–64 (1968)

Siedler,G., Hatje,G.: Temperatur, Salzgehalt und Dichte. In: Meereskunde der Ostsee, 43–60. Magaard,L., Rheinheimer,G. (eds.) Berlin-Heidelberg-New York: Springer, 1974

Simidu,U., Aiso,K.: Occurrence and distribution of heterotrophic bacteria in sea water from Komagara Bay. Bull. Jap. Soc. Sci. Fish. **28**, 1133–1141 (1962)

Skerman,V.B.D.: A Guide to the Identification of the Genera of Bacteria. Baltimore: Williams and Wilkins Co., 1967

Sneath,P.H.A.: Some thoughts on bacterial classification. J. Gen. Microbiol. **17**, 184–200 (1957a)

Sneath,P.H.A.: The application of computers to taxonomy. J. Gen. Microbiol. **17**, 201–226 (1957b)

Sneath,P.H.A.: The construction of taxonomic groups. Symp. Soc. Gen. Microbiol. **12**, 289–332 (1962)

Sneath,P.H.A.: Vigour and pattern in taxonomy. J. Gen. Microbiol. **54**, 1–11 (1968)

Sokal,R.R., Sneath,P.H.A.: Principles of numerical taxonomy. San Francisco: Freeman, 1963

Steel,K.J.: The oxidase reaction as a taxonomic tool. J. Gen. Microbiol. **25**, 297–306 (1961)

Zobell,C.E.: Marine microbiology. Waltham, Mass.: Chronica Botanica 1946

Zobell,C.E., Upham,H.C.: A list of marine bacteria including descriptions of sixty new species. Bull. Scripps Inst. Oceanogr. **5**, 239–292 (1944)

14. Analysis of Actively Metabolizing Bacterial Populations with the Autoradiographic Method

H.-G. HOPPE

Brackish water areas are often characterized by fluctuations in the salt content as well as chemical and biological species composition. This variability is caused by varying oceanic and fresh water influence in near coast regions (see Chaps. 2 and 3).

Bacterial populations in brackish water therefore are composed of real, well-adapted, brackish water bacteria (Meyer-Reil, 1974) and fluctuating quantities of freshwater or marine bacteria (see Chaps. 1 and 11). The metabolic activity of bacteria not adapted or tolerant to brackish water conditions may be reduced by different factors of the unusual environment. Some bacteria will die after a more or less long period of survival.

In water bodies consisting of mixed water masses of different qualities, the metabolic activity of the individual microorganism therefore is a significant criterium to detect bacteria which play a role in substrate turnover of brackish water. The total amount of bacteria as determined by staining microscopy may include a greater or less number of dead or inactive organisms which are of interest as food for filter-feeders and in the calculation of total microbial biomass. Saprophytic bacteria, forming colonies on nutrient media, seem to indicate pollution and patches of high nutrient in coastal waters.

The amount of actively metabolizing heterotrophic bacteria, however, should bear the most obvious relation to bacterial uptake parameters and growth rates.

Identification of actively metabolizing heterotrophic bacteria which are able to break down easily degradable substances such as amino acids and sugars has been realized by new autoradiographic methods. (Hoppe, 1974, 1976). By these methods both the substrate uptake qualities of single bacterial cells (micro-auto-radiography) and of bacterial colonies isolated and grown on agar media or nutrient pads (macro-autoradiography) can be investigated.

The relatively high percentage (up to 8% from the active microorganisms) of colony-forming bacteria in inshore areas requires a reliable method to detect the uptake properties of different nutrients of these bacteria. This would enable the investigator to follow fluctuations in the composition of the population and to ascertain adaptations of the population to dominating nutrients in the water.

The recommended methods for the detection of substrate metabolism in bacteria species include some possible errors. Acid formation during sugar assimilation by bacteria may be too weak to indicate the utilization of the compound. Auxanographic tests might be disturbed by growth of the bacteria with supplementary substances such as yeast extract. Slight uptake of toxic substances is often not to be distinguished from substrate tolerance.

These errors are avoided by a new macro-autoradiographic method introduced by Kokke (1970,a,b) and developed by Hoppe (1974). The analysis of substrate uptake properties of colony-forming bacteria might be of more use for microbial ecology in aquatic environments than species and morphological determination, especially when chemists are in future able to determine the quantities of single organic compounds in the sea water which will enable the microbiologists to find correlation between the concentration of certain nutrients and the development of bacteria.

14.1 Material and Methods

14.1.1 Micro-Autoradiographic Method for the Determination of Active Bacteria Cells

The application of the autoradiographic method in microbial ecology is relatively new. T.D.Brock (1967) was one of the first to use this technique to determine the generation time of certain bacteria. Saunders (1972) and Munroe and Brock (1968) investigated heterotrophic uptake of organic compounds by algae. An autoradiographic test to determine the metabolism of several metals by yeasts and toxic substances (e.g., DDT) by bacterial colonies was developed by Kokke et al. (1970). Ramsey (1974) evaluated the rate of actively metabolizing bacteria growing on *Elodea canadensis* leaves. She found a relation of 1–26%:17–45%:100% between colony-forming bacteria, active bacteria and the total number of bacteria. All these approaches were based on the application of only one labeled ^{3}H-substrate to label the organisms for autoradiographic procedure. It is clear that only a limited number of bacteria could be detected in this way. Peroni and Lavarello (1975) therefore used ^{32}P-phosphate as a label for the total number of actively metabolizing microorganisms by in situ experiments. Their method, advantageous as it may seem, proved to be difficult in routine experiments.

We therefore elaborated a simple autoradiographic method for the determination of actively metabolizing heterotrophic bacteria (Hoppe 1976). This method is based on the labeling of bacteria by a standardized mixture of 15 tritium-labeled amino acids, a filtration process on Nuclepore filters and autoradiography performed on stripping film. In this description we give the newest and simplified modification of the improved method (Fig. 14.1):

In relation to the expected number of active bacteria, 1 to 5 ml of the water sample are pipetted into a sterile glass vial. Per 1 ml sample 10 μCi of ^{3}H-amino acid mixture are added. One of the sample parallels is fixed immediately by addition of 0.1 ml of formaldehyde (35%) per ml sample. This control serves to observe adsorption or contamination of the label. Then the vials are incubated for 3 h at in situ or standard temperature (20° C) on a laboratory shaker. After this the remaining vials are fixed in the same manner as above and 30 ml sterile isotonic water are added to all samples in order to prevent adsorption on the Nuclepore filter, and to obtain an even distribution of the bacteria in the water

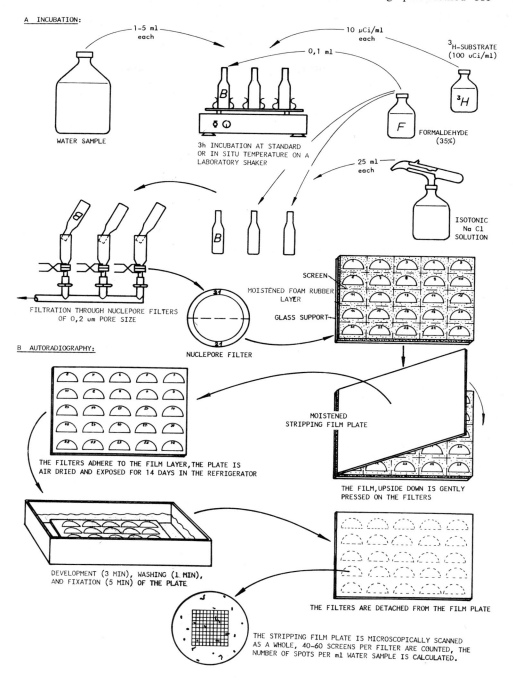

Fig. 14.1 A and B. Micro-autoradiographic technique for the determination of actively metabolizing heterotrophic bacteria

sample. Before filtraton the 0.2 μm Nuclepore filter and frit filter support are wetted with a few drops of detergent water mixture. The water is filtered through the Nuclepore filter at a vacuum pressure not exceeding 0.2 atm to avoid damage to cells. After this procedure the filters are air-dried and can be stored for several days.

As a preparation for the following autoradiographic process, the filters are cut into two pieces and one half of the filter is placed on a foam rubber layer, moistened with sterile distilled water. This rubber layer has the same size as the stripping film plate and is provided with a screen for 25 filters. When all filters are attached to the wet rubber the stripping film plate is wetted in the dark for 1 min and pressed on to the rubber layer. As a rule, all filters will adhere to the film plate on separating it from the rubber. The stripping film plate is then air-dried and exposed light-protected in the refrigerator for 14 days.

By this simple procedure 25 filters can be exposed on one plate and laborious stripping of the film from the support and wrapping the film piece around the specimen is avoided. It must be stressed that films should be stored according to manufacturers' instructions because otherwise the film might become detached from the support during development and become wrinkled after the drying process. Other methods have been published in Roger's comprehensive review *Techniques of Autoradiography*, 1973. After exposure, the film should be allowed to adapt slowly to room temperature. Time for development (Kodak, D 19) was 3 min, followed by a short dipping in distilled water and a subsequent fixation of 5 min followed by a 3-min water bath. Some of the filters will become detached from the film during this procedure; the others are stripped from the film during watering with a pincette.

After air-drying of the whole film plate, the images on the plate are examined with bright field optics (× 400 to 1000). Silver grain aggregations upwards of five grains are registered as a spot caused by a labeled bacterium. The number of actively metabolizing heterotrophic bacteria is calculated from the following formula:

$$NAB\,\mathrm{ml}^{-1} = \frac{x \cdot A}{V \cdot a}$$

NAB = number of active heterotrophic bacteria
x = mean value of the spots per screen
A = effective area of the filter
V = volume of water sampler
a = the area on the filter corresponding to the area of the screen.

14.1.2 Description of a Macro-Autoradiographic Method to Determine Physiological Groups of Active Bacteria Colonies

The macro-autoradiographic method to determine the substrate uptake of bacterial colonies has already been published (Hoppe, 1974) and will therefore be described only briefly (Fig. 14.2): Depending on the bacterial content of the water sample, 10 ml of the water sample or a suitable dilution are filtered through a

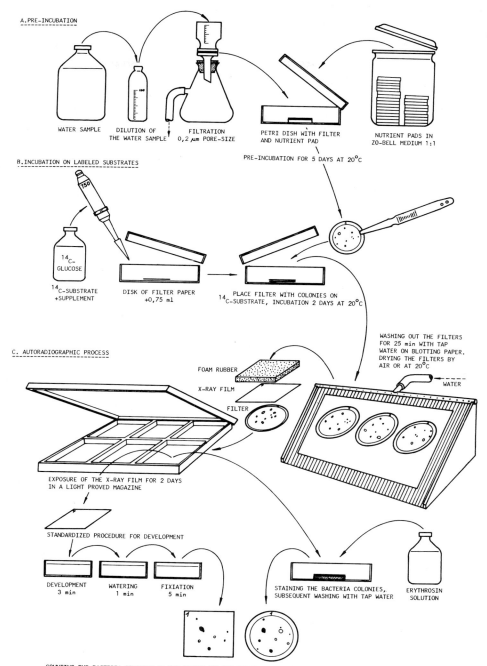

A. PRE-INCUBATION

WATER SAMPLE   DILUTION OF THE WATER SAMPLE   FILTRATION 0,2 μm PORE-SIZE   PETRI DISH WITH FILTER AND NUTRIENT PAD   NUTRIENT PADS IN ZO-BELL MEDIUM 1:1

PRE-INCUBATION FOR 5 DAYS AT 20°C

B. INCUBATION ON LABELED SUBSTRATES

^{14}C-GLUCOSE

^{14}C-SUBSTRATE +SUPPLEMENT   DISK OF FILTER PAPER +0,75 ml   PLACE FILTER WITH COLONIES ON ^{14}C-SUBSTRATE, INCUBATION 2 DAYS AT 20°C

WASHING OUT THE FILTERS FOR 25 min WITH TAP WATER ON BLOTTING PAPER. DRYING THE FILTERS BY AIR OR AT 20°C

WATER

C. AUTORADIOGRAPHIC PROCESS

FOAM RUBBER
X-RAY FILM
FILTER

EXPOSURE OF THE X-RAY FILM FOR 2 DAYS IN A LIGHT PROVED MAGAZINE

STANDARDIZED PROCEDURE FOR DEVELOPMENT

DEVELOPMENT 3 min   WATERING 1 min   FIXIATION 5 min

STAINING THE BACTERIA COLONIES, SUBSEQUENT WASHING WITH TAP WATER   ERYTHROSIN SOLUTION

COUNTING THE BACTERIA COLONIES ON THE FILTER AND THE CORRESPONDING BLACK SPOTS ON THE X-RAY FILM. CALCULATION OF THE NUMBER OF COLONIES PER ml AND THE PERCENTAGE OF BACTERIA WITH UPTAKE PROPERTIES FOR THE ^{14}C-SUBSTRATE.

Fig. 14.2 A–C. Macro-autoradiographic technique for the determination of substrate uptake by heterotrophic bacterial colonies

0.2 μm membrane filter. The number of parallels is as high as the number of substrates to be tested. The filters are placed on nutrient pads soaked with Zo-Bell's medium 2216 E and incubated at 20° C for five days (pre-incubation). During this period small colonies appear on the filters. After this pre-incubation the filters are transferred to pieces of blotting paper wetted with 0.5 μCi of ^{14}C-substrate. The carbon content of 0.5 μCi is adjusted to 0.5 mg C per filter with unlabeled substrate in order to exceed the threshold concentration. Incubation on ^{14}C-substrates lasted two days at 20° C.

After this procedure, the incubated filters are watered on blotting paper with tap water for 30 min to eliminate surplus ^{14}C-substrate. Then the filters are air-dried and can be stored for several weeks. For autoradiographic exposure the filters are pressed to X-ray film pieces in a special light-protected device. After two days' exposure, filter pieces are developed for 3 min, rinsed with water and fixed for 5 min, followed by watering for 25 min.

The black spots on the film represent colonies with active uptake mechanisms for the selected ^{14}C-compound.

14.2 Results

14.2.1 Annual Cycle of the Actively Metabolizing Heterotrophic Bacteria in the Kiel Fjord and the Kiel Bight

The results of analysis of heterotrophic bacterial populations were obtained on cruises in the western Baltic Sea during 1974/75 and the Limfjord, a brackish water area of northern Denmark connecting the Baltic and the North Sea. The special hydrographic situation of the western Baltic Sea and especially the Kiel Bight has already been described in Chapters 2 and 3. It should be mentioned that allochthoneous bacteria are introduced in this area by a small river (Schwentine), the sewage outlet of the town of Kiel, terrestrial runoff, and by intensive navigation.

To give an idea of the autoradiographs to be evaluated, first some figures (Figs. 14.3, 14.4) of tritium-labeled bacteria and algae are demonstrated. Each spot on the film represents an aggregation of silver grains caused by a bacterium or other planktonic organism with uptake of the offered substrate. Background grains are always present, but they do not disturb the evaluation. Adsorption on detritus is detectable by greater density of background grains above their area.

Figure 14.5 shows the seasonal fluctuation of heterotrophic actively metabolizing bacteria at Stations 1 and 2 of the Kiel Fjord and Station 5 of the central Kiel Bight in comparison with the colony-forming bacteria from the same region. The results from the months February, March, and May cannot be compared with the other data because these values were obtained with other substrates (glucose, aspartic acid). The most evident observation from the curves is the slight difference of active bacteria counts between the polluted inner Fjord station (St. 1) and unpolluted offshore station (St. 5). This would mean that the amount of active bacteria is little affected by increasing salt content and decreasing supply of dissolved organic matter in offshore regions. Seasonal fluctuations in the amount

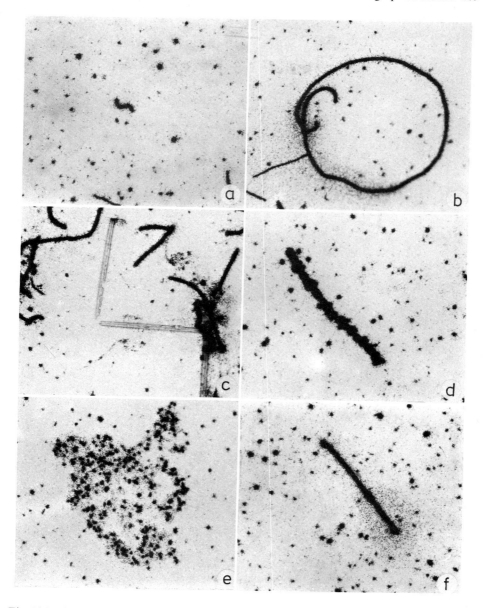

Fig. 14.3a–f. Micro-autoradiographs of tritium labeled microorganisms from a brackish water sample taken from the inner Kiel Fjord (St. 1), ×1400. (a) *Spirillum*-like bacteria cell, rods and cocci of different size. Usual autoradiography of bacteria from the research area of the Kiel Fjord. (b) Thread-like bacteria, only observed in polluted areas with a high standing stock of phytoplankton. (c) Bacteria clumps attached to *Asterionella* fragments. (d) Bacteria attached to a heavily labeled filament of blue-green algae (*Anabaena* sp.). (e) A membraneous detrital particle inhabited by bacteria microcolonies. (f) A filamentous bacterium showing partial accumulation of labeled substances in his surroundings (perhaps slime)

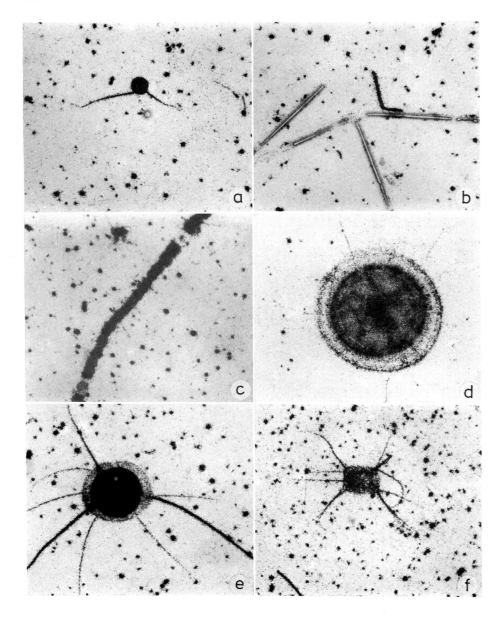

Fig. 14.4a–f. Micro-autoradiographs of tritium labeled planktonic organisms from a brackish water sample from the inner Kiel Fjord (St. 1), × 1400. (a) Thraustochytrium-like organism (zoospore). Active cells of lower fungi were very seldom observed in the investigated brackish water region. (b) Threadlike bacterium "creeping" on an *Asterionella* sp. fragment, as frequently observed in this water sample. (c) Heavily labeled *Anabaena* sp. filament. Note weak labeling of auxanospores. (d) Labeled *Coscinodiscus* sp. exhibiting different degrees of labeling within the cell. (e) Strong labeling of a centric diatom (*Thalassiosira* sp.) Note labeling of filament and slime capsule. (f) Weakly labeled *Chaetoceros* sp.

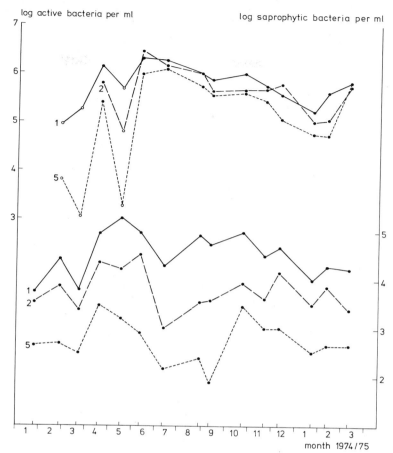

Fig. 14.5. Seasonal distribution of actively metabolizing bacteria as determined by micro-autoradiography *(upper part)* and saprophytic bacteria *(lower part)*. Stations: *1*: Reventlou-Brücke, polluted inner Kiel Fjord; *2*: Laboe, mouth of the Kiel Fjord; *5*: central Kiel Bight, relatively unpolluted

of actively metabolizing bacteria are low in comparison to colony counts and do not seem to be influenced by short-term variations of the salt content of water masses and other physical as well as chemical parameters. Activity or inactivity of bacteria cells in brackish water is obviously related to the seasonal alteration of water temperature. They do not exhibit distinct maxima of development in correlation with algal development, as could be demonstrated for colony-forming saprophyte bacteria (see Chap. 11).

These observations may lead to the conclusion that actively metabolizing heterotrophic bacteria, as detected by our autoradiographic method, represent mainly autochthoneous brackish water or marine bacteria which are able to metabolize at a low level of nutrimental supply. Autoradiographs of the small fractions (0.2–0.4 μm pore size) of separately filtrated bacteria revealed that these

Table 14.1. Seasonal and regional distribution of bacteria in the Kiel Bight 1974/75[a]

	Jan. 21, 1974	Feb. 28	March 21	April 18	May 16	June 11	July 11
NAB	—	90,759 +	180,703 +	$1,389 \cdot 10^3$	$476 \cdot 10^3 +$	$2,083 \cdot 10^3$	$1,931 \cdot 10^3$
		—	—	$630 \cdot 10^3$	$61 \cdot 10^3 +$	$2,789 \cdot 10^3$	$1,439 \cdot 10^3$
		6,514 +	1,137 +	$261 \cdot 10^3$	$2 \cdot 10^3 +$	$963 \cdot 10^3$	$1,213 \cdot 10^3$
PC	5,900	27,600	5,700	91,600	184,266	93,400	23,600
	5,180	7,450	2,385	23,347	17,053	33,400	1,083
	434	488	309	3,120	1,627	812	150
PC % of		30.4	3.2	6.6	38.7	4.5	1.2
NAB		—	—	3.7	29.0	1.2	0.1
		7.3	27,0	1.2	87.0	0.1	0.01
NAB % of		4.0	11.2	27.1	9	34.6	41.9
TNB		—	—	13.1	2	47.6	49.3
		0.6	0.2	17.0	0.1	55.3	55,1
NAB %[b]		4	7	67	23	100	93
		—	—	23	2	100	52
		0.5	0.1	22	0.2	79	100
PC %[c]	3	15	3	50	100	18	13
	16	22	7	70	51	100	3
	11	16	10	100	52	26	5
NAB %[d]		100	100	100	100	100	100
		—	—	45	13	134	75
		7.2	0.6	19	0.4	46	63
PC %[e]	100	100	100	100	100	100	100
	88	27	42	25	9	36	5
	7	1.8	5	3	0.9	0.9	0.6

Average calcula-tions	∅ NAB 944,818	100%	∅ PC 51,903	100%	∅ PC% of NAB	5.5%
	796,727	84%	9,772	19%		1.2%
	450,273	48%	1,005	2%		0.2%

NAB: Number of active bacteria per ml as determined by ^{3}H-micro-autoradiography. PC: Plate counts of saprophytic bacteria colonies per ml grow on Zobell's medium prepared with water of 14‰ salinity. TNB: Total number of bacteria per ml as determined by fluorescent microscopy.

[a] In the columns of 3 data the first was always obtained from Station 1 (inner Kiel Fjord 2 m) the second from Station 2 (Laboe 2 m) and the third from Station 5 (centre of the Kiel Bight, 2 m). In the average calculations all data except those marked with + were integrated. + these data were obtained by other substrates than ^{3}H-amino acid mixture.

[b] Seasonal distribution of active bacteria in percent of the highest number of these bacteria during the investigation period.

[c] Seasonal distribution of saprophytic bacteria in % of the highest number of these bacteria during the investigation period.

[d] Regional distribution of active bacteria in % of Station 1, inner Kiel Fjord.

[e] Regional distribution of saprophytic bacteria in % of Station 1, inner Kiel Fjord.

Table 14.1 (continued)

Aug. 29	Sept. 12	Oct. 24	Nov. 21	Dec. 10	Jan. 23, 1975	Feb. 12	March 10
$989 \cdot 10^3$	$757 \cdot 10^3$	$1,008 \cdot 10^3$	$567 \cdot 10^3$	$385 \cdot 10^3$	$171 \cdot 10^3$	$422 \cdot 10^3$	$691 \cdot 10^3$
$1,106 \cdot 10^3$	$437 \cdot 10^3$	$468 \cdot 10^3$	$476 \cdot 10^3$	$633 \cdot 10^3$	$106 \cdot 10^3$	$115 \cdot 10^3$	$565 \cdot 10^3$
$538 \cdot 10^3$	$353 \cdot 10^3$	$417 \cdot 10^3$	$273 \cdot 10^3$	$123 \cdot 10^3$	$57 \cdot 10^3$	$55 \cdot 10^3$	$700 \cdot 10^3$
82,266	54,000	98,666	32,400	48,066	10,400	19,600	17,000
3,490	3,833	8,487	6,110	14,533	3,188	7,470	2,500
243	75	2,933	1,207	1,256	332	460	460
6.3	7.1	9.8	5.7	12.5	4.6	4.6	2.5
0.3	0.88	1.8	1.3	2.3	6.5	6.5	0.5
0.05	0.02	0.7	0.4	1.0	0.8	0.8	0.07
25.4	39.2	37.6	33.4	26.0	17.8	25.0	52.4
45.3	35.5	19.8	21.9	26.8	—	—	—
21.7	32.2	23.4	23.1	10.2	15.8	8.6	40.7
47	36	48	27	18	8	20	33
40	16	17	17	23	4	4	20
44	29	24	23	10	5	5	58
45	29	54	18	26	0	11	9
10	11	25	18	44	10	22	8
8	2	94	39	40	11	15	15
100	100	100	100	100	100	100	100
112	58	45	84	164	62	27	82
54	47	41	48	32	33	13	104
100	100	100	100	100	100	100	100
1.2	7	9	19	30	31	38	15
0.3	0.1	3	4	3	3	2	3

very small bacteria which are characteristic for the offshore marine environment seem to be as active as larger inshore bacteria.

In Table 14.1 we look closer to the statistics of active bacteria and the relation of this group to colony-forming bacteria and the total number of bacteria as revealed by fluorescense staining. The counts of February, March, and May are based on the autoradiographic determination of bacterial glucose or aspartic acid uptake, respectively. The values of inshore and offshore stations for the bacterial uptake of these substrates differ greatly. This may indicate that larger inshore bacteria can be sufficiently labeled by one substrate only because substrate-governed actual uptake velocity is greater than that of offshore bacteria. The average number of active bacteria in the polluted brackish water area of the Kiel Harbor is about 950,000 ml^{-1} ($= 100\%$) in the surface layer. It decreases to 84% in the mouth of the Kiel Fjord and about 50% in the middle of the Kiel Bight. In recomparison to this, colony-forming bacteria decrease from 100% to 2% at the same stations. While they represent 5.5% of the active bacteria in the polluted harbor, they are only 0.2% in the offshore region. Though colony-forming bacteria seem to be larger than the majority of the active bacteria, their biomass in offshore regions represents only a small fraction of the total active bacteria biomass. In such areas therefore nonculturable bacteria seem to play the major part in remineralization and substrate uptake of organic matter.

The proportion of colony-forming bacteria of the total number of active bacteria in offshore regions increases during winter. This observation is in line with Rheinheimer (1965) and Hoppe (1972) who presume a prolonged time of survival in brackish water for allochthoneous colony-forming microorganisms.

A comparison between the total number of bacteria and the actively metabolizing bacteria demonstrates the influence of water temperature on the activity of bacteria in the sea. During June and July, up to 55% of the bacteria are active in the turnover of organic soluble substances in the brackish water. The rate of active bacteria decreases continuously during autumn and winter to 9%. In this connection should be mentioned that only bacterial cells with a high level of uptake activity can be detected by autoradiography, due to the low efficiency of tritium autoradiography. According to Rogers (1973) only 11% of the radiation causes a silver grain in the X-ray film. Our values for active bacteria therefore do not indicate that the other bacteria are completely inactive or even dead. However the low uptake rate of these bacteria seems to be unimportant in relation to the uptake of detectable cells.

The size distribution of active bacteria could be demonstrated by fractionated filtration by means of Nuclepore filters (Hoppe 1976) with 0.2, 0.4, 0.6, 0.8, 1, 3, 5, and 8 μm pore size. The highest amount of bacteria (71%) of the total number of active bacteria was retained in the size class 0.4–0.6 μm in polluted inshore water. In the unpolluted part of the Kiel Bight size classes of 0.4–0.6 μm (45%) and 0.2–0.4 μm (46%) dominated.

14.2.2 Distribution of Some Physiological Bacteria Groups in Different Brackish Water Biotopes

Physiological groups of heterotrophic bacteria colonies were determined by means of macro-autoradiography. ^{14}C-Substrates to be utilized by the bacteria were selected in respect of their degradability and water solubility. Glucose, xylose and lactose were chosen as easily degradable water-soluble substances, fat and uric acid as less soluble substrates, more resistant towards bacterial breakdown. Of considerable interest is of course the mineralization of toxic compounds such as phenol or pesticides (DDT). Though many bacteria are able to produce vitamins and excrete them into the medium under certain conditions, the abundance of bacteria from the vitamin supply (riboflavine) was tested.

In a cruise of the brackish water area of the Limfjord (Denmark) it was our purpose to obtain an idea of the magnitude of the physiological groups described above and to evaluate their role in the most important biotops, water column, sediment and neuston. As can be seen from Table 14.2, glucose was utilized by nearly the entire heterotrophic bacterial population. An insignificant decrease

Table 14.2. Physiological groups of the bacterial populations from the Limfjord (1973) as revealed by macro-autoradiography (in % of the total population)

^{14}C-Substrate	Station 1 m						Sediment				Neuston		
	1	3	5	6	8	11	1	6	11	13	1	6	11
Glucose	100	100	100	96	96	100	100	100	100	100	86	85	89
Xylose	22	43	70	57	100	73	56	67	88	48	50	55	63
Lactose	64	44	29	61	100	6	100	84	66	91	64	63	78
Phenol	4	0	8	9	3	0	6	21	(3)	19	0	8	10
DDT	0	0	0	0	25	3	13	0	—	18	0	0	0
Riboflavine	0	7	10	25	82	0	64	52	4	—	9	30	—
Uric acid	33	14	23	3	21	12	9	6	36	19	10	7	—
Fat	54	31	27	30	0	53	30	14	26	3	56	30	50

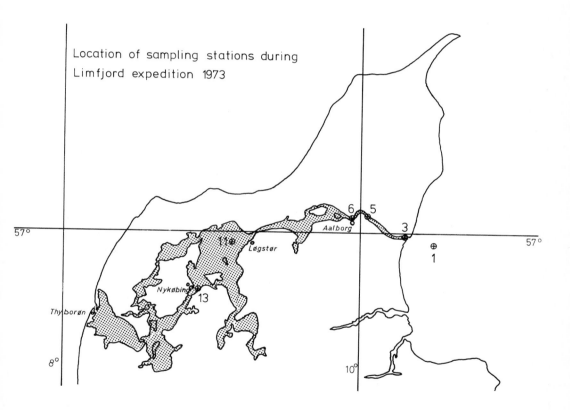

Location of sampling stations during Limfjord expedition 1973

was observed in the neuston. This may be explained by the concentration of bacteria with specialized uptake mechanisms in the uppermost water-air interphase which reveal no significant glucose uptake. On the average xylose and lactose were taken up by about half of the bacterial population present in the water samples. The percentage of bacteria with uptake mechanisms for these compounds of the total number of colony-forming bacteria shows a wide range, depending on the variety and dominance of bacteria species in the samples. The amount of the bacteria utilizing phenol was smaller than 10% of the whole population. High concentrations of these bacteria were found in some sediment cores. This observation may indicate destruction of phenolic compounds of the humic acid type in this biotope. According to the amount of microorganisms, significant DDT destruction seems to take place only in the sediment and some polluted water areas. From these observations, it may be concluded that destruction of extremely resistant organic compounds is located predominantly in the upper sediment layer.

During the monthly cruises in the Kiel Bight (1973–1975) physiological bacteria groups with substrate uptake mechanisms of several carbohydrates (glucose, xylose, saccharose, maltose, lactose), aspartic acid, Na-acetate, glucosamine, glycine, fat, phenol, DDT, uric acid, glycollic acid and riboflavine were determined. It is obvious that most of the groups show seasonal fluctuations over a wide range. Unfortunately we have no possibility of finding explanations for this alteration because reliable measurements of the concentration of most of these compounds in the sea water do not exist. Although some values exist, it is not proved whether all the substrate is available to bacterial destruction. Some nutrients may be enclosed into complexes and thus become resistant to degradation. For this reason Table 14.3 gives values of the average magnitude of the groups besides two data demonstrating the extremes during the investigation period.

As observed in the Limfjord, glucose was also taken up by the total colony-forming bacteria flora in the Kiel Bight; glucose uptake is therefore not mentioned in the table. Saccharose was taken up by an average of 94% of the bacteria. The mean population size of maltose-degrading bacteria was 83%, while xylose and lactose were taken up by 81% and 71% respectively. It is well known that lactose breakdown is relatively seldom found in aquatic bacteria; it is a special faculty of some Enterobacteriaceae, especially *Escherichia coli*. However, these observations are based on auxanographic or acid-formation experiments. Our autoradiographic results show that a much larger range of bacteria is capable of degrading lactose. Soluble starch as well as the amino sugar glucosamine are taken up by nearly all bacterial colonies. The same is true of aspartic acid and Na-acetate, utilization of acetate by bacteria is rather seldom reported in the literature on the subject. Our autoradiographic studies revealed generally a wider spectrum of uptake properties of aquatic bacteria than expected from previous taxonomic investigations.

The population size of bacteria degrading stable substances or other unusual compounds was much smaller than the population with uptake mechanisms of water-soluble easily degradable substances.

Fat (Na-butyrat) was taken up by an average of 30% of the bacteria. A clear reduction of the population size of bacteria with uptake of phenol, uric acid and riboflavine from the inner Kiel Fjord to the open sea area of the central Kiel Bight was observed in some water samples. This might be due to the fact that bacteria with mechanisms to take up these substrates may be predominantly allochthoneous bacteria of limnetic or terrestrial origin. While autochthoneous bacteria are seldom adapted to these substrates, the population with corresponding properties will increase in inshore areas.

Table 14.3. Physiological groups of the colony-forming bacteria of the Kiel Bight (1973/75) as revealed by macro-autoradiography in % of the total population

| ¹⁴C-substrate | Inner Kiel Fjord (Habor, St. 1) | | | | | | | | Offshore Kiel Bight (Sts. 3, 5) | | | | | | | |
| | Surface | | | | Sediment | | | | Surface | | | | Sediment | | | |
	min.	max.	average	n	min.	max.	average	n	min.	max.	average	n	min.	max.	average	n
Xylose	32	100	77	19	57	100	91	12	25	100	74	19	41	100	81	12
Fructose	—	—	93	1	—	—	100	1	—	—	100	1	—	—	—	—
Galactose	11	70	41	12	2	100	66	12	1	100	40	12	3	100	59	12
Saccharose	79	100	95	5	—	—	100	1	69	100	91	16	76	100	88	12
Lactose	24	100	71	19	20	100	75	12	17	100	68	19	34	100	73	12
Maltose	77	94	86	2	—	—	—	—	65	92	79	2	—	—	—	—
Glucosamine	—	—	90	1	—	—	—	—	—	—	—	—	—	—	—	—
Soluble starch	90	100	95	2	—	—	100	1	97	100	99	2	—	—	100	1
Na-acetate	49	100	94	18	47	100	90	12	55	100	93	18	56	100	82	12
Glycerol	—	—	83	1	—	—	—	—	—	—	93	1	—	—	—	—
Glycolic acid	1	100	34	12	1	70	30	12	1	62	31	12	2	38	13	12
Uric acid	0	100	28	19	1	55	23	19	0	100	29	19	6	77	33	12
Aspartic acid	94	100	97	5	—	—	—	5	91	100	97	5	—	—	—	—
Fat	5	65	18	19	20	60	37	19	0	60	25	19	9	69	41	12
Phenol	0	100	21	20	9	100	66	20	0	80	14	20	2	80	24	12
DDT	0	21	11	12	0	2	1	12	2	4	3	12	2	5	3	12
Riboflavine	10	89	34	17	10	80	40	12	0	69	23	17	2	93	44	12

14.3 Discussion on the Role of Actively Metabolizing
Bacteria in Brackish Water Areas

In connection with our comprehensive study of brackish water microbiology, many unresolved questions have arisen. Subsequently we will discuss some problems which bear upon the relationship between the heterotrophic active bacteria and bacterial groups as determined by autoradiography and related parameters as well as environmental factors.

In our autoradiographic experiments we always ran a blank fixed with a small amount of formaldehyde. After this procedure, performed immediately before incubation with ^{3}H-substrates, no spot-like accumulation of radioactivity could be detected on X-ray film. This means that radiochemicals were free from active bacteria and the organisms of the water sample were completely inactivated by fixation. Adsorption on bacteria and anorganic material such as diatom skeleton was too low to be detected by this method and thus could not disturb the evaluation of the results. A slight increase of silver grains was only observed associated with large detrital particles and algal filaments. It cannot be decided whether this radioactivity was due to adsorption or sample water which could not be washed out of the capillarious structure of particles.

The majority of active heterotrophic bacteria was not attached to particles throughout the year. After the breakdown of algal or zooplankton populations these organic particles are colonized rapidly and completely by bacteria, as appears true of some dominating species. Completely inorganic particles were not colonized by microorganisms in the water column. Autoradiographic observation indicates that fresh organic detritus is a microbiotope of considerable reproduction and substrate-uptake activity for bacteria. While the amount of colony-forming bacteria is probably influenced by the number of colonized particles, the total amount of actively metabolizing bacteria is not obviously altered by this process. This may be due to the fact that in relation to the high number of free-living active cells normally found, the amount of particle-colonizing bacteria is only a few %. A considerable part of these microorganisms will sedimentate rapidly together with the particles and can be detected in "Sinkstoff" traps (Iturriaga, 1977).

In contrast to colony forming bacteria, the total number of actively metabolizing heterotrophic bacteria in brackish waters shows no remarkable decrease from polluted inshore to less polluted offshore areas. The same observation was confined for the total counts of bacteria by Zimmermann (1975; see Chap. 10). This would mean that the majority of active bacteria is not influenced substantially by terrestrial bacteria and nutrient runoff, pollution effects, and changing environmental factors such as salinity or algal development. This may lead to the conclusion that most of the active heterotrophic bacteria in brackish waters are well-adapted autochthoneous organisms. Their characteristics are small size (mean volume 0.2 μm^3 in relation to colony-forming bacteria, mean volume 0.3 μm^3; Hoppe, 1976), salt tolerance within brackish water salinities and strong nutrient uptake at in situ nutrient concentrations during the warm season. In general, autoradiographic observations revealed no significant differences between grain densities per unit cell volume associated with very small bacteria from offshore regions or larger bacteria from harbor water. This finding may be appropriate to find an explanation for the divergence between maximal heterotrophic activity and the total number of active bacteria in polluted and unpolluted areas. First, bacterial count and biomass relation will not be constant in different water types. Though uptake per biomass unit seems to be constant, maximal uptake rates will increase unproportionally towards cell counts in polluted waters. Secondly, we have to assume that in offshore brackish water areas, a smaller amount of active bacteria reveals detectable uptake mechanisms for single substrates such as glucose in relation to amino acid mixture uptake than in polluted inshore areas. This may be due to the greater uptake of large inshore bacteria. In this connection, uptake of colony-forming bacteria should be mentioned. Autoradiographic uptake experiments showed general uptake of glucose, aspartic acid and even acetate by these microorganisms. This fact may demonstrate the probable influence of this bacteria group on quantitative uptake experiments: while only a varying portion of the total number of active bacteria is able to show detectable uptake of simple, easily degradable substrates, the whole population of relatively large colony-forming bacteria shows uptake mechanisms of these substrates.

The main criterium for seasonal development of active heterotrophic bacteria as revealed by autoradiography proved to be water temperature. Numbers of active bacteria, as well as the total number of bacteria, accumulate during the warm season and decrease significantly during winter. Short-term variations in nutrient supply caused by algal blooms or temporary pollution seem to have less effect on the total number of active bacteria than on colony-forming saprophytic bacteria. It should be mentioned that our results were obtained at a standard incubation temperature of 20° C, as is usual in agar plate incubation. At in situ incubation temperature we expect even a lower number of detectable active bacteria during winter because the threshold concentration of radioisotope which can be detected on X-ray film in this procedure is constant.

Bacteria population analysis of colony-forming saprophytic bacteria enables the investigator to find biotopes of special microbial uptake activities. Our observations indicate that bacteria with uptake mechanisms of resistant substrates are enriched in air-water interphase (neuston) and in the sediment. In a comparison of inshore and offshore brackish water areas, bacteria with uptake properties of resistant substrates appear more frequent in polluted areas. Easily degradable water soluble substrates are taken up by the same proportion of colony-forming bacteria in all biotopes. Comparable investigations of nutritional requirements of bacteria were performed by Berland et al. (1976a,b) in front of the Rhone outlet. Their results were obtained from isolated bacteria pure cultures which were cultivated on a medium prepared with artificial sea water and enriched with different nutrimental sources. Briefly, the percentage of bacterial strains from the whole collection which was supported by the different substrates was found to be 3.5% for vitamin B_{12}, 10% for biotin, 14% for thiamine (33% riboflavine), up to 38% for glucose, galactose and saccharose (ca. 95%, 52%, 91%), about 35% for maltose (82%), 34% for lactose (69%) and 27% for xylose (75%), 32% for glycerol (94%), 36% for glucosamine (92%), 72% for asparagine and acetate (97%, 91%). In this reproduction, only results for those substrates were selected which were also tested in our investigations; our average results from 1974/1975 are inserted in parentheses. Our findings are in general two to three times higher than those of Berland et al. (1976 a, b, c). This may be explained by the dominance of few species in bacterial populations causing the high uptake percentage in our autoradiographic experiments, while these organisms may be ranked with seldom-occurring bacteria in Berland's calculations. On the other hand, methodical differences should not be ignored. In my opinion measurements of growth and even acidification of the medium are more rough parameters of substrate uptake and utilization than the detection of small quantity uptake by autoradiography. Observation of species composition demonstrates that most of the colony-forming bacteria are able to decompose water-soluble compounds while only a few bacteria are able to utilize other substrates (DDT 5%, uric acid 23%, glycolic acid 27%). In offshore areas these specialized microorganisms are less frequent than in polluted inshore waters. Otherwise this would mean that the dominance of few species in inshore areas is lower than in the open sea.

The presented autoradiographic methods for the study of bacterial population in brackish waters are a tool of experimentation in microbial ecology as already pointed out by Brock and Brock (1966). The methods may be used to follow successions of bacterial development as well as adaptation towards supplemented or naturally occurring substances, especially toxic compounds. The distribution of labeled bacteria in a closed system may be investigated, as has already been tried by Berlin and Rhylander (1963) and the active metabolizing „Aufwuchs" of detrital particles as well as living cells may be studied. In fungal research the method offers a possibility to study zones of active growth e.g., substrate uptake, and the location of certain substrates in the cell (Kleeff et al., 1969). Substrate uptake of single microbial cells, as well as transport pathways, may be studied by grain counting of spot evaluation by automatized image analysis.

References

Berland, B. R., Bonin, D. J., Durbec, J.-P., Maestrini, S. Y.: Bactéries hétérotrophes aérobies prélevées devant le Delta du Rhône. II-Determination des exigences nutritionelles. Comparison avec des souches provenant d'autres biotopes. Hydrobiol. **49**, 123–128 (1976a)

Berland, B. R., Bonin, D. J., Durbec, J.-P., Maestrini, S. Y.: Bactéries hétérotrophes aérobies prélevées devant le Delta du Rhône. III. Utilisation potentielle de différents substrats organiques comme source de carbone. Hydrobiol. **50**, 3–10 (1976b)

Berland, B. R., Bonin, D. J., Durbec, J.-P., Maestrini, S. Y.: Bactéries hétérotrophes aérobies prélevées devant le Delta du Rhône. IV. Besoins en vitamines et liberation de ces substances. Hydrobiol. **50**, 167–172 (1976c)

Berlin, M., Rylander, R.: Autoradiographic detection of radioactive bacteria introduced into seawater and sewage. J. Hyg. **61**, 307–315 (1963)

Brock, M. L., Brock, T. D.: The application of microautoradiographic technique to ecological studies. Mitt. Intern. Verein. Limnol **15**, 1–29 (1968)

Brock, T. D.: Bacterial growth rate in the sea: direct analysis by thymidine autoradiography. Science, **155**, 81–83 (1967)

Brock, T. D., Brock, M. L.: Autoradiography as a tool in microbial ecology. Nature (London) **209**, 734–736 (1966)

Hoppe, H.-G.: Untersuchungen zur Ökologie der Hefen im Bereich der westlichen Ostsee. Kieler Meeresforsch. **28**, 54–77 (1972)

Hoppe, H.-G.: Untersuchungen zur Analyse mariner Bakterienpopulationen mit einer autoradiographischen Methode. Kieler Meeresforsch. **30**, 107–116 (1974)

Hoppe, H.-G.: Determination and properties of actively metabolizing heterotrophic bacteria in the sea investigated by means of micro-autoradiography. Mar. Biol. **36**, 291–302 (1976)

Iturriaga, R.: Mikrobielle Aktivität des Sinkstoffaufwuchses in der westlichen Ostsee. Thesis Univ. Kiel (1977)

Kleeff, van B. H. A., Kokke, R., Nieuwdorp, P. J.: Radioisotope uptake by and localization in yeasts. Ant. v. Leeuwenhoeck **35**, Suppl.: 9–10 (1969)

Kokke, R.: Autoradiography as a tool for the detection and isolation of microbes. Ant. v. Leeuwenhoeck **36**, 189 (1970a)

Kokke, R.: DDT: its action and degradation in bacterial populations. Nature (London) **226**, 577–978 (1970b)

Meyer-Reil, L.-A.: Untersuchungen über die Salzansprüche von Ostseebakterien: Temperatureinflüsse und Adaptation. Bot. Mar. **17**, 1–15 (1974)

Munro, A. L. S., Brock, T. D.: Distinction between bacterial algal utilization of soluble substances in the sea. J. Gen. Microbiol. **51**, 35–42 (1968)

Peroni, C., Lavarello, D. A.: Microbial activities as a function of water depth in the Ligurian Sea: an autoradiographic study. Mar. Biol. **30**, 37–50 (1975)

Ramsay, A. J.: The use of autoradiography to determine the proportion of bacteria metabolizing in an aquatic habitat. J. Gen. Microbiol. **80**, 363–373 (1974)

Rheinheimer, G.: Mikrobiologische Untersuchungen in der Elbe zwischen Schnackenburg und Cuxhaven. Arch. Hydrobiol. Suppl. Elbe-Aestuar **29**, 181–251 (1965)

Rogers, A. W.: Techniques of autoradiography. Amsterdam-London-New York: Elsevier 1973

Saunders, G. W.: Potential heterotrophy in a natural population of *Oscillatoria agardhii* var. *isothrix* SKUJA. Limnol. Oceanogr. **17**, 704–711 (1972)

Zimmermann, R.: Entwicklung und Anwendung von fluoreszenz- und rasterelektronenmikroskopischen Methoden zur Ermittlung der Bakterienmenge in Wasserproben. Thesis Univ. Kiel (1975)

15. Heterotrophic Activity

K. GOCKE

Besides measuring number and biomass of heterotrophic microorganisms, the determination of the activity of these organisms is of high priority in microbial ecology. (In this study the term "microbial activity" will be restricted to the breakdown of dissolved organic substances by heterotrophic microorganisms and the resulting formation of microbial biomass). In some cases the number, or even better, the biomass of the active microorganisms is directly related to the activity. In complex systems as e.g., brackish water environments like the Kiel Bight and Kiel Fjord, it is necessary to perform direct measurements of the activity itself, since hydographical conditions are changing so rapidly.

Techniques for such measurements on dense cultures as used for example in physiological or biochemical studies are most often not suited to ecological research. The low density and hence low activity of natural microbial populations require extremely sensitive methods. Every measurement itself alters the environmental conditions to a certain degree, introducing an artificial change in the bacterial activity. Thus, we are confronted with a two-fold problem; first, the method has to be very sensitive, and second, it should not disturb the system.

The most widely used techniques for the assessment of the microbial activity at least partly fullfilling these qualifications are based on the studies of Parsons and Strickland (1962) and Williams and Askew (1968). The former authors describe a method similar to that for the determination of the primary production. They add a defined amount of ^{14}C-labeled glucose or acetate to the water sample. After incubation the incorporated radioactivity is determined by filtering the organisms.

The uptake velocity is given by

$$v = \frac{f}{t}(S_n + A) \tag{1}$$

v = rate of uptake (μg C l^{-1} h^{-1}); f = fraction of the added isotope which is taken up; t = incubation time (h); S_n = natural concentration of the substrate under study (μg C l^{-1} h^{-1}); A = added substrate.

For the calculation of v one has to know the natural concentration S_n of the substrate in question. Since this value is quite difficult to measure, Parsons and Strickland (1962) determined instead the maximum uptake velocity, or "relative heterotrophic potential". To obtain this parameter, they added the labeled substance in high excess over the natural concentration (250 μg C l^{-1} versus only a few μg l^{-1}), so that $(S_n + A) \approx A$. Furthermore, they showed that the uptake

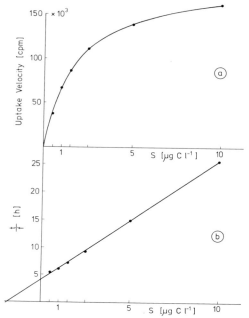

Fig. 15.1a and b. Uptake of glucose by the natural microbial population in the inner Kiel Fjord (April 18, 1974). Saturation curve (a) and Lineweaver-Burke plot (b)

velocity is dependent on the concentration and has the form of a saturation curve. This relationship between uptake velocity and substrate concentration is analogous to the velocity of enzymatic reactions as a function of the substrate concentration.

The mathematical expression of these reactions is

$$v = V_{max} \cdot \frac{S}{K + S} \tag{2}$$

V_{max} = maximum uptake velocity ($\mu g\, C\, l^{-1}\, h^{-1}$); K = half-saturation constant ($\mu g\, C\, l^{-1}$); S = substrate concentration ($\mu g\, C\, l^{-1}$) as sum of $S_n + A$.

By combining Equations (1) and (2) one obtains the linear relationship (Lineweaver-Burke transformation)

$$\frac{t}{f} = \frac{K_t + S_n}{V_{max}} + \frac{A}{V_{max}}. \tag{3}$$

In this equation K is replaced by K_t (transport "constant").

Figure 15.1 represents both the saturation curve and the Lineweaver-Burke plot of a glucose uptake experiment performed in the inner Kiel Fjord (St. 1). As shown, three parameters can be obtained graphically or with the aid of a computer:

1. The maximum uptake velocity, V_{max}, of a given substrate by the natural microbial population. This parameter is a measure of the relative size of the microbial population able to utilize this substrate. V_{max} enables one to compare the heterotrophic activities in different bodies of water.

2. The sum of the transport "constant" and the natural concentration of a given substrate, $K_t + S_n$. As a sum this parameter sets the upper limit for each of its two constituents.

3. The turnover time, T_t, of a given substrate. This is the time required by the natural microbial population for the complete uptake of an amount of the substrate which is equal to its natural concentration. This value is of special interest as it indicates the intensity of heterotrophic utilization of different substances. In conjunction with a knowledge of the natural concentration, the flux rate of a substrate can be calculated.

Using the technique of Parsons and Strickland (1962), which was further improved by Wright and Hobbie (1966) several studies of heterotrophic activity have been performed in marine and fresh water environments. To give an impression of the great diversity of heterotrophic activity in different areas, some data are compiled in Table 15.1. These data are only momentary pictures, not reflecting seasonal changes. Furthermore, the microbial uptake of several other substrates, which are not mentioned here, was included in these works. However, these few works depict clearly the great variability of heterotrophic activity in

Table 15.1. Heterotrophic activity at various areas

Location	Substrate	V_{max} $\mu g\,Cl^{-1}h^{-1}$	T_t h	$K_t + S_n$ $\mu g\,Cl^{-1}$	References
Tropical Atlantic 800 km offshore	glucose	0.07		15	Vaccaro and Jannasch (1966)
Tropical Atlantic shelf	glucose	0.02		60	Vaccaro and Jannasch (1966)
Eastern tropic. Pacific	glucose aspartate	0.0006–0.054 0.002 –0.009		15 –275 4.3– 88	Hamilton and Preslan (1970)
Western north Pacific	glucose aspartate	0.006 0.002	6,000 10,000	19 34	Seki et al. (1972)
Kuroshio current	glucose aspartate	0.003 0.003	2,700 6,000	9 17	Seki et al. (1972)
Subartic Pacific	glucose aspartate	0.009 0.006	1,300 6,500	12 35	Seki et al. (1972)
Woods Hole dock water	glucose	0.11		1.6	Vaccaro and Jannasch (1966)
Tokyo Bay	glucose aspartate	7.2 1.2	8.7 19	62 23	Seki et al. (1975)
Shimoda Bay (Estuary)	glucose aspartate	9.2 1.4	31 36	284 51	Seki et al. (1975)
Pamlico River (Estuary)	glucose	1.3–3.8			Hobbie and Crawford (1969)

The data of Seki et al. (1972, 1975) and Hobbie and Crawford (1969) refer to gross uptake, the other to net uptake.

different marine areas. In fresh water biotopes the maximum uptake velocity showed a variability range of up to four orders of magnitude between highly eutrophic ponds and oligotrophic arctic lakes. Rodhe et al. (1966) noted an extremely low value for V_{max} of 8×10^{-4} µg glucose l^{-1} h^{-1} in northern Swedish lakes whereas Allen (1969) observed maximum uptake velocity of 20 µg glucose l^{-1} h^{-1}. Also the turnover times vary between 15 min up to 10,000 h.

In contrast to many studies in which the above method yielded a large amount of information, there are several others where the method failed (Vaccaro and Jannasch, 1967; Vaccaro, 1969; Hamilton and Preslan, 1970; Overbeck, 1975). In these cases it could be shown that the Lineweaver-Burke plot of the substrate uptake by the natural microbial population resulted in an S-shaped curve instead of a straight line. These authors mainly interpret their findings as a result of heterogeneity of the bacterial populations.

Williams (1973) performed some model calculations to answer the question how the Lineweaver-Burke plot changes when instead of a pure culture (analogous to an isolated enzyme) a mixed population with different transport "constants" and uptake velocities is given. The calculation showed no influence on the linearity of the plot at high substrate concentration even when the values for K_t and V_{max} varied by several orders of magnitude among the different subpopulations. However, at low substrate concentrations (less than or equal to K_t), the substrate uptake by the subpopulation having the smallest K_t outweighs the other subpopulations. In the graphical representation the "straight" line of the Lineweaver-Burke plot therefore bends towards the x-axis. This means that the values for $K_t + S_n$ and T_t obtained with the described method are generally too high.

Our own experiments (Gocke, 1977) performed in the Baltic Sea proved the nonlinearity of the Lineweaver-Burke plot (Fig. 15.2) especially for oligotrophic areas with low heterotrophic activity (central Baltic Sea).

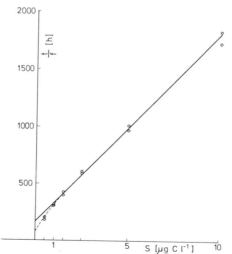

Fig. 15.2. Uptake of glucose by the natural microbial population in the central Baltic Sea (May, 1975). *Broken line* indicates the curving down of Lineweaver-Burke regression line

The curving was less often observed in coastal areas where activities were generally much higher. Thus, it can be concluded that the results obtained by the described technique are satisfactory at least in relatively eutrophic environments like the Kiel Bight and Kiel Fjord.

To avoid these difficulties and to obtain a method capable of working regardless of the trophic status of the area, Williams and Askew (1968) developed a technique which is in many respect easier to handle. However, the method permits only the turnover time to be determined. These authors add such a small amount of labeled substrate to the sample that it might be regarded as negligible. Rearrangement of Equation (1) then gives the turnover time:

$$\frac{t}{f} = \frac{S_n}{v} = T_t. \tag{4}$$

Detailed theoretical and experimental comparisons of the two methods were performed by Wright (1974) and Gocke (1977).

15.1 Material and Methods

Samples were taken by means of a sterile water sampler at Station 1 (inner Kiel Fjord) from 2-m and 10-m depth and at Station 5 (central Kiel Bight) from 2-m, 10-m and 18-m depth. Measurements were performed under sterile conditions not later than 30 min (St. 1) or 2 h (St. 5) after taking the samples. During the transport these were stored at in situ temperatures.

15.1.1 Determination of V_{max}, T_t and $(K_t + S_n)$

The method used is based on the technique of Wright and Hobbie (1966). A detailed description is given by Gocke (1977). The uptake of glucose was studied at all depths of the two stations, whereas the uptake of aspartate and acetate was confined to the 2-m samples.

Six different concentrations of uniformly labeled substrate (0.5; 1.0; 1,5; 2,5; 5.0; 10.0 µg C l^{-1}) were pipetted into 50-ml samples. A seventh sample with 1.5 µg C l^{-1} was fixed with 0.15 ml formalin and was used as a blank. The samples were incubated at in situ temperature for 2 h in the dark. Then the microbial activity was arrested by fixing with 0.15 ml formalin. The samples were filtered through membrane filters with a pore size of 0.2 µm and the radioactivity counted in a scintillation counter. The parameters V_{max}, T_t and $K_t + S_n$, as well as their 95% confidence limits, were calculated with the aid of a computer using the Lineweaver-Burke equation. The data were rejected if the correlation coefficient was below that required for the 95% probability level. The parameters calculated are related only to the net uptake of substrate because respiration studies for the three compounds were not included in the study. This means that the gross uptake V_{max} would be higher and T_t shorter; $K_t + S_n$ is not affected. The method is presented in Figure 15.3.

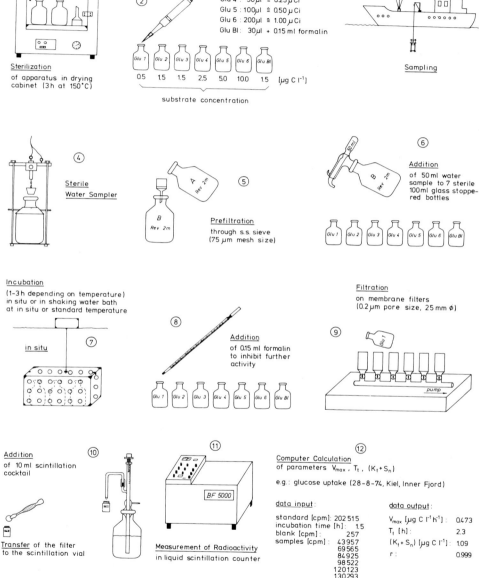

Fig. 15.3. Scheme of the technique for the determination of V_{max}, T_t and $K_t + S_n$

15.1.2 Determination of the Turnover Time of an Amino Acid Mixture

The method used is basically a combination of the techniques of Williams and Askew (1968) and Hobbie and Crawford (1969). The final concentration of the uniformly labeled ^{14}C-amino acid mixture pipetted to 100-ml samples was 0.2 μg $C l^{-1}$. The composition of the mixture was (by radioactivity): ala, 10.0%; arg, 6.5%; asp 9.0%; glu 12.5%; gly, 5.0; ile, 5.0%; leu, 12.0%; lys, 5.5%; phe, 7.0%; pro, 6.0%; ser, 5.0%; thr, 6.0%; tyr, 3.5%; val, 7.0%. One sample out of four was fixed by adding 0.3 ml formalin and served as a blank. The samples were incubated for 2 h at in situ temperature in the dark. For the determination of the substrate respired, half of the sample volume of each flask was used, from which the $^{14}CO_2$ was blown off and absorbed in a scintillation vial. The net uptake was obtained by filtering the other half of the sample volume. Thus, filtering an acidified sample was omitted (Griffith et al., 1974). The procedure is described in detail by Gocke (1976). A graphical presentation is given in Figure 15.4. The turnover time is calculated according to Equation (4).

The composition of the labeled AA mixture is different from that of the natural AA mixture. The error thus introduced regarding the turnover time is not greater than 25%. The percentage respiration is hardly affected by the difference in the composition. This can be proved by experiments performed with an AA mixture similar to the natural one (Gocke, unpubl.). In the present work the values for the turnover time are not corrected.

15.2 Horizontal and Vertical Distribution of the Heterotrophic Activity

15.2.1 Spatial Distribution of the Maximum Uptake Velocity

Concerning net uptake, the monthly measurements show that acetate is incorporated with the highest, glucose with an intermediate and aspartate with the lowest velocity. Figure 15.5 shows the annual average values. Since the percentage respiration of aspartate is considerably greater than that of glucose (Gocke, 1976), the gross uptake velocity for both substances is nearly the same. However, the gross uptake of acetate exceeds that of glucose and aspartate.

The measurements show, as expected, appreciably higher uptake velocities in the inner Kiel Fjord (St. 1) than in the central Kiel Bight (St. 5). On the average, the ratio for the 2-m samples was found to be 6.4:1 for glucose, 6.1:1 for aspartate (the disproportionately high value for St. 5 in September is omitted), and 7.6:1 for acetate. Occasionally, considerably higher ratios were found (see Table 15.2).

The increase of V_{max} in the inner Kiel Fjord is generally gradual and runs parallel to the degree of eutrophication. Usually the eutrophication and hence V_{max} is highest in the innermost part of the Fjord. Exceptions are observed only when (due to special hydrographic conditions) sewage water is driven out into the Kiel Bight (Gocke, 1974a).

The stratification of the maximum uptake velocity has been studied in the case of glucose. Only at Station 1 (inner Kiel Fjord) was an appreciable variation with

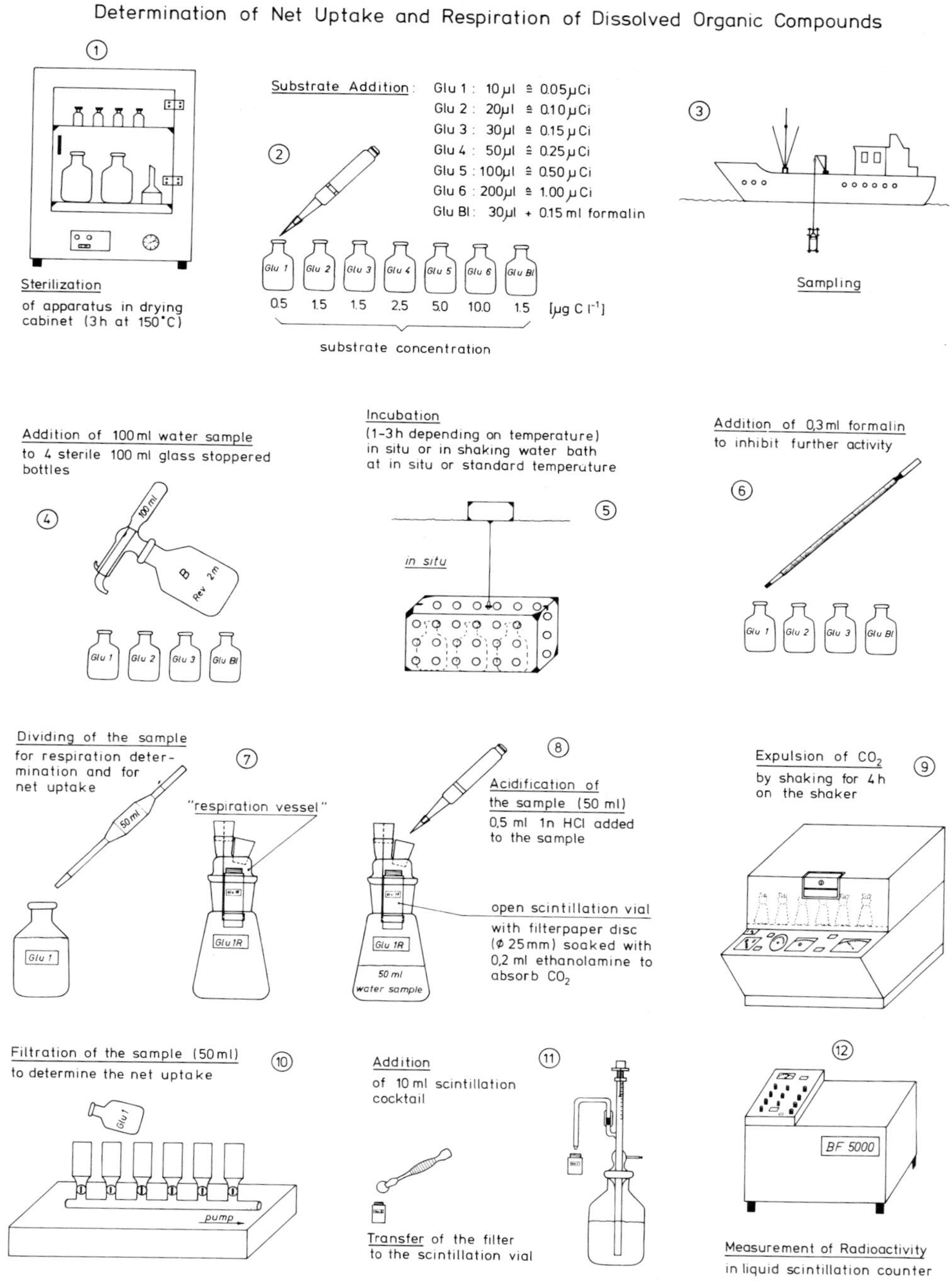

Determination of Net Uptake and Respiration of Dissolved Organic Compounds

①

Substrate Addition:

Glu 1 :	10 μl	≙ 0.05 μCi
Glu 2 :	20 μl	≙ 0.10 μCi
Glu 3 :	30 μl	≙ 0.15 μCi
Glu 4 :	50 μl	≙ 0.25 μCi
Glu 5 :	100 μl	≙ 0.50 μCi
Glu 6 :	200 μl	≙ 1.00 μCi
Glu Bl:	30 μl	+ 0.15 ml formalin

②

③

Sampling

Glu 1   Glu 2   Glu 3   Glu 4   Glu 5   Glu 6   Glu Bl

0.5   1.5   1.5   2.5   5.0   10.0   1.5   [μg C l^{-1}]

substrate concentration

Sterilization

of apparatus in drying cabinet (3h at 150°C)

Addition of 100 ml water sample
to 4 sterile 100 ml glass stoppered bottles

④

Glu 1   Glu 2   Glu 3   Glu Bl

Incubation
(1–3h depending on temperature) in situ or in shaking water bath at in situ or standard temperature

⑤

in situ

Addition of 0,3 ml formalin
to inhibit further activity

⑥

Glu 1   Glu 2   Glu 3   Glu Bl

Dividing of the sample
for respiration determination and for net uptake

⑦

"respiration vessel"

Glu 1

Glu 1R

⑧

Acidification of the sample (50 ml)
0,5 ml 1n HCl added to the sample

Glu 1R

50 ml
water sample

open scintillation vial with filterpaper disc (⌀ 25 mm) soaked with 0,2 ml ethanolamine to absorb CO_2

Expulsion of CO_2
by shaking for 4h on the shaker

⑨

Filtration of the sample (50 ml)
to determine the net uptake

⑩

pump

Addition
of 10 ml scintillation cocktail

⑪

Transfer of the filter to the scintillation vial

⑫

BF 5000

Measurement of Radioactivity
in liquid scintillation counter

Fig. 15.4. Scheme of the technique for the determination of T_t and the percentage respiration of a dissolved organic compound

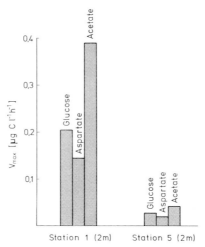

Fig. 15.5. Average values of V_{max} for glucose, aspartate and acetate in the inner Kiel Fjord (St. 1) and the central Kiel Bight (St. 5)

Table 15.2. Maximum uptake velocity ($\mu g\, C\, l^{-1}\, h^{-1}$) in the inner Kiel Fjord (St. 1) and in the central Kiel Bight (St. 5)

	Glucose					Aspartate		Acetate	
Station	1		5			1	5	1	5
Depth	2 m	10 m	2 m	10 m	18 m	2 m	2 m	2 m	2 m
Date									
Feb. 28, 1974	0.046	0.039	0.015	0.013	0.017	0.033	0.018	0.146	—
March 21	0.095	0.102	—	0.005	0.006	0.070	—	0.442	—
April 18	0.465	0.314	0.039	0.045	0.148	0.296	0.024	1.044	—
May 16	0.452	0.059	0.025	0.019	0.011	0.360	0.027	0.795	0.098
June 11	0.291	0.140	0.046	0.030	0.027	0.230	0.045	0.346	—
July 11	0.134	0.136	0.031	0.041	0.028	0.134	0.030	0.218	0.024
Aug. 29	0.663	0.140	0.055	0.040	0.046	0.376	—	1.003	0.094
Sept. 12	0.180	0.152	0.051	0.038	0.053	0.155	0.293	0.372	0.090
Oct. 24	0.228	0.078	0.032	0.049	0.063	0.220	0.020	—	0.022
Nov. 21	0.024	0.042	0.018	0.020	0.021	0.029	0.009	0.076	0.015
Dec. 10	—	0.016	—	—	—	0.034	—	—	—
Jan. 23, 1975	0.030	0.030	0.006	0.005	0.010	0.023	0.010	0.059	0.010
Feb. 12	0.031	0.036	0.004	0.004	0.010	0.034	0.007	0.119	0.009
March 10	0.030	0.048	0.018	0.015	0.004	0.030	0.015	0.066	0.015

depth observed. The average variation range for all samples taken from 2-m to 10-m depth is about 2; the actual values are 0.205 and 0.095 $\mu g\, C\, l^{-1}\, h^{-1}$, respectively. More pronounced changes were found from May to October parallel to distinct variations of the chlorophyll a concentration. In contrast to these results, only slight vertical variations of V_{max} were observed at Station 5 (central Kiel Bight). The exceptionally high value at 18 m (April 1974) might be explained by an unusually high load of resuspended sediment caused by special hydrographic conditions. The annual average values of the maximum uptake velocity for glucose are: $0.028 \, \mu g \, C \, l^{-1} \, h^{-1}$ (2 m), $0.025 \, \mu g \, C \, l^{-1} \, h^{-1}$ (10 m), and $0.034 \, \mu g \, C \, l^{-1} \, h^{-1}$ (18 m).

It is generally accepted that bacteria play a dominant role in the uptake of organic solutes. Consequently the large variations of the maximum uptake velocity between the surface samples of the central Kiel Bight and the inner Kiel Fjord must be caused by such factors as quantitative and qualitative composition and physiological state of the bacterial populations. Furthermore, the physical and chemical conditions of the stations could play a significant role. Several of these factors were studied as part of this joint investigation. Results concerning the distribution of single fractions and of the total bacterial population—certainly a very heterogeneous group of organisms—are given in Chapters 10, 11, 12, and 14. It is certainly worthwhile to present some of these results and to discuss their impact on the distribution of the maximum uptake velocity.

On an annual basis, the total number of bacteria (direct counts) at Station 1 (inner Kiel Fjord) is typically 2.1 times higher than at Station 5 (central Kiel Bight). Thus the increase in the inner fjord is on the average not very pronounced in comparison with the increase of V_{max}. Since it is difficult or impossible to differentiate microscopically between active, and dead or inactive bacteria, a closer agreement of the ratios of V_{max} and the number of active bacteria between the two stations should be expected. Nevertheless, the ratio for active bacteria is only slightly higher than for the total number of bacteria.

The discrepancy between bacterial numbers and V_{max} cannot be explained by differences of the physical and chemical conditions at both stations since temperature, salinity and oxygen concentration vary only slightly. Thus it is reasonable to assume that significant qualitative differences exist between the bacterial populations of the central Kiel Bight and the inner Kiel Fjord.

This assumption is supported by the results of the studies on saprophytic bacteria (cf. Chap. 11). It can be shown from yearly records that the average number of saprophytic bacteria is about 50 times higher in the inner Kiel Fjord than in the central Kiel Bight, whereas the total number of bacteria increases only by a factor of about 2. The role of saprophytic bacteria in the breakdown of organic matter is usually regarded to be of minor importance, since this "group" of bacteria represents only a small fraction of the total bacterial population in most areas (Jannasch, 1969; Schmidt, 1973; Herbland and Pagés, 1976). However, in the inner Kiel Fjord the number of saprophytic bacteria is relatively high, and their fraction of the total population is much greater (up to 2.5%) than in offshore waters of the Baltic Sea (Gocke, 1977).

If one compares the situation in the inner Kiel Fjord with that in the Kiel Bight one finds (as already stated) that the maximum uptake velocity is about 6.7 times higher and that the total number is only 2.1 times higher. The abundance of saprophytic bacteria on the other hand is about 100 times higher than in the inner Kiel Fjord. The discrepancy between maximum uptake velocity and the total number of bacteria suggests that the saprophytic bacteria play a more prominent role than expected from their small share within the total population. This assumption is supported by a previous study (Gocke, 1975a) in the inner Kiel Fjord, where short-term variations of V_{max} and the number of saprophytic bacteria were significantly correlated.

It should also be pointed out that the bacterial population at Station 1 (inner Kiel Fjord) could be better adapted to the uptake of low molecular organic substances. This might be caused by differences in the composition of the dissolved organic material between the eutrophicated inner Kiel Fjord and the much less eutrophic central Kiel Bight.

15.2.2 Spatial Distribution of the Sum of Transport "Constant" and Natural Substrate Concentration $(K_t + S_n)$

Since growth—and consequently activity—of heterotrophic bacteria is largely dependent on the supply of easily degradable organic compounds, it should be expected that the concentrations of these substances in the inner Kiel Fjord exceed those of the Kiel Bight to a significant extent. This should be reflected in the values of the parameter $K_t + S_n$. Contrary to expectation, the differences in $K_t + S_n$ between Station 1 (inner Kiel Fjord) and Station 5 (central Kiel Bight) are on the average very small (see Table 15.3). A correlation between the level of eutrophication of the area and the value of $K_t + S_n$ does not seem to exist. Concerning aspartate, we even found a somewhat higher average value of $K_t + S_n$ at the central Kiel Bight.

Generally the value of $K_t + S_n$ of acetate is higher than for the two other substrates studied. This was also observed by Wright and Hobbie (1966), Allen (1969), Wright (1975). $K_t + S_n$ of glucose is on the average somewhat smaller than for aspartate. Differences in the natural concentrations or in the value of the

Table 15.3. The sum of the transport "constant" and the natural substrate concentration ($\mu g \, C \, l^{-1}$) in the inner Kiel Fjord (St. 1) and the central Kiel Bight (St. 5)

	Glucose					Aspartate		Acetate	
Station	1		5			1	5	1	5
Depth	2 m	10 m	2 m	10 m	18 m	2 m	2 m	2 m	2 m
Date									
Feb. 28, 1974	1.10	1.06	0.84	0.86	2.18	1.21	4.21	4.30	—
March 21	0.90	0.83	—	1.28	3.15	2.92	—	5.41	—
April 18	1.89	0.93	0.40	0.56	0.76	0.72	1.05	7.11	—
May 16	1.44	0.58	1.32	0.91	4.27	2.33	3.12	7.87	21.5
June 11	0.81	0.85	0.63	0.40	0.40	2.67	3.22	6.48	—
July 11	0.74	1.02	1.16	0.81	0.88	2.70	4.49	5.61	4.11
Aug. 29	4.70	0.84	2.76	1.10	1.67	1.44	—	11.29	5.33
Sept. 12	2.78	1.33	1.11	1.39	1.39	1.77	4.47	2.86	2.18
Oct. 24	1.20	1.72	0.54	1.33	1.23	2.52	2.31	—	2.49
Nov. 21	0.74	1.02	1.26	0.85	1.27	0.89	0.92	3.25	3.66
Dec. 10	—	0.99	—	—	—	3.47	—	—	—
Jan. 23, 1975	0.87	0.79	1.09	0.51	1.00	1.69	3.07	2.94	4.13
Feb. 12	1.12	0.89	1.44	0.97	1.68	1.53	5.39	4.31	3.15
March 10	1.00	1.30	2.04	1.13	0.73	1.66	1.06	4.67	4.24

transport "constant" of these two substrates may account for this observation. One also has to consider that the uptake system for glucose seems to be specific (Wright and Hobbie, 1966), while this is not the case for aspartate (Burnison and Morita, 1973).

The results of determination for $K_t + S_n$ of glucose and acetate, obtained in this study, are in good agreement with data of Wright and Hobbie (1966) for an oligotrophic lake. (Aspartate was not included in their study). Other authors found values which are sometimes higher by an order of magnitude (cf. Table 15.1). Seki et al. (1975) obtained a value of 284 µg C l⁻¹ for glucose in the surface water of the polluted Shimoda Bay (Japan), in contrast to maximally 4.7 µg Cl⁻¹ found in samples of the inner Kiel Fjord in this study. The relatively low values of $K_t + S_n$ obtained in this study for the Kiel Bight and Kiel Fjord consequently indicate good adaptation of the bacterial populations to the uptake of very low concentrations of dissolved organic substances.

15.2.3 Spatial Distribution of the Turnover Time

The turnover times of the three substrates studied show considerable differences between Station 1 (inner Kiel Fjord) and Station 5 (central Kiel Bight). Without exception the turnover times measured at Station 5 are longer than at Station 1 (see Table 15.4). On the average, ratios of 3.5:1 for glucose, 4.6:1 for aspartate, and 5.6:1 for acetate were found. Although at present no data on the natural concentrations of the substrates are available, one can assume that the uptake of these compounds given in units of µg Cl⁻¹ is considerably higher in the eutrophic inner Kiel Fjord than in the Kiel Bight. If we assume that the concen-

Table 15.4. Turnover time (h) of glucose, aspartate and acetate in the inner Kiel Fjord (St. 1) and in the central Kiel Bight (St. 5)

	Glucose					Aspartate		Acetate	
Station	1		5			1	5	1	5
Depth	2 m	10 m	2 m	10 m	18 m	2 m	2 m	2 m	2 m
Date									
Feb. 28, 1974	24.1	27.7	56.1	65.3	127	36.8	234	29.4	—
March 21	9.4	8.8	—	277	523	41.4	—	12.2	—
April 18	4.1	3.0	10.3	12.4	5.1	2.4	44.7	6.8	—
May 16	3.2	9.9	52.2	49.4	387	6.5	118	9.9	219
June 11	2.8	6.1	13.7	13.4	15.1	11.6	72.4	18.7	—
July 11	5.6	7.6	37.2	19.9	31.1	20.2	149	25.7	174
Aug. 29	7.1	6.1	50.4	27.3	36.5	3.8	—	11.3	56.4
Sept. 12	15.5	8.1	21.6	36.6	26.1	11.4	15.2	7.7	24.3
Oct. 24	5.3	22.7	16.8	26.8	19.5	11.5	113	—	112
Nov. 21	31.2	24.4	69.7	41.9	60.5	31.2	97.7	50.0	237
Dec. 10	—	63.4	—	—	—	102		—	
Jan. 23, 1975	29.6	27.0	167	79.7	96.5	74.2	297	50.1	429
Feb. 12	35.7	24.4	395	295	166	44.6	811	36.1	361
March 10	33.5	27.0	112	73.6	182	54.9	105	71.1	276

Table 15.5. Turnover time (h) of an amino acid mixture in the inner Kiel Fjord (St. 1) and in the central Kiel Bight (St. 5)

Station	1		5		
Depth	2 m	10 m	2 m	10 m	18 m
Date					
Feb. 28, 1974	32.5	49.9	122	101	151
March 21	10.0	8.0	16.7	238	259
April 18	3.1	5.7	41.7	33.5	10.7
May 16	2.5	7.5	140	56.9	26.5
June 11	3.6	10.6	37.8	24.3	18.7
July 11	5.1	6.4	19.6	12.0	23.4
Aug. 29	2.9	7.3	11.7	18.6	13.9
Sept. 12	4.6	4.4	17.0	26.5	13.7
Oct. 24	2.7	11.4	29.7	16.6	23.6
Nov. 21	28.3	45.8	67.6	47.0	29.8
Dec. 10	22.2	17.0	134	119	165
Jan. 23, 1975	25.6	9.6	62.5	47.6	34.9
Feb. 12	12.4	8.0	65.8	103	54.1
March 10	23.8	22.7	17.7	22.7	26.7

trations available to the heterotrophic bacteria of the three substrates under investigation are about the same at the two stations (see above), then the ratios for the uptake would be similar to those for the T_t.

The vertical variation of the turnover time for glucose is far less pronounced than the horizontal. For both the inner Kiel Fjord and the central Kiel Bight somewhat longer turnover times are found close to the bottom than at the 2-m depth, analogous to the maximum uptake velocities. It should be noted that the actual turnover times are somewhat shorter if the gross uptake is determined. However, since all values will be reduced by a similar percentage, this has no effect on the spatial differences.

In addition to the turnover times of the three single compounds, the turnover time of a mixture of free dissolved amino acids was determined. In this case measurements of the respiration of this mixture were included in the study. Thus the turnover times presented in Table 15.5 are related to the gross uptake. For the horizontal and vertical variations of the T_t for the mixture, similar conclusions as above for those of the single compounds are valid. On an average the turnover time in the central Kiel Bight is about 5.2 times longer than in the Kiel Fjord, whereas the vertical differences are considerably smaller.

15.3 Seasonal Distribution of Heterotrophic Activity

15.3.1 Seasonal Distribution of Maximum Uptake Velocity

The annual variations of the maximum uptake velocity of glucose, aspartate and acetate are shown in Figure 15.6. Obviously there is a remarkable similarity between the maximum uptake velocity of the three compounds. The same obser-

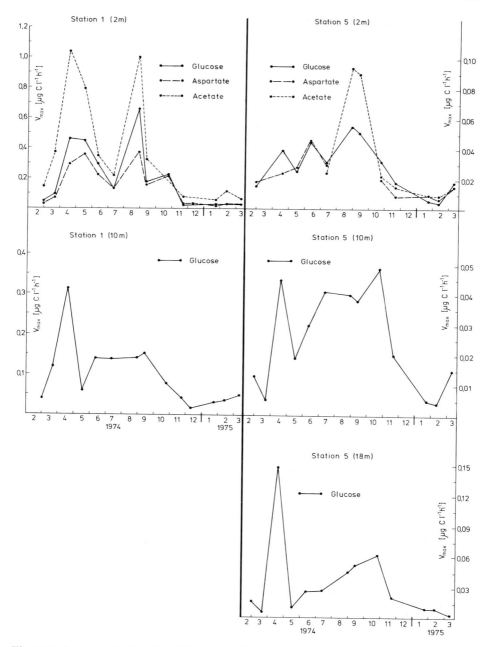

Fig. 15.6. Seasonal distribution of V_{max} in the inner Kiel Fjord (St. 1) and the central Kiel Bight (St. 5)

vations were obtained with previous studies at other stations in the Kiel Fjord (Gocke, unpubl.). It can be concluded therefore, that a (probably large) fraction of the bacterial population is able to take up all the three substrates studied. If the uptake caused by distinct subpopulations were restricted to only one of the substrates it would have to be concluded that these subpopulations are present in nearly the same relation throughout the year. However, since the compounds studied are easily degradable the first assumption seems to be valid. Studies performed by Hoppe (1974) show that almost all of the saprophytic bacteria of the studied area take up glucose as well as aspartic acid or acetate (cf. Chap. 14).

Figure 15.6 shows further that the net uptake velocity of acetate is almost always considerably higher than that of the two other substrates. This is especially remarkable for Station 1 (inner Kiel Fjord), where the heterotrophic activity is generally high. At Station 5 (central Kiel Bight), with much smaller activity, a few exceptions can be seen. The average annual maximum uptake velocities (net uptake) at the inner Kiel Fjord (2-m depth) are: acetate $0.390 \, \mu g \, C \, l^{-1} \, h^{-1}$; glucose $0.205 \, \mu g \, C \, l^{-1} \, h^{-1}$; aspartate $0.145 \, \mu g \, C \, l^{-1} \, h^{-1}$. The gross uptake values are: acetate $0.527 \, \mu g \, C \, l^{-1} \, h^{-1}$; glucose $0.266 \, \mu g \, C \, l^{-1} \, h^{-1}$; aspartate $0.284 \, \mu g \, C \, l^{-1} \, h^{-1}$. These values are based on measurements of the percentage respiration performed in later studies (Gocke, unpubl.). Thus, in the eutrophic inner Kiel Fjord, acetate is taken up about twice as fast as glucose. In the central Kiel Bight the differences in uptake velocity are far less marked. Investigations of other authors in eutrophic lakes showed also considerably higher uptake rates of acetate than of glucose (Allen, 1969, 1973; Francisco, 1971; Wright 1975). In contrast to these studies Parsons and Strickland (1962) found a reverse relationship on the Canadian westcoast.

The maximum uptake velocity shows pronounced seasonal variations (see Fig. 15.6). With possibly the exception of the 2-m sample of Station 5 (central Kiel Bight), where some analyses had to be rejected, distinct peaks of V_{max} at all depths were found for both stations in April, followed by a strong decrease. Due to stratification, the agreement between surface and depth samples was less pronounced during summer. The surface samples show another distinct peak in August/September.

The relation between the maximum uptake velocity and the water temperature at Station 1 can be seen in Figure 15.7. The maximum temperature coincides approximately with the summer peak of the heterotrophic activity. The decrease during fall also runs parallel for both parameters. On the other hand, it is obvious that the spring peak of V_{max} still occurs at relatively low temperatures. This shows that temperature plays a large role, but clearly is not the only factor determining the changes of V_{max} during the year.

Wright and Hobbie (1966) found a value of Q_{10} (the factor by which V_{max} increases when the incubation temperature is increased by $10°$ C) for the maximum uptake velocity of 2.2. This is in good agreement with my own observations (Gocke, unpubl.). Thus, an increase in temperature of about $15°$ C between summer and winter should lead to a rise of V_{max} by about a factor of 3–4, even if the bacterial density of the samples were constant. The observed variations of V_{max} by more than one order of magnitude thus suggest seasonal changes in size and composition of the bacterial population (cf. Chaps. 10 and 11).

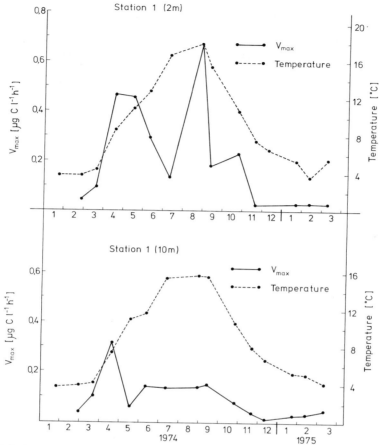

Fig. 15.7. Relationship between V_{max} (glucose) and temperature in the inner Kiel Fjord (St. 1)

The relationship between the seasonal variations of the concentration of chlorophyll a, the bacterial biomass, and the maximum uptake velocity of glucose in 2-m samples of the inner Kiel Fjord (St. 1) and the central Kiel Bight (St. 5) are shown in Figure 15.8. At Station 1, a rapid increase of all three parameters is observed in April. However, in summer the peaks of V_{max} and bacterial biomass follow the chlorophyll maximum with a delay of several weeks. A possible explanation could be that sampling in July might have been performed at the start or in the early stages of an algal bloom when conditions for bacteria were unfavorable due to inhibition. Later, in August after the breakdown of the algal bloom, the concentration of labile organic substances increased and led to an intensive development of bacteria. A similar delay was probably found in March 1975. The temporal connections between phytoplankton and bacteria found in the inner Kiel Fjord was not observed in the central Kiel Bight. One of the reasons for this is certainly that the time intervals between the samplings were too long for exact interpretation of the complicated interactions between both groups of organisms.

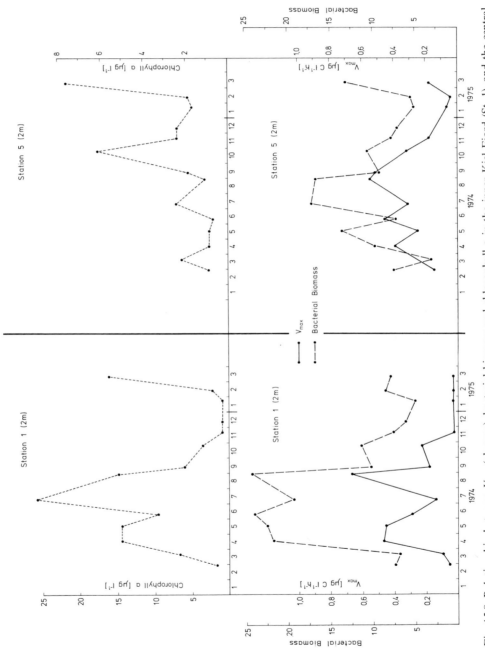

Fig. 15.8. Relationship between V_{max} (glucose), bacterial biomass and chlorophyll a in the inner Kiel Fjord (St. 1), and the central Kiel Bight (St. 5)

Despite the imperfect results obtained at the central Kiel Bight, the following simplified scheme is proposed as a general rule for the whole area under study: organic material is released by phytoplankton during all stages of development, especially during stationary growth phase and breakdown of an algal bloom (Gocke, 1970; Steinberg, 1975; Stabel, 1976). This organic material regulates development and activity of the bacteria, thus bacterial activity runs parallel to the growth of algae or, more probably, follows with a certain delay. Since this scheme holds true with great certainty for the eutrophic inner Kiel Fjord, it has to be concluded that even in this area despite the many anthropogenetic influences (waste water, etc.) the amount of organic substances formed by autochthonous processes surpasses that which is supplied from allochthonous sources.

In connection with these studies on the temporal relationship between chlorophyll a and V_{max}, it should be taken into consideration how much of the heterotrophic uptake of organic solutes is due to bacteria or to phytoplankton. Several authors have studied this problem, and most of them conclude that the uptake by phytoplankton plays a minor role when compared to bacterial uptake (Wright and Hobbie, 1966; Munro and Brock, 1968; Williams, 1970; Sorokin, 1971; Bennett and Hobbie, 1972; Derenbach and Williams, 1974). On the other hand, heterotrophic uptake of dissolved organic substances by algae could be demonstrated (Saunders, 1972; Hoppe, 1976). However, previous studies in the inner Kiel Fjord (Gocke, 1975b) revealed that by far the major part of glucose supplied in natural concentrations is taken up by bacteria.

15.3.2 Seasonal Distribution of the Turnover Time

The seasonal variations of the turnover times of glucose, aspartate and acetate are shown in Figure 15.9. In general, short turnover times were observed from April to October. This coincides roughly with the period during which the water temperature exceeds 8–10° C. In late fall and winter rather long T_ts up to more than 800 h (aspartate at St. 5) have been measured. A basically similar behavior was found in respect to the season for all three substrates studied.

Usually the turnover times at Station 5 are much longer than at Station 1. The turnover times of glucose at the inner Kiel Fjord differ by a factor of about 20 during the year. Allen (1969) observed similar seasonal variations in the eutrophic Swedish lake Lötsjön. At the less productive central Kiel Bight the seasonal changes were found to be more pronounced than at the eutrophic inner Kiel Fjord. Andrews and Williams (1971) determined turnover rates of glucose (turnover rate is the reciprokal value of the turnover time given as %) in the English Channel, where seasonal differences of more than two orders of magnitude were found. Variations of about the same magnitude were observed by Wright and Hobbie (1966) at Lake Erken (Sweden). It is generally assumed that the seasonal changes of T_t are mainly caused by changes of the actual uptake velocity, and only to a smaller degree by variations of the natural concentrations of substrate. Thus, the relatively small variation in turnover times at the eutrophic inner Kiel Fjord indicates that in eutrophic and in polluted areas the decrease of heterotrophic activity during winter is less pronounced than in less eutrophic areas.

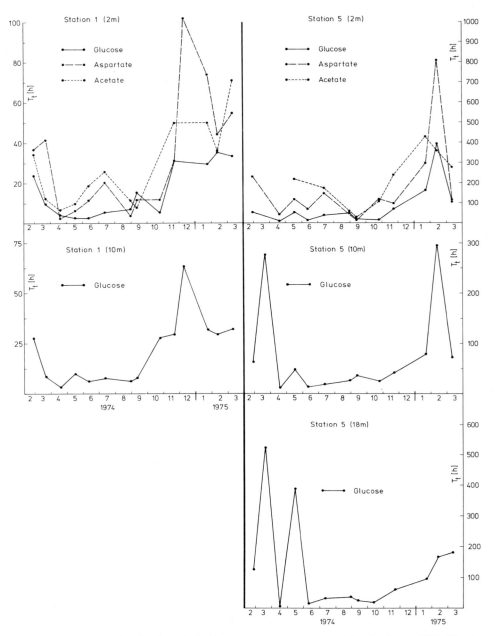

Fig. 15.9. Seasonal distribution of T_t (glucose, aspartate, acetate) in the inner Kiel Fjord (St. 1) and the central Kiel Bight (St. 5)

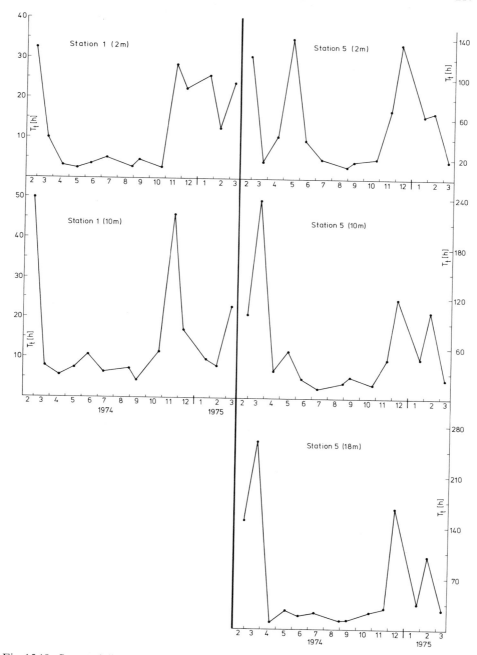

Fig. 15.10. Seasonal distribution of T_t (amino acid mixture) in the inner Kiel Fjord (St. 1) and the central Kiel Bight (St. 5)

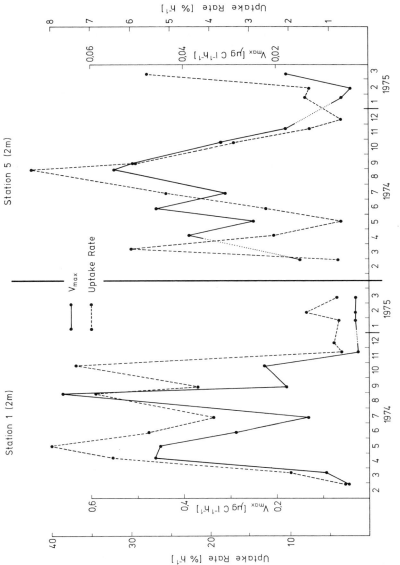

Fig. 15.11. Relationship between the maximum uptake velocity (V_{max}) of glucose and the turnover rate (T_t) of an amino acid mixture in the inner Kiel Fjord (St. 1) and the central Kiel Bight (St. 5)

Figure 15.10 shows the seasonal variations of the turnover time of an amino acid mixture. Here, a similar behavior was found concerning the T_ts of the other substrates studies; when the turnover time of the AA mixture is converted to turnover rates, a clear relationship between this parameter and the maximum uptake velocity of glucose is obvious (see Fig. 15.11). This can only be explained by the fact that the concentration of the sum of the dissolved free amino acids available to the bacteria is relatively constant throughout the year. Thus the actual uptake velocity of these substances is more or less a content part of the potential uptake velocity.

Andrews and Williams (1971) determined the turnover rate, the natural concentration, and the percentage respiration of glucose in the English Channel. Thus it was possible to calculate the annual flux rate of glucose and the resulting formation of bacterial biomass. The value obtained for the annual flux rate was $8 \, \text{g C m}^{-2}$ and the formation of bacterial biomass resulting from the uptake of glucose amounted to ca. $5.4 \, \text{g C m}^{-2}$.

In the present study annual averages of the turnover time of glucose due to net uptake were calculated. The values were: 15 h (St. 1, inner Kiel Fjord, 2 m); 17.7 h (St. 1, 10 m); 73.3 h (St. 5, central Kiel Bight, 2 m); 72.9 h (St. 5, 10 m), and 96.5 h (St. 5, 18 m). Since the concentrations of glucose were not determined, the annual production of bacterial biomass can only be estimated. The annual average value of $K_t + S_n$ may help in estimating the concentration of glucose available to the bacteria. On the average $K_t + S_n$ amounted to about $1.2 \, \mu\text{g Cl}^{-1}$ for both the inner Kiel Fjord and the central Kiel Bight. Half of this value might be due to the natural concentration of glucose. Andrews and Williams (1971) determined glucose concentrations in the English Channel. They obtained values of 0.16–$2.3 \, \mu\text{g}$ Cl^{-1}. Thus the bacterial biomass production per year, given a concentration of glucose of $0.6 \, \mu\text{g Cl}^{-1}$, is estimated to be $3.3 \, \text{g C m}^{-2}$ at the inner Kiel Fjord and $1.3 \, \text{g C m}^{-2}$ at the central Kiel Bight. This, of course, is the production due only to the uptake of a single compound, namely glucose.

15.3.3 Seasonal Distribution of the Sum of Transport "Constant" and Natural Substrate Concentration $(K_t + S_n)$

Although considerable annual variations of $K_t + S_n$ were observed, a relationship to temperature is not evident. The parameter runs parallel to some extent to the maximum uptake velocity, but this is restricted to V_{max} of glucose and acetate and is only seen at the inner Kiel Fjord (see Fig. 15.12). The different behavior of $K_t + S_n$ of aspartate might be due to the fact that this amino acid is not taken up by a transport enzyme which is specific to aspartate. Variations in $K_t + S_n$ can be caused by changes in either the transport "constant", or the natural substrate concentration, or by simultaneous variations of both parameters. Since high concentrations of dissolved organic compounds certainly induce higher uptake rates, the observed parallel between the maximum uptake velocities and the $K_t + S_n$ values for glucose and acetate might be due to higher concentrations of these two compounds. However, it is also possible that, when high peaks of V_{max} were observed, distinct bacterial groups with high transport "constants" dominate the uptake of glucose and acetate. Since at present the natural concentrations of the

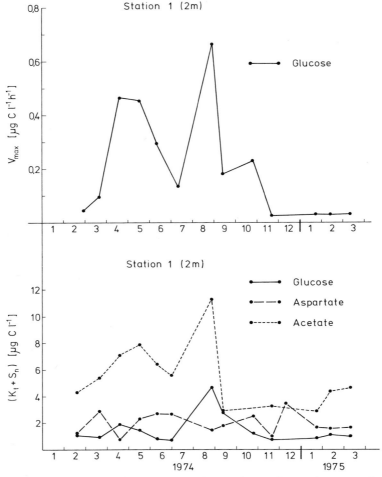

Fig. 15.12. Seasonal distribution of $K_t + S_n$ and its relation to the maximum uptake velocity of glucose in the inner Kiel Fjord (St. 1)

three substrates studied are not known for the Kiel Bight and Kiel Fjord, a choice between the two possibilities mentioned would be largely speculative.

Of considerable interest is a comparison between regional and seasonal variations in chlorophyll a concentration and the value for $K_t + S_n$. Since ultimately the phytoplankton produces the dissolved organic substances, a relationship between these two parameters would be expected. It is interesting to note that $K_t + S_n$ varies maximally by one order of magnitude, whereas the seasonal and regional differences of the chlorophyll a concentration are much greater. Since the parameter $K_t + S_n$ gives at least some idea of the size of the natural substrate concentration, the relatively small changes of $K_t + S_n$ suggest the presence of a mechanism which stabilizes the variations of the concentrations of dissolved organic substrates on a low level (cf. Andrews and Williams, 1971). At this low level, a balance between release and uptake of organic substances is achieved which can be disturbed only for short periods of time. This controlling function clearly can be attributed to the activity of heterotrophic microorganisms.

References

Allen, H. L.: Chemo-organotrophic utilization of dissolved organic compounds by planktonic algae and bacteria in a pond. Intern. Rev. ges. Hydrobiol. **54**, 1–33 (1969)

Allen, H. L.: Dissolved organic carbon: patterns of utilization and turnover in two small lakes. Intern. Rev. ges. Hydrobiol. **58**, 617–624 (1973)

Andrews, P., Williams, P. J. LeB.: Heterotrophic utilization of dissolved organic compounds in the sea. III. Measurement of the oxidation rates and concentrations of glucose and amino acids in sea water. J. Mar. Biol. Ass. U.K. **51**, 115–125 (1971)

Bennet, M. E., Hobbie, J. E.: The uptake of glucose by *Chlamydomonas* sp. J. Phycol. **8**, 392–398 (1972)

Burnison, B. K., Morita, R. Y.: Competitive inhibition for amino acid uptake by the indigenous microflora of Upper Klamath Lake. Appl. Microbiol. **25**, 103–106 (1973)

Derenbach, J. B., Williams, P. J. LeB.: Autotrophic and bacterial production: fractionation of plankton populations by differential filtration of samples from the English Channel. Mar. Biol. **25**, 263–269 (1974)

Francisco, D. E.: Glucose and acetate utilization by the natural microbial community in a stratified reservoir. Ph. D. Thesis, Univ. North Carolina at Chapel Hill (1971)

Gocke, K.: Untersuchungen über Abgabe und Aufnahme von Aminosäuren und Polypeptiden durch Planktonorganismen. Arch. Hydrobiol. **67**, 285–367 (1970)

Gocke, K.: Methodische Probleme bei Untersuchungen zur mikrobiellen Stoffaufnahme in Gewässern. Kieler Meeresforsch. **30**, 12–23 (1974a)

Gocke, K.: Untersuchungen über den Einfluß des Salzgehaltes auf die Aktivität von Bakterienpopulationen des Süß- und Abwassers. Kieler Meeresforsch. **30**, 99–106 (1974b)

Gocke, K.: Studies on short-term variations of heterotrophic activity in the Kiel Fjord. Mar. Biol. **33**, 49–55 (1975a)

Gocke, K.: Untersuchungen über die Aufnahme von gelöster Glukose unter natürlichen Verhältnissen durch größenfraktioniertes Nano- und Ultrananoplankton. Kieler Meeresforsch. **31**, 87–94 (1975b)

Gocke, K.: Respiration von gelösten organischen Verbindungen durch natürliche Mikroorganismen-Populationen. Ein Vergleich zwischen verschiedenen Biotopen. Mar. Biol. **35**, 375–383 (1976)

Gocke, K.: Untersuchungen über die heterotrophe Aktivität in der zentralen Ostsee. Mar. Biol. **40**, 87–94 (1977)

Gocke, K.: A comparison of methods for determining the turnover times of dissolved organic methods. Mar. Biol. (1977) (in press)

Griffith, R. P., Hanus, F. J., Morita, R. Y.: The effect of various water-sample treatments on the apparent uptake of glutamic acid by natural marine microbial populations. Can. J. Microbiol. **20**, 1261–1266 (1974)

Hamilton, R. D., Preslan, J. E.: Observations on heterotrophic activity in the Eastern tropical Pacific. Limnol. Oceanogr. **15**, 395–401 (1970)

Herbland, A., Pagés, J.: Note on the variability of heterotrophic activity measurements by the ^{14}C method in sea water. Mar. Biol. **35**, 211–214 (1976)

Hobbie, J. E., Crawford, C. C.: Bacterial uptake of organic substrate: new methods of study and application to eutrophication. Verh. intern. Verein. theor. angew. Limnol. **17**, 725–730 (1969)

Hoppe, H.-G.: Untersuchungen zur Analyse mariner Bakterienpopulationen mit einer autoradiographischen Methode. Kieler Meeresforsch. **30**, 107–116 (1974)

Hoppe, H. G.: Determination and properties of actively metabolizing heterotrophic bacteria in the sea, investigated by means of micro-autoradiography. Mar. Biol. **36**, 291–302 (1976)

Jannasch, W.: Current concepts in aquatic microbiology. Verh. intern. Verein. Limnol. **17**, 25–39 (1969)

Munro, A. L. S., Brock, T. D.: Distinction between bacterial and algal utilization of soluble organic substances in the sea. J. Gen. Microbiol. **51**, 35–42 (1968)

Overbeck, J.: Distribution pattern of uptake kinetic responses in a stratified eutrophic lake (Plußsee ecosystem study IV). Verh. intern. Verein. Limnol. **19**, 2600–2615 (1975)

Parson, T. R., Strickland, J. D. H.: On the production of particulate organic carbon by heterotrophic processes in the sea. Deep Sea Res. **8**, 211–222 (1962)

Rodhe, W., Hobbie, J. E., Wright, R. T.: Phototrophy and heterotrophy in high mountain lakes. Mitt. intern. Verein. Limnol. **16**, 302–313 (1966)

Saunders, G. W.: Potential heterotrophy in a natural population of *Oscillatoria agardhii* var. *isothrix* Skuja. Limnol. Oceanogr. **17**, 704–711 (1972)

Schmidt, E. L.: The traditional plate count technique among modern methods. Chairman's summary. Bull. Ecol. Res. Comm. Stockholm **17**, 453–454 (1973)

Seki, H., Nakai, T., Otobe, H.: Regional differences on turnover rate of dissolved materials in the Pacific Ocean at summer 1971. Arch. Hydrobiol. **71**, 79–89 (1972)

Seki, H., Yamaguchi, Y., Ichimura, S.: Turnover rate of dissolved organic materials in a coastal region of Japan at summer stagnation period of 1974. Arch. Hydrobiol. **75**, 297–305 (1975)

Sorokin, J. J.: On the role of bacteria in the productivity of tropical oceanic waters. Intern. Rev. ges. Hydrobiol. **56**, 1–48 (1971)

Stabel, H.-H.: Gebundene Kohlenhydrate als stabile Komponenten im Schöhsee und in *Scenedesmus*-Kulturen, Thesis. Univ. Kiel 1976

Steinberg, Ch.: Schwer abbaubare, stickstoffhaltige gelöste organische Substanzen im Schöhsee und in Algenkulturen, Thesis Univ. Kiel 1975

Vaccaro, R. R.: The response of natural microbial populations in seawater to organic enrichment. Limnol. Oceanogr. **14**, 726–735 (1969)

Vaccaro, R. R., Jannasch, H. W.: Studies on heterotrophic activity in sea water based on glucose assimilation. Limnol. Oceanogr. **11**, 596–607 (1966)

Vaccaro, R. R., Jannasch, H. W.: Variations in uptake kinetics for glucose by natural populations in sea water. Limnol. Oceanogr. **12**, 540–542 (1967)

Williams, P. J. LeB.: Heterotrophic utilization of dissolved organic compounds in the sea. I. Size distribution of population and relationship between respiration and incorporation of growth substrates. J. Mar. Biol. Ass. U. K. **50**, 859–870 (1970)

Williams, P. J. LeB.: The validity of the application of simple kinetic analysis to heterogenous microbial populations. Limnol. Oceanogr. **18**, 159–165 (1973)

Williams, P. J., Askew, C.: A method of measuring the mineralization by microorganisms of organic compounds in sea water. Deep Sea Res. **15**, 365–375 (1968)

Wright, R. T.: Mineralization of organic solutes by heterotrophic bacteria. In: Effect of the Ocean Environment on Microbial Activities, pp. 546–565 Colwell, R. R., Morita, R. Y. (eds.), Baltimore-London-Tokyo: University Park Press (1974)

Wright, R. T.: Studies on glycolic acid metabolism by freshwater bacteria. Limnol. Oceanogr. **20**, 626–633 (1975)

Wright, R. T., Hobbie, J. E.: Use of glucose and acetate by bacteria and algae in aquatic ecosystems. Ecology **47**, 447–464 (1966)

16. Bacterial Growth Rates and Biomass Production

L.-A. Meyer-Reil

Bacteria contribute to the cycle of matter and serve as a nutrient source for filter-feeders in natural waters. The extent to which this occurs will be dependent on growth activity and biomass production of the bacterial populations.

Only very few detailed studies concerning bacterial growth rates have been presented. Weyland (1966), Jannasch (1969) and Hendricks (1972) determined the growth rates of marine and enteric bacterial strains in chemostat experiments. Straskrabova-Prokesova (1966) and Godlewska-Lipowa (1970, 1972) studied the generation time of aquatic bacterial populations on membrane filters and in closed containers, respectively. Measurements of the growth rates of attached aquatic bacteria in the natural environment were carried out by Bott and Brock (1970), Brock (1971) and Bott (1975).

Studies on the biomass production depending on cell division are very few in number. Most of the data available deal with the determination of the standing crop bacterial biomass. By using conversion factors, bacterial biomass was concluded from the assimilation of labeled glucose (Seki, 1970), the determination of ATP (Holm-Hansen and Paerl, 1972) or the lipopolysaccharide concentration (Watson unpubl. data, Dexter et al., 1975). Bacterial growth rates and biomass production based on the heterotrophic assimilation of CO_2 were determined by Kusnetsov and Romanenko (1966) and Romanenko (1973). Information on the direct determination of bacterial growth rates and biomass production by using light microscopy have been given by Sorokin (1969), Rodina (1972), and Straskrabova and Sorokin (1972).

The direct measurement of bacterial growth and production rates includes two main procedural difficulties: recognition of microorganisms (especially small cells and cells attached to detritus), and cultivation of bacterial populations under natural conditions. We were able to overcome part of these difficulties by incubating natural bacterial populations in a flow system and following the growth by fluorescence microscopy. Surface water samples were taken monthly over a one-year period at two stations in the Kiel Fjord (St. 1) and the Kiel Bight (St. 5). The following points have been studied in detail: (1) the portion of individual subpopulations on the growth and production rate of the total population, (2) the influence of temperature on growth activity, and (3) the influence of water quality on growth activity.

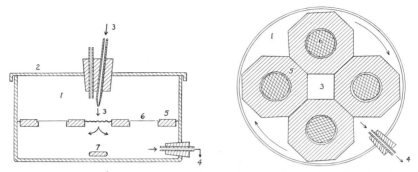

Fig. 16.1. Culture apparatus. *Left:* cross section. *Right:* top view. *1*: breeding chamber; *2*: lid of the chamber; *3*: water inlet; *4*: water outlet; *5*: swimming ring; *6*: filter; *7*: magnetic stirring bar. (According to Meyer-Reil, 1975)

16.1 Material and Methods

16.1.1 Sampling Procedure and Processing the Samples

Samples were collected monthly from a depth of 2 m at Station 1 (Reventlou Brücke, Kiel Fjord) and Station 5 (KBM II, central Kiel Bight) in sterile glass flasks using ZoBell water samplers, and stored in insulated boxes until they were processed in the laboratory.

Portions of the water samples were suspended in filter-sterilized water from the same station and filtered through 0.2 μm Nuclepore membrane filters. Prior to autoclaving, the filters were washed several times in boiling distilled water. Four filters were placed on swimming rings in the breeding chamber of the flow system and incubated under direct contact with filter-sterilized water from the same station. The flow rate of about 500 ml day^{-1} was controlled by a peristaltic pump (Desaga, type 132100). The flow system used (cf. Fig. 16.1) is a modification of the system developed by Kunicka-Goldfinger and Kunicki-Goldfinger (1972). Details are described by Meyer-Reil (1975). Parallel incubations were carried out at the in situ temperature for all samples, at 20° C (for samples taken from March to July and from November to February) and at 5° C (for samples taken from August to October), and samples from one station were incubated with water from the other station.

16.1.2 Assay Analysis

Single filters were removed periodically from the flow system, fixed on paper pads saturated with 2% formalin, air-dried, stained with acridine orange (see Zimmermann and Meyer-Reil, 1974; cf. also Chap. 10) and examined by fluorescence microscopy using a Zeiss Universal Microscope (BG 12, ×2; FL 500; BF 50; epifluorescence condensor III RS, Osram HBO 200; oculars ×12.5; intermediate magnification 1.25; Neofluar objective ×100). Microphotographs were taken with a Zeiss CS-matic camera using Agfapan Professional 400 film. Each filter was cut into four equal wedges with two alternate wedges used for counting. A total of 60 microscopic grids or fields were counted, chosen at approximately even intervals between the filter periphery and the center. The average cell density was 16 cells per grid. Only bodies with distinct fluorescence (orange or green), clear outline and recognizable bacterial shape were counted as bacterial cells. For the final analysis those filters were used which showed distinct cell division with limited, countable numbers of cells per microcolony. Filters fixed immediately after filtration and those treated as a sample, but rinsed with filter-sterilized seawater, served as controls. During the counting procedure separate counts were made for single cells and colony-forming cells (both attached and not attached to detritus) and filamentous cells. The sum of the separate counts equalled the total numbers of cells. The determination of the number of cells per filament was based on an average cell length of 0.8 μm, which was most frequently observed. Groups of three or more uniform cells were classified as colonies.

For the control and the bacterial populations incubated at in situ temperature, a size analysis of the cells was carried out in a limited number of microscopic fields (normally 15). Spherical cells were divided into four size classes (diameter between 0.2 and 0.8 μm) and rod-shaped cells into 18 size classes (length between 0.2 and 2.0 μm, width between 0.2 and 0.8 μm). Assuming a spherical shape for cocci and a cylindrical shape for rods, the corresponding volume for each size class was calculated. By multiplying cell volume by numbers, the bacterial volume of each size class, and the total bacterial volume in the water sample was determined. Bacterial biomass (mg) was calculated from the specific gravity of bacterial cells (s.g. equal to 1). Growth rates and biomass production were reported as increases in cell numbers and bacterial biomass ml^{-1} day^{-1}, respectively. The calculation of the generation time of the total population was according to Ivanoff (1955), the calculation of the generation time of cells capable of growth (colony-forming cells) was according to Straskrabova-Prokesova (1966).

16.2 Growth Activity and Biomass Production

Similar curves were observed for the seasonal fluctuations of bacterial numbers and biomass values for both stations. On an annual average, bacterial numbers and biomass were found to be twice as high for Station 1 near the shore in the inner Kiel Fjord as compared to Station 5 off the shore in the central Kiel Bight (see Table 16.1; cf. Chap. 10). Generally maxima and minima in cell numbers show up also in biomass values. However, the absolute amount of bacterial biomass was higher in summer and fall than in spring, due to an increase of larger rods during the summer. Single cells (not attached to detritus) accounted for the highest percentage of cell numbers and biomass (77–97%). Single cells attached to detritus (normally less than 5% of the total population) generally showed the tendency to increase in summer and fall. Greater numbers of filamentous cells occurred only in spring and summer. Colony-forming cells were found only related to maxima in the total number of cells (see Figs. 16.2, 16.3). Rod-shaped cells normally accounted for about 30% of the total number of cells, but for about 70% of the total biomass. These data are in the same range as the data reported by Ferguson and Rublee (1976). In contrast to the direct counts the number of colony-forming units showed great seasonal fluctuations (see Table 16.1).

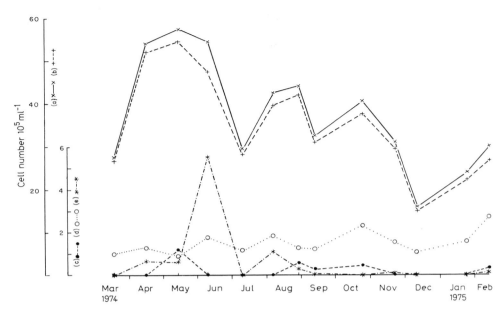

Fig. 16.2. Station 1 (Kiel Fjord). Seasonal changes of bacterial numbers. *a*: total number of cells; *b*: single cells not attached to detritus; *c*: colony-forming cells; *d*: single cells attached to detritus; *e*: filamentous cells

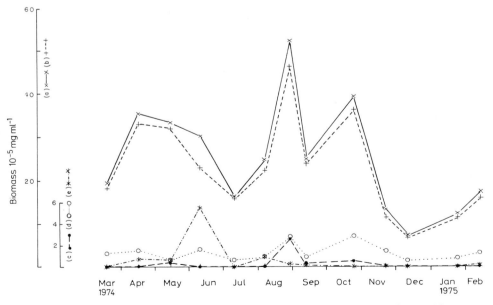

Fig. 16.3. Station 1. Seasonal changes of bacterial biomass. Legend see Figure 16.2

Table 16.1. Microbiological growth parameters. The range of the data measured during March 1974 to February 1975 is reported

	Station 1	Station 5
Colony-forming units (plate counts) (% of the total number of cells)		
natural seawater agar	0.04–1.3	0.0003–0.05
natural seawater agar (with nutrients)	0.1–8.4	0.01–0.2
Total number of cells (direct counts) (10^5 cells ml^{-1})	16–57 (37)	8–27 (17)
Total biomass (10^{-5} mg bacterial biomass ml^{-1})	8–52 (25)	4–19 (12)
Number of cells capable of growth (flow system) (% of the total number of cells)	0.2–0.6 (0.4)	0.1–1.7 (0.4)
Increase of the total number of cells (10^5 cells ml^{-1} day^{-1})		
July–October	6.7–13.7 (9.9)	0.2–4.4 (1.5)
November–June	0–3.0 (1.3)	0–0.9 (0.3)
Annual average (10^{13} cells m^{-3} y^{-1})	17	3
Generation time (h)		
Total population		
July-October	70–111 (88)	105–1,510 (811)
November–June	0–1,980	0–3,040
Cells capable of growth (flow system)		
July–October	7.7–13.4 (11.0)	11.9–71.4 (36.0)
November–June	15.2–37.2 (26.9)	0–114 (40.2)
Annual average	20.8	38.7
Biomass production (10^{-5} mg bacterial biomass ml^{-1} day^{-1})		
June–October	11.7–52.0 (25.9)	1.0–5.7 (2.5)
November–May	0.2–9.6 (7.0)	0–0.8 (0.2)
Annual average (g bacterial C m^{-2} y^{-1})	57	9
Primary production (g phytoplankton C m^{-2} y^{-1})	200[a]	60[b]

Mean values in parentheses.   [a] Probst, pers. comm.   [b] Literature see Horstmann, 1972.

Very low or even negative growth rates (increase in cell numbers ml^{-1} day^{-1}) and biomass production (increase in biomass ml^{-1} day^{-1}) were measured from late fall to early summer for both stations (see Table 16.1) Growth rates and biomass production drastically increased during summer and early fall. Colony-forming cells accounted for the highest percentage of the increase in numbers and biomass (see Figs. 16.4, 16.5). At the offshore station (St. 5), colonies attached to detritus dominated; at the station near the shore (St. 1) those not attached to detritus dominated. Rod-shaped cells were generally responsible for the highest percentage of the increase in cell numbers and biomass.

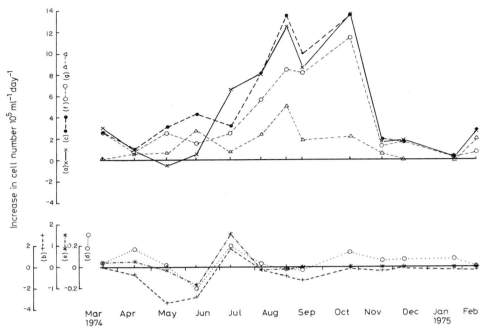

Fig. 16.4. Station 1. Seasonal changes of the growth activity after incubation at in situ temperature. Legend *a* to *e* see Figure 16.2; *f*: colony-forming cells (not attached to detritus); *g*: colony-forming cells (attached to detritus)

16.3 Generation Time and Influence of Temperature on Growth Activity

The generation time of cells capable of growth (colony-forming cells) was much lower and showed less seasonal fluctuation compared to the generation time of the total population (see Table 16.1). In contrast to in situ temperature, elevation of the temperature to 20° C (March to July and November to February) generally increased the average growth rates of the total population by 400% (St. 1) and 300% (St. 5). In early summer, fall, and winter the growth rates increased, whereas in spring the growth rates decreased after elevation of the temperature to 20° C. On the other hand, reduction of the temperature to 5° C (August to October) decreased the average growth rates of the total population to 27% (St. 1) and 5% (St. 5).

16.4 Influence of Quality of Water on Growth Activity

Incubation of bacterial populations from the station near the shore (St. 1) with water from the station offshore (St. 5) generally decreased the growth rates (annual average decrease 19%). However, incubation of populations from Station 5 with water from Station 1 led to a decrease of the growth rates during March to August and January to February and to an increase during September to Decem-

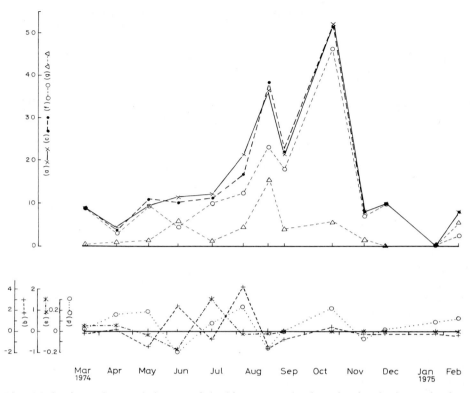

Fig. 16.5. Station 1. Seasonal changes of the biomass production after incubation at in situ temperature. Legend see Figure 16.4

ber (annual average increase 140%). During the summer the growth of micro-colonies attached to detritus is promoted by incubation of water samples from Station 1 with water from Station 5. However, incubation of bacterial populations from Station 5 with water from Station 1 increased the number of microcolonies not attached to detritus. Individual subpopulations (single cells attached and not attached to detritus and filamentous cells) from Station 1 were greatly influenced by incubation with water from Station 5. Their growth curves showed similarities to the growth curves of the corresponding subpopulations from Station 5 incubated with water from the same station.

The spectrum of microcolonies observed on the membranes seemed to be larger in spring than during any other season of the year. A much larger variety of colony types was growing on the membranes in the flow system as compared to the spectrum of isolates from agar plates (cf. Chap. 13).

Figure 16.6 gives an example of the spectrum of colonies obtained from one water sample (St. 1, March 21, 1974). Algal debris and detritus were colonized by one type or different types of bacterial cells. Small spherical cells (0.2–0.4 μm in diameter) grew exclusively in transparent clouds of detritus or bacterial slime (cf. Fig. 16.7). As shown by their formation of colonies and their constant cell size, these cells are obviously not starvation forms.

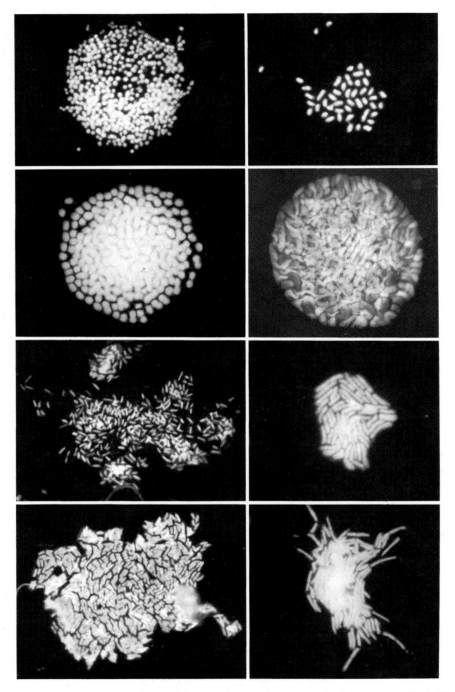

Fig. 16.6. Spectrum of colonies growing on the membranes in the flow system (St. 1, Kiel Fjord, March 21, 1974), × 2000

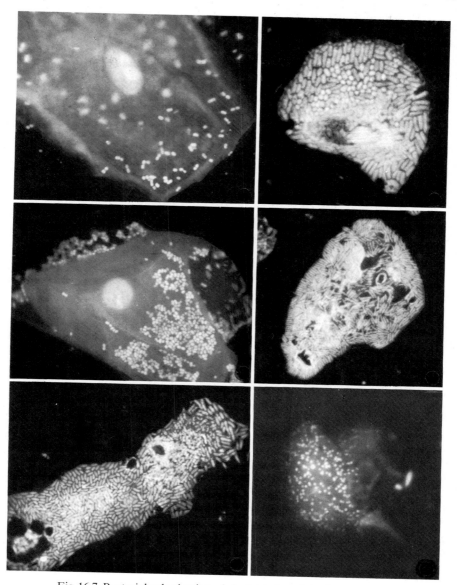

Fig. 16.7. Bacterial colonization of algal debris and detritus, ×2000

16.5 Discussion

The presented data show that the growth activity of a dynamic bacterial population is characterized inadequately by the generation time of the total population. Mainly in spring, the decrease in the number of cells of individual subpopulations was not always compensated by the increase in cell numbers caused by cell division. Frequently the total number of cells increased only insignificantly or was found to be even lower than the control counts. As a result of long generation times (up to 3000 h) even negative values were measured, although a considerable number of cells capable of growth was present (see Table 16.1).

The generation time of the cells capable of growth (colony-forming cells) provides more detailed information on the growth activity of a bacterial population. The generation time measured (St. 1, 21 h; St. 5, 39 h) is in the range of the generation time for marine periphytic bacteria and single marine bacterial strains reported in the literature (between 2.0 and 200 h, see Kriss and Rukina, 1952; Kriss and Lambina, 1955; ZoBell, 1963; Jannasch, 1969).

The growth activity of single subpopulations cannot be concluded from the growth activity of the total population. During most of the year the number of single cells not attached to detritus decreased after incubation. Sieburth et al. (1974) suggested that these unattached cells might be "nothing more than transients liberated from a richer substrate which are starving to death while waiting for another surface to colonize". Cells attached to detritus normally showed growth activity during most of the year, even when negative growth rates were measured for the total population. Providing both a higher nutrient concentration and an attachment surface, detritus is important for growth and metabolic activity of bacteria (ZoBell, 1943; Jannasch and Pritchard, 1972; Wiebe and Pomeroy, 1972; Corpe and Winters, 1972; Corpe, 1974; Hendricks, 1974).

For the station near the shore in the inner Kiel Fjord (St. 1) a significant correlation could be shown for the number of microcolonies growing on the membranes (a measurement for the growth activity of a bacterial population) and other parameters (total number of cells, colony-forming units on plates, maximum velocity of substrate uptake). In contrast, at the station off the shore in the central Kiel Bight (St. 5), the number of microcolonies correlate only with the maximum velocity of substrate uptake (see Table 16.2). This is obviously dependent on differences in both the bacterial populations and the methods used for the activity determinations. The water at the station near the shore is relatively polluted, including a broad spectrum of nonsensitive cells which show comparable activities even by using quite different methods for the activity determinations. However, at the station off the shore, comparable activities could be measured only by using those techniques which do not appreciably alter the natural environment. For a detailed discussion of the differences between the two stations based on two-state correlation analysis, series analysis, and time series analysis, see Chapter 19.

In comparison to in situ temperature, elevation of the temperature to 20° C led to an intensification of the influence of both growth-promoting and growth-limiting factors on the growth activity. Reduction of the temperature to 5° C led to an attenuation of this influence. The data indicated that the bacterial populations were not optimally adapted to the prevailing water temperature and that the temperature was a growth-regulating factor during most of the year.

Besides the temperature, the quality of water plays an important role in bacterial growth activity. The data reported cannot be explained by differences in the nutrient content of the water alone. It is suggested that during most of the year at the station offshore a bacterial population adapted to lower nutrient concentra-

Table 16.2. Correlation coefficients between the number of microcolonies growing on the membranes in the flow system and other parameters

	Correlation coefficients[a]	
	Station 1	Station 5
1. Cell numbers (direct counts)	0.83+	0.02
2. Colony-forming units (plate counts)		
a) Natural seawater agar	0.85+	0.07
b) Natural seawater agar (with nutrients)[b]	0.41	−0.48
c) ZoBell agar[c]	0.80+	−0.59
3. Number of active bacteria (micro-autoradiography)[d]	0.44	0.25
4. Maximum velocity of uptake[e]		
a) Glucose	0.83+	0.72+
b) Aspartic acid	0.93+	0.83+
c) Acetate	0.78+	0.58

[a] + significant correlation coefficient (95% confidence level).
[b] 0.05% Bacto-peptone, 0.01% yeast extract.
[c] Aged seawater/aqua dest. 1:4. Calculations based on data given by Rheinheimer (Chap. 11).
[d] Calculations based on data given by Hoppe (Chap. 14).
[e] Calculations based on data given by Gocke (Chap. 15).

tion was prevailing and/or that water from the station near the shore was exerting a growth-limiting effect on the populations of the station off the shore.

During spring, relatively high growth activities were measured when the level of cell numbers in the water samples was low. Relatively low or even negative growth rates were measured when the level of cell numbers in the water samples was high. The same was found occasionally for the relationship between cell numbers and growth activity of individual subpopulation (single cells attached to detritus, also filamentous cells and spherical cells). Differences in the nutrient concentration alone (e.g., exhaustion of nutrients caused by high cell numbers) are not sufficient to explain these observations. Further investigation is needed to clarify whether cell density in natural populations could be controlled by regulation factors.

An average biomass production of 57 g bacterial carbon $m^{-2} y^{-1}$ (St. 1, Kiel Fjord) and 9 g bacterial carbon $m^{-2} y^{-1}$ (St. 5, Kiel Bight) was calculated. These data are the same order of magnitude as the primary production by phytoplankton as reported in the literature: 200 g carbon $m^{-2} y^{-1}$ (Kiel Fjord, Probst, compare to Chap. 7), and 60 g carbon $m^{-2} y^{-1}$ (Kiel Bight, Horstmann, 1972). It is problematic to compare these data with the data for bacterial biomass production reported in the literature. The calculations given by ZoBell (1963) are based on an average bacterial biomass of 2×10^{-12} g and an average generation time for the total population of 24 h. However, as shown in this paper, these values are much too high. The data of Sorokin (1974) are based on biomass production measured in closed containers (see Godlewska-Lipowa, 1969). It is well known that great fluctuations occur in these containers and that the growth of mainly larger rods is promoted (see Kunicki-Goldfinger, 1974).

The biomass and biomass production data reported emphasize the role of bacteria as an important nutrient source for filter-feeders. According to Sorokin (1974) filter-feeding invertebrates need concentrations of 0.1–0.3 g wet bacterial biomass m^{-3} for their normal feeding. Zooplankton and other coarse filter-feeding organisms can use only aggregates, not single cells as a nutrient source (Sorokin, 1972). The importance of bacterial aggregates for the food chain was pointed out by Seki (1972). The percentage of bacterial biomass in aggregates (cells attached to detritus and colonies) was relatively low in the controls (about 10%) and increased drastically after incubation due to the formation of micro-colonies (to about 60% of the total biomass). Under natural conditions bacterial aggregates will be removed relatively quickly by predators and the sedimentation process.

The poor results obtained by Daley and Hobbie (1975) with the staining technique described by Zimmermann and Meyer-Reil (1974) were obviously due to the authors' difficulties in repeating our technique and the use of an unwettable batch of filters. It must generally be doubtful that better qualitative and quantitative results can be obtained by using cellulose ester membranes, where bacterial cells are trapped in all filter layers.

Compared to the natural environment, the flow system used, like every other assay device for the incubation of bacterial populations, must be an artificial system. The adsorption of nutrients at the surfaces in the flow system, the higher cell density on the membranes, and the subjectivity to a certain degree in the microscopic analysis have to be considered. However, incubation of bacterial populations in a flow system is close to simulating natural conditions. The method reported in this paper is to date the only direct approach to estimate bacterial growth activity and biomass production.

References

Bott, T. L.: Bacterial growth rates and temperature optima in a stream with fluctuating thermal regime. Limnol. Oceanogr. **20**, 191–197 (1975)

Bott, T. L., Brock, T. D.: Growth and metabolism of periphytic bacteria: Methodology. Limnol. Oceanogr. **15**, 333–342 (1970)

Brock, T. D.: Microbial growth rates in nature. Bacteriol. Rev. **35**, 39–58 (1971)

Corpe, W. A.: Periphytic marine bacteria and the formation of microbial films on solid surfaces. In: Colwell, R. R., Morita, R. Y. (eds.) Effect of the Ocean Environment on Microbial Activities, 397–417. Baltimore-London-Tokyo: University Park Press, 1974

Corpe, W. A., Winters, H.: Hydrolytic enzymes of some periphytic marine bacteria. Can. J. Microbiol. **18**, 1483–1490 (1972)

Daley, R. J., Hobbie, J. E.: Direct counts of aquatic bacteria by a modified epifluorescence technique. Limnol. Oceanogr. **20**, 875–882 (1975)

Dexter, S. C., Sullivan, J. D., Williams III, Jr., J., Watson, S. W.: Influence of substrate wettability on the attachment of marine bacteria to various surfaces. Appl. Microbiol. **30**, 298–308 (1975)

Ferguson, R. L., Rublee, P.: Contribution of bacteria to standing crop of coastal plankton. Limnol. Oceanogr. **21**, 141–145 (1976)

Godlewska-Lipowa, W. A.: Relationship between the generation time of a group of bacteria in water, and the exposure time and capacity of flasks. Bull. Acad. Pol. Sci., Ser. Sci. Biol. **17**, 233–237 (1969)

Godlewska-Lipowa, W. A.: Generation time of a group of bacteria in the water of Mazurian Lakes. Pol. Arch. Hydrobiol. **17**, 117–120 (1970)

Godlewska-Lipowa, W. A.: The effect of temperature on the generation time of a bacterial community in lake water. Bull. Acad. Pol. Sci., Ser. Sci. Biol. **20**, 653–656 (1972)

Hendricks, C. W.: Enteric bacterial growth rates in river water. Appl. Microbiol. **24**, 168–174 (1972)

Hendricks, C. W.: Sorption of heterotrophic and enteric bacteria to glass surfaces in the continuous culture of river water. Appl. Microbiol. **28**, 572–578 (1974)

Holm-Hansen, O., Paerl, H. W.: The applicability of ATP determination for estimation of microbial biomass and metabolic activity. In: Melchiorri-Santolini, U., Hopton, J. W. (eds.) Detritus and its Role in Aquatic Ecosystems. 149–168. Mem. Ist. Ital. Idrobiol., 29 Suppl. 1972

Horstmann, U.: Über den Einfluß von häuslichem Abwasser auf das Plankton in der Kieler Bucht. Kieler Meeresforsch. **28**, 178–198 (1972)

Ivanoff, M. V.: The method of estimation of bacterial biomass in the water body. Microbiologia **24**, 79–89 (1955)

Jannasch, H. W.: Estimations of bacterial growth rates in natural waters. J. Bacteriol. **99**, 156–160 (1969)

Jannasch, H. W., Pritchard, P. H.: The role of inert particulate matter in the activity of aquatic microorganisms. In: Melchiorri-Santolini, U., Hopton, J. W. (eds.), Detritus and its Role in Aquatic Ecosystems. 289–308 Mem. Ist. Ital. Idrobiol. 29 Suppl. (1972)

Kriss, A. E., Lambina, V. A.: Rapid increase of microorganisms in the ocean in the region of the North Pole. (In Russian). Usp. Sov. Biol. **39**, 366–373 (1955). (Cited after ZoBell 1963)

Kriss, A. E., Rukina, E. A.: Biomass of microorganisms and their rate of reproduction in oceanic depths. (In Russian). Zurn. Obshch. Biol. **13**, 346–362 (1952). (Cited after ZoBell 1963)

Kunicka-Goldfinger, W., Kunicki-Goldfinger, W. J. H.: Semicontinuous culture of bacteria on membrane filters. I. Use for the bioassay of inorganic and organic nutrients in aquatic environments. Acta Microbiol. Pol. Ser. B **4**, 49–60 (1972)

Kunicki-Goldfinger, W. J. H.: Methods in aquatic microbiology. A story of apparent precision and frustrated expectations. Pol. Arch. Hydrobiol. **21**, 3–17 (1974)

Kusnetsov, S. I., Romanenko, W. I.: Produktion der Biomasse heterotropher Bakterien und die Geschwindigkeit ihrer Vermehrung im Rybinsk-Stausee. Verh. intern. Ver. Limnol. **16**, 1493–1500 (1966)

Meyer-Reil, L.-A.: An improved method for the semi-continuous culture of bacterial populations on Nuclepore membrane filters. Kieler Meeresforsch. **31**, 1–6 (1975)

Rodina, A. G.: Methods in Aquatic Microbiology. Colwell, R. R., Zambruski, M. S. (eds.) Baltimore-London-Tokyo: University Park Press, 1972

Romanenko, V. I.: Abundance and production of bacteria in Latvian lakes. Verh. intern. Ver. Limnol. **18**, 1306–1310 (1973)

Seki, H.: Microbial biomass on particulate organic matter in seawater of the euphotic zone. Appl. Microbiol. **19**, 960–962 (1970)

Seki, H.: The role of microorganisms in the marine food chain with reference to organic aggregate. In: Melchiorri-Santolini, U., Hopton, J. W. (eds.) Detritus and its Role in Aquatic Ecosystems. 245–259 Mem. Ist. Ital. Idrobiol., 29 Suppl. 1972

Sieburth, J. McN., Brooks, R. D., Gessner, R. V., Thomas, C. D., Tootle, J. L.: Microbial colonization of marine plant surfaces as observed by scanning electron microscopy. In: Colwell, R. R., Morita, R. Y. (eds.) Effect of the Ocean Environment on Microbial Activities. 418–432. Baltimore-London-Tokyo: University Park Press, 1974

Sorokin, Y. I.: Bacterial production. In: Vollenweider, R. A. (ed.) A Manual on Methods for Measuring Primary Production in Aquatic Environments. IBP Handbook No. 12, 128–146. Philadelphia, PA.: F. A. Davis Co. 1969

Sorokin, Y. I.: Evaluation of the aggregation level of planktonic bacteria. In: Sorokin, Y. I., Kadota, H. (eds.) Techniques for the Assessment of Microbial Production and Decomposition in Fresh Waters. IBP Handbook No. 23, 76. Oxford: Blackwell Scientific Publications (1972)

Sorokin, Y. I.: Bacterial production in bodies of water. In: Kuznetsova, I. (ed.) General Ecology, Biocenology, Hydrobiology Vol. I., 37–80. Boston, MA: G. K. Hall and Co. (1974)

Straskrabova-Prokesova, V.: Seasonal changes in the reproduction rate of bacteria in two reservoirs. Verh. intern. Ver. Limnol. **16**, 1527–1533 (1966)

Straskrabova, V., Sorokin, Y. I.: Determination of cell size of micro-organisms for the calculation of biomass. In: Sorokin, Y. I., Kadota, H. (eds.) Techniques for the Assessment of Microbial Production and Decomposition in Fresh Waters. IBP Handbook No. 23, 48–50. Oxford: Blackwell Scientific Publications 1972

Weyland, H.: Untersuchungen über die Vermehrungsrate mariner Bakterien in Seewasser. Veröff. Inst. Meeresforsch. Bremerh. (Sonderbd.) **2**, 245–253 (1966)

Wiebe, W. J., Pomeroy, L. R.: Microorganisms and their association with aggregates and detritus in the sea: a microscopic study. In: Melchiorri-Santolini, U., Hopton, J. W. (eds.) Detritus and its Role in Aquatic Ecosystems. 325–352 Mem. Ist. Ital. Idrobiol., 29 Suppl. 1972

Zimmermann, R., Meyer-Reil, L.-A.: A new method for fluorescence staining of bacterial populations on membrane filters. Kieler Meeresforsch. **30**, 24–27 (1974)

ZoBell, C. E.: The effect of solid surfaces on bacterial activity. J. Bacteriol. **46**, 38–59 (1943)

ZoBell, C. E.: Domain of the marine microbiologist. In: Oppenheimer, C. H. (ed.) Symposium on Marine Microbiology 3–24. Springfield, Ill.: C. C. Thomas 1963

17. Nitrification

H. Szwerinski

Winogradsky (1890) defined nitrification as the biological oxidation of ammonia to nitrate. Ammonia is oxidized in two steps: the oxidation of ammonia to nitrite is carried out for example by *Nitrosomonas* sp., the oxidation of nitrite to nitrate by *Nitrobacter* sp.. These organisms are chemoautotrophic bacteria which do not metabolize organic compounds.

Besides this, several heterotrophic bacteria and fungi are capable of oxidizing nitrogen compounds, inorganic nitrogen compounds such as e.g., ammonia and nitrite, but also a variety of organic nitrogen substances. Therefore nitrification has been redefined by Verstraete and Alexander (1973) as ... "the conversion of inorganic or organic nitrogen from a reduced to a more oxidized state".

In the Kiel Fjord and the Kiel Bight, the concentration of the inorganic nitrogen compounds, especially ammonia and nitrate, showed characteristic seasonal changes. Very low concentrations were measured during spring, summer and early fall (see Chap. 4). From October to December the concentrations increased slowly, followed by a rapid increase from January to February. In the same period the amount of ammonia liberated from proteolysis processes decreased. According to Hamilton (1964) the nitrite and nitrate formation in the sea cannot be explained by abiotic processes as the photochemical oxidation of ammonia to nitrite and nitrate. As there are only few small rivers flowing into the Kiel Bight, the nitrate increase during winter cannot come from the land. Therefore, autochthonous nitrifying organisms must be responsible for the ammonia oxidation to nitrite and nitrate.

During the last ten years several different species of autotrophic nitrifying bacteria have been isolated from seawater and brackish water (Watson, 1965; Watson and Waterbury, 1971; Koops et al., 1976). Thomsen (1910) already described the isolation of an ammonia-oxidizing bacterium from the sediment of the Kiel Fjord. Rheinheimer (1967) usually observed nitrifying activity in sediment samples and in water samples taken 1 m above the sediment from the Kiel Bight. He seldom detected it in surface water samples. According to Rheinheimer (1965) in the Elbe Estuary, nitrite and nitrate are mainly formed by autotrophic nitrifying bacteria. It had been demonstrated that several heterotrophic bacteria, fungi and actinomycetes isolated from soil and fresh water can also nitrify (Eylar, and Schmidt, 1959; Alexander et al., 1960; Laurent, 1971; Verstraete and Alexander, 1972, 1973; Gode and Overbeck, 1972; Witzel, 1973). In contrast to autotrophic nitrification, carbohydrate concentrations of at least 3 mg C l^{-1} (Verstraete and Alexander, 1973) are necessary for the heterotrophic nitrification process to occur.

Natural carbohydrate concentration in the water of the western Baltic Sea are several orders of magnitude below the necessary concentration (about 20 μg dissolved free carbohydrates per l according to Dawson (pers. comm.). Therefore heterotrophic nitrification cannot be expected to occur in the water.

These investigations were carried out to show seasonal changes in the nitrification potential and to correlate these with changes in the concentration of the inorganic nitrogen compounds ammonia, nitrite and nitrate.

17.1 Material and Methods

As there is no method to measure directly and routinely the in situ activity of nitrifying bacteria in sea water, a modified enrichment procedure (Rheinheimer, 1965) was used for the determination of the potential activity for nitrite oxidation. Because of the fact that the potential activity for ammonia oxidation (measured as increase of nitrite after two weeks) reached only very low levels, the potential activity for nitrite oxidation (measured as decrease of nitrite after two weeks) proved to be a better method to determine the nitrifying potential.

Water and sediment samples were collected monthly over one year range at Stations 1 and 5. Five hundred ml of each water sample were enriched with 10 mg NO_2^--N, 12 mg K_2HPO_4 and 25 mg $NaHCO_3$ (simplified nitrification medium according to Carlucci and Strickland, 1968). To determine the potential activity for nitrite oxidation in sediment 0.1 cm^3 of surface mud sediment was inoculated into 500 ml of aged seawater (diluted with distilled water, salinity 16‰). This medium was enriched with minerals (see above). The nitrite decrease was tested by the diazo coupling procedure (Grasshoff, 1976) after an incubation time of two weeks at 20° C. The results were averaged from three parallels.

17.2 Potential Activity for Nitrite Oxidation in the Kiel Fjord and the Kiel Bight

Figures 17.1 and 17.2 show the potential activities for nitrite oxidation measured in 1 l seawater and 1 cm^3 sediment from January 1974 to March 1975 with the values of the inorganic nitrogen compounds ammonia, nitrite and nitrate at Stations 1 and 5.

The potential activity for nitrite oxidation measured in 1 cm^3 sediment at Station 1 in the inner Kiel Fjord, as well as at Station 5 in the central Kiel Bight, was usually ten times higher than in 1 l water from the same station. From January 1974 to March 1975 at Station 1 the nitrification potential of sea water from a depth of 2 m and of the sediment was changing as shown in Figure 17.1: the highest values were measured in January 1974. They corresponded with the nitrate maximum of the investigation period. One month later, during spring phytoplankton bloom, the potential activity for nitrite oxidation in water, as well as in sediment, had dropped to very low levels. This rapid decrease cannot be explained by nutrient shortage caused by phytoplankton uptake, as there was still enough ammonia and nitrite in the water.

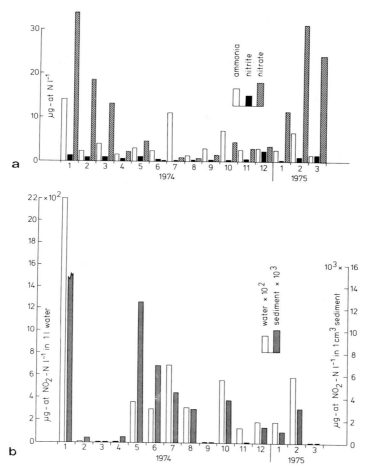

Fig. 17.1. (a) Inorganic nitrogen concentrations in the Kiel Fjord (St. 1) in 2-m depth from Jan. 1974 to March 1975. (b) Potential activity for nitrite oxidation in the Kiel Fjord (St. 1) in 2-m depth and in the sediment from Jan. 1974 to March 1975. For the sediment sample taken in January, 1974 only a minimum value for the potential activity for nitrite oxidation could be recorded, because the substrate added was totaly used up during the incubation period

High potential activities could be measured again when the bloom was beyond its maximum in May 1974 and became decomposed, which is indicated by decreasing values in the concentrations of the following parameters: chlorophyll, lipids, albumin, particulate nitrogen, total carbon, carbohydrates (see Chap. 5). At the same time the ammonia and nitrate values increased.

The nitrite oxidation rates of the water reached about 30% of the January values. In the sediment they were nearly as high as in January 1974. From June to September 1974, nitrite oxidation rates of the sediment decreased to zero. Oxygen shortage in the sediment could have reduced nitrification potential during this time.

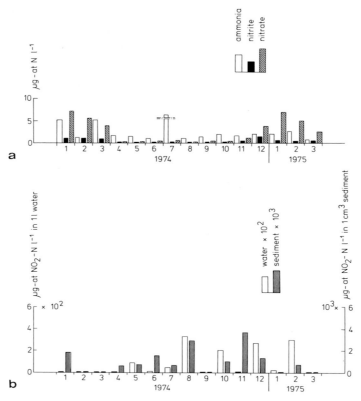

Fig. 17.2. (a) Inorganic nitrogen concentration in the central Kiel Bight (St. 5) in 10-m depth from Jan. 1974 to March 1975. (b) Potential activity for nitrite oxidation in the central Kiel Bight (St. 5) in 10-m depth and in the sediment from Jan. 1974 to March 1975

Corresponding with increased ammonia concentrations, the potential activity of the water reached maxima in July and October 1974, and in February, 1975.

The winter maximum of the potential activity for nitrite oxidation in February 1975 in both water and sediment was about 70% lower than the values measured in January 1974. This could have been caused by lower ammonia and nitrite concentrations. (The ammonia concentration in Feb. 1975 was 50% lower, the nitrite value 30% lower than in Jan. 1974). At the beginning of the phytoplankton bloom in March 1975, the values of the nitrification potential decreased to zero again.

The concentrations of the organic and inorganic nutrients measured in the water of the Kiel Bight were much lower than in the Kiel Fjord (Fig. 17.2). During the investigation period the ammonia concentration of the water at Station 5 was about 30–50% lower than at Station 1. Generally the values of the potential activity for nitrite oxidation were also lower, compared to those at Station 1.

On an average a decrease of about 80% from the Kiel Fjord to the central Kiel Bight was calculated.

From January to April 1974 no nitrification could be measured in the water. From May to August the potential activity for nitrite oxidation rose slowly and reached its first maximum. After a period of changing activities the nitrification activity had a second maximum in February 1975. In January 1974 fairly high potential activities in the sediment were followed by a period of no measurable activity from February until March. In April it rose again to reach a second maximum in August. The highest values of the potential activity in sediment were measured in November 1974. From January to March 1975 very low activities were observed.

17.3 Discussion of the Results

There are several problems concerning the enrichment method for the determination of the potential activity for ammonia and nitrite oxidation.

During an incubation time of more than few hours, the microbial population of a water sample enclosed in a bottle changes strongly (Kunicki-Goldfinger, 1974). According to Johnson and Sieburth (1976) ecologically unimportant nitrifiers are selected against species that are most active in the environment using enrichment procedures. Moreover several nitrifying species are killed by unnatural high substrate concentrations which must be added to the sample to measure nitrite and nitrate formation from ammonia.

Obviously ammonia-oxidizing bacteria are more sensitive to laboratory conditions than nitrite-oxidizing bacteria. The potential activity for ammonia oxidation reached only very low levels.

Nevertheless, to measure nitrification in habitats with low nutrient levels like the Kiel Bight and even in the Kiel Fjord, it is necessary to incubate the water sample for at least 14 days. The diazo coupling procedure for the determination of nitrite is not sensitive enough to indicate small changes in nitrite concentration formed or consumed during a few hours. In situ rates of the oxidation of nitrite cannot be measured by the enrichment method, which only describes the tendency of the nitrification rate during a year.

The results of this examination demonstrate that the potential activity for nitrite oxidation depends on several different factors.

Except during spring phytoplankton bloom in the Kiel Fjord (St. 1) it was usually correlated with the ammonia concentration. Although there was still enough ammonia and nitrite, nitrification rates at once dropped to very low levels when spring phytoplankton bloom started. This could also be observed at Station 5 in the central Kiel Bight. The nitrification potential might have been inhibited by compounds secreted by spring phytoplankton. In summer, increased temperatures enhanced nitrite oxidation rates, provided enough substrate and oxygen. In the Elbe Estuary the potential activity for ammonia oxidation was correlated with temperature (Rheinheimer, 1965), whereas the potential activity for nitrite oxidation did not show seasonal rhythmus. During summer nitrite usually accumulated in the water. Braune and Uhlemann (1968) observed increasing nitrite values in river water with rising temperatures. According to Laudelout et al. (1974, 1976), temperatures above 15° C, inadequate aeration and low pH-values favor nitrite accumulation in the water. In contrast to observations in the Elbe Estuary (Rheinheimer, 1965) and in the Saale River (Braune and Uhlemann, 1968) the natural level of nitrite in the Kiel Bight and in the Kiel Fjord is usually very low (0–1.0 µg-at NO_2-N l^{-1}; see Fig. 4.4). Obviously nitrite and nitrate formation in the Baltic Sea is still balanced.

In the Kiel Fjord the highest potential activities for nitrite oxidation were measured during winter. In the Elbe Estuary decreasing potential activities were observed during this time. According to Rheinheimer (1965), nitrifying bacteria in the Elbe Estuary are mostly allochthonous, coming from soil and sewages, and are rather inactive at low temperatures.

The nitrifying population of the Kiel Bight and the Kiel Fjord on the other hand continued nitrifying at winter temperatures. High potential activities during late winter which could be observed especially at Station 1 were correlated with high nitrate concentrations. Together with the isolation of an obligate halophilic *Nitrosomonas* sp. from the water of the Eckernförde Bight, this might be a sign that nitrification is mainly responsible for the oxidation of ammonia to nitrate.

Furthermore, it could be demonstrated that nitrification must occur primarily in the sediment. The potential activity measured in 1 cm³ surface mud sediment was about ten times higher than that in 1 l water, caused by much higher concentrations of nutrients in the sediment than in the water. Possibly a great portion of nitrite and nitrate in water is oxidized in sediment and liberated into water by diffusion and mixing processes. Decreasing nutrient concentrations from the Kiel Fjord to the Kiel Bight were accompanied by decreases in the potential activity for nitrite oxidation. This can also be observed in several microbiological parameters, as for example with the number of the saprophytic bacteria (Chap. 11), and the uptake rates of organic compounds (Chap. 15).

References

Alexander, M., Marshall, K. C., Hirsch, P.: Autotrophy and heterotrophy in nitrification. 7th Intern. Confr. Soil Ci. **3**, 586–591 (1960)

Braune, W., Uhlemann, R.: Studien zum Einfluß der Temperatur auf Ammonifikation und Nitrifikation im Flußwasser. Intern. Rev. ges. Hydrobiol. **53**, 453–468 (1968)

Carlucci, A. F., Strickland, J. D. H.: The isolation, purification, and some kinetic studies of marine nitrifying bacteria. J. Exptl. Mar. Biol. Ecol. **2**, 156–166 (1968)

Eylar, O. R. Jun., Schmidt, E. L.: A survey of heterotrophic microorganisms from soil for ability to form nitrite and nitrate. J. Gen. Microbiol. **20**, 473–481 (1959)

Gode, P., Overbeck, J.: Untersuchungen zur heterotrophen Nitrifikation im See. Zeitschrift für Allgem. Mikrobiol. **12**, 567–574 (1972)

Grasshoff, K.: Methods of Seawater Analysis. — Weinheim-New York: Verlag Chemie 1976

Hamilton, R. D.: Photochemical processes in the inorganic nitrogen cycle of the sea. Limnol. Oceanogr. **9**, 107–111 (1964)

Johnson, P. W., Sieburth, J. McN.: In situ morphology of nitrifying-like bacteria in aquaculture systems. Appl. Environm. Microbiol. **31**, 423–432 (1976)

Koops, H.-P., Harms, H., Wehrmann, H.: Isolation of a moderate halophilic ammonia-oxidizing bacterium, *Nitrosococcus mobilis nov.* sp. Arch. Microbiol. **107**, 277–282 (1976)

Kunicki-Goldfinger, W. J. H.: Methods of aquatic microbiology. A story of apparent precision and frustrated expectations. Pol. Arch. Hydrobiol. **21**, 3–17 (1974)

Laudelout, H., Lambert, R., Fripiat, J. L., Pham, M. L.: Effet de la température sur la vitesse d'oxydation de l'ammonium en nitrate par des cultures mixtes de nitrifiants. Ann. Microbiol. (Inst. Pasteur) **125B**, 75–84 (1974)

Laudelout, H., Lambert, R., Pham, M. L.: Influence du pH et de la pression partielle d'oxygène sur la nitrification. Ann. Microbiol. (Inst. Pasteur) **127A**, 367–382 (1976)

Laurent, M.: La nitrification autotrophe et hétérotrophe dans les écosystèmes aquatiques. Ann. Inst. Pasteur, Paris **121**, 795–810 (1971)

Rheinheimer, G.: Mikrobiologische Untersuchungen in der Elbe zwischen Schnackenburg und Cuxhaven. Arch. Hydrobiol. Suppl. Elbe Aestuar **29**, II, 181–251 (1965)

Rheinheimer, G.: Ökologische Untersuchungen zur Nitrifikation in Nord- und Ostsee. Helgoländer Wiss. Meeresunters. **15**, 243–252 (1967)

Thomsen, P.: Über das Vorkommen von Nitrobakterien im Meer. Kieler Meeresforsch. **11**, 1–27 (1910)

Verstraete, W., Alexander, M.: Heterotrophic nitrification in samples from natural environments. Naturwissenschaften **59**, 79–80 (1972)

Verstraete, W., Alexander, M.: Heterotrophic nitrification in samples of natural ecosystems. Environm. Sci. Technol. **7**, 39–42 (1973)

Watson, S. W.: Characteristics of a marine nitrifying bacterium, *Nitrosocystis oceanus* sp. n. Limnol. Oceanogr. **10** (supplement), 274–289 (1965)

Watson, S. W., Waterbury, J. B.: Characteristics of two marine nitrite-oxidizing bacteria *Nitrospina gracilis nov. gen. nov. sp.* and *Nitrococcus mobilis nov. gen. nov. sp.* Arch. Mikrobiol. **77**, 203–230 (1971)

Winogradsky, S.: Sur les organisms de la nitrification C. R. Acad. Sci. (Paris) **110**, 1013–1016 (1890)

Witzel, K.-P.: Untersuchungen zur Physiologie heterotropher Nitrifikanten und ihr Vorkommen in ostholsteinischen Seen. Thesis Univ. Kiel (1973)

18. Desulfurication and Sulfur Oxidation

J. Schneider

Brackish water areas such as estuaries and fjords often create favorable conditions for the activity of sulfate-reducing bacteria in the marine environment.

Being strictly anaerobic, these organisms gain energy for their life processes by the transport of electrons from organic substrates to sulfate (which is abundant in sea water). The most conspicuous end-product of this process is hydrogen sulfide, which can accumulate in bottom waters. With ferrous salts it forms dark compounds (black color of anaerobic sediments).

Reduced sulfur compounds are oxidized in marine environments primarily by *Thiobacillus* sp. and by *Beggiatoa* and *Thiothrix* sp. (*Thiobacillus denitrificans* can oxidize H_2S under anaerobic conditions with nitrate), and by the colored green and purple bacteria, which are strictly anaerobic. The first group is especially active in aphotic water layers containing hydrogen sulfide which are in contact with more oxygenated water (border layers under stagnant conditions), while the latter group is restricted to euphotic anaerobic layers with hydrogen sulfide content.

The Baltic Sea is characterized by special hydrographic conditions which may result in the formation of anoxic zones in the bottom water layers: by the coincidence of water masses of different salinity and the additional influence of water temperature (see Chap. 3), stabile thermo-haloclines develop, which prevent the exchange of water and consequently the influx of oxygen into the deeper water. In the fjords and estuaries, the runoff from land (especially from agricultural activities and sewage inlets) causes a rise of the oxygen demand of the bottom water, directly or indirectly.

Regions of the Baltic Sea where these biological processes of sulfur reduction and oxidation take place are primarily the deep basins in the central area of the Baltic (Gotland deep 249 m, Farö deep 205 m) and holes in lagoons and fjords situated mostly in the middle and western parts of the Baltic Sea. Microbiological investigations of more than sporadic character regarding the organisms involved in these processes have been performed only in the fjords and bays of the western Baltic (Bansemir, 1970; Bansemir and Rheinheimer, 1974; Schneider unpubl.). The Gotland deep has also been studied intensively in its chemical, hydrographical and microbiological aspects (Fonselius, 1962; Gieskes and Grasshoff, 1969; Seppänen and Voipio, 1971). According to these authors a general increase of salinity of the waters of the Baltic Sea as a whole is to be observed, with the consequence that the stability of the halocline becomes stronger and the mixing of the water masses in the depths with oxygenated surface water decreases. The final effect is that stagnant zones with a considerable content of H_2S enlarge. Thus, an increase of the activity of sulfur bacteria of these areas can be supposed. The first intensive microbiological study on the activity of sulfur bacteria in the western Baltic was that of Bansemir and Rheinheimer (1970) who investigated water and sediment samples from the Schlei, a narrow fjord of the Kiel Bight with a steep gradient of salinity towards its inner parts and a rather eutrophic condition of the water. The results of this study can be summarized as follows: the hydrogen sulfide content in the sediment, especially of deep holes, was high, whereas in the water, H_2S could never be demonstrated. The numbers of sulfate-reducing microorganisms (*Desulfovibrio* sp.), therefore, were considerably higher in the sediment than in the water, with MPN counts (Most Probable Number) of 3500–17,000 bacteria ml^{-1} in the sediment and 100–1000 ml^{-1} in water samples, respectively. Although sulfate-reducing bacteria could be demonstrated in the water throughout the year and at all stations, their activity and number seemed to remain reduced in consequence of the high oxygen content of the water. Sulfur-oxidizing microorganisms (especially *Thiobacillus* sp.) were also present in the water and in the sediment; their activity in water seemed to be correlated to salinity. Experiments in the laboratory demonstrated that the activity (measured by the oxidation of thiosulfate) was reduced in water of high salinity. In this connection the publications of Fenchel and Riedl (1970) and Jørgensen and Fenchel (1974) may be of interest. In field and laboratory studies these authors investigated the complex sulfide system in marine sand bottoms, including quantitative studies of plants and animals, chemical and physical parameters, and the evaluation of an artificial sulfide system, especially in regard to the rate of sulfate reduction.

A deep hole in the innermost part of the Kiel Fjord was studied by Bansemir (1970) and Bansemir and Rheinheimer (1974). Here considerable amounts of organic substrates accumulated (partly oily products, partly sewage), and periods of stagnant conditions during the summer and autumn months prevented the exchange of the bottom water. The number of sulfate-reducing microorganisms in the always anaerobic sediment in the uppermost cm reached 100,000 cm^{-3} during periods of stagnation and was reduced to ca. 5000 cells cm^{-3} during the winter, while in the water only about 20 cells ml^{-1} could be counted. The number of saprophytic bacteria in the sediment fluctuated between 6,000,000 and 600,000 cells cm^{-3}. The amounts of hydrogen sulfide in the bottom water (22 m) during one investigation period was in a range from 0.3 mg H_2S l^{-1} water (with a daily increase from 0.07 to 0.22 mg H_2S l^{-1}). The authors concluded that the hydrogen sulfide was mainly produced by sulfate-reducing bacteria—most of it by *Desulfovibrio desulfuricans*, the percentage of the spore-forming *Desulfotomaculum nigrificans* was only 1% of the total sulfate-reducing microorganisms. The decomposition of proteins containing sulfur was of minor importance, and this process occurred primarily in the uppermost cm of the sediment.

During stagnant water conditions, the H_2S migrated up into the overlaying water. This process was interrupted, however, when oxygen-containing water from the Kiel Bight mixed with the water of the inner Kiel Fjord. The sulfur oxidizing microorganisms, *Thiobacillus* sp., *Beggiatoa* and *Thiothrix* sp. have regularly been found in the water and the sediment of the deep hole. The photosynthetic green and purple bacteria did not play a role in the sulfur cycle of the investigated locality, probably because the light did not penetrate into the deeper hydrogen sulfide-containing water layers.

According to Bansemir (1970) in the water only 1–5 cells ml^{-1} and in the sediment approximately 500 cells ml^{-1} of the genus *Thiobacillus* could be demonstrated. Obviously these organisms concentrated at the border layer of oxygenated and of hydrogen sulfide-containing water.

In the course of the intensive microbiological investigations of the Kiel Fjord and Kiel Bight during 1974 and 1975, the occurrence and fluctuation of sulfate-reducing bacteria in water and sediment was also studied. Parts of the samples of the general microbiological program collected on monthly cruises were processed in the manner described below. In addition to Stations 1 and 5, Station 1a in the innermost part of the Kiel Fjord (at ca. 1 mile distance from Station 1) was chosen, that is the above-mentioned "deep hole" (Bansemir and Rheinheimer, 1974). Thus three different habitats could be studied: (1) the Station 1a "deep hole" (23 m water depth) in the inner Kiel Fjord with a restricted water exchange, extended periods of anoxic conditions near the bottom, and a strong accumulation of organic substrates; (2) Station 1 (12 m), with a better water exchange than Station 1a, but still with a great amount of organic substrates in the sediment, sufficient to cause a considerable production of H_2S; (3) Station 5 (22 m) in the central Kiel Bight, with good water exchange throughout the year and a muddy sediment.

The samples (water or sediment) were processed on the ship immediately after collection. The dilutions were prepared in sea water of appropriate salinity and under anaerobic conditions (the dilution flasks were flooded with N_2 before use). One ml of each dilution was mixed with a solidifying medium for sulfate-reducing bacteria (Miller, 1969) in screw cap vials, and incubated at $+30°$ C. After three weeks, black colonies were counted and the number of viable sulfate-reducing bacteria computed according to the MPN procedure (per ml water or per g dry weight of sediment). The content of hydrogen sulfide in the water samples was determined according to Fonselius (1962). The results are compiled in Table 18.1. As the figures show, there were only very few sulfate-reducing bacteria active in the water, even at Station 1a ("deep hole") which in general presented the highest numbers. In contrast, the sediment of all stations contained high numbers of these organisms, throughout the period of investigation. The results of Station 5 in the central Kiel Bight show that, although the water is much more moved and oxygenated here than at the other two stations, this could not prevent the development of a remarkable number of sulfate-reducing bacteria in the sediment, which could be demonstrated throughout the year. However, at no time was the primary oxygen content of the bottom water low enough to permit the existence of hydrogen sulfide in the water itself.

Generally, the highest number of sulfate-reducing microorganisms was found during the summer months, beginning with June and ending approximately in August/September, in water samples as well as in the sediment, although there are exceptions, for example in March, 1974, Stations 5 and 1 (sediment). The very low count of August, 1974 (St. 1a, sediment) of 2.2 cells g^{-1} is probably caused by a methodical failure.

Table 18.1. Numbers of sulfate reducing bacteria in the water (ml⁻¹) and the sediment (g⁻¹) at three stations of the Kiel Fjord (Sts. 1, 1a) and the Kiel Bight (St. 5)

Station	Depth m	1974 March 21 / Feb. 11ᵃ	April 18 / —	May 16 / May 7ᵃ	June 11 / June 6ᵃ	July 11 / July 16ᵃ	Aug. 29 / Aug. 21ᵃ	— / Sept. 25ᵃ	Dec. 10	1975 Jan. 23 / Jan. 21ᵃ	Feb. 12 / Feb. 19ᵃ	March 19ᵃ
5	2 / 20	no H₂S and no sulfate-reducing bacteria demonstrable										
	Sediment	82,000	800	800	216,600	15,000	22,000		3,000	0	5,000	
1	2 / 10		0.2 / 0.2	0.2 / 0.2	2.2 / 1.7	8 / 7	11 / 8		5 / 1	1.7 / 2	0 / 0	
	Sediment	11,300	7,000	6,000	464,000	70,000	174,000		47,000	48,000	0	
1a ("deep hole")	2 / 22	3.3 / 2.3		2.3 / 0.7	11 / 22	34 / 54	0 / 0	5 / 34		13 / 2	0 / 0	3 / 1
	Sediment	22,500		1,000	15,000	138,400	(2.2)	77,400		14,000	14,000	100,000

ᵃ Samples collected at Station 1a.

From the low number of sulfate-reducing bacteria found in the water of each station, it can be supposed that these organisms were hardly active, because of the oxygen content of the water. These bacteria were probably whirled up from the ground into the overlaying water. These organisms seem not to be sufficiently sensitive to oxygen to be killed, and possibly a more or less extended period of inactivation precedes the final death. In this connection the observations of Bansemir and Rheinheimer (1974) on the indifference of *Desulfovibrio* to oxygen are of interest. Cells of this organism were often found in the uppermost water layer in higher concentrations than in the bottom water. They had obviously been transported into the fjord by a polluted river where they had already covered some distance in aerated river water. The insensitivity to oxygen of *Desulfovibrio* strains isolated from this area could be confirmed by laboratory experiments. This problem is also discussed by Kimata et al. (1955), who found *Desulfovibrio* in oxic ocean waters (see also Seki, 1972).

References

Bansemir, K.: Die H$_2$S-Bildung in einer Vertiefung der Kieler Innenförde. Thesis Univ. Kiel (1970)

Bansemir, K., Rheinheimer, G.: Bakterielle Sulfatreduktion und Schwefeloxidation. In: Chemische, mikrobiologische und planktologische Untersuchungen in der Schlei im Hinblick auf deren Abwasserbelastung. Kieler Meeresforsch. **26**, (2), 170–173 (1970)

Bansemir, K., Rheinheimer, G.: Bakteriologische Untersuchungen über die Bildung von Schwefelwasserstoff in einer Vertiefung der inneren Kieler Förde. Kieler Meeresforsch. **30**, 91–98 (1974)

Fenchel, T. M., Riedl, R. J.: The sulfide system: a new biotic community underneath the oxidized layer of marine sand bottoms. Mar. Biol. **7**, 255–268 (1970)

Fonselius, S. H.: Hydrography of the baltic deep basins. Rep. of the Fishery Board of Sweden, Ser. Hydrogr. **13**, 41 (1962)

Gieskes, H., Grasshoff, K.: A study of the variability in the hydrochemical factors in the Baltic Sea on the basis of two anchor stations Sept. 1967 and May 1968. Kieler Meeresforsch. **25**, 105–132 (1969)

Jørgensen, B. B., Fenchel, T.: The sulfur cycle of a marine sediment model system. Mar. Biol. **24**, 189–201 (1974)

Kimata, M., Kadota, H., Hata, Y., Tajima, T.: Studies on the marine sulfite reducing bacteria. I. Distribution of marine sulfate reducing bacteria in the coastal waters receiving a considerable amount of pulp-mill drainage. Bull. Japan. Soc. Sci. Fisheries **21**, 102–108 (1955)

Miller, L. P.: In Methods in Microbiology, Norris, I. R., Ribbons, D. W. (eds.) London and New York: Academic Press 1969

Seki, H.: Formation of anoxic zones in seawater. In: Biological Oceanography of the Northern Pacific Ocean. Takenouchi, Y. (ed.) Idemitsu Shoten, Tokyo, 487–493 (1972)

Seppänen, H., Voipio, A.: Some bacteriological observations made in the northern Baltic. Merentutkimuslait. Julk./Havsforskningsinst. Skr. No. **233**, 43–48 (1971)

19. Comparative Analysis of Data Measured in the Brackish Water of the Kiel Fjord and the Kiel Bight

M. Bölter, L.-A. Meyer-Reil, and B. Probst

The intensive investigation of the seasonal fluctuations of planktonic, microbiological and chemical parameters in the brackish water of the Kiel Fjord and Kiel Bight (cf. Chaps. 3–18) yielded a great number of individual data. Based on these data a statistical analysis was carried out for the station in the inner Kiel Fjord (St. 1) and the central Kiel Bight (St. 5), in order to show further relationships between the individual parameters measured.

Only very few detailed studies concerning the microbiology of an ecosystem by comparative data analysis have been presented (Brasfield, 1972; Faust et al., 1975; Sayler et al., 1975). Most of the data available are restricted to the measurement of "important" individual parameters, which were compared by two-state correlation coefficients. In many studies the influence of temperature, salinity or inorganic nutrients on the total bacterial population or specific bacterial groups are described (Kadota, 1956; Rheinheimer, 1966, 1968; Seki 1966; Bonde 1968; Gundersen et al., 1972; Lehnberg, 1972; Meyer-Reil, 1973, 1974; Hoppe, 1974; Faust et al., 1975; Ferguson and Rublee, 1976).

Only very few investigations deal with the influence of planktonic parameters on cell numbers (Lear, 1961; Seki and Taga, 1963; Seki, 1970; Tanaka et al., 1974). In most of the studies static parameters (standing crop) were measured. However, only the measurement of rates provides information on the flux in an ecosystem. For a detailed comprehensive discussion of relationships between planktonic, microbiological and chemical parameters see Melchiorri-Santolini and Hopton, 1972; Rosswall, 1972; Stevenson and Colwell, 1973; Colwell and Morita, 1974.

For the comparative analysis of the data, different methods have been used. Among these the multiple linear correlation analysis and/or the two-state correlation analysis have been most often applied (Seki, 1966; Brasfield, 1972; Faust et al., 1975; Sayler et al., 1975). The analysis of time-dependent parameters requires the application of the time-series analysis, which allows a statistical analysis of the relationships between two time-dependent data series (Wallis and Roberts, 1969). From the understanding of the total number of parameters as a statistical population, it follows that the important factor of the time series of the parameters measured would be missed. Then a descriptive statistical analysis of the seasonal fluctuations would be impossible. Therefore, besides two-state correlation analysis and series comparison, mainly time-series analysis was applied to interpret the various relationships between the individual parameters measured.

Introductorily, a rough abstraction of the brackish water ecosystem in the Kiel Bight is presented with special reference to microorganisms (cf. Fig. 19.1). For this model the energy language of Odum (1969) was chosen. Thick lines represent the parameters measured. Based on the symbols, the energy language offers the possibility of showing energetic relations in the food web. The model facilitates the set up of differential equation systems for simulating fluctuations of individual parameters. By using his energy language and subsequently the mathe-matical description of energy fluxes, Odum (1969) tried to offer a box system for differential equations. Recently a model was used by Jansson (1972) to describe the brackish water ecosystem of the Baltic Sea.

19.1 Methods Applied for the Comparative Analysis of the Results

For the comparative analysis of the parameters measured in this study, the following three methods were used: two-state correlation, series comparison and time-series analysis. The aim of the analysis was to demonstrate parallelisms between the time-dependent parameters measured.

19.1.1 Two-State Correlation Analysis

Two-state correlation analysis (Weber, 1961) was carried out to reduce the data for the time-consuming time-series analysis. Those correlation coefficients were chosen which show a significant correlation on at least the 5% confidence limit.

19.1.2 Series Comparison

Series comparison was based on the iterations between the values of the individual parameters measured. Values were coded as 1 if they increase as against the previously measured value, if they decrease, they were coded as 2. Code 3 means that there was no change as against the previous value measured. The code is independent of the absolute values of the data series. If no value was measured, the previously measured value was compared with the next following value.

According to the complete data series a maximum of $m-1$ iterations can be observed (m = number of data measured). If $n_{(1)}$ is the number of elements coded with 1 and $n_{(2)}$ is the number of elements coded with 2, then $n = n_{(1)} + n_{(2)}$. Code series of ..., $1, 3, 1, 1, ...$ were evaluated as one iteration.

Fluctuations of the elements ($1, 2$) by chance were proved according to Weber (1961) since $n_{(1)}, n_{(2)} < 20$.

Some data showed a large number of iterations that was unlikely, whereas the iterations of other data were too small to meet the requirements of the 5% confidence limit.

For a comparison between two data series the number of corresponding iterations ($1, 2,$ or 3) was counted. The percentage of similarity is given by

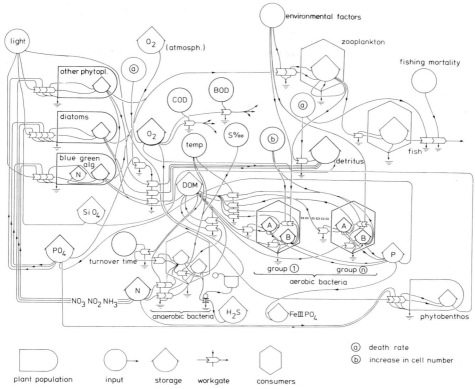

Fig. 19.1. Coarse abstraction of the brackish water ecosystem Kiel Bight with special reference to microorganisms. *Thick lines* represent the parameters measured. For details cf. Odum, 1969. The aerobic bacterial population is portioned into the subpopulations 1 … n and each of them into A and B. A indicates the metabolizing part of the population and B the metabolizing *and* actively growing part of the total population

$U = U_A/U_S \times 100$, where U_A is the number of corresponding iterations and U_S the number of codes compared. Consequently, only positive correlations can be demonstrated by this method. Tables 19.4, 19.5 and Figure 19.3 present the conditions with $U \geq 75\%$, since this level is needed to obtain a comparison with two-state correlation coefficients on the 5% confidence limit (Bölter, unpubl. data).

19.1.3 Time-Series Analysis

Parallel to the method described above, time-series analysis according to the method of Morgenstern (1959) and Pfanzagl (1963) is dependent upon the time-dependent increase or decrease of parameters. Values increasing as compared to the value previously measured were coded as *1*, decreasing values as *0*. Therefore the individual parameters is characterized by the sequence $\delta_1, \delta_2, …, \delta_n$, where δ_i is *1* or *0*, respectively. Let $\varepsilon_1, \varepsilon_2, …, \varepsilon_n$ be an analog sequence for a second

Table 19.1. Two examples for the relationship between time depending parameters based on time series analysis, showing parallelism between the parameters particulate carbon and particulate nitrogen (a), and nonparallelism between the parameters bacterial biomass and turnover time of amino acids (b). Asterisk marks the number of agreements between the non permutated data series

a) Number of agreements	Number of agreements after permutation	b) Number of agreements	Number of agreements after permutation
0	0	0	0
1	16	1	144 *
2	176	2	720
3	200 *	3	1,296
4	128	4	720
5	56	5	0
6	0	6	0
7	0	7	0
8	0		

parameter, then $T = \sum \delta_i \varepsilon_i$. T represents the number of intervals of the two parameters with increasing values, and therefore T serves as a measurement for the parallelism between the two time-dependent parameters. A method for randomization is needed, which does not disturb the autocorrelation of the two data series. This holds true for permutation of the iterations (definition: uninterupted sequence of 1 or 0) of the total number of the codes 0 and 1, separately. Otherwise, a fusion of iterations and therefore an increase of autocorrelation would occur. Randomization is carried out by preservation of the iterations for both series separately. By combination of the two individual time series based on $(\delta_1, \delta_2, ..., \delta_n)$ and $(\varepsilon_1, \varepsilon_2, ..., \varepsilon_n)$, respectively, the T value can be determined. The resulting distribution of T serves as a basis for the evaluation of the T value actually observed. An example of parallelism and nonparallelism, respectively, is given in Table 19.1. The number of agreements originally occurring is marked with an asterix. Pfanzagl (1963) found that the distribution of T resulting from the above randomization corresponds with a standard distribution, presumely the number of iterations is not too small, or single iterations are not extremely great. Details are described by Probst (1973). Theoretical investigations are lacking. Randomization of four 0 iterations and three 1 iterations results in $4!3! = 144$ series. The comparison with a second parameter consisting of two 1 iterations and three 0 iterations ($2!3! = 12$ series) yields in 1728 T values, since each of the first series has to be compared with each of the second series. Therefore the permutations require long run times on the computer, especially if a long time series and frequent fluctuations exist. This was the main reason for applying only those data series to the time-series analysis, which (1) at least correlate on the 5% confidence limit by using two-state correlation coefficients, and (2) show more than 75% similarity by using series comparison. However, from the remaining data, less than 6% of the random samples show parallelism based on time-series analysis without correlation on the 5% limit.

    All calculations were performed on the X 8 and PDP 10 of the computer center of Kiel University.

19.1.4 Arrangement of the Parameters Measured

For the representation and the discussion of the results it proved to be necessary to arrange the individual parameters measured into individual groups. Generally, the arrangement followed from the nature of the parameters measured (planktonic data, seston and detritus, particulate organic matter, dissolved inorganic matter, cell numbers, activity measurements). Other parameters were examined separately according to their nature and function in the system (temperature, salinity, chemical oxygen demand, spores, nitrification potential).

19.1.5 Representation of the Results

The total raw data measured are summarized in Table 19.2 (St. 1, Kiel Fjord, water depth 2 m and 10 m) and Table 19.3 (St. 5, Kiel Bight, water depth 2 m and 18 m). The correlation matrices (Tables 19.4 and 19.5) include two-state correlation coefficients, as well as series comparison and time-series analysis. Figure 19.1 shows a rough abstraction of the ecosystem Kiel Bight with special reference to microorganisms. The parameters measured are represented by thick lines. Table 19.1 gives an example of parallelism and nonparallelism, respectively, between the time-dependent individual parameters based on time-series analysis. For Station 1 (2 m) the relationships between the individual parameters are demonstrated, based on correlation coefficients (Fig. 19.2), series comparison (Fig. 19.3), and time-series analysis (Fig. 19.4). Figures 19.5–19.7 are based on time-series analysis and demonstrate the relationships between the individual parameters measured at Station 1 (10 m, Fig. 19.5), Station 5 (2 m, Fig. 19.6) and Station 5 (18 m, Fig. 19.7).

19.2 Results

For the station in the Kiel Fjord (St. 1, 2 m), various relationships were found between microbial activity (substrate uptake, turnover time, number of active cells) and the following parameters: temperature, particulate organic matter (POM; carbon, nitrogen, carbohydrates, proteins), and dissolved inorganic matter (DIM; nitrite, nitrate). Particulate lipids, phosphate, ammonia, and oxygen showed no relationships to other parameters. Furthermore, activity parameters related to cell numbers (total numbers of cells, total biomass, coliform and chitinoclastic bacteria) as well as to seston content and detritus area. Saprophytic bacteria correlated only with the number of yeasts. As was expected, close relationships existed between primary production and POM (carbon, nitrogen and proteins). Only a limited number of correlations was found between ATP, DHA, and other activity parameters. From Figures 19.2–19.4 the separate role of yeasts, spores, nitrification potential, and chemical oxygen demand (COD) becomes obvious. For salinity only a correlation with seston content could be shown. Within the compartments, interrelations were found only for activity parameters, planktonic parameters (phytoplankton numbers and chlorophyll a) and cell numbers (total number of cells, total biomass).

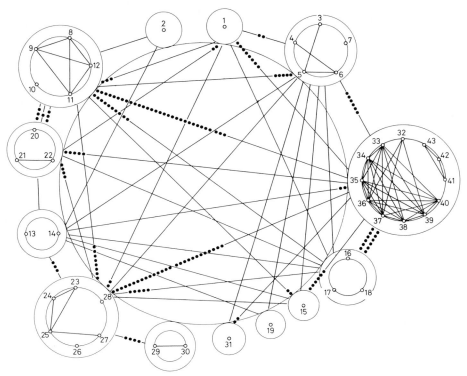

Fig. 19.2. Station 1, Kiel Fjord (2 m). Relationships based on two-state correlation coefficients between the individual parameters measured. *Black dots* represent the number of relationships found between the individual compartments. For code numbers cf. Table 19.2

From the various relationships found by correlation coefficients only 20% could be verified by series comparison, and 33% by time-series analysis. Mainly the close correlations between POM and ATP, DHA, and BOD, as well as the interrelationships within the individual compartments (DIM, POM, cell numbers) found by correlation coefficients must be objected by time-series analysis. Comparing series analysis and time-series analysis, 22% of the correlations could be confirmed. However, most of the important relationships between the individual compartments could also be found by using correlation coefficients and series comparison.

In contrast to the surface samples of Station 1, the 10-m samples showed a different pattern in the relationships between the parameters measured (cf. Fig. 19.5). The close correlation between activity parameters and temperature, DIM, and POM, found at a water depth of 2 m is lacking at 10 m. Although very few activity parameters were measured, these can be expected to be valid for other activity parameters. Again, the close correlation between primary production, chlorophyll a and POM (carbon, nitrogen, proteins) is obvious. Single parameters for which no correlation was found in the surface water (2 m), correlate with other parameters in deeper water (10 m): number of yeasts with particular lipids and

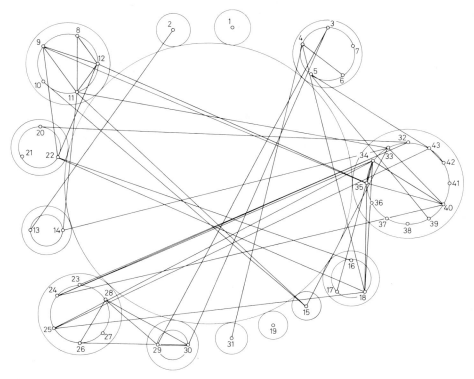

Fig. 19.3. Station 1, Kiel Fjord (2 m). Relationships based on series comparison between the individual parameters measured. For code numbers cf. Table 19.2

turnover time of glucose. Interrelationships between the parameters within the individual compartments as they were found for the surface water, are practically nonexistent at 10 m. No correlation was found between total number of yeasts and red yeasts, chlorophyll a and primary production. Again, no correlation between salinity and other parameters could be shown.

At the station in the central Kiel Bight (St. 5, 2 m) close relationships between chlorophyll a and POM (carbon, nitrogen, carbohydrates, proteins) are obvious (cf. Fig. 19.6). Furthermore, the total number of cells, as well as the total microbial biomass, correlate with DIM (nitrite, nitrate) on the one hand and activity parameters (turnover time of glucose, aspartic acid) on the other. Although there is no explanation at present, the relationships between spores and oxygen, carbohydrates and saprophytes should be mentioned.

In contrast to the surface sample of Station 5, a different correlation pattern was found in a water depth of 18 m (cf. Fig. 19.7). The important role of oxygen in deeper water overlying the sediment becomes obvious. Oxygen correlates with various parameters: particulate carbon and carbohydrates, chlorophyll a, and ATP. Furthermore, ATP is strongly connected with POM (nitrogen, carbohydrates). The close relationships between chlorophyll a and POM found at a water

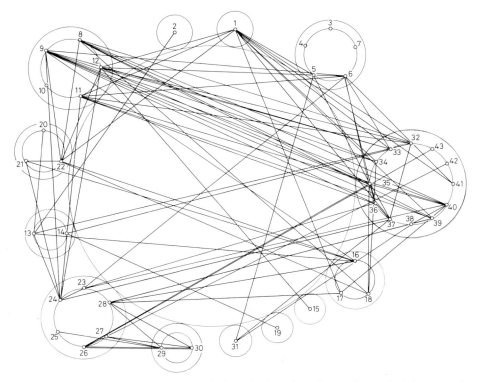

Fig. 19.4. Station 1, Kiel Fjord (2 m). Relationships based on time series analysis between the individual parameters measured. For code number cf. Table 19.2

depth of 2 m could not be confirmed at a water depth of 18 m. However, a relationship between chlorophyll a and the following parameters could be shown: particulate carbon, oxygen, maximum velocity of uptake of glucose, and number of chitinoclastic bacteria. For specific bacteria groups the following correlations were found: saprophytes correlate with particular lipids, and the number of chitinoclastic bacteria is related to temperature.

19.3 Discussion

The statistical analysis of the results was based on the three methods mentioned above (two-state correlation coefficients, series comparison, time-series analysis). Correlation coefficients were chosen in order to reduce the data for the time-series analysis. Correlation coefficients provide only a pilot information on relationships between individual time-dependent parameters. Mainly in the case of strongly structured parallel time-dependent data, autocorrelation may interfere with relationships actually existing between different parameters. For example, this always holds true for nonlinear relationships.

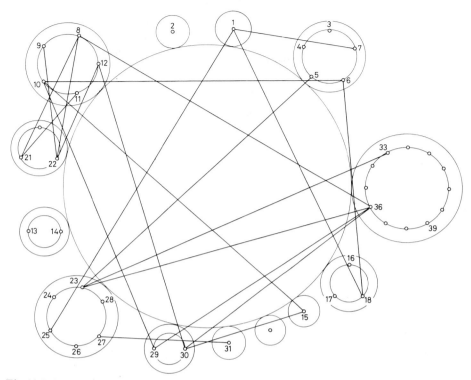

Fig. 19.5. Station 1, Kiel Fjord (10 m). Relationships based on time series analysis between the individual parameters measured. *Numbers* represent the parameters measured. For code numbers cf. Table 19.2

Series comparisons and time-series analysis were carried out without taking into account the absolute values measured for the individual parameters. By comparing the parallelism of curves, time-series analysis substitutes the term parallelism by the term correlation. In contrast to series comparison, time-series analysis compensates fluctuations by change.

For some of the relationships between individual parameters, parallelism by time-series analysis or series comparisons could be shown, but the parameters did not show correlation on the 5% confidence limit (cf. Tables 19.4 and 19.5). This is mainly due to the fact that, in contrast to the calculation of the correlation coefficients, series comparisons and time-series analyses were carried out without taking absolute values into account. The existence of nonlinear relationships between individual parameters could be another explanation.

Based on the parameters measured, one could expect the following relationships between the main compartments: plankton as primary producers should be dependent on temperature as well as dissolved inorganic matter (DIM). Primary production should strongly influence the level of particulate organic matter (POM). Bacterial activity and cell numbers should be controlled by temperature as well as by POM, DIM, and BOD. A strong relationship should exist between

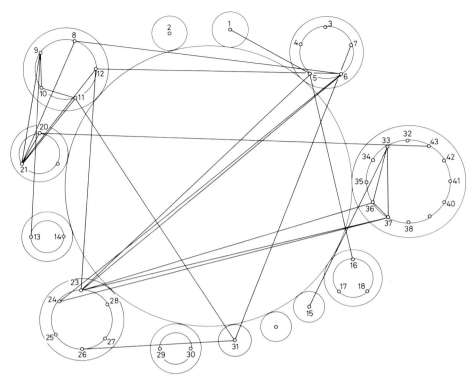

Fig. 19.6. Station 5, Kiel Bight (2 m). Relationships based on time series analysis between the individual parameters measured. *Numbers* represent the parameters measured. For code numbers cf. Table 19.3

cell numbers and activity. Between single compartments, as well as between individual parameters, a different relationship pattern could be expected. For example, activity in nature should be related directly to temperature, since the slow constant increase of temperature during spring and summer should be accompanied by a similar increase in metabolic activity. Indirect relationships between two parameters could be expected if the relationship between two parameters is dependent on a third parameter. Furthermore, a time lack between the increase in one parameter and the reaction of a second parameter could exist. This pattern is typical for the relationship between phytoplankton and bacteria maxima (Rheinheimer, 1975). It must be pointed out, however, that only direct relationships could be detected by the method used in this study (see above).

Most of the correlations were found for the surface water of Station 1 (Kiel Fjord). Of the relationships that were expected between the compartments, most could be confirmed by the correlations found. Primary production depending on light and temperature led to an increase in POM. Temperature, POM, and DIM (nitrite, nitrate) stronlgy influence microbial activity, as well as the total number of cells. Various relationships exist between the individual activity parameters. For all other stations investigated (St. 1, 10 m; St. 5, 2 and 18 m), less correlations

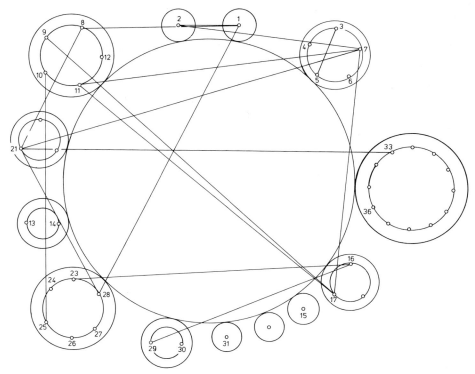

Fig. 19.7. Station 5, Kiel Bight (18 m). Relationships based on time series analysis between the individual parameters measured. *Numbers* represent the parameters measured. For code numbers compare Table 19.3

could be shown, and less of the relationships that were expected between the compartments could be confirmed. Close relationships between planktonic data (chlorophyll a) and POM still exist. However, the direct influence of POM, DIM and temperature on microbial activity found at Station 1 (2 m) does not exist. For Station 1 (10 m) and Station 5 (2 m), a similar correlation pattern could be shown. For both stations, correlations between the total number of cells and activity parameters on the one hand, and DIM (nitrite, nitrate) on the other hand are obvious. In addition, nitrate relates to individual POM parameters. The correlation pattern found at Station 5 (18 m) differs from that of all other stations. Oxygen as a limiting factor becomes obvious. The close relationship between ATP and POM shows that the energy available is related to POM.

The station in the Kiel Fjord (St. 1, 2 m) differs from all other stations by its homogeneous pattern. After the planktonic bloom in spring, the phytoplankton stock remains relatively constant until fall, thus providing a relatively constant nutrient source (cf. Chap. 5 and 7). In addition, the station is greatly influenced by land and ship traffic. Possibly, a broad spectrum of nonsensitive cells is present which show comparative activities, as demonstrated by using quite different methods for the activity determinations. A relatively high percentage of cells (and possibly of the total activity) are saprophytes, adapted to higher nutrient concentrations. All these points may be responsible for the high number of direct relationships which were found at this station. Station 5 (Kiel Bight) possesses a more heterogeneous pattern. A succession of different short-term individual plankton blooms can be observed, depending on short fluctuations of the physical and chemical parameters. Thus the nutrient source for bacteria is more totally dependent on plankton. Microbial activity obviously becomes more related to a summary of suitable parameters rather than to individual parameters. Therefore, direct relationships between individual parameters and microbial activity are rarely observed. Under these conditions the time interval of sampling was too great to follow direct relationships. Furthermore, indirect relationships and a possible time lack between short-term plankton blooms and bacterial activity could be important. Inhibition and promotion of bacterial activity and short-term plankton blooms might be another factor to be considered (Bell et al., 1974).

Most of the data available in the literature deal with the relationship between very few individual parameters based on correlation coefficients. Long-term observations, as well as a comparative analysis of the relationships between a broad spectrum of parameters in nearshore and offshore regions, is practically lacking. As could be shown in this study, from the various relationships found by correlation coefficients, only a certain percentage (varying from station to station) could be verified by time-series analysis. Therefore, a comparison with all data reported in the literature is limited.

The relationships between planktonic data and POM in brackish water is well known from the literature (Derenbach, 1969; Lenz, 1974; v. Bodungen, 1975; v. Bröckel, 1975). Independent of the type of water studied, the same relationships were found for open oceans (Zeitzschel, 1973) as well as for lakes (Menon et al., 1972). In ocean profiles, total particulate carbon, nitrogen, ATP and chlorophyll showed similar curves (Holm-Hansen, 1969). Investigations concerning the relationship between bacterial activity and cell numbers on the one hand and POM and DIM on the other are very few in number. Seki (1970) reported a correlation between particulate carbon and microbial biomass. However, based on time-series analysis, this relationship could only be confirmed for the station in the Kiel Fjord (St. 1, 2 m), where a relatively high constant phytoplankton stock was observed. For upwelling areas, Castellvi and Ballester (1974) reported a correlation between primary production and bacterial activity. In our studies, only for the station in the Kiel Bight (St. 5, 18 m) a correlation could be shown between chlorophyll a and the maximum velocity of glucose uptake. For the upwelling area off the West African Coast Watson (pers. comm.) found a correlation between bacterial biomass and the amount of glucose oxidized. In accordance with our results, the investigations of Ferguson and Rublee (1976) revealed no correlation between the total number of cells determined by epifluorescence microscopy and temperature, salinity or ATP. It must be pointed out that for none of the stations a correlation could be shown between salinity and cell number or cell activity in our studies, although the salinity of the brackish water region investigated showed great fluctuations (cf. Tables 19.2, 19.3). However, bacteria isolated from the Kiel Bight show a broad spectrum of salt optima within the fluctuating salinity of this area (Meyer-Reil, 1973, 1974). Most of the data reported in the

Table 19.2. Raw data measured at Station 1 (Kiel Fjord)

Date	1 Temperature (°C)		2 Salinity (S‰)		3 Phosphate (µg-at PO_4-P l^{-1})		4 Ammonia (µg-at NH_3-N l^{-1})		5 Nitrite (µg-at NO_2-N l^{-1})		6 Nitrate (µg-at NO_3-N l^{-1})	
	2 m	10 m	2 m	10 m	2 m	10 m	2 m	10 m	2 m	10 m	2 m	10 m
Jan. 24, 1974	3.70	3.60	15.26	17.76	1.947	1.630	14.143	14.064	1.286	1.125	33.634	26.893
Feb. 14	4.35	3.75	16.45	17.58	1.871	2.010	9.000	6.464	1.414	1.200	28.586	16.371
Feb. 28	3.70	3.80	16.77	17.02	3.803	1.732	2.393	2.293	1.029	1.121	18.550	19.064
March 21	4.40	4.10	15.60	16.37	3.135	1.230	4.071	5.714	0.969	0.969	13.343	17.886
April 18	8.60	7.30	13.66	15.06	0.794	0.358	1.493	2.064	0.589	0.279	2.325	2.636
May 16	10.90	9.60	14.10	15.06	5.216	0.984	3.143	3.829	0.913	0.254	4.687	2.671
June 11	12.80	11.60	15.25	16.66	1.061	2.123	2.343	2.286	0.400	0.350	0.000	0.964
June 25	17.70	17.00	15.95	15.95	1.000	1.600	0.629	4.007	0.250	0.429	0.550	1.057
July 11	16.70	15.40	16.40	16.79	1.423	1.219	11.029	2.400	0.150	0.150	0.900	0.761
Aug. 7			19.62	20.54	2.823	1.806	2.857	4.929	0.300	0.500	0.191	1.050
Aug. 29	17.70	15.80	15.30	20.67	0.650	3.148	1.286	5.236	0.400	0.250	0.832	0.607
Sept. 12	15.50	15.70	18.50	19.86	1.539	1.539	2.918	2.171	0.350	0.357	1.414	1.786
Oct. 24	10.50	10.50	17.32	18.25	2.040	1.118	6.871	3.807	0.482	0.214	4.500	1.714
Nov. 21	7.50	7.90	17.17	17.53	1.729	1.513	2.714	4.004	0.600	0.600	3.021	1.471
Dec. 10	6.50	6.60	17.86	18.12	3.282	1.508	2.957	2.793	2.286	2.057	3.536	5.979
Jan. 23, 1975	5.30	5.20	20.40	20.40	1.755	1.755	2.714	3.714	0.430	0.450	11.250	12.086
Feb. 12	3.60	5.10	15.00	19.23	1.530	1.563	6.514	12.000	0.920	0.800	30.879	23.457
March 10	5.50	4.10	13.13	16.63	6.865	11.584	1.569	1.851	1.500	1.232	23.946	16.821

Table 19.2 (continued)

Date	7 Oxygen (mg l⁻¹) 2 m	10 m	8 Carbon (µg l⁻¹) 2 m	10 m	9 Nitrogen (µg l⁻¹) 2 m	10 m	10 Lipids (µg l⁻¹) 2 m	10 m	11 Carbohydrates (µg l⁻¹) 2 m	10 m	12 Proteins (µg l⁻¹) 2 m	10 m	13 Seston (µg l⁻¹) 2 m	10 m
Jan. 24, 1974	10.98	10.93	322		27		125	(663)	103	81	222	1270	5310	5740
Feb. 14	7.97	7.19												
Feb. 28	9.77	11.20	332	343	43	43	151	262	164	160			3800	4200
March 21	10.92	8.41	635	732	94	87	100	119	206	212	642	526	3960	7620
April 18	10.92	11.61	1785	1000	313	163	312	130	953	431	1584	1000	5210	3080
May 16	11.74	9.24	1318	508	206	76	103	21	594	150	1200	516	7480	3090
June 11	8.80	6.92	1182	670	178	87	170		533	433	1078	538	7580	6660
June 25	10.95	9.14												
July 11	9.25	5.51	1774	1134	315	199	(6)	126	800	365	1974	1290	6110	5700
Aug. 7	5.00	5.85	1108	372	207	66	104	32	477	138	1012	400	2790	2300
Aug. 29	9.52	2.67	1612	464	280	76	194	64	866	237	1776	468	4170	2250
Sept. 12	8.54	7.27	859	412	151	76	111	56	245	175	772	390	2970	2020
Oct. 24	8.73	8.92	628	630	99	104	230	244	281	225	656	662	3150	3030
Nov. 21	8.99	7.11	433	368	64	52	63	67	230	145	404	298	2470	1920
Dec. 10	7.67	7.71	380	327	58	53	22	27	77	101	292	223	1920	1610
Jan. 23, 1975	8.06	9.66	590	285	46	37	100	91	166	162	254	282	2860	2110
Feb. 12	11.30	9.56	399	382	55	43	90	130	186	191	320	231	2340	2520
March 10	12.75	8.57	805	646	143	97	288	191	434	184	800	592	3700	3110

Table 19.2 (continued)

Date	14 Detritus ($mm^2\,ml^{-1}$)		15 COD ($mg\,l^{-1}$)		16 BOD ($mg\,l^{-1}$)		17 ATP ($10^{-2}\,\mu g\,l^{-1}$)		18 DHA Extinction (495 nm) incubation time 1h sample volume 1 l		19 Nitrification potential ($\mu g\,NO_2$-$N\,l^{-1}$ $(14\,d)^{-1}$)	
	2 m	10 m	2 m	10 m	2 m	10 m	2 m	10 m	2 m	10 m	2 m	10 m
Jan. 24, 1974	3.30	1.31	0.325	0.267	4.13	3.39	5.7	13.1			15,500	
Feb. 14					0.39							
Feb. 28	0.33	0.30	0.986	0.649	5.70	7.85	17.9	22.1	0.047	1.030		0
March 21	1.97	2.65	0.766	0.526	3.47	0.74	22.6	24.5	0.372	1.260		0
April 18	1.67	0.60	0.893	0.848	3.73	4.14			0.531	2.750		0
May 16	1.34	0.93	0.888	0.722	5.63	1.84	49.8	50.2	0.156	1.633		
June 11	0.66	1.34	0.879	0.764	3.27	1.42	49.6	49.9	0.100	1.963	2,700	
June 25					5.56	4.02					2,100	
July 11	0.56	1.20	0.651	0.564	5.84	1.27	27.3	19.0	0.433	2.466	4,800	
Aug. 7					5.95	3.99	23.0	5.1				
Aug. 29	0.70	1.00	0.876	0.682	3.71	1.07	116.4	18.5	0.237	1.610	2,200	
Sept. 12	0.29	0.94	0.576	0.541	2.95	1.92	73.0	11.6	0.076	2.810	0	
Oct. 24	1.09	0.38	0.691	0.617	2.37	2.16	18.3	18.2	0.246	1.336	3,900	
Nov. 21	0.79	2.69	0.679	0.620	1.12	0.03	7.4	17.9	0.010	0.984	900	
Dec. 10	0.25	0.49	0.497	0.643	0.71	1.30	10.9	13.6	0.118	1.233	1,300	
Jan. 23, 1975	0.46		0.516	0.674	0.05	1.24	3.3	4.0	0.021	0.532	1,300	
Feb. 12	0.50		0.638	0.557	2.45	1.70	23.5	11.1	0.186	1.153	4,100	
March 10	1.36		0.636	0.552	3.54	1.91	42.7	73.6	0.020	0.935	0	

Table 19.2 (continued)

Date	20 Planktonic cell number ($N \times 10^3 \, l^{-1}$) 2 m	21 Chlorophyll a ($\mu g \, l^{-1}$) 2 m	10 m	22 Primary production ($mgC \, m^{-3} \, h^{-1}$) 2 m	6 m	23 Total number of bacteria (direct counts) ($N \times 10^6 \, ml^{-1}$) 2 m	10 m	24 Total biomass of bacteria ($mgC \, m^{-3}$) 2 m	10 m	25 Saprophytes ($cfu \, ml^{-1}$) 2 m	10 m
Jan. 24, 1974	14.8	0.9	1.2			2.01	1.29	12.8	7.6	13,600	7,200
Feb. 14										4,600	62,500
Feb. 28	2.2	1.7	1.2			1.93	1.34	7.3	5.1	27,600	21,300
March 21	183.0	2.1	2.3	3.34	0.81	1.55	1.89	6.9	9.9	15,900	22,300
April 18	4,642.0	14.4	8.9	23.10	1.15	5.34	3.90	21.7	19.7	91,600	58,800
May 16	161.0	14.2	2.3	7.54	0.22	5.26	2.58	22.5	10.6	184,266	30,600
June 11	21,000.0	9.5	5.6	16.85	0.55	5.25	3.59	24.0	13.3	122,667	48,267
June 25										19,934	95,334
July 11	5,086.0	25.8	14.7	122.63	83.84	3.95	4.19	19.4	17.5	47,066	24,600
Aug. 7	2,299.0	17.7	4.0							39,600	19,934
Aug. 29	754.0	14.8	1.5	55.46	5.47	3.90	2.52	24.2	9.8	82,266	25,000
Sept. 12	73.9	6.0	3.4	23.89	7.48	1.97	2.65	10.2	11.5	54,000	65,200
Oct. 24	157.0	3.7	2.4	13.65	0.35	2.72	1.70	11.4	10.1	138,134	59,600
Nov. 21	194.0	0.9	0.5			1.73	5.68	7.6	(25.0)	37,000	49,200
Dec. 10	25.4	0.9	0.6			1.51	1.57	6.1	6.2	48,066	42,534
Jan. 23, 1975	131.0	0.8	0.7	0.81	0.23	0.96		5.0		11,667	10,467
Feb. 12	969.0	2.3	1.5	1.02	0.16	1.69		8.6		19,667	23,867
March 10	2,116.0	16.1	9.0			1.32		7.8		18,000	17,000

Table 19.2 (continued)

Date	26 Coliforms (cfu l⁻¹)		27 Cellulolytic bacteria (MPN l⁻¹)		28 Chitinoclastic bacteria (cfu ml⁻¹)		29 Total number of yeasts (cfu l⁻¹)		30 Number of red yeasts (cfu l⁻¹)		31 Spores (cfu ml⁻¹)	
	2 m	10 m	2 m	10 m	2 m	10 m	2 m	10 m	2 m	10 m	2 m	10 m
Jan. 24, 1974	49,000	10,500	0.1	0.1			4,150	19,900	350	9,850		
Feb. 14	49,000	4,500					3,100	1,450	200	100		
Feb. 28												
March 21	46,500	17,500	1.0	0.1	50	60	3,150	3,550	350	350		
April 18	6,500	1,000	1.0	0.1	110	20	1,300	0	50	0	3	10
May 16	61,000	500	0.1	1.0	40	8	5,350	100	500	0	6	30
June 11	56,500	6,500	10.0	10.0	110	25	3,100	800	400	150	7	1
June 25	26,500	17,000	1.0	1.0	70	80	400	100	50	0	4	0
July 11	75,500	15,500					1,000	750	250	50	7	0
Aug. 7	2,500	0	1.0	10.0	90	110	14,300	6,550			10	3
Aug. 29	84,000	2,500					1,100	200	150	50	9	3
Sept. 12	135,000	61,500	1.0	0.1	110	190	100	200	50	100	2	5
Oct. 24	935,000	69,500	1.0	1.0		220	5,200	2,750	1,100	600	3	3
Nov. 21	128,500	60,500	10.0	1.0	4	40	2,000	2,550	350	300	10	3
Dec. 10	90,500	79,500	10.0	1.0	20	100						
Jan. 23, 1975	48,500	59,000	0.1		30	10	1,400	2,850	300	850	80	30
Feb. 12	38,333	22,500	0.01	0.1	20	40	1,150	800	0	0	20	20
March 10	325,000	25,500	1.0	1.0	70	30	2,200	1,950	450	700		

Table 19.2 (continued)

Date	32 Active cells (microautoradiography) (N ml⁻¹)	33 V_{max} glucose (μg Cl⁻¹ h⁻¹)		34 V_{max} aspartic acid (μg Cl⁻¹ h⁻¹)	35 V_{max} acetate (μg Cl⁻¹ h⁻¹)	36 Turnover time (glucose) (h)		37 Turnover time (aspartic acid) (h)
	2 m	2 m	10 m	2 m	2 m	2 m	10 m	2 m
Jan. 24, 1974								
Feb. 14		0.046	0.039	0.033	0.146	24.1	29.7	36.8
Feb. 28		0.095	0.102	0.070	0.442	9.9	8.8	41.4
March 21		0.465	0.314	0.296	1.044	4.1	3.0	2.4
April 18		0.452	0.059	0.360	0.795	3.2	9.9	6.5
May 16		0.291	0.140	0.230	0.346	2.8	6.1	11.6
June 11	2,083,254							
June 25								
July 11	1,930,796	0.134	0.136	0.134	0.218	5.6	7.6	20.2
Aug. 7		0.663	0.140	0.376	1.003	7.1	6.1	3.8
Aug. 29	989,446	0.180	0.152	0.155	0.372	15.5	8.1	11.4
Sept. 12	756,824	0.228	0.078	0.220		5.3	22.7	11.5
Oct. 24	1,008,300	0.024	0.042	0.029	0.076	31.2	24.4	31.2
Nov. 21	567,381		0.016	0.034			63.4	102.0
Dec. 10	385,455	0.030	0.030	0.023	0.059	29.6	27.0	74.2
Jan. 23, 1975	171,173	0.031	0.036	0.034	0.119	35.7	24.4	44.6
Feb. 12	422,269	0.030	0.048	0.030	0.066	33.5	27.0	54.9
March 10	690,600							

Table 19.2 (continued)

Date	38 Turnover time (acetate) (h)	39 Turnover time (pool of free amino acids) (h)		40 Number of cells capable of growth ($N \times 10^4\ ml^{-1}$)	41 Generation time (h)	42 Increase in cell number ($N \times 10^5\ ml^{-1}\ d^{-1}$)	43 Biomass production ($10^{-5}\ mg\,ml^{-1}\ d^{-1}$)
	2 m	2 m	10 m	2 m	2 m	2 m	2 m
Jan. 24, 1974							
Feb. 14							
Feb. 28	29.4	32.5	49.9				
March 21	12.2	10.0	8.0	0.72	28.8	3.0	9.0
April 18	6.8	3.1	5.7	1.84	27.6	0.9	4.4
May 16	9.9	2.5	7.5	3.44	29.5	0	9.6
June 11	18.7	3.6	10.6	1.53	15.2	0.5	11.7
June 25							
July 11	25.7	5.1	6.4	0.92	7.7	6.7	12.3
Aug. 7				2.08	10.1	8.0	21.3
Aug. 29	11.3	2.9	7.3	2.32	12.5	12.5	36.7
Sept. 12	7.7	4.6	4.4	1.52	13.4	8.7	21.3
Oct. 24		2.7	11.4	1.68	11.3	13.7	52.0
Nov. 21	50.0	28.3	45.8	0.80	19.1	1.7	8.0
Dec. 10		22.2	17.0	0.60	23.3	1.9	10.0
Jan. 23, 1975	50.1	25.6	9.6	0.48	37.2	0.2	0.2
Feb. 12	36.1	12.4	8.0	0.48	34.7	2.6	7.9
March 10	71.1	23.8	22.7				

Table 19.3. Raw data measured at station 5 (Kiel Bight). (Parameters 22 and 39 were not measured at this station)

Date	1			2			3			4		
	Temperature ($^\circ$C)			Salinity ($S^o/_{oo}$)			Phosphate (μg-at PO_4-P l^{-1})			Ammonia (μg-at NH_3-N l^{-1})		
	2 m	10 m	18 m	2 m	10 m	18 m	2 m	10 m	18 m	2 m	10 m	18 m
Jan. 24, 1974	3.00	2.90	2.60	15.51	16.77	19.54	1.374	1.031	3.321	4.007	5.186	4.793
Feb. 14	10.10	3.10	3.30	16.58	17.08	19.84	1.179	0.790	1.040	4.429	5.071	6.429
Feb. 28	2.90	3.00	3.20	16.52	16.39	18.66	0.881	3.577	3.632	0.900	1.136	1.164
March 21	3.70	4.40	3.10	15.60	16.24	16.49	2.710	2.710	2.090	3.571	5.143	4.000
April 18	7.30	6.80	5.40	15.31	14.68	16.21	0.206	0.171	0.258	0.651	1.737	1.791
May 16	10.10	8.70	6.40	14.61	15.93	17.81	0.485	0.713	1.174	1.507	1.543	2.914
June 11	12.30	12.20	11.60	16.02	16.15	22.42	0.379	0.303	0.652	1.400	0.971	1.259
June 25	17.20	15.70	10.50	14.92	15.89	22.45	0.610	0.240	0.700	1.257	0.864	7.700
July 11	15.50	15.50	15.10	18.45	18.32	20.82	1.016	0.864	0.610	2.286	49.143	9.714
Aug. 7												
Aug. 29	17.45	17.50	15.10	10.73	14.34	22.24	0.203	0.590	1.019	1.021	0.929	1.950
Sept. 12	15.90	15.70	15.60	14.75	18.70	20.96	0.431	0.332	0.513	21.239	1.391	1.629
Oct. 24	10.36	10.34	11.20	16.92	17.45	18.51	2.342	2.306	1.419	2.739	2.043	1.254
Nov. 21	7.50	7.45	8.20	17.66	17.79	18.18	1.189	1.189	1.405	1.466	1.561	1.873
Dec. 10	6.50	6.50	7.00	17.08	17.08	18.12	1.020	0.020	1.952	1.479	1.971	1.479
Jan. 23, 1975		5.10	5.00	20.32	20.64	20.77	1.507	1.445	2.209	2.429	1.971	6.000
Feb. 12	4.10	3.70	4.80	10.13	10.64	20.45	0.625	0.609	1.135	2.366	2.657	1.886
March 10	3.90	3.30		11.55	13.33	20.26	2.574	3.555	2.966	1.174	0.737	2.254

Table 19.3. (continued)

Date	5 Nitrite (μg-at NO_2-N l^{-1})			6 Nitrate (μg-at NO_3-N l^{-1})			7 Oxygen (mg l^{-1})			8 Carbon (μg l^{-1})		
	2 m	10 m	18 m	2 m	10 m	18 m	2 m	10 m	18 m	2 m	10 m	18 m
Jan. 24, 1974	0.964	0.964	0.857	5.893	7.197	11.679	11.80	11.42	10.85	111	91	173
Feb. 14	0.977	0.926	0.600	6.051	5.589	5.914	11.14	8.90	6.69			
Feb. 28	0.907	0.907	0.986	6.807	5.743	8.757	12.03	11.99	10.87			
March 21	0.771	0.771	0.600	3.957	3.957	4.071	12.30	12.02	11.70	326	195	655
April 18	0.043	0.054	0.161	0.243	0.175	1.039	11.81	12.14	11.54	335	337	481
May 16	0.050	0.050	0.152	0.293	0.293	3.048	11.04	10.93	7.82	402	378	369
June 11	0.100	0.050	0.050	0.529	0.407	0.613	9.79	9.94	9.22	364	364	229
June 25	0.054	0.054	0.107	0.575	0.496	0.443	9.41	9.75	6.98	442	419	285
July 11	0.050	0.050		0.411	0.625	0.321	9.25	9.22	8.62			
Aug. 7										507	453	403
Aug. 29	0.150	0.140	0.160	0.054	0.161	0.107	9.24	9.64	3.74	476	650	888
Sept. 12	0.064	0.054	0.107	0.182	0.342	0.297	9.66	6.19	5.96	466	473	815
Oct. 24	0.450	0.380	0.600	0.418	0.268	0.107	9.89	9.77	9.40	917	957	463
Nov. 21	1.429	1.429	1.600	0.836	1.013	1.329	8.00	8.02	6.67	485	453	298
Dec. 10	0.550	0.500	0.500	3.929	3.821	2.364	9.47	8.94	9.68	505	431	380
Jan. 23, 1975	0.200	0.300	0.700	6.629	6.893	10.000	10.98	10.54	10.55	368	338	495
Feb. 12	0.096	0.471	0.386	5.155	4.727	13.944	11.76	12.05	10.48	210	260	319
March 10				0.257	2.507	15.621	13.26	12.87	8.88	583	632	207

Table 19.3. (continued)

Date	9 Nitrogen (µg l⁻¹)			10 Lipids (µg l⁻¹)			11 Carbohydrates (µg l⁻¹)			12 Proteins (µg l⁻¹)		
	2 m	10 m	18 m	2 m	10 m	18 m	2 m	10 m	18 m	2 m	10 m	18 m
Jan. 24, 1974	15	11	20	127	134	35	32	39	75	108	74	124
Feb. 14												
Feb. 28	53	30	66	122	62	176	178	146	296	328	152	700
March 21	55	58	59	48	61	63	157	157	187	316	324	464
April 18	74	60	36	83	141	397	176	185	157	434	360	362
May 16	47	55	39	64	171	43	170	142	151	304	358	260
June 11	66	65		38	73	42	232	235	167	408	390	242
June 25												
July 11	82	74	62	166	365	85	246	235	232	464	440	412
Aug. 7												
Aug. 29	62	87	104	46	70	75	335	480	770	294	490	586
Sep. 12	59	72	110	61	40	29	280	341	534	366	468	686
Oct. 24	126	134	71	247	154	121	675	576	239	754	840	464
Nov. 21	67	65	38	44	33	77	376	227	116	342	366	238
Dec. 10	56	63	46	50	50	59	255	233	166	316	328	286
Jan. 23, 1975	49	43	62	79	90	73	146	150	174	279	285	392
Feb. 12	28	30	41	58	82	96	108	135	120	168	126	233
March 10	93	116	26	190	247	250	371	289	122	524	692	125

Table 19.3. (continued)

Date	13 Seston (μg l^{-1})			14 Detritus (mm^2 ml^{-1})		15 COD (mg l^{-1})			16 BOD (mg l^{-1})		
	2 m	10 m	18 m	2 m	10 m	2 m	10 m	18 m	2 m	10 m	18 m
Jan. 24, 1974	1230	1230	1510	0.21	1.26	0.302	0.296	0.319	3.92	3.33	2.09
Feb. 14									3.17	0.40	
Feb. 28	2850	1360	7700	0.16	0.19	0.525	0.457	0.766	8.24	8.72	7.81
March 21	1690	1930	2940	0.37	0.77	0.863	0.736	0.668	4.29	3.15	2.09
April 18	1380	1200	1510	0.37	0.33	0.616	0.503	0.593	3.51	4.27	3.98
May 16	1560	2150	1690	0.36	3.64	0.602	0.599	0.673	3.09	3.16	2.37
June 11	2050	2680	2190	0.30	0.16	0.736	0.789		2.32	2.89	2.79
June 25									2.85	2.48	1.85
July 11	1970	1390	1480	0.40	0.51	0.606	0.413	0.357	2.38	3.28	2.21
Aug. 7											
Aug. 29	3300	3420	1820	0.26	1.68	0.662	0.569	0.619	0.81	2.27	0.96
Sept. 12	1620	1850	3840	0.16	1.05	0.508	0.533	0.354	2.72	0.10	1.22
Oct. 24	3820	3160	1750	0.60	0.70	0.495	0.507	0.470	3.18	2.77	3.76
Nov. 21	1820	1840	1620	0.48	0.31	0.503	0.522	0.633	0.96	0.11	0.11
Dec. 10	1600	1590	3520	0.37	0.75	0.670	0.529	0.583	9.21	0.33	1.10
Jan. 23, 1975	3240	2990	5060	0.76		0.516	0.507	0.525	2.29	1.71	2.13
Feb. 12	1280	1080	3830	0.16		0.518	0.498	0.499	1.65	2.22	1.94
March 10	1920	2250	2010	0.44		0.521	0.506	0.552	2.16	3.12	1.22

Table 19.3. (continued)

Date	17 ATP (10^{-2} µg l^{-1})			18 DHA Extinction (495 nm) incubation time 1 h sample volume 1 l	19 Nitrification potential (µg NO$_2$-N l^{-1} (14 d)$^{-1}$)	20 Planktonic cell number (N × 10^3 l^{-1})	21 Chlorophyll a (µg l^{-1})			23 Total number of bacteria (direct counts) (N × 10^6 ml^{-1})	
	2 m	10 m	18 m	2 m	10 m	2 m	2 m	10 m	18 m	2 m	18 m
Jan. 24, 1974	26.6	24.0	8.6		0	5.9	0.4	0.5	0.7	0.38	0.70
Feb. 14											
Feb. 28	6.4	8.0	2.7	0.026	0	11.9	0.9	0.7	1.1	1.99	0.80
March 21	28.9	36.5	20.4	0.063	0	183.0	2.2	1.9	2.1	0.61	0.52
April 18				0.012	0	77.0	0.9	1.1	1.3	1.60	2.05
May 16	27.5	46.7	42.6		600	83.0	0.9	1.4	1.4	1.81	1.79
June 11	55.9	45.1	8.7	0.040	50	244.0	0.7	1.4	0.8	1.78	1.89
June 25											
July 11	3.7	7.2	3.7	0.120	300	1641.0	2.4	2.3	1.9	2.22	2.99
Aug. 7											
Aug. 29	16.4	43.8	64.6	0.195	2300	167.0	1.1	1.9	4.8	2.22	1.97
Sept. 12	32.0	55.0	82.3	0.022	0	1283.0	1.9	2.2	4.0	1.10	1.47
Oct. 24	74.4	64.8	44.1	0.176	1400	195.0	6.1	5.6	2.5	1.82	2.74
Nov. 21	23.3	19.1	4.5	0.004	0	39.4	2.4	2.1	0.6	1.21	1.06
Dec. 10	19.1	20.0	2.3	0.022	1900	59.0	2.4	2.4	0.5	1.24	0.99
Jan. 23, 1975	6.7	5.8	2.8	0.064	940	181.0	1.7	1.8	1.9	0.67	
Feb. 12	9.2	7.1	4.1	0.049	2140		1.9	1.0	1.0	0.64	
March 10	50.3	76.0	16.2	0.301	0	1911.0	7.6	16.6	1.9		

Table 19.3. (continued)

Date	24 Total biomass of bacteria (mg C m^{-3})		25 Saprophytes (cfu ml^{-1})			26 Coliforms (cfu l^{-1})			27 Cellulolytic bacteria (MPN ml^{-1})		28 Chitinoclastic bacteria (cfu ml^{-1})	
	2 m	18 m	2 m	10 m	18 m	2 m	10 m	18 m	2 m	18 m	2 m	18 m
Jan. 24, 1974	4.9	3.4	434	221	680	120	710	920	0.01	0.01		
Feb. 14			1098	720	409	0	10	0	0	0.1	2	2
Feb. 28	4.8	2.8	1875	775	368	0	40	0	0.01	1.0	2	2
March 21	2.0	1.5	531	227	428	120	0	10	0	0.1	0	3
April 18	6.2	11.1	3959	2860	3612	500	0	0	0.1	1.0	0	20
May 16	8.7	9.4	1627	1261	1360	10	10	40	0	10.0		55
June 11	4.6	8.4	812	857	529	0	0	0	0.1		25	
June 25			228	337	300	2590	100	20	0			20
July 11	11.0	8.8	336	380	246	10	20	200	0	0.1	10	
Aug. 7												
Aug. 29	10.7	11.3	263	107	174	60	7	7	0		50	20
Sept. 12	5.9	6.1	604	579	377	600	1070	250	0.1	0.1	0	110
Oct. 24	6.9	10.1	3070	1895	2944	1160	3950	7450	0.1	1.0	2	30
Nov. 21	5.0	3.9	1207	1132	687	2280	3780	3090	0	0.1	0	70
Dec. 10	4.6	3.3	1257	1523	790	630	530	140	0	0	3	2
Jan. 23, 1975	3.3		400	367	337	970	920	1900	0	1.0	0	0
Feb. 12	3.6		660	761	1297	140	100	50	0.01	1.0	30	0
March 10			1240	379	700	800	20000	480	0	0	0	20

Table 19.3. (continued)

Date	29 Total number of yeasts (cfu l⁻¹)			30 Number of red yeasts (cfu l⁻¹)			31 Spores (cfu ml⁻¹)		32 Active cells (microautoradiography) (N ml⁻¹)	33 V_{max} glucose (µg C l⁻¹ h⁻¹)		
	2 m	10 m	18 m	2 m	10 m	18 m	2 m	18 m	2 m	2 m	10 m	18 m
Jan. 24, 1974	130	365	225	30	10	20						
Feb. 14	10	10	25	5	0	0						
Feb. 28										0.015	0.013	0.017
March 21	5	20	20	5	10	5	0	0			0.005	0.006
April 18	0	0	0	0	0	0	1	10		0.039	0.045	0.148
May 16	500	930	0	60	10	0	0	3		0.025	0.019	0.011
June 11	0	160	25	0	30	0	1	20	963,024	0.046	0.030	0.027
June 25	20	45	15	10	10	0						
July 11	155	145	165	60	80	65	0	1	1,212,683	0.031	0.041	0.028
Aug. 7												
Aug. 29	110	100	10	0	0	0	10	10	538,289	0.055	0.040	0.046
Sept. 12	225	520	30	0	0	0	1	0	352,563	0.051	0.038	0.053
Oct. 24		495	40	15	15	0	10	0	416,652	0.032	0.049	0.063
Nov. 21	10	10	10	5	0	0	10	10	272,807	0.018	0.020	0.021
Dec. 10							3	1	123,008			
Jan. 23, 1975	40	40	60	20	0	0	2	1	57,352	0.006	0.005	0.010
Feb. 12	40	0	40	0	0	0	0	4	55,183	0.004	0.004	0.010
March 10	95	155	0	15	30	0	1	5	700,152	0.018	0.015	0.004

Table 19.3. (continued)

Date	34 V_{max} aspartic acid (μg C l^{-1} h^{-1}) 2 m	35 V_{max} acetate (μg C l^{-1} h^{-1}) 2 m	36 Turnover time (glucose) (h) 2 m	10 m	18 m	37 Turnover time (aspartic acid) (h) 2 m
Jan. 24, 1974						
Feb. 14						
Feb. 28	0.018		56.1	65.3	127.0	234.0
March 21				277.0	523.0	
April 18	0.024		10.3	12.4	5.1	44.7
May 16	0.027	0.098	52.2	49.4	387.0	118.0
June 11	0.045		13.7	13.4	15.1	72.4
June 25						
July 11	0.030	0.024	37.2	19.9	31.1	149.0
Aug. 7						
Aug. 29		0.094	50.4	27.3	36.5	
Sept. 12	0.293	0.090	21.6	36.6	26.1	15.2
Oct. 24	0.020	0.022	16.8	26.8	19.5	113.0
Nov. 21	0.009	0.015	69.7	41.9	60.5	97.9
Dec. 10						
Jan. 23, 1975	0.010	0.010	167.0	79.7	96.5	297.0
Feb. 12	0.007	0.009	395.0	295.0	166.0	811.0
March 10	0.015	0.015	112.0	73.6	182.0	105.0

Table 19.5. Station 5 (Kiel Bight). Correlation matrices based on two-state correlation coefficients ($+/-$), series comparison (○), and time series analysis (□). For code numbers compare Table 19.3

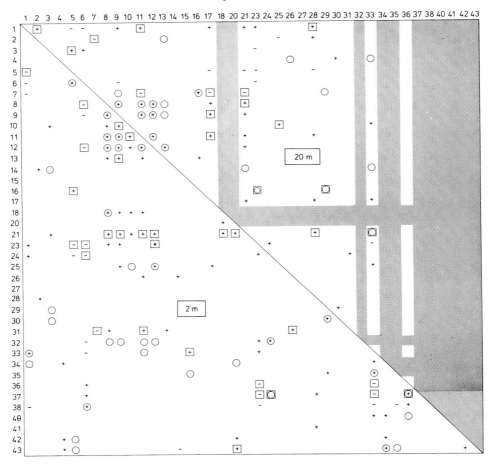

important parameters, e.g., zooplankton and dissolved organic matter (DOM) should be included in further studies. For the stations with a more heterogenous pattern, short-term investigations may be the choice to interpret the influence of different parameters on the ecology of microorganisms in brackish waters.

References

Bell, W. H., Lang, J. M., Mitchell, R.: Selective stimulation of marine bacteria by algal extracellular products. Limnol. Oceanogr. **19**, 833–839 (1974)

Bodungen, B. v.: Der Jahresgang der Nährsalze und der Primärproduktion des Planktons in der Kieler Bucht unter Berücksichtigung der Hydrographie, Thesis, Univ. Kiel (1975)

Bonde,G.J.: Studies on the dispersion and disappearance phenomena of enteric bacteria in the marine environment. Rev. Intern. Océanogr. Méd. **9**, 17–44 (1968)

Brasfield,H.: Environmental factors correlated with size of bacterial populations in a polluted stream. Appl. Microbiol. **24**, 349–352 (1972)

Bröckel,K.v.: Der Energiefluß im pelagischen Ökosystem vor Boknis Eck (Westl. Ostsee), Reports Sonderforschungsbereich 95 Univ. Kiel **10** (1975)

Castellvi,J., Ballester,A.: Activité hétérotrophique bactérienne en rapport avec les conditions hydrologiques des systèmes marines. Théthys **6**, 189–202 (1974)

Colwell,R.R., Morita,R.Y. (eds.): Effect of the ocean environment on microbial activities, Baltimore-London-Tokyo: University Park Press, 1974

Derenbach,J.B.: Partikuläre Substanz und Plankton an Hand chemischer und biologischer Daten gemessen in den oberen Wasserschichten des Gotland-Tiefs im Mai 1968. Kieler Meeresforsch. **25**, 279–289 (1969)

Faust,M.A., Aotaky,A.E., Hargadon,M.T.: Effect of physical parameters on the in situ survival of *E. coli* MC-6 in an estuarine environment. Appl. Microbiol. **30**, 800–806 (1975)

Ferguson,R.L., Rublee,P.: Contribution of bacteria to standing crop of coastal plankton. Limnol. Oceanogr. **21**, 141–145 (1976)

Gundersen,K., Mountain,C.W., Taylor,D., Ohye,R., Shen,J.: Some chemical and microbiological observations in the Pacific Ocean off the Hawaiian Islands. Limnol. Oceanogr. **17**, 524–531 (1972)

Holm-Hansen,O.: Determination of microbial biomass in ocean profiles. Limnol. Oceanogr. **14**, 740–747 (1969)

Hoppe,H.-G.: Untersuchungen zur Analyse mariner Bakterienpopulationen mit einer autoradiographischen Methode. Kieler Meeresforsch. **30**, 107–116 (1974)

Jansson,B.-O.: Ecosystem approach to the Baltic problem. Bull. Ecol. Res. Com./NFR **16**, 7–82 (1972)

Kadota,H.: A study of marine aerobic cellulose-decomposing bacteria. Mem. Coll. Agric. Kyoto **74** (Fish. Ser. 6), 1–128 (1956)

Lear,D.W.: Occurrence and significance of chitinoclastic bacteria in pelagic waters and zooplankton. Bact. Proc. **61**, 47 (1961)

Lehnberg,B.: Ökologische Untersuchungen an agar- und zellulosezersetzenden Bakterien aus Nord- und Ostsee. Thesis Univ. Kiel (1972)

Lenz,J.: Untersuchungen zum Nahrungsgefüge im Pelagial der Kieler Bucht. Der Gehalt an Phytoplankton, Zooplankton und organischem Detritus in Abhängigkeit von Wasserschichtung, Tiefe und Jahreszeit. Habilitationsschrift Univ. Kiel (1974)

Melchiorri-Santolini,U., Hopton,J.W. (eds.): Detritus and its role in aquatic ecosystems. Mem. Ist. Ital. Idrobiol. 29, Suppl. 1972

Menon,A.S., Glooschenko,W.A., Burns,N.M.: Bacteria-phytoplankton relationships in Lake Erie. Proc. 15th Conf. Great Lakes Res., 54–101 (1972)

Meyer-Reil,L.-A.: Untersuchungen über die Salzansprüche von Ostseebakterien. Bot. Mar. **16**, 65–76 (1973)

Meyer-Reil,L.-A.: Untersuchungen über die Salzansprüche von Ostseebakterien: Temperatureinflüsse und Adaptationen. Bot. Mar. **17**, 1–15 (1974)

Morgenstern,O.: International Financial Transactions and Business Cycles. Princeton Univ. Press 1959

Odum,H.T.: An energy circuit language for ecological and social systems: Its physical basis. Progr. Rep. U.S. At. Energy Com. **1** (40–1)—3666, 3–90 (1969)

Pfanzagl,J.: Über die Parallelität von Zeitreihen. Metrika **6**, 100–113 (1963)

Probst,B.: Auswertung ökologischer Parameter, die 1966 auf Feuerschiff P 8 beobachtet wurden. Dipl.-Arbeit, Univ. Kiel 1973

Rheinheimer,G.: Einige Beobachtungen über den Einfluß von Ostseewasser auf limnische Bakterienpopulationen. Veröff. Inst. Meeresforsch. Bremerh., Sdbd. **2**, 237–244 (1966)

Rheinheimer,G.: Beobachtungen über den Einfluß von Salzgehaltsschwankungen auf die Bakterienflora der westlichen Ostsee. Sarsia **34**, 253–262 (1968)

Rheinheimer,G.: Mikrobiologie der Gewässer. Jena: Fischer, 1975

Rosswall,T. (ed.): Modern methods in the study of microbial ecology Bull. Ecol. Res. Com. 17 (1972)

Saylor,G.S., Nelson,J.D., Justice,A., Colwell,R.R.: Distribution and significance of fecal indicator organisms in the upper Chesapeake Bay. Appl. Microbiol. **30**, 625–638 (1975)

Seki,H.: Seasonal fluctuations of heterotrophic bacteria in the sea of Aburatsubo Inlet. J. Oceanogr. Soc. Jap. **22**, 93–104 (1966)

Seki,H.: Microbial biomass on particulate matter in seawater of the euphotic zone. Appl. Microbiol. **19**, 960–962 (1970)

Seki,H., Taga,N.: Microbial studies on the decomposition of chitin in the marine environment. I, II. J. Oceanogr. Soc. Jap. **19**, 101–111, 143–161 (1963)

Stevenson,L.H., Colwell,R.R. (eds.): Estuarine microbial ecology, Columbia,S.C.: Univ. South Carolina Press 1973

Tanaka,N., Nakanishi,M., Kadota,H.: Nutritional interrelation between bacteria and phytoplankton in a pelagic ecosystem. In: Effect of the Ocean Environment on Microbial Activities. Colwell,R.R., Morita,R.Y (eds.) Baltimore-London-Tokyo: University Park Press, 1974

Wallis,W.A., Roberts,H.V.: Methoden der Statistik, Hamburg: Rowohlt, 1969

Weber,E., Grundriß der biologischen Statistik, Jena: Fischer 1961

Zeitzschel,B. (ed.): The biology of the Indian Ocean, Berlin-Heidelberg-New York: Springer 1973

20. Conclusion

G. RHEINHEIMER

In contrast to most ecosystem investigations carried out up to the present in the marine area, this study is mainly concerned with heterotrophic microorganisms, especially the bacteria. The importance of bacteria for the cycle of matter and for the food chain has been well known for a long time. However, bacteriological parameters have not been sufficiently included in most of the research programs, for which reason relatively few bacteriological data are available. Only in the most recent, still unpublished, ecosystem investigations at present still being carried out in some European countries and in the USA are bacteriological parameters included to a larger extent. More knowledge is available concerning the role of bacteria in the lake ecosystems (see Overbeck, 1972; Wetzel, 1975).

This volume should help to gain better information on the microbial aspect of the sea. Despite all difficulties and problems of such a program, extensive microbiological data series for a brackish water environment are presented and compared with hydrographic, chemical and planktological data. It must be pointed out that intensive methodological work was necessary prior to starting the program. Afterwards a certain time was needed for the interpretation of the comprehensive data set. Therefore, this study should be regarded not only as a summary of our results and interpretations, but also as a suggestion for further investigations.

Although most of the data presented in this volume are from the Kiel Bight area, the results allow not only an insight into the microbial ecology of this most western part of the Baltic Sea, but also of similar brackish water environments in the temperate climatic zone.

From the results of this study many relations may be shown between the individual microbiological parameters, as well as between these and the hydrographic and chemical parameters. Yet these represent only a small part of the various relations for which correlations can be found as in Chapter 19. Besides indirect relationships, those which show a time lag play a particularly important role, such as, for example, the relation between the development of phytoplankton and saprophytic bacteria.

The interpretation of the relationships between the various parameters is made more difficult by the changeability of the meteorological and hydrographic conditions in the area of investigation, and likewise in many other brackish water areas.

The instability of the hydrographic conditions can be regarded as an essential characteristic of brackish water regions, since these are for the most part estuaries situated between the limnic and marine areas (see Chap. 3). Most typical for these are the more or less strong fluctuations in salinity. As a rule these can occur periodically as well as nonperiodically. The nonperiodic changes in the salt content, e.g., in the western Baltic Sea, can be so great that at times those occurring periodically are masked. The instability of the area investigated must therefore be accepted, in spite of all the difficulties involved, and may be regarded as an example of many other brackish water areas.

Another problem is presented by the meteorological conditions during the time of investigation, since these show considerable differences from year to year. Thus the year 1974 was characterized by relatively small changes in temperature, as a result of the mild winter and moderately warm summer (see Chap. 2). Therefore, neither very low temperatures in the winter nor high summer temperatures were measured in the water of the Kiel Bight (cf. Chap. 3). However, the year of investigation does not show such great deviations from the long-term meteorological mean values as the years 1975 and 1976, which were too low in average rainfall, with too many hours of sunlight and correspondingly high temperatures in summer.

For many parameters comparisons could be made with earlier and, in a few cases, also with more recent investigations in the same area and in neighboring regions. Thus for the interpretation of the results it was possible to take into consideration a much greater time span, so that the knowledge gained is greater than that usually obtained from time-limited investigations. For a number of parameters (saprophyte numbers, concentration of inorganic nutrients, seston and its main components) earlier results were confirmed—among others, certain differences could be found (primary production, distribution of cellulolytic bacteria) for which, as a rule, explanations could be given, mainly by the different meteorological conditions. This expanding of the interpretation possibilities also benefited the studies on bacterial activity carried out for the first time with new methods, and allowed conclusions to be drawn here with greater certainty.

Of particular importance is the fact that for the various parameters, investigations made within shorter time intervals can likewise be included, so that also in this respect further information for the interpretation of the results is made available (see Chap. 15).

An unexpected result of this study, leading to a revision of our knowledge, is the very small amount of bacteria attached to detritus particles (cf. Hopton and Melchiorri-Santolini, 1972). The main values are below 5% of the total bacterial number in 2-m depth at the five stations investigated and below 10% overground (see Table 10.8). Only 20% of the particles were colonized by microorganisms (see Chap. 10). Therefore, although the bacteria cells attached to detritus are larger than those living free in the water, they can only play a limited role either in the food chain or in the cycle of matter in the water body of the Kiel Bight and similar brackish water areas.

Autoradiographic observation showed, however, that fresh organic detritus is a microbiotope of considerable reproductive and substrate uptake activity for bacteria, while inorganic particles are almost free of bacteria (see Chaps. 10 and 14). The detritus sedimentates rather quickly in the shallow water of the western Baltic, as could be found by Zeitzschel (1965) and Iturriaga (1977) with "Sinkstoff" traps.

Therefore, most of the degradable particulate matter will be decomposed in the uppermost zone of the sediment. Especially the aerobic zones of mud sediments are habitats of large and actively metabolizing microbial populations. Another, however, very restricted area of enlarged bacterial development is the air–water interface of the neuston, where besides fats, hydrocarbons, and other nonwater-soluble liquids, particulate organic matter of low specific density is concentrated. In both these zones bacteria which are able to attack resistant substrates are enriched (see Chap. 14).

It may be concluded that in the shallow brackish water area investigated the easily degradable dissolved organic matter is mainly decomposed in the water column, while the more resistant nonwater-soluble substrates are mainly decomposed in the air–water and water–sediment interfaces. In deeper waters, however, more of the organic material of detritus is decomposed in the water body itself, because of the longer way for the particles from the photic zone to the ground and the consequent longer time for bacteria to attach and to reproduce. Therefore, the detritus particles show a denser colonization of microorganisms in depths of more than 20 m.

Investigations on heterotrophic activity revealed a good adaptation of the microflora to the uptake of low concentrations of dissolved organic substances, not only in the rather clean central Kiel Bight but also in the relatively eutrophicated Kiel Fjord (see Chap. 15).

The average bacterial biomass production calculated proved to be approximately 30% of the primary production in the rather eutrophicated Kiel Fjord and approximately 15% in the central Kiel Bight (see Chap. 16).

Many parameters show more or less distinct seasonal cycles which may be regarded as typical for coastal waters of temperate climatic zones. This is particularly true for the concentration of inorganic nutrients (see Chap. 4) and basically also for the distribution and production of the phytoplankton, as well as for the saprophytic bacteria and those parameters connected with them (see Chaps. 5, 7, 11, 15). However, particularly in the primary production, short-term summer maxima may occur in addition to the characteristic spring and later summer–fall maxima. This is most likely due to the strong fluctuations in the hydrographic conditions of the area investigated (cf. Chap. 3). During the period of investigation yet a third peak was registered on Juli 11, 1974. With a series of samples taken at closer time intervals, probably still further peaks could have been determined. This can be concluded from similar investigations made in other years. However, the overall view of all results obtained shows that the greatest development of phytoplankton and bacteria occurs in the spring and autumn. Thereby a time lag in the saprophytic bacteria peaks can be seen. In contrast, a lively zooplankton development can be determined during the summer months. It may thus be assumed that the microbiological conditions in relatively unstable areas such as the Kiel Bight are basically similar to those in other coastal waters, but show stronger fluctuations, especially in the summer. These affect above all the primary production, and to a lesser extent also the processes of remineralization (see Chaps. 7 and 15). However, the influence of short-term fluctuations in the nutrient concentration on the total number of bacteria, or the number of active bacteria due to plankton blooms and wastewater is relatively minimal (see Chaps. 10 and

14). This is connected with the greater activity of heterotrophic microorganisms at the relatively high summer water temperatures, which can rapidly effect the decomposition of phytoplankton exudates.

The total bacterial numbers, as well as the numbers of active heterotrophic bacteria, growth rates, and biomass production increase during the warm season and decrease significantly during winter. Thus they have a distinct maximum in summer. The main reason for seasonal development of active bacteria proved to be water temperature (see Chaps. 14 and 15).

However, temperature does not influence the number of heterotrophic bacteria forms or species, as could be revealed by taxonomic analysis of the saprophytic bacteria isolated from the Kiel Fjord and Kiel Bight (see Chap. 13). On the other hand the population changes significantly during the seasons, e.g., greater numbers of filamentous cells occur only in spring and summer, star-forming agrobacteria have maxima in late fall, and to a lesser extent also in spring (see Chaps. 1 and 16).

The species composition of plankton algae shows seasonal and regional changes. The number of algae species has its maximum in summer (see Chap. 8).

A few specialized groups of microorganisms also have only one maximum, however in late summer or fall. This is, for example, the case with the chitinoclastic bacteria (see Chap. 12) and has also been determined during earlier investigations for the cellulolytic bacteria (Lehnberg, 1972). A distinct correlation exists here between the substrate availability (chitin, cellulose) and the increase of those microorganisms which are able to utilize these compounds as food. Although this relationship between substrate availability and the amount of corresponding bacteria can be disturbed in unstable waters, or masked, as was the case for example with cellulolytic bacteria during the investigation year 1974/75, in the long run, however, it is always clearly recognizable.

A comparable dependence also exists between waste materials and the bacteria decomposing them. This holds true, for example, with urea, hydrocarbons and phenols, as has been shown during investigations carried out in the Kiel Fjord and Kiel Bight and other brackish water areas (see Steinmann, 1974; Rheinheimer, 1975; Iturriaga and Rheinheimer, 1972).

Especially during the warm seasons, the input of such substances will cause a rapid increase of the corresponding microorganisms.

When the supply of waste material occurs on a regular basis, temperature dependent differences in the amount of the corresponding specialized bacteria can result during the course of the year. The activity of these bacteria is generally very low at water temperatures below 5° C, so that their numbers decrease in the winter and increase again with the warming up of the water in spring.

The situation is much more complex, however, when along with the waste materials the corresponding specialized bacteria enter into the coastal waters. These are for the most part nonhalophilic forms which can survive for only a limited time in brackish and sea water. The survival time is greatest at low temperatures in the winter and decreases when the temperatures rise (see Chaps. 1 and 11). Therefore, the yearly cycle of these bacteria in the more heavily polluted inner Kiel Fjord is very different from that in the relatively clean Kiel Bight. Thus, according to Iturriaga and Rheinheimer (1972) and Hoppe (1974), the number of phenol-degrading bacteria, for example, decreased strongly from March to Juli 1971 in the inner Kiel Fjord—whereas in the Kiel Bight they clearly increased during the same time.

The coastal waters normally contain a population of mostly halophilic specialists which bring about the breakdown of waste materials, whereas the imported allochthonous (nonhalophilic) forms only have a small share in the process. Corresponding to their longer survival time at lower water temperatures, however, the numbers of the allochthonous bacteria increase during the winter in more heavily polluted waters—while the halophilic forms at the same time decrease, due to their lower activity. With the rising temperatures in the spring and summer the opposite development takes place.

The sporadic input of waste materials such as, for example, the oils which enter the sea from ships, leads as a rule to a rapid increase of active hydrocarbon-degrading bacteria during the warm seasons; this occurs much more slowly in the winter. Thus seasonal influences are also effective in this case—however, the irregular substrate input remains decisive. A seasonal cycle in the distribution of these bacteria is not present in this case.

Yet seen as a whole, the investigations treated in this volume show that the influence of the waste load on the bacteriological situations are above all of an indirect nature. Thus, contrary to all expectations, the total bacteria counts determined by means of fluorescence microscopy in the Kiel Fjord and Kiel Bight differ only relatively slightly from one another (see Chap. 10). The saprophyte numbers, on the other hand, show very large differences (see Chap. 11). On the basis of yearly averages, they decrease from Station 1 to Station 5 by 1/50 whereas the former only decrease by 1/2. The saprophyte numbers therefore reflect the waste load of a body of water more clearly—which is likewise the case with yeast and coliform counts (see Chaps. 9 and 11).

Yet the yearly cycle of total saprophyte numbers shows with the two peaks in spring and autumn that here for the most part an indirect influence exists, in which the development and production of the phytoplankton play a decisive role. The organic substances made available through the phytoplankton thus influence the development of the saprophytic bacteria far more than the organic waste material which enters into the water of the Kiel Fjord and similar coastal waters (e.g., the Solent estuary, Williams, pers. comm.) along with waste water and refuse.

To a considerable extent these are compounds which are relatively difficult to break down—they often reach the sediments and are finally more or less reminer-alized on the sea bottom according to the oxygen supply present. Accordingly in the uppermost zones of muddy sediments very high saprophyte numbers may be found (cf. Chaps. 11 and 18). The direct influence of waste materials on the microflora is thus probably much greater on the sediment surface than in the water. This shows, for example, the distribution of phenol-decomposing bacteria. Their number normally is much higher in sediments than in the water column. Corresponding to the strong bacterial activity oxygen deficiency and hydrogen sulfide production may occur (see Chap. 18). On the other hand aerobical sediment surfaces are the main location of nitrification (oxydation of ammonia to nitrite and nitrate; see Chap. 17). The inorganic plant nutrients released from the sediments reach the water again and influence the phytoplankton development.

Although altogether 52 parameters were measured in this study, of which 43 could be used for comparative analysis, this material is not large enough to allow an explanation of all the relations between the microorganisms and the many factors efficient in their biotope. This was to be expected because such research programs are limited by staff and equipment (see Chap. 1).

The application of macro- and micro-autoradiography, assay analysis, scanning electron microscopy, numerical taxonomy and the comparative analysis of data have enlarged our knowledge concerning bacterial activity in coastal waters considerably. The results of this study were used for the construction of a model for the brackish water ecosystem with special reference to the function of the auto- and heterotrophic microorganisms (see Fig. 19.1). The model gives an idea of the energy fluxes within the ecosystem.

From the beginning of our program we also intended to gain experience for similar investigations in other waters and for further research in our area, to enlarge our knowledge of the role of microorganisms in the marine ecosystem. Therefore, it might be useful to present some proposals for future investigations on microbial ecology.

Additionally to the parameters measured in this study, zooplankton production and the concentration of some dissolved organic compounds, such as amino acids and sugars, should be determined. Besides monthly sampling, at least temporarily samples should also be taken at short intervals. This is necessary especially at times of high microbiological activity—e.g., during the development of phytoplankton blooms in spring, the growth of zooplankton in summer and the breakdown of phytoplankton populations in late autumn. Of course, such additional investigations can hardly be carried out simultaneously with an extensive long-term investigation like ours in the Kiel Bight. However, these could follow after a more orientative research program of this kind—even if it is not possible to do this immediately. Very important for enabling comparisons is, however, to carry out the same program and to use as many of the methods proved suitable as possible. Besides the field work, additional experiments in the laboratory are necessary.

One of the questions to be answered is the bacterial colonization of detritus, especially the origin of the particles, the adsorption of organic nutrients and the mechanism of bacterial attachment. Furthermore, the relationships between primary and secondary producers, especially the role of zooplankton, have to be investigated. More knowledge is also necessary of the relations between the waste load and plankton development on the one hand, and bacterial growth on the other. An important problem is in what way activity and development of heterotrophic microorganisms are influenced by waste water of different quantity and quality. Nearly nothing is known about the mutual relationships between bacterial populations in water and sediments. Detailed knowledge is needed about the dynamics of the decomposition processes in water and sediments, about bacterial growth and grazing and about the energy flux in the food chain.

The list of questions gives evidence that concentrated work is necessary for years before the energy flux within an ecosystem can be expressed in terms of well-founded figures. This volume shows possible ways and methods and may be a first step toward answering the problems presented above.

References

Hoppe, H. G.: Untersuchungen zur Analyse mariner Bakterienpopulationen mit einer autoradiographischen Methode. Kieler Meeresforsch. **30**, 10–116 (1974)

Hopton, J. W., Melchiorri-Santolini, U. (eds.): Detritus and its role in aquatic ecosystems. Pallanza: Mem. Ist. Ital. Idrobiol. Vol. 29 (1972)

Iturriaga, R.: Mikrobielle Aktivität des Aufwuchses von Sinkstoffen in der Kieler Bucht. Thesis Univ. Kiel (1977)

Iturriaga, R., Rheinheimer, G.: Untersuchungen über das Vorkommen von phenolabbauenden Mikroorganismen in Gewässern und Sedimenten. Kieler Meeresforsch. **28**, 213–218 (1972)

Lehnberg, B.: Ökologische Untersuchungen an aeroben agar- und zellulosezersetzenden Bakterien in Nord- und Ostsee. Thesis Univ. Kiel (1972)

Overbeck, J.: Zur Struktur und Funktion des aquatischen Ökosystems. Ber. Dtsch. Botan. Ges. **85**, 553–577 (1972)

Rheinheimer, G.: Mikrobiologie der Gewässer. 2nd ed. Jena-Stuttgart: Fischer, 1975

Steinmann, J.: Ökologische Untersuchungen zum bakteriellen Abbau von Harnstoff und Harnsäure in Gewässern. Thesis Univ. Kiel (1974)

Wetzel, R. G.: Limnology. Philadelphia: Saunders, 1975

Zeitzschel, B.: Zur Sedimentation von Seston, eine produktionsbiologische Untersuchung von Sinkstoffen und Sedimenten der westlichen u. mittleren Ostsee. Kieler Meeresforsch. **21**, 55–80 (1965)

Subject Index

Ecological Studies

Analysis and Synthesis
Editors: W.D.Billings, F.Golley, O.L.Lange,
J.S.Olson

**Springer-Verlag
Berlin Heidelberg New York**

This book describes the development of a
mechanistic simulation model for
Narragansett Bay (Rhode Island USA) and its
use in ecosystem analysis. Such models
provide a synthesis of analytical data on the
rates of photosynthesis, feeding, nutrient
uptake and excretion respiration, reproduction, growth and other processes of many
species and groups of organism. The Narragansett Bay model serves as a useful case
study for systems ecologists in general and
also provides a general treatment of the dynamics of plankton-based aquatic ecosystems. Discussions of the biological and
ecological bases as well as the mathematical
concepts involved in the model and descriptions of the development of the computer
algorithm are also included.

Together with Volume 25 by G. Rheinheimer,
*Microbial Ecology of a Brackish Water
Environment*, these two books represent a
comprehensive study of coastal marine
ecosystems.

Springer-Verlag
Berlin
Heidelberg
New York